East Aegean

Rod Heikell
Editor Lucinda Heikell

Imray Laurie Norie & Wilson Ltd

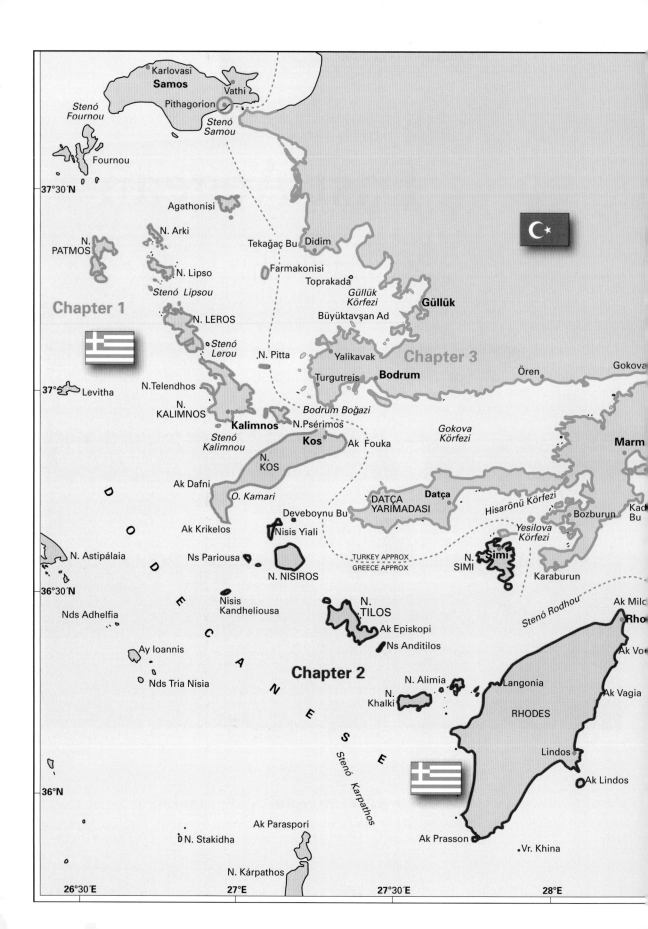

East Aegean

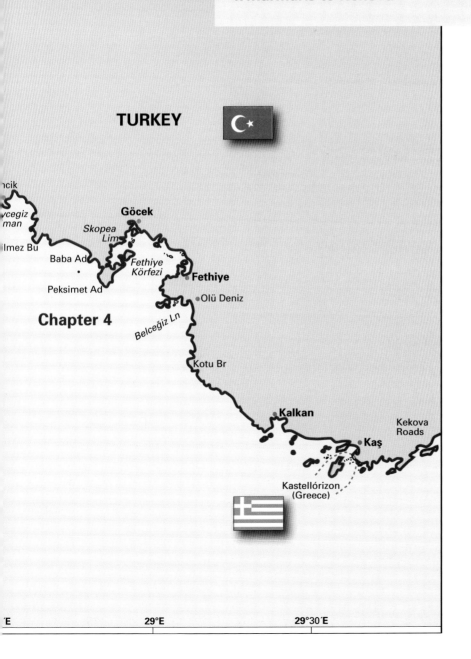

TURKEY

ncik

vcegiz
man

Imez Bu

Göcek

Skopea
Lim

Baba Ad

Fethiye
Körfezi

Fethiye

Peksimet Ad

Olü Deniz

Chapter 4

Belceğiz Ln

Kotu Br

Kalkan

Kekova
Roads

Kaş

Kastellórizon
(Greece)

E

29°E

29°30´E

Published by
Imray, Laurie, Norie & Wilson Ltd
Wych House St Ives Cambridgeshire PE27 5BT England
☎ +44(0)1480 462114
Fax +44(0)1480 496109
Email ilnw@imray.com
www.imray.com
2012

First edition 2007
Second edition 2012

A catalogue record for this book is available from the British Library.

ISBN 978 184623 374 6

CAUTION

Every effort has been made to ensure the accuracy of this book. It contains selected information and thus is not definitive and does not include all known information on the subject in hand; this is particularly relevant to the plans, which should not be used for navigation. The author believes that his selection is a useful aid to prudent navigation, but the safety of a vessel depends ultimately on the judgement of the navigator, who should assess all information, published or unpublished.

PLANS

The plans in this guide are not to be used for navigation. They are designed to support the text and should at all times be used with navigational charts.

CORRECTIONAL SUPPLEMENTS

This pilot book will be amended at intervals by the issue of correctional supplements. These are published on the internet at our web site www.imray.com and may be downloaded free of charge. Printed copies are also available on request from the publishers at the above address.

This work has been corrected to February 2012

Printed in Singapore by Star Standard Industries (PTE) Ltd

Contents

Preface

When talking about Greece and Turkey these days *A Tale of Two Cities* comes to mind in his 'It was the best of times, it was the worst of times, it was the age of wisdom, it was the age of foolishness, it was the epoch...'. Greece is in the grip of a recession and its economy has had to be bailed out by a massive injection of Euros. The Greeks themselves are living in austere times. Friends of many years have phoned and emailed describing the dire situation they face. Across the water in Turkey the economy is booming and the Turks have embraced sailing and the sailing lifestyle with the result that marinas and yacht facilities have mushroomed.

And yet. And yet, this is a tale of two cities. In the very first pilot I wrote I mentioned that as far as the Greeks living on the islands and towns and villages outside Athens are concerned, the capital of Greece is another country that has little to do with life and living outside its environs. No one can know exactly what will happen in the future, but the likely scenario is that life around the islands and coasts of Greece will go on much as it has for aeons. Everyone still has to earn a living, keep the taverna open, provide yacht facilities, get on with life. It will be hard for the Greeks for years to come and I imagine Yanni, Theo and Spiro will be bending my ear for hours over more than a few glasses.

In Turkey the economy may be booming, yet those who live along the coast and have dealings with things nautical are tearing their hair out over the directives from Ankara. At the time of writing visiting yachtsmen get only a 90 day visa out of 180 days. Interpretation of the new legislation on the 90/180 day rule has see-sawed from an on-again-off-again scenario for yachtsmen and with luck and a little clarification things may change. The new 'blue card' scheme governing the discharge of black and grey water has also exercised yachtsmen, though in practice it may not be as onerous as it reads. It's another wait and see that marina managers, charter operators, yacht service companies and the average Turkish yachtsman I talked to along the coast late 2011 are as confused about as visiting yachties are.

If this all sounds dire, it isn't. Cruising around the Dodecanese and the Turkish coast in the autumn of 2011 was a constant delight. In *Skylax* we started in Samos at the top of the Dodecanese and sailed to the bottom at Rhodes. Then we sailed up the Turkish coast from Kaş to Didim Marina after a bit of racing in the Göçek Autumn Regatta. Along the way we amended plans and drew new ones. We have sounded harbours and climbed up steep hill-sides to get photos. We checked information and revised old notes. And we had the most wonderful time. Sometimes newspaper headlines and angry forumites can distort just what life on the water is like here. The Greek Dodecanese is still a wonderful cruising area with some delightful tavernas along the way. The Turkish coast is now more chichi with more marinas, but the welcome is still great and there are places to get away from it all. And yes, we will be sailing around the area and further afield next year and I expect it all to be little different from the last time.

Rod Heikell, London 2012

Acknowledgements

Lu sailed the long days around Greece and Turkey with me and tackled a few high hills for photos when I elected to have a coffee after breakfast. Funny how the angle vis-a-vis the sun often means a morning photo. Without her input this book would not be as rounded as it is. Kadir Kir (KK) took many of the wonderful aerial photos for the chapters on Turkey and is as always his own sparky affable self. Many thanks also to Can Polat and the team in Didim Marina for their care and attention and for making us feel at home. Can Surekli and the guys at Yachtworks have done wonderful things to *Skylax* to keep her sound and safe while sailing long miles. Hasan Kacmaz is the same bundle of energy providing information on marinas old and new with good cheer and fare. Thanks to Theo in Samos for his welcome and pointing us to good tavernas. To Alexis and Dina of the Leros YC thanks for your hospitality and the neatest YC in the Med. Next time we will use the spinnaker in the Round Leros Race.

Yusuf Civilekoglu as always provided succinct and accurate information for Turkey. Special thanks also to Zafer Ergül and Özgür Ugan at Marmaris Netsel Marina, Akbulut Kahraman at Marinturk Göçek, Onur Ugan at D-Marin Göçek, Burak Ardahan at Fethiye Marina, and Tuncay Özses at Kas Marina. Also Agmar Marina, Leros Marina, and Kós Marina in Greece. Hasan, Wilma and Aziz Simsek at Budget Sailing in Göçek were so welcoming it felt like home. Also to Smiley's in Kas, and Genevieve and Stephen s/y *Pi*, for their warm hospitality. Andy and Nan upped the level in the Göçek Autumn Regatta and didn't mind too much about being kidnapped for the bumpy trip back up to Didim.

We would also like to thank everyone who sent in information and updates for this new edition. Thanks to the CA and RCC members for their updates; Giles and Daphne Youngs S/Y *Amari*, John Marsh, Alan Gardner and Gillie Green, and Martin Walker. Also Kit Power, Maurizio Cosano, David and Elaine Royal, Gerard Mennetrier, Theo Spoor, Jean Marc Aumaitre, Konstantin Panitsas, and Rudolf Gwalter S/Y *Moira DMM*. Toni Font sent some additional photos and info from the Dodecanese.

William Wilson, Elinor Cole and Clare Georgy wrapped the book up into what you see here.

Other books by Rod Heikell

Imray Mediterranean Almanac (editor) (Imray)
Mediterranean Cruising Handbook (Imray)
Mediterranean France and Corsica Pilot (Imray)
The Adlard Coles Book of Mediterranean Cruising
Mediterranean Sailing
Greek Waters Pilot (Imray)
Ionian (Imray)
West Aegean (Imray)
Italian Waters Pilot (Imray)
Turkish Waters and Cyprus Pilot (Imray)
The Turquoise Coast of Turkey
The Danube – A River Guide (Imray)
Yacht Charter Handbook
Indian Ocean Cruising Guide (Imray)
Dorling Kindersley Eyewitness Companion to Sailing (contributor)
Mediterranean Islands (contributor)
Sailing in Paradise: Yacht Charter Around the World (Adlard Coles)
Ocean Passages and Landfalls (with Andy O'Grady) (Imray)

Key to quick reference guides

Shelter
A Excellent
B Good with prevailing winds
C Reasonable shelter but uncomfortable and sometimes dangerous
O In calm weather only

Mooring
A Stern-to or bows-to
B Alongside
C Anchored off

Fuel
A On the quay
B Nearby or delivered by tanker
O None or limited

Water
A On the quay
B Nearby or delivered by mini-tanker
O None or limited

Provisioning
A Excellent
B Most supplies can be obtained
C Meagre supplies
O None

Eating out
A Excellent
B Average
C Poor
O None
(*Note* These ratings are nothing to do with the quality of food served in restaurants, but relate only to the numbers of restaurants.)

Plan
• Harbour plan illustrates text

Charges
Charges are for the daily high season rate for a 12m yacht, at the exchange rates current when this volume went to press, with approximate exchange rates. For smaller or larger yachts make an approximate guesstimate.

1 No charge
2 Low cost, under €25
3 Medium cost, €25–40
4 High cost, €41–55
5 Very high cost, over €55
6 Highest cost, €70–100

Introduction

About the Eastern Mediterranean

History

One of the problems I constantly encounter in the Aegean is putting historical events into perspective. When did the Venetians colonise the Aegean? And where? When was the Classical period in Greek antiquity? Who were the Myceneans? When did the modern Turkish Republic come about? I am not going to elaborate on any of these, but I have assembled the following historical order of things in Greece and Turkey (with a slight bias to the eastern Aegean) to give some perspective to historical events. For more details about dates and places, and for explanations of what went on, the reader will have to consult other sources.

Neolithic Period

Little is known of early Neolithic life in the Aegean. Around 6500BC early Stone Age settlers crossed the Bosphorus to mainland Europe and probably used primitive boats and rafts to get to islands close to the Asian shore. A Neolithic city dating back to 7000BC has been discovered at Çatal Hoyuk near Konya, and numerous wall-paintings, including the earliest known landscape, have been uncovered. Around 4000BC Mesopotamia was settled and soon after the Nile delta was under the Egyptian Pharaohs. In the islands the Cycladic civilisation was well established by 4000BC and from the wide distribution of their distinctive geometric designs we know that there was communication between the islands on a regular basis.

Minoan Period (2000 to 1450BC)

Around 2500BC new colonists moved down into Greece from the Balkans and Turkey, bringing bronze weapons and tools with them. The Minoan civilisation was concentrated on Crete and Thíra, where pottery and metalwork were brought to a high art, as was the art of comfortable and civilised living. The Minoans colonised few places, appearing happy to police the seas with their vessels and so procure order and peace while permitting other peoples to go about their business. The civilisation ended abruptly around 1450BC, probably from one of the biggest volcanic eruptions known, when Thíra exploded and a tsunami estimated to be 70ft high, together with earthquakes and ash, destroyed the civilisation overnight.

Medusa at Myra

Mycenean Period (1500 to 1100BC)

With the demise of the Minoans the Myceneans, a Greek-speaking race based at Mycenae in the Argolid, stepped into the power vacuum. These are the Acheaens of Homer, and the Trojan War, fought around 1200BC, is thought to be a battle caused by the Myceneans seeking trade outlets in the Black Sea. Cities along the Aegean coast of Asia Minor and the important island cities

Many of the ancient harbours were built on or near river mouths and silted over time. This is the meandering river at Andraki which caused the harbour for ancient Myra to silt

like Kós and Rhodes are listed in the Iliad according to their contribution of ships and men. While this was going on in the Aegean, a people known as the Hatti built Bronze Age cities on the central Anatolian plateau. They in turn were succeeded by the Hittites. Around the eastern Mediterranean the Phoenicians were the maritime nation, making big leaps transporting cargoes between their own and other colonies. The Myceneans were displaced by the Dorians, who invaded from the north bringing with them Iron Age technology.

Greek Civilisation (1100 to 200BC)

This title covers a multitude of developments. From around 1100 to 900BC the Greek 'Dark Age' wiped out not only culture, but also written language. While the Greek-speaking Dorians existed in this dark twilight, the Phoenicians from the Levant (Syria, Lebanon and Israel) took control of the sea routes. By 800BC a new written language was emerging and Homer, possibly a native of Khios or present-day Izmir, penned the *Iliad* and the *Odyssey*. From 750 to 500BC (the Archaic or Classical period) city-states (Pólis) sprang up all over the Greek islands and along the coast of Asia Minor, some more powerful than others, some in alliance with others, but all trading with one another and bound together in a loose defence pact. Indigenous peoples along this coast – the Carians, Lydians and Lycians – were Hellenised and became client colonies of Greece. Colonies were established all around the Mediterranean and in the Black Sea. Ionia on the coast of Asia Minor was pre-eminent in its contributions to science and philosophy and Herodotus, the 'father of history', was born in Halicarnassus (Bodrum) in 480BC.

The ancients left their debris all up and down the coast

Throughout the ages Asia Minor has been the terminus for spices brought from the east to be transported on to the west

The Persian Wars and the Hellenic Period (500 to 200BC)

In the late 6th century BC the Persians moved west and subdued the coast of Asia Minor. The Persian threat pulled the Greek city-states together around Athens and cemented the Delian league, based around the tiny island of Delos in the Cyclades. The Hellenic period arrived with the final defeat of the Persians and the establishment of Athens as the power base. The Battle of Salamis was instrumental in rebuffing the Persians and establishing Athens as the centre of things Greek. The Peloponnesian War (431–404BC) between Athens and Sparta divided the islands and the city-states, causing much hardship for the inhabitants if their government opted for the wrong side at the wrong time as the war raged back and forth. The war weakened both Athens and Sparta, leaving the way open for Phillip II of Macedonia, and later his son Alexander the Great, to take control of ancient Greece, though little changed under the Greek-educated Alexander.

The Romans (200BC to AD295)

A weak Greece was easy prey for the Romans and they declared war on Phillip V of Macedonia in 202BC. Octavius defeated Antony and Cleopatra at Actium near Preveza and after a decade of infighting cemented the Roman Empire into a whole. It was the Romans who first called the mainland region Asia Minor. Roman rule had little cultural influence on Greece, whereas everything Greek, from architecture to cuisine, had a profound effect on the Roman way of life. Greek cities were largely autonomous, owing allegiance to Rome, and Greek remained the official language. In AD295, weakened by attacks from tribes on the edges of the empire and beset by difficulties within, Diocletian split the empire into two.

Grumpy Roman at Bodrum

Byzantium (AD330 to 1204)

The foundation of Constantinople and the rise of Byzantium marks the rise of the first Christian Empire. Byzantine rule was constantly beset by invasions from the north and south. The Slavs, Avars, Goths, Huns, Vandals and Bulgars came down from the north, while the Saracens sailed across from the south. The islands were depopulated and towns and villages contracted in size and moved away from a precarious shoreline. At times the Byzantines drove the invaders out, but as Ottoman power grew, the empire shrank away from its island territory in Greece.

The Venetians (1204 to 1550)

In 1204 the Fourth Crusade sacked Constantinople (ostensibly an ally!) and parts of the Byzantine Empire were parcelled out to adventurers from the European nobility. The Venetians, who had transported the crusaders, emerged with a large chunk of Byzantine territory as their prize. In the eastern Aegean the Venetians and Genoese vied for chunks of real estate so that the riches of the east, especially spices, could be transported to the west. The Knights of St John, displaced from the Levant, settled in Rhodes in 1310 and effectively colonised the nearby islands and adjacent mainland coast. In 1522 Suleiman the Magnificent evicted them from Rhodes and they went to Malta.

The Turks

Around AD1000 Turkic-speaking Seljuks moved into Anatolia and organised themselves into a potent fighting and political force. In 1300 Osman founded the Ottoman dynasty in Anatolia and had soon supplanted the Seljuks to become the major player in the area. In 1453 the Ottomans captured Constantinople, renamed it Istanbul, and ended Byzantine power in the area. By the end of the 16th century most of Greece was under Turkish control. Around the Peloponnese and the Aegean islands the Venetians continued to battle for territory, though it was a losing battle against the omnipotent Turk.

The Venetians left the Lion of St Mark scattered all over the Aegean

The Greek War of Independence (1822 to 1830)

In 1821 the Greek flag was raised at Kalavrita in the Peloponnese. In 1822 the Turks massacred 25,000 people on the island of Khios and so aroused Greek passions that many took up arms against them. The war was effectively won when a combined English, French and Russian fleet destroyed the larger Turkish and Egyptian fleet at Navarino. The provisional capital of newly liberated Greece was at Aígina until it was moved to Navplion in 1828. Athens was made the capital in 1834.

Statues and portraits of Atatürk, founder of the modern Turkish Republic, will be found everywhere in Turkey

Modern Turkey

During the First World War Greece and Italy were on the side of the Allies and Turkey on the Axis side. After the Allies won the war much Turkish territory in present-day Greece was given to Greece, although the Dodecanese went to the Italians. The Greeks, emboldened by the war and encouraged by some of the Allies, invaded Turkey in 1919. Mustafa Kemal (Atatürk) rallied the Turkish army at Ankara and pushed the Greeks back to the coast. By September 1922 the last of the Greeks troops were in Smyrna (Izmir) and the Turks fired the city to flush them out. Mustafa Kemal went on to found the modern Turkish Republic and in 1922 the first of the great population exchanges began, with Greeks from Turkey returned to Greece and Turks in Greece returned to Turkey. Mustafa Kemal went on to create a secular state and by the time he died in 1938 he had introduced a written constitution, votes for women and the Roman alphabet to replace the Arabic, and abolished the fez and polygamy. He was a truly remarkable man and is honoured all over Turkey to this day. In 2005 Turkey was accepted as a candidate member of the EU, although full ratification is inextricably linked to the Cyprus question.

In the crash of 2008–10 Turkey's economy was little affected and the industrial base, particularly construction, automotive and electronics, has powered ahead compared to the EU. Turkey under the AKP (Justice and Development Party) has moved towards union with Europe even though there have been some concerns on both sides.

Modern Greece

The newly born Greek Republic got off to a shaky start, and after a series of assassinations the western powers put a Bavarian prince on the throne. He proved an insensitive and unpopular ruler and was deposed by a popular revolt in 1862. In 1863 a new ruler, George I from Denmark, was chosen, and the British relinquished control of the Ionian islands to encourage support. The boundaries of Greece expanded, with the acquisition of Thessaly and the Epirus in 1881 and Macedonia and the northern Aegean islands in the Balkan wars (1912–13). Greece fought on the side of the Allies in the Second World War and obtained the last of her territory, the Dodecanese, from the Italians at the end of the war. Civil war split the country until 1947 when a conservative government was elected. In 1967 the army took power with the notorious junta of the Colonels, which ushered in seven years of autocratic and harsh rule. Democracy returned in 1974 with Karamanlis. The first socialist government, PASOK, under Papandreou, was elected in 1981. In 1986 Greece joined the European Community and in 2004 the Olympic Games returned to Greece after a long absence.

In the last few decades power has oscillated between the two main parties, Nea Democratia on the right and Pasok on the left. As I write Greece is in the grip of a major recession, with government debt running at 160% of GDP. It has needed the combined forces of the EU (principally the Germans), the ECB and the IMF to lend the government €240 billion so far, and more may be needed. The government has imposed severe austerity measures to bring the budget deficit down and this has led to riots and strikes in Athens.

At present an interim coalition government is trying to steer Greece through the debt crisis, although an election will be held in April. It is not inconceivable that Greece could exit the euro zone with dramatic fiscal results for the ordinary Greek on the streets. Although times are undoubtably hard for Greeks, it is likely that, away from the cities, visitors will continue to enjoy typical Greek hospitality.

Things Greek

Language

It should be remembered that the Greek spoken today (Demotic Greek) is not ancient Greek, though it is largely derived from it. Anyone with a knowledge of ancient Greek will be able to pick up a little over 50% of the Greek spoken today, though the pronunciation may not be what you expect. Rendering Greek into the Roman alphabet also presents some difficulties.

Although at first it seems impossible to master, the Greek alphabet can be conquered with a little persistence, and common words and phrases to get you by in the tavernas and bars and on the street can be picked up by ear. One of the obstacles to learning Greek is that you so often come across someone speaking English that the need to learn Greek evaporates. However, if you can even only learn a few phrases, such as 'hello' and 'goodbye' and 'how are you?', the effort will be repaid, especially in out-of-the-way places. A few useful phrases will be found in the Appendix.

The Greek Orthodox church

For someone from the West, from the world of Roman Catholicism and Protestantism, the churches and the black-robed priests of the Greek Orthodox church seem to constitute another religious world; and so indeed it is. Until the last meeting of the Council of Nicaea in 787, the western and eastern branches of the church had stumbled along together, growing apart but outwardly united. Post-Nicaea the churches grew apart, partly on doctrinal issues but mostly, one suspects, because of the geographical and cultural isolation between Rome and Constantinople. In Rome they spoke mostly Latin, in Constantinople Greek. In the west priests were celibate, in the east they married. In Rome the Pope was infallible, in Constantinople articles of faith were decided by a council of bishops. In the west the spirit of God came from the Father and the Son, in the east from the Father.

The Orthodox cross against an azure blue sky: a typically Greek aspect

The overthrow of Constantinople by the Turks in 1453 had a far-reaching effect on Orthodoxy, and the Russian branch finally severed its connections with the Greek parent church. In Greece under the Turks the church was allowed to continue, and it later became a focus of rebellion against the occupiers.

Today the church, although much weakened in this secular age, still permeates Greek life. For the Greeks the big event of the year is not Christmas, but Easter, *Paskha*. The date of Easter is reckoned in a different way to that in the west, and the celebration is focused on the Resurrection rather than the Crucifixion. On Good Friday a service marks the descent from the Cross and the *Epitafion* containing the body of Christ is paraded through the streets. In some places an effigy of Judas Iscariot is burnt or blown up. This latter can be a spectacular event, as Greek men love playing with dynamite and the effigy is inevitably stuffed with it. All Greek homes brew up a soup from the offal of the lamb which is to be eaten on the Resurrection (depending on your inclination the soup may be tasty or you may have problems sampling even a spoonful of assorted organs).

Late on Saturday night there is the *Anestisi* mass to celebrate Christ's return. In the church all the lights are turned out, and then from behind the altar screen the priest appears with a lighted candle and proceeds to light the candles of those in the church. Everyone responds with *Kristos Anesti* (Christ

Papas

is risen) and there is a procession with the lighted candles through the streets to the sound of firecrackers and skyrockets, or any other explosive devices that are to hand. This is not a good time to be in trouble at sea as a lot of out-of-date flares are used up, though don't be tempted yourself as it is against the law to do so and there have been prosecutions. The traditional greeting at this time is *Kronia Polla* ('Many years' or 'Long life'). In the home boiled eggs, traditionally dyed red, are dished out and the normal sport is to bet your egg against the others, in the manner of conkers, or to surprise your friends with a solid rap on the head with the egg to crack the shell.

There are many local saints' days in the villages and towns, and the whole place will often close down for them even if they are not on the list of state holidays. Greeks normally celebrate not their birthday but the day of the saint they are named after – their name-day. In some churches there are icons to a saint reckoned to provide an above-average service, and these will have numerous votive offerings. Many of these are simple affairs: a pressed metal disc showing what blessing is required, whether for an afflicted limb, safety at sea, a newborn baby or a family house. Some of the older votive offerings are more ornate and elaborate: sometimes a painting or a model of a ship where thanks are given for survival at sea, or a valuable brooch or piece of jewellery for some other blessing. Greek churches are wonderful places, the *iconostasis* always elaborate and adorned, and the interior a dark and mystical place. It constantly amazes me that even in the most out-of-the-way places, on a rocky islet or a remote headland, every church and chapel and shrine will be newly whitewashed and cleaned, with an oil lamp burning or ready to burn in it.

Food

Greek food is not for the gourmet, but rather is plain wholesome cooking that goes with the climate and the Greek idea that a meal is as much a social occasion as a culinary experience. This is not, I emphasise, to say that Greek food is not enjoyable. I love the unadulterated flavours of charcoal-grilled fish with a squeeze of lemon over it, or a *salata horiatiki*, the ubiquitous mixed salad swimming in olive oil and peppered with *feta* and black olives – the simplicity of the combination of ingredients brings out the best in them. In some restaurants and in Greek family cooking you will come across dishes that have been lost in the tourist areas, where either the lethargy of taverna owners or the demands of visitors for a bland 'international' cuisine revolving round steak and chips has removed them from the menu. Some of the island tavernas still have a dish or two specific to the island or region, such as fish *à la Spetsiota*, but for the majority the dishes on the menu are those which are simply prepared and cooked, including a few favourites such as *moussaka* and *stifadho*.

Taverna with a view

The principal meal in Greece is the midday meal and most oven-cooked dishes are prepared in the morning for this meal. In the evening these dishes will simply be partially reheated and served up overcooked and lukewarm, or banged into the microwave so they are scalding hot. Restaurants in Greece are categorised as either an *estiatorio* (a restaurant), a taverna (a simple tavern), or a *psistaria* (a restaurant specialising in freshly prepared food, mostly grilled meat), but the distinctions between these have now become so blurred that most restaurants call themselves tavernas.

The menu in a taverna will often be quite exhaustive, but only those dishes that are available that day will have prices alongside. In most Greek tavernas you will be invited into the kitchen or to a counter displaying the food to make your choice, a handy convention that gets over the problem of knowing what it is you are ordering from the menu. Only in the smarter restaurants will you be requested to order from the menu, and there will normally be an English translation on the menu, or on a board on the wall to help you out.

A typical Greek meal will be a starter and main course, with other side dishes ordered at random. Dessert is not normally served in a taverna, although you may get fresh fruit or yogurt. When ordering, don't order everything at the same time as it will all arrive at once, or sometimes

Dinner and drinks by the water

you will get the main course first and the starter second. Often the food will be just warm, having been set aside to cool as Greeks believe hot food is bad for you – a belief that has some backing from the medical community. If you get everything in order and hot (and things have improved in recent years) you are on a winner. If you don't, just order another bottle of wine and settle yourself in for the evening like the Greeks around you – after all, what have you got to do that's so important after dinner?

Wine

Greek wine is a source of mystery to most western oenophiles. There are grape varieties in Greece which few have ever encountered before. The production is so inconsistent that wines vary radically from year to year and most of the wines are oxidised or maderised. Storing wine properly is virtually unknown and most wine is new wine, and until 1969 there was no real government control over wines of a specific origin. To compound all of this, wine will

'Bakery'

often be sitting in a shop window where it gets a dose of sunlight every day. Given all these problems it is amazing that some Greek wine is as good as it is. And these days some of it is very good. On the plus side, Greek oenology is on the mend and given the climatic conditions, the interesting grape varieties, and the excellent results of a few wine producers who have imported new wine-making technology and nurtured their product, the prospect for the future is good. Already some excellent wines are being produced in the Peloponnese, northern Greece and on some of the islands. I suggest you just experiment with some of the wines, until you find something to your taste and in your price range. Local wines have much improved and some *xema* ('locally made') can be bought in bulk from some supermarkets and minimarkets. You can also order loose wine in a taverna by the kilo or half kilo (essentially a litre or half litre), and much of it is eminently quaffable.

Vines for wine-making were growing in Greece before anyone in France or Spain had ever seen or heard of the plant or its product. Estimates vary, but probably sometime around the 13th to the 12th centuries BC Greek viticulture was well established. The mythic origins of the introduction of the vine are associated with Dionysus and trace the route of the vine from India and/or Asia to Greece. Dionysus was said to be the son of Zeus and Semele (daughter of Cadmus, King of Thebes) who was brought up in India by the nymphs and taught the lore of the vine and wine-making by Silenus and the satyrs (sounds

Libation to the gods. It's always wise to make a libation to Aeolus and Poseidon for fair winds and calm seas

a wonderful childhood to me). He journeyed from India across Asia Minor to Greece, bringing the vine and accompanied by a band of followers.

One can imagine a religious cult growing up around wine. The visions and hallucinations from imbibing it could only have been supernatural, and the introduction of it to Greece would have been unstoppable, hence its incorporation into the mythic universe of the ancients. The Homeric Hymn to Dionysus tells of his journey around the islands distributing the vine and describes vine leaves sprouting from the masthead of his ship. Nor is it surprising that the cult of Dionysus was associated with the release of mass emotion, was a fertility cult, and that the Dionysian Festival included wild uninhibited dancing and at times violence and sacrifice – all things associated in one way or another with alcohol today.

There is no way we can know what ancient wine was like. It was referred to by its place of origin, thus Pramnian, Maronean, Khian, Thasian, and Koan wine were mentioned by name much as we mention a Bordeaux or Côtes du Rhône today. Whether or not it was all resinated, as in the ubiquitous *retsina* surviving today, is unknown. Most likely amphoras of wine were sealed with a resin mixture to prevent oxidation and this imparted a flavour to the wine. Over time it was assumed that the resin itself, and not the exclusion of oxygen, prevented wine going sour and oxidising and so resin was added directly to the wine to produce *retsina*. It is unfortunate that many people only get to drink bottled *retsina* today, as the stuff from the barrel is superior and should be drunk as a new wine. Much of the bottled *retsina* and some of the barrel *retsina* is simply bad wine that can only be made to taste palatable by resinating it.

There are also a number of Muscats that are considered to be good quality, though they are not to my taste. The Samos Muscat from the island is considered the best, although Muscat of Cephalonia and Muscat of Patras produced by Achaia Clauss also get a mention. Sweet red liqueur wine vaguely resembling port is produced from the Mavrodaphne grape and Mavrodaphne of Patras (produced by Achaia Clauss) and Mavrodaphne of Cephalonia are passable port-type wines. Many of the local wine shops have a local Mavrodaphne in stock and this is often acceptable.

Retsina

Much of the ubiquitous *retsina* found in Greece is made from the savatiano grape, grown in Attica and brewed and bottled there for the mass market. As I have indicated, the bottled variety is best avoided and *retsina* should be drunk fresh from the barrel. *Retsina* should really be drunk with *mezes* and not with a full meal, but in practice you drink it with whatever you want.

Although *retsina* is traditionally identified with Attica and the savatiano grape, in fact it is made all over Greece from a variety of grapes. Normally the grapes are gathered in September and after mashing go straight into the barrels with the must and the pine resin. Around 2kgs of resin which the locals collect goes into a 1,000-litre barrel. The wine ferments for around 40 days before fermentation is stopped. Most of the barrels are old, often around 40–50 years old, and if a barrel should give bad wine it is immediately burnt. The *retsina* should always be drunk as a new wine within a year.

Things Turkish

Language

Turkish is a language that shares its roots with few others, Azerbaijani being one, though it may also be connected to Hungarian and Finnish. When Atatürk did away with the Arabic script he got a group of prominent linguists together to adapt it to the Roman alphabet and to simplify it. The result is a language that is basically fairly phonetic and if you follow the rules for pronouncing a letter and say a word, you have a good chance of getting it right. Many modern terms have been borrowed directly from English and French and expressed in a Turkish form. Thus a *bufe* is a buffet, *otel* is an hotel, *bira* is a beer, *viski* is whisky, and so on. For vocabulary the *Berlitz Turkish For Travellers* has everything the visitor needs.

There are a few useful Turkish words and a guide to pronunciation of the Turkish alphabet in the Appendix.

Islam and Mosques

Although Turkey has been a secular state since Atatürk's reforms, 98% of Turks are Muslims, though some are not all that devout and Islam in Turkey is a much gentler religion than the fundamentalism found in Iran next door. Muslims believe in everything in the Bible, particularly the Old Testament, except that Jesus is regarded as a prophet and not the son of God. After Jesus came Mohammed, who was the last and greatest of the prophets and to whom God communicated the final revelations, which are written down in the Qur'an (Koran). The word Islam means 'submission to God's will', and at the beginning of daily prayers the call from the minaret is: 'there is no god but God, and Mohammed is his prophet'. To be a Muslim you should say this phrase, (and understand what it means), pray five times daily at the set times, give alms to the poor, observe the fast of Ramadan and make a pilgrimage to Mecca if possible.

A Muslim must not eat pork or drink wine. The latter is normally interpreted as a prohibition on alcohol in general, though the less devout say Muhammad said nothing about *raki* and beer. No image can be worshipped, and images that might possibly be venerated have been vigorously destroyed by the faithful. This accounts for the general paucity of portraits in Islamic art.

Unlike in some Muslim countries, visitors can enter a mosque in Turkey, as long as the proper etiquette is observed and permission from the Imam is obtained. While the Turkish coast has no grand mosques like those in Istanbul, Bursa and Konya, there are interesting examples in Izmir, Milas, Mugla and Fethiye. You should remove your shoes before entering a mosque, a purely practical rule designed to keep the carpets inside clean for worshippers. You should be modestly attired: no shorts, short skirts or tatty clothes, and women should cover their hair and shoulders with a scarf. Do not take photographs using a flash or talk loudly. Avoid visiting a mosque on Friday, which is the Muslim holy day.

98% of Turks are Muslims but Turkey itself is a secular state

Festivals

Though Turkey uses the Gregorian calendar for most things, Islamic festivals are fixed using the Islamic calendar (based on a lunar month and thus 11 days shorter than the Gregorian year). Consequently, the dates of Islamic festivals change from year to year. There are two major Islamic holidays: the first is Kurban bayrami, the 'Feast of the Sacrifice', which remembers Abraham's willingness to sacrifice his son. Most families buy a sheep which is paraded around before the big day, when it is ritually slaughtered and the feast takes place. Meat is distributed to the poor who cannot afford to slaughter a sheep. There is much celebration and everything usually closes down for it. The second festival is Şeker bayrami, the 'sugar festival', celebrating the end of Ramadan and a month of fasting for the faithful. At these times the coast is packed with Turks on holiday celebrating the festivals, and every restaurant is packed full.

Hammams

The Turkish steam bath or *hammam* was an essential part of every Turkish community. The Ottoman hammam developed from the Roman bath, but with the number of chambers reduced to two instead of four. The central bath-house has a dome over it studded with thick bottle glass which lets smoky shafts of light into the misty atmosphere of the baths. In the middle of the bathhouse there is a circular marble platform on which you sit or lie,

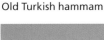
Old Turkish hammam

or where the brave are pummelled with a Turkish massage. The latter are fairly violent affairs compared with the gentler European-type massage, though recipients always insist they feel good afterwards. Around the edge of a hammam are cubicles with hot and cold running water where you wash dirt and grime off before relaxing on the central platform.

A hammam leaves you feeling wonderfully relaxed and often quite sleepy. There are different times for men and women, with men getting the lion's share of the time available in male-dominated Turkey. In the main towns around the coast (Bodrum, Muğla, Marmaris, and Fethiye) you will find hammams; ask where they are located at the tourist information office.

Food

Turkish cuisine has been praised as the best in the eastern Mediterranean, and so it is. The traditional cuisine scores from combining a wealth of basic raw ingredients in novel ways to make dishes which often have novel names. The most memorable of the names are *imam bayaldi*, 'the Imam fainted' (aubergine with tomatoes and onions) and a sweet pastry soaked in honey called 'lady's navel'. Aubergine features a lot in Turkish cooking and it was said that in Istanbul you could tell when the aubergine season started from the fires that swept through the city – fires caused by the hot oil from fried aubergine dishes spilling over and igniting. Over 40 dishes are attributed to this purple vegetable. Females also figure a lot in the naming of dishes, particularly desserts, with names like 'lady's thigh', 'lady's breasts', 'lady's fingers', and so on through most of the anatomy.

Mezes are superb in Turkey and can make a meal in themselves. You will commonly come across *cacik* (yoghurt with cucumber and garlic), *patliçan salata* (pureed aubergine mixed with yoghurt), *taramasalata* (red fish roe with yoghurt and garlic), *pilaki* (white beans in a vinaigrette sauce), *dolma* (stuffed vine leaves), *borek* (white cheese or mincemeat wrapped in filo pastry and deep-fried), *Amerikan salata* (potato salad with mayonnaise, also called Russian (*Rus*) salad), *coban salata* (a mixed salad meaning literally 'shepherd's salad'), and many more – depending on the chef's inclination and ability – such as fish salads, pickled octopus, fiery tomato and onion purees, and the celebrated *imam bayaldi*. Soups are usually on offer at lunchtime and the most popular are lentil and rice soups, meat broths, and vegetable soups. Special shops serve only *Iskembe corbasi*, tripe soup, which is a sovereign remedy for hangovers in the eastern Mediterranean. Friends who live in Turkey swear by it, but however bad my hangover I've steadfastly refused to believe that tripe soup could cure it.

Doner kebab, but superior to any kebab you will have outside Turkey

Cooked dishes like stews and oven dishes are prepared at lunchtime and kept hot until the evening, so the best time to have them is at midday when they are fresh. Most of the dishes combine meat, usually lamb, with vegetables to produce dishes like *salcali kofte* (meatballs in a sauce with vegetables), or *kuzu ve patliçan guveç* (a lamb and aubergine stew). This is usually accompanied by pilau rice or bulgur (*pilav*). Some restaurants specialise in *kebap*, of which there are several varieties depending on where they originated. The *doner kebap* is cooked on a slowly revolving vertical spit and the cook slices meat off it with a long knife. Usually the meat comes on a bed of rice with a salad garnish and a piquant tomato sauce or yoghurt according to your taste. *Adana kebap* is spiced with hot peppers, *Urfa kebap* comes with sliced onions and black pepper, and *Bursa* or *Iskender kebap* comes on chopped *pide* bread with yoghurt and butter. Beef usually comes as *bonfile* or *biftek*, small steaks grilled over charcoal. *Şiş kebap* is grilled lamb on a skewer and *şiş kofte* is meatballs.

Fish is not cheap in Turkey and you should enquire about the price beforehand. It is sold by weight, so before it is cooked the *patron* will weigh it and give you a price. Usually it comes fried or grilled, though in some places more ambitious dishes and sauces are prepared. Enquire to see if one of my favourites, a lemon and dill sauce, can be prepared. Usually your grilled or fried main course will come with French fries, a legacy of increasing tourism in this area. Instead you may like to order rice or bulgur *pilav*.

Lahmaçun is a type of *pide* – roll it up with a salad filling inside and enjoy

Sadly, in some of the larger resorts the traditional cuisine is being subordinated to blander 'international' dishes that the restaurateurs think the tourists want (unfortunately some of them do like their steak-and-eggs-and-chips). Fast-food places have also sprouted in the resorts and the Turks have taken to these with a vengeance, ensuring that they are here to stay.

Desserts are not generally served in restaurants and for the traditional sweet sticky desserts you will usually have to go to a patisserie. However, a restaurant will usually have fresh fruit; depending

Fresh fish on offer, but it will not be cheap *Kadir Kir*

on what is in season it may be peaches, apples, pears, grapes, oranges or melon. As far as I am concerned a plate of honeydew melon beats sticky sweets any day. The sticky sweets are almost identical to those found in Greece and parts of the Middle East: *baklava* (flaky pastry stuffed with nuts in a honey syrup), and *kadayif* (shredded wheat with nuts in the same sweet syrup). Some of the patisseries make a variety of chocolate and sponge cakes, but on the whole these are too sweet for my taste. *Dondurma* (ice cream) is also popular and is often sold on the streets by colourfully attired vendors who make a great show of their prowess at flicking scoops of ice cream into the cone.

Drinks

Although the Turks introduced coffee to Europe, it is not the national drink. That privilege is accorded to *çay* and all over Turkey you will find *çay* shops serving the little tulip-shaped glasses of strong amber tea. It is always drunk without milk and, usually sweet, though the sugar lumps come separately so you can determine how sweet you want it to be. In some tea shops you can get 'apple tea' made with dried apples, and *ada çay*, 'Island tea', made from sage and reputed to cure everything from a tummy upset to a cold. In most *çay* shops you can get *Türk kahve*, Turkish coffee, a small cup of concentrated brew with the grounds in the bottom of the cup. Nescafé and even expressos and cappuccinos are also obtainable in some cafés and *çay* shops in the larger and more cosmopolitan spots, a reflection of the demands of tourism on the coast.

Beer is brewed in Turkey, with Efes and Tuborg the two most common brands. The beer is a light, slightly bitter pilsener, eminently drinkable on hot summer days. Wines are mediocre at best in Turkey and also highly taxed. For reds try Villa Doluca, Dikmen, and Buzbag. For whites try Villa Doluca, Cankaya, and Kavak. Although you can get used to them, mostly because the alternative is highly priced imports, the wine is not great, consistency is not always what it should be and the bottle that follows, of the same brand and vintage, may not be anything like the first.

If there is a national drink after *çay*, it is *raki*, the clear aniseed flavoured spirit similar to Greek ouzo and French pastis. With water it turns a milky white colour. Some Turks drink prodigious quantities of the stuff, but newcomers should beware of the kick hiding behind the pleasant aniseed flavour. Other hard spirits such as gin, vodka and brandy are also manufactured in Turkey by the state distiller Tekel. The brandy is terrible, more akin to cough mixture than brandy as we know it. Imported spirits are available but expensive.

Apart from all this alcohol, caffeine and tannin, there are excellent fruit juices. Most of the good brands are concentrated 100% juice and are excellent. Cherry, peach, and apple are commonly available. Spring water (*su*) is available everywhere and will often be put on the table in a café or restaurant as a matter of course. If you want fizzy mineral water ask for *maden sodasi*. One other drink you will come across is *ayran*, yoghurt mixed with water and salt. Though I love yoghurt, and Turkish yoghurt is good stuff, *ayran* is something I can't get on with. Turks drink a lot of it, but most foreigners try it only once.

Carpets and kilims

To give advice on buying a carpet or kilim is impossible; in the end you should not be concerned with whether or not you have obtained a bargain, but whether you like the piece. Good carpets and kilims are not cheap even for Turks, and for exceptional pieces you will be looking at thousands of pounds. But for a substantially lower sum you can buy a good carpet or kilim at less than the price in Europe, though only at around one-third off European prices. Buy a carpet or kilim because you like it and have a place to put it in your home, and not in the mistaken belief that you can sell it on and make money in Europe or elsewhere. Carpet and kilim wholesalers buying in bulk get a bigger discount than you can.

There are a number of pointers to help you on your way to getting a good piece. Examine the carpet to determine how close the weave is. The finer the weave – that is, the more knots there are per square centimetre – the better the quality and the higher the price. Examine the colours on the surface and then part the pile and look at the root of the fibres. If the colour is darker at the roots there is a good chance the piece has been acid-washed to look older; this shortens its life by weakening the fibres and decreases its value. Genuinely old pieces that have faded have an even gradation of colour through each fibre and a different feel from the coarseness an acid-wash gives.

Take the piece outside to look at it in daylight, which will give you a better idea of the colours than the soft lights in the shop. Artificial dyes have been used since the 1890s and despite the salesman's assurance that the piece has 100% vegetable dyes, this is unlikely. Take a handkerchief or a bit of cloth of some sort, preferably white, dampen a corner and drag it across the carpet. If the artificial dyes have not been fixed properly you will pick up colour on the damp cloth. Pre-1890 pieces are very expensive indeed and are nearly all collector's items. The carpet should have a different hue when looked at from opposite ends as the pile is orientated one way or the other. It is not a bad idea to get hold of one of the small books on carpets for sale in Turkey, to get some idea of regions and colours and patterns, but it won't make you into an expert and the carpet dealer will know this.

Haggling over the price is a ritual and you should never pay the asking price. Go around a number of shops to see what sort of price you can get down to for similar pieces and to get an idea of patterns and colours and the 'look' of a carpet. Kilims, the flat woven rugs, are different again and it is mostly a matter of comparing like pieces and prices. It's worth spending some time over buying a piece and the time spent looking is enjoyable in itself. Usually the dealer will offer you çay or coffee, but don't feel obliged to make a purchase because of this. All this bother is well worth it. You will be buying something which is hand-crafted, beautiful and functional. A good Turkish carpet or kilim will most likely go on giving service after you have shuffled off.

Background basics in Greece

Getting to the Dodecanese

By air

Anyone coming to the Dodecanese will probably be flying into Samos, Kós or Rhodes. These are the three major airports for charter and budget airline flights from Europe and for onward flights from Athens Spata Airport. Easyjet fly to Athens and to Kós and Rhodes in the summer. Other major airlines like BA and Olympic also do discounted flights.

There are several internal flights a day to and from Spata and the airports on Samos, Kós and Rhodes, though these are frequently booked out so it pays to book internal flights in advance rather than turning up and hoping to get on one. As well as Olympic Airways there is Aegean Airlines which operates from Spata to Kós and Rhodes.

See www.olympic-airways.com and www.aegeanair.com

From Spata you can also go to Piraeus to take a ferry down to the Dodecanese. (For information on ferries see below.)

Athens Airport (Spata)

The new Athens International Airport is located at Spata, 27km NE of Athens, and is connected by a new motorway to the Athens ring road. You can get to and from the airport in a number of ways.

Taxi The taxi rank is inside the airport perimeter and for two or more people this is arguably the easiest way to get anywhere. A taxi into Athens costs around €40–50.

Bus A number of buses connect to various destinations, as follows:

E94 connects the Ethniki Amina metro station with the airport. Passengers can transfer from the metro line to the airport bus at this departure point.

Some tips on charter and budget airline flights

- Some companies will sell-one way flights and others only a return flight. Paradoxically, some return flights are cheaper than the one-way flight, so if you are on a one-way leg you can just discard the return.
- Some companies will sell a flight bundled with accommodation for only marginally more than the flight. Some of these bundled deals put you in the tourist ghetto from hell, but at times the accommodation can be useful if you are hauled and need to work with the boat on the hard.
- All charter flights will have transfers included in the flight and this is the easiest way of getting to your destination, especially at some ungodly hour in the morning.
- Check the yacht charter operators for flights as well as the major package holiday tour operators. Sunsail and Neilson usually have flight options.
- Budget airlines operate on the first-in-cheapest-flight system. The first 10% of seats will be at the cheapest price, rising through tranches to the last 10% at the most expensive price.
- At times it is worth booking in advance if a flight is very cheap and you 'think' it is around the time you will go out.
- Leaving flights to the last minute doesn't work and you are better off looking at charter flights where prices can get cheaper as the departure date gets closer.
- Try scheduled airlines as well. Many of the major carriers have been forced to do cheap deals in order to compete with no-frills budget airlines like Easyjet. Major carriers will not usually fly to smaller airports but you can always get a connecting flight from a major airport to the smaller one.

E95 Syntagma Square – Airport Express has its departure point at the centre of Athens (Syntagma Square) and goes via Vas. Sofias Avenue, Mesogion Avenue and Attiki Odos before it terminates at the airport.

E96 Piraeus – Airport Express starts from the centre of Piraeus (Karaiskaki Square) and via Posidonos Avenue, Varis-Varkizas, and Varis-Koropiou Roads and then terminates at the airport.

KTEL Express to Rafina A daily service operates between the airport and Rafina approximately every 40 minutes from 0600 to 2100.

A ticket is about €3 and is valid for 24 hours' travel on all public transport.

For more detailed information on buses you can look at AUTO (Athens Urban Transport Organisation) on www.oasa.gr

Rail The rail connection from the airport to join up with the Athens metro was completed for the 2004 Olympics. It costs around €8 to downtown Athens where you can change to the metro running to Piraeus. The metro link to the airport is due to open soon.

Samos Airport

Samos Airport lies just 3km west of Pithagorion, the main yachting base on Samos. Charter flights go to Samos in the summer though not as frequently as Kós and Rhodes. There are also internal flights from Spata Airport. It is a short taxi ride into Pithagorion, the best option as buses are infrequent.

Kós Airport (Hippocrates)

Kós Airport is located near the middle of the island about 26km from Kós town. Numerous charter flights go to Kós, as do budget airlines Easyjet and Ryanair (the latter via a European hub). Easyjet and Ryanair only fly in the summer, typically April to October. If you are on a charter flight you

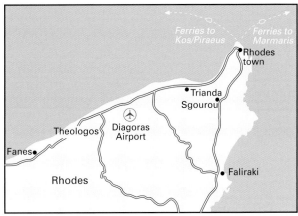

KOS AIRPORT

RHODES AIRPORT

will need to get to Kós town as many of the charter flights will be shuttling their passengers off to resort hotels in other parts of the island. Buses leave from the airport for Kós town every couple of hours or so and will cost approximately €3.50. A taxi will cost around €20. Olympic flights are met by a bus that goes to Kós town and also leave from the Olympic Office in Kós town two hours before a flight.

Rhodes Airport (Diagoras)

Rhodes Airport is situated near Paradissi village approximately 17km from Rhodes town. Numerous charter flights go to Rhodes, as do budget airlines Easyjet and Ryanair (the latter via a European hub). Easyjet and Ryanair only fly in the summer, typically April to October. If you are on a charter flight there may be a transfer to Rhodes town or somewhere close. Buses leave regularly from opposite the north car park at the airport to Rhodes town (0600 to midnight). A taxi will cost around €15–20 to Rhodes town.

Hire motorbikes are the cheapest way to get around and can be found on the major islands: just keep your wits about you when dealing with local traffic

Getting around

Ferries

Passenger and car ferries all leave from Piraeus, with a few exceptions. Passenger ferries operate on a regular basis to the Cyclades and then on down to the Dodecanese. Some ferries visit more ports than others and some are definitely faster than others. If you book on one of the major ferry lines like Blue Star it is roughly an 8-hour trip to Kós on the fast ferry. Most of these ferries will do a run from Piraeus that includes Siros, Léros, Pátmos and then Kós and Rhodes, though there may be a few other stops en route at places like Kalimnos. The slower ferries will stop at a lot more islands en route and the trip will take a lot longer. Ferries to Samos run through the northern Cyclades to Karlovasi and/or Vathi.

Around the Dodecanese smaller ferries and a few hydrofoils operate between the islands, complementing the service of the bigger Piraeus ferries. In most of the islands it is fairly easy to find out what services are operating where and book a ticket on the spot in that place.

Buses

Local bus services vary widely around the larger islands in the Dodecanese, but even the best of the services are infrequent. To get about by bus you will need to check departure times the day before and to exercise a little (and sometimes a lot of) patience and budget to allow fairly large chunks of time if you are going to get around this way.

Taxis

Most of the islands have taxis in the major centres, or you can phone for one. Fares are reasonable as long as there is a meter and it works, or the price is roughly agreed on first. In some of the more touristy spots visitors are fleeced by drivers, but on the whole little of this goes on now.

Hire cars and bikes

In many of the tourist resorts you can hire a car or jeep, or a motorbike-cum-scooter of some description. Hire cars and jeeps are expensive in Greece and unless there are two or more people it is not really worth it unless you are feeling frivolous.

In Greece a supermarket is really a minimarket and a minimarket is very 'mini'

Hire motorbikes come in all shapes and sizes, from battered Honda 50s to 500cc brutes. The operator will normally check your licence and/or hold your passport. The reliability of hire bikes varies considerably, with some bikes only a year or so old and others still struggling along after years of battering by would-be TT riders. On the whole I have found even the older Honda/Suzuki/Yamaha step-through 50s or 80s to be the most reliable, and the larger tyres (compared with scooters) make them safer on gravel roads.

All of the operators charge you for insurance, but read the small print as it doesn't seem to cover you for very much. You are expected to return the bike if it breaks down and to pay for any damage to the bike if you have an accident. Bear in mind that Greece has the highest accident rate in Europe after Portugal and that on a bike you are

vulnerable to injury. Even coming off on a gravel road at relatively low speed can cause serious gravel burns, so despite the heat it is best to wear long trousers and solid footwear. Roads on the islands are usually tarmac for the major routes and gravel for the others. Despite all these warnings a hire bike is the best way to get inland and with care you can see all sorts of places it would be difficult to get to by car.

The shop that sells the evening tipple

Walking

There are some fine walks around the islands. The main problem is finding a good map, as most locally produced maps should be treated with a healthy scepticism. Tracks which have long since disappeared will be shown and new tracks omitted. The best policy is to set out with the spirit of exploration uppermost and plan not necessarily to arrive somewhere, but rather to dawdle along the way. This mode of walking is encouraged by the energy-sapping heat of the summer. Take stout footwear, a good sun-hat, sunglasses, sunblock cream and, most importantly, a bottle of water.

Shopping and other facilities

Provisioning

In all but the smallest village you will find you can obtain basic provisions, and in the larger villages and tourist areas there will be a variety of shops catering for your needs. In larger towns and tourist resorts there are now big-name supermarket chains like Carrefour, Lidl and Alpha Beta. Unfortunately these are often on the outskirts of town so it is a long walk to get to them. Greece now has a lot more imported goods from the other EU countries and you will be able to find familiar items, such as peanut butter, bacon, breakfast cereals and even baked beans in the larger supermarkets and specialist shops. Imported items are, of course, more expensive than locally produced goods. Shopping hours are roughly 0800–1300 and 1630–2000, though shops will often remain open for longer hours in the summer if there are customers around, especially in tourist spots.

Meat is usually not hung for long and can be butchered in a peculiarly eastern-Mediterranean way – if you ask for a chicken to be quartered the butcher picks up his cleaver and neatly chops it into four lumps. In larger centres more attentive butchers and the supermarkets will produce cuts you can readily recognise. Salami and bacon are widely available in minimarkets.

In more out-of-the-way places fruit and veg trucks will do the rounds

Fish is generally expensive except for smaller varieties. Some fish, like red snapper and grouper, are very expensive and prawns and crayfish have a hefty price tag, except off the beaten track. Farmed fish, usually sea bass and bream, are cheaper. In many places you can now find frozen fish and crustaceans, usually imported from places like Brazil or SE Asia. Menus should show if the fish is fresh or frozen.

Fruit and vegetables Fresh produce used to be seasonal, but now EU imports mean more is available longer. It is wise to wash fruit and vegetables before eating them raw.

Bread Greek bread straight out of the oven is delicious, but it doesn't keep well. Bakers are a growth industry in Greece and even small villages often have a good bakers with all sorts of bread, from white through all shades of brown. They will also often have mini-pizzas, cheese or spinach pies, bacon and egg pies, filled croissants, in fact whatever the baker thinks he can sell.

Staples Many items are often sold loose. Some staples, loose or packaged, may have weevils.

Cheese Imported cheeses such as edam or gruyère are now widely available courtesy of the EU. Local hard cheeses can also be found and feta is available everywhere.

Yogurt I think Greek yogurt is the best in the world. Use it instead of salad dressing or cream.

Canned goods Local canned goods (particularly canned fruit) are good and cheap. Canned meat is usually imported and expensive.

Coffee and tea Instant coffee is comparatively expensive. Local coffee is ground very fine for 'Greek coffee' and tends to clog filters. Imported ground coffee is available. Good tea bags can be hard to find.

Wines, beer and spirits Bottled wine varies from the very good to the terrible and is not consistent, usually because it is not stored properly. Wine can be bought direct from the barrel in some larger villages and towns and at least you get to taste before you buy. *Retsina* is also available bottled or from the barrel. Beer is brewed under licence (Amstel and Heineken are the most common), is a light lager type and is eminently palatable. Local spirits, ouzo (not dissimilar to pastis) and Greek brandy, often referred to by the most common brand name as just Metaxa, are good value and can be bought bottled or from the barrel.

Banks

The major credit cards (Mastercard and Visa), debit cards and charge cards (American Express and Diners Club) are accepted in the larger towns and tourist resorts. Many use 'chip and pin' card readers, but you may be asked for a signature as well. You may need your passport for identification. All of the larger towns and tourist resorts have an ATM, (automatic teller machine or 'hole-in-the-wall machine'), which will give you cash from the major credit and debit cards such as Visa or MasterCard with a pin number. Many UK debit and credit cards charge you for foreign purchases and cash withdrawals at anything up to 2% of the amount. The exchange rate set by the bank is also often loaded by up to 3%. Some credit cards and a few debit cards are charge-free, and it is worth looking at these if you are a regular traveller to Euro countries. Prepaid cards, usually under the MasterCard umbrella and allied to a UK bank or building society, are another way to reduce these charges. You load the card with Euros by transferring money from your bank account at an agreed rate, and it then allows you to spend the money up to the amount you have on the card, either by withdrawing cash or spending as you would normally with MasterCard. The exchange rate for cards like FairFX and Caxton is usually better than that of the major banks, they do not charge to transfer the money, and only a small fixed charge is made for cash withdrawals. It means that you can transfer funds at a known exchange rate, so you know exactly how much you are spending. You can reload the card easily using the internet or by phone. You do need to be careful of how much you load

Public Holidays

Jan 1	New Year's Day
Jan 6	Epiphany
Mar 25	Independence Day
May 1	May Day
Aug 15	Assumption
Oct 28	Okhi ('No') Day
Dec 25	Christmas Day
Dec 26	St Stephen's Day

Movable
First Day of Lent
Good Friday
Easter Monday
Ascension

In addition many of the islands or regions have local saints' days when a holiday may be declared and some shops and offices will close.

as the law regarding repayment of funds should the card company go bust is ambiguous, to say the least.

For smaller places carry cash. Banks are open from 0800–1300 Monday to Friday.

Telecommunications

IDD code for Greece 30. IDD code for UK 44.

Landline telephones You can direct dial from almost anywhere in Greece. The landline system is not bad and international calls usually work seamlessly. Calls can be made at an OTE office or at a periptero using a metered phone, or at a kiosk using a prepaid phone card available in many shops or peripteros. Competition between phonecard companies mean that call rates are good. This is one of the cheapest ways to make international calls.

Mobile phone and data communications Greece has an excellent 3G and GSM network which means you get a decent signal on your mobile phone almost anywhere, including out sailing some distance off the coast. Many people now use smartphones with call and data packages arranged with their UK provider that can be used for calls, email, social networking and internet browsing. Most people are unaware of their data usage as they stream videos from YouTube, BBC iPlayer or similar, play online games, or tweet and post on social networks. When roaming on foreign networks you will need to be.

EU rulings have forced mobile phone companies to reduce their roaming call and data rates, although costs are still considerably higher than at home – your home allowances will not work abroad. And don't forget that it is still normal for you to be charged to receive calls.

Provided your phone is unlocked for using abroad it will automatically pick up the local signal, which if 3G will mean data as well. You may want to disable data roaming until you know the costs as many smartphone applications are set to update automatically and can run up huge roaming charges that you are unaware of. Some providers allow you to prepay for roaming packages, both calls and data, which allow you to control your budget. Even if you have bought a data add-on remember that many apps use up sizeable chunks of your data allowance running in the background. Turn off any that you do not need, and consider using Wi-Fi to update stuff when you are in a café.

A 'roaming' EU data add-on to your existing phone contract costs around £10 a month, with a reasonable download limit for emails and light internet use. Check with your provider as roaming data charges vary enormously, and without an agreement it is possible to run up huge bills. Once it is all set up, you have all the convenience of receiving email, or checking weather forecasts wherever you are, and with some packages you can use your phone as a modem so you can use your laptop.

Wireless Internet Access (Wi-Fi) using a laptop computer or smartphone Many marinas, hotels, cafés, bars, libraries and internet cafés have Wi-Fi networks, some of which are provided free of charge, or unsecured; others require a password. Subscribers may pay a one-off connection charge and/or 'pay-as-you-go' for minutes/hours/days of online access. Costs are reasonable for a fast connection, and you don't need to run up unseen bills on your phone.

Most new laptops and smartphones have built-in wireless modems and will 'search' automatically for available Wi-Fi networks. All you need to do is to identify which network you wish to connect to, and put in a password if requested. Once connected, you can access email, social networks and internet –

pretty much as you would at home; but remember that unsecured public networks do carry some security risks so make sure you have a decent firewall installed.

A separate Wi-Fi aerial which plugs into your laptop will enable you to pick up signals at greater distances, so you can 'surf' in the anchorage should you wish.

Note Wi-Fi is a generic term used here to describe all wireless networks.

Data access using a local SIM card and a laptop Most local phone companies offer pay-as-you-go SIM cards with data capability, which will utilise 3G technology to give you broadband speed if the network is capable. You can use the SIM card in a local or unlocked mobile phone, or in a dedicated USB 'dongle'. If using a dongle you simply plug in and go. If you use a phone you will need to connect to the computer using either a cable or Bluetooth technology. Your UK phone is probably 'locked' to your UK service provider so you can't use a different SIM card in it.

The advantage of using a phone is that if a 3G network is not available you can also use the GPRS system – not as fast but adequate for email and light surfing. Much is written elsewhere on the ins and outs of both systems, but generally costs are linked to data quantity downloaded/uploaded, and can be arranged on a daily or monthly basis. Shop around the various companies, and in many larger towns the staff will have a good knowledge of the options and will be able to get you what you want. Costs are generally higher than using Wi-Fi networks, but you have the advantage of being able to use it anywhere where you have a phone signal. You could even use it to make cheap local calls!

Internet cafés Many quite small places have an internet café these days and if you have an internet webmail provider then it takes little time to download and send mail, using a USB stick if you need to save stuff. Costs are usually low and of course connection rates are high with many places on broadband or ASDL connections. As mentioned above, many internet cafés also have a Wi-Fi network, or a cable network which you can use your laptop or smartphone to connect to.

Voice over Internet Protocol (VoIP) Using a laptop with a broadband connection and a simple headset, many people use VoIP to make telephone calls. You need to subscribe to a VoIP provider, and set up an account and username to use the service. Call charges are a fraction of those incurred using a phone, and calls between subscribers of the same provider are free. The downside for travellers is the need to be connected to a broadband network, and it is generally not practical to use on mobile data roaming packages. It is best used with a reasonable Wi-Fi connection. Skype is probably the best known service, although there are now many companies offering similar services.

Background basics in Turkey

Getting to Turkey

By air

Most people coming to this part of Turkey will be flying with a charter or budget airline to Bodrum or Dalaman Airport. There are also charter and budget airline flights to Izmir and Antalya. Easyjet fly to Izmir, Bodrum and Dalaman in the summer. Other major airlines like BA and Turkish Airlines also do discounted flights. Charter flights originate from a number of airports in the UK and other countries: Sweden, Finland, Germany, France and Russia. In the UK the major operators are Thomson, First Choice, MyTravel, and Thomas Cook who fly from a number of UK airports. Charter flights operate only in the summer, usually from May to October, with the majority of flights on weekends.

Scheduled flights operate to Istanbul, Izmir and Antalya and you can then get an internal flight with Turkish airlines or Pegasus to Bodrum and Dalaman airports. Easyjet and Pegasus also fly from Istanbul to the UK.

Bodrum Airport The airport is 33km from Bodrum, about half an hour to Bodrum town and around two hours to Marmaris. A number of charter airlines fly here as well as budget airline Easyjet. Easyjet only fly in the summer, typically April to October. If on a charter flight try to arrange the transfer before you fly. Alternatively a taxi is around 50 YTL from the airport to Bodrum. Havas airport buses run to and from Bodrum when internal flights are arriving or departing (€8).

Dalaman Airport Charter airlines and budget airline Easyjet fly to Dalaman. Easyjet only fly in the summer, typically April to October. Dalaman Airport is near the town of Dalaman which is around 35km from Göcek and 50km from Fethiye. From Dalaman it is 30 minutes to Göcek, under an hour to Fethiye, about 1½ hours to Marmaris, and around four hours to Bodrum. Try to arrange a transfer beforehand as it is difficult to find many buses stopping in Dalaman and the taxi drivers here run a bit of a cartel with fixed prices. A taxi is around 75 YTL from the airport to Göcek.

Istanbul Sabiha Gokcen Airport

Situated on the Asian side of the Bosphorus. Budget airlines like Easyjet and Pegasus fly here all year round. Charter airlines also fly here. You can connect from Bodrum or Dalaman with internal flights with Pegasus, Onur or Turkish Airlines.

Antalya Airport

Charter and budget airlines like Easyjet fly here in the summer. Internal flights to other airports with Pegasus, Onur and Turkish Airlines.

TURKISH AIRPORTS IN EAST AEGEAN

By sea

Daily ferries run from the Greek islands to Turkey: from Rhodes to Marmaris, Kós to Bodrum and Turgutreis, Samos to Kuşadasi, Khios to Çeşme, and from Lesvos to Ayvalik. If you arrive on a charter flight in Greece and spend more than one day in Turkey you may be prevented from using the return portion of your ticket in Greece. On a scheduled flight to Greece you will have no problems in this respect.

Getting around

Bus

Bus and minibus (*dolmuş*) are the most widespread form of public transport in Turkey. Different companies run scheduled buses around most of the coast described here, and to the smaller villages you can get a *dolmuş*, small minibuses that leave when they are full or nearly so. The large buses are all fairly modern, mostly Mercedes assembled in Turkey. You can book a seat on the bus in advance and on popular routes it is worth doing this. Some of the driving is a little aggressive so it is best to sit towards the back where you cannot see what is happening on the road up ahead. On board there will be bottled water courtesy of the bus company (ask for *su*), and lemon cologne is liberally distributed at intervals to keep you smelling nice on the journey. On some major routes Wi-Fi is available. The bus will stop every two hours or so for the toilet, snacks, and *çay*.

The larger towns will have a central bus station (*otogar, otobus terminali,* or *otobus garaji*) that buses leave from. As you get further down the coast, buses get less frequent, and from Fethiye around the coast to Antalya there are only a few scheduled services. *Dolmuş* fill in where the larger buses leave off. To get to many of the smaller villages there will only be a *dolmuş* service and you must squeeze in with the locals, bags of fruit and vegetables, sacks of flour, and whatever else has been purchased in town – *dolmuş* literally means 'stuffed', and the minibuses often are.

Turkey is the market garden of the eastern Mediterranean and the markets have some of the best fruit and vegetables in the region

Car

This is the best way of exploring many of the more remote inland places mentioned in this book. You can hire cars at Izmir, Kuşadasi, Bodrum, Marmaris, Fethiye, and Antalya. Hire cars are not cheap in Turkey and neither is fuel, and it is best to get a deal with unlimited kilometres. It may be that you can get a better deal before you leave with a Fly-Drive package which usually works out substantially cheaper than buying the flight and hiring the car separately. You require only a licence from your own country to drive in Turkey.

There are few problems driving on the roads in Turkey and for the most part driving is a pleasure. However, there are a few pointers for the newcomer driving in Turkey for the first time. Trucks and cars cannot be relied on to turn in the direction they are signalling: a vehicle turning left will usually indicate left and then pull over onto the hard shoulder until the road is clear. (It is not normal, except where marked, to pull into the middle and turn left.) Driving at dusk and at night is not recommended. As well as herds of sheep or goats or the odd cow or donkey on the road, there are also unlit vehicles; horse and carts, tractors and trailers, motorbikes and the odd truck and car. Sometimes a tractor and trailer or a cart exhibits a single white light at the rear, which can be confusing. The main roads along the coast are good, well paved affairs, and the roads are being improved all the time with a number of motorways under construction.

By contrast some of the minor roads are very rough, ill-made affairs, often a single lane with just gravel and a lot of pot-holes, and at worst dirt or clay tracks which are passable in the summer (with due care and attention) but are often impassable after heavy rain in the spring and autumn. One thing you will have to get used to is using the horn to warn pedestrians, cyclists, and other drivers of your presence before overtaking. Likewise, anyone overtaking you will give a toot on the horn to let you know he is there. Driving in Turkey, especially in towns and cities, is a much more raucous business than in comparatively sedate Europe.

Taxis

Taxis are all metered and you should make sure the meter is on to avoid exorbitant demands at the end of the trip. If there is no meter or the driver says the meter is broken, agree on the fare for the trip first. There are agreed tariff rates for intercity and intracity journeys and a tariff card should be available. Overall, taxis are cheap and the service polite and good-humoured. Incidentally, Turks do not tip taxi drivers unless some extra service has been provided, so there is no need for you to do so.

Shopping and other facilities

Provisioning

Turks are natural entrepreneurs and you will be able to get basic provisions in even the smallest village. If a dozen yachts call somewhere in a season you will likely find a minimarket with an eccentric range of products depending on what the owner thinks yachties want. In the larger centres you will find numerous minimarkets with all sorts of goods imported from the EU and these days you can get good cheeses, bacon and French wine, though it all comes at a price. There are also some supermarket chains, notably Migros, Carrefour and Tansas, sometimes in a marina or otherwise close by the town centre, where you will find a wide range of local and imported goods. Shopping hours are roughly 0830–1400 and 1600–1930 Monday to Saturday though many of the smaller minimarkets are open longer if there is demand.

Meat Relatively expensive though usually nicely butchered. Lamb chops will be butterflied and steak trimmed of excess fat. It is often not hung for long but is generally tender for all that. One tip, if you are buying mince ask the butcher to put it through the mincer just once as he is generally used to doing it several times to make finely minced meat for kofte and kebabs.

Fish No longer cheap, and prized fish like grouper is expensive. Crayfish and prawns are also expensive. Other types of fish, especially mackerel and tunny in season, are good value. Fish from fish farms, predominantly sea bass and bream, is a lot cheaper than the wild variety and farmed shellfish, predominantly mussels, are also available.

Fruit and vegetables Excellent throughout the year and comparatively cheap. The choice is seasonal, though more is now grown in greenhouses so 'seasons' are longer. In more out-of-the-way places you will find small stalls selling almonds, seasonal fruit like apricots, bananas, and pomegranates, and excellent honey.

Staples Most basics can be found, although some items, such as rice and pasta, tend to be of poor quality unless you buy imported brands. Larger towns and tourist resorts now have European supermarkets Carrefour, Migros and even Tesco.

Al fresco dining on *Skylax* with fresh produce from the local markets. Most things can be found these days and it's interesting to experiment as well

Public Holidays

Jan 1
New Year's Day

Apr 23
Children's Day

May 1
May Day

May 19
Youth Day

May 27
Freedom and Constitution Day

Aug 30
Victory Day

Oct 29, 30
Republic Days

Where the holiday falls on a weekend the following Monday will be a holiday.

Movable

Şeker bayrami
(Sugar festival)

Kurban bayrami
(Fast of sacrifice)

Regulations and documentation
GREECE

Documents Passport. Yacht registration papers. VAT receipt or other proof of payment. You may be asked for proof of competence to handle a yacht such as the RYA ICC or Yachtmaster.

Customs (Telenion) Greece as part of the EU comes under EU legislation regarding the payment of VAT.

Non-EU boats should report to customs at the first Port of Entry.

Entry formalities All yachts entering Greece must go to a Port of Entry. A Greek courtesy ensign and, for non-EU registered yachts, a 'Q' flag should be flown.

Passport control, health, customs and port police must be visited in order.

Note Interpretation and implementation of the regulations regarding foreign (and particularly non-EU registered) yachts in Greece varies in different ports.

Pleasure Craft Traffic Document (DEKPA)

All yachts cruising in Greek Waters must have a valid Traffic Document. These are purchased on entry along with the Cruising Permit (if required) and are valid for fifty ports of call. A Traffic Document should be presented to port police on entering and leaving each port where it will be stamped. Cost c.€30

Transit log

A Customs record for non-EU yachts. It is valid for six months, with a further six months on application. The transit log must be surrendered on leaving Greece. There is no charge for the transit log, although most non-EU vessels are liable for the Special Reciprocal Charge (see below).

Other charges

Compulsory customs processing fee €15

Solidarity tax for sailors social security €15

Special reciprocal charge

(Non-EU yachts only) €15 per metre (valid for three months and levied at the end of the period.)

Port dues

Each time a yacht moors in a Greek harbour, the skipper should visit the Port Police to get the DEKPA stamped, and to pay port dues. The dues are made up of two parts, a docking fee and a mooring fee. (See below).

Thus a 12m yacht mooring stern-to should pay a total of €9.42 per day including tax. The reality in some of the busier places is that a representative will come along the quay once a day to collect a flat fee of around €10. Since many of these town quays now have good access to water, and sometimes electricity, this doesn't seem to be an unfair arrangement.

Greek Cruising Tax

Law 3790, introduced for all motor yachts over 10m and yachts over 15m that remain in Greek waters for over 40 days. As yet the tax has only been implemented a handful of times and it is reported to have been axed.

Cost for 15m motorboat: €5,000

Cost for 15m yacht: €3,000

Notes

1. Port dues are usually included in marina berthing fees.

2. It is reported that if a yacht has proof of an annual contract with a marina they do not have to pay the docking fee, as it is understood that this is included in the annual marina fee.

In practice

In many ports you will not be asked for port dues. In others the port police or a deputised official will come down to ask you for the fee and you are legally bound to pay it. I find the attitudes of some who complain about having to pay a €10 fee (in fact it can vary from €8–12 or so depending on the computation) churlish, to say the least, when marina and port fees in other countries are so much higher. A smile and treating the port police and officials like human beings goes a long way to keeping things sweet – and this is a sweet place to be.

Insurance

1. All yachts must have insurance for liability for death or injury for those on board and any third party for a minimum of €295,000.

2. Insurance for liability for damage of at least €145,000.

3. Liability for pollution resulting from an incident of €90,000.

4. A certificate of insurance translated into Greek.

Ports of entry in the Eastern Aegean

Ayios Nikólaos (Crete)
Khíos (Eastern Sporades)
Kós (Dodecanese)
Pátmos (Dodecanese)
Pithagorion (Sámos) (Eastern Sporades)
Rhodes (Dodecanese)
Sitia (Crete)

Fees (€ in 2010)	Docking Fee	Mooring (Stern-to)	(Alongside)
Charter yacht	0·07/m	0·08/m/day	0·11/m/day
Private yacht >5m with cabin	0·30/m	0·36/m/day	0·45/m/day
Private boat >5m open boat	0·04/m	0·36/m/day	

Regulations and documentation
TURKEY

Documents Passport. Most foreign nationals, including UK citizens, need to obtain a visa. In some cases they are free, others must pay a modest fee. In 2011 a visa cost £10 for UK passport holders. Visas are typically multiple entry and are issued for 90 days for all EU, N American and Australasian citizens. New visa restrictions have been introduced which permit a maximum stay of 90 days in 180 days. After 90 days in Turkey visitors must leave the country for at least 90 days. Special exemptions for yachtsmen have been sought, but at the time of writing the restrictions stand. Yacht registration papers. You may be asked for proof of insurance and proof of competence to handle a yacht such as the RYA ICC or Yachtmaster's certificate.

Customs All yachts entering Turkey must do so at one of the designated Ports of Entry (*see below*). A transit log will be issued by customs and in 2011 it cost US$30. It is valid for one year, or one continuous visit, or until the yacht is laid-up, whichever happens first. On issue you must list your intended itinerary and crew list in the transit log, and changes to either must also be recorded and authorised by the harbourmaster at the time of the change. When leaving Turkey with the yacht you must surrender the transit log, even if you intend to return to Turkey at any time.

New harbour dues must be paid on entry to Turkey for vessels over 11 NRT (this equates to yachts around 10–12m LOA). The dues are around 7 YTL for vessels up to 45 NRT. The payment process can only be done by an agent who may also complete all clearance procedures at the same time. Agent charges vary from €50–150 so ask around before committing to one agent, and make sure you know what is included. Most agents will charge in the region of €80–100 which includes all fees. Some marinas are also able to complete the new payment and clearance procedures.

There are plans to make it possible for the tonnage fees to be paid on the internet with a debit or credit card so the transit log can be completed online without the need for an agent. This is not possible at the time of writing.

Extended stays Heavy fines are imposed for overstaying your visa, even by one day. Those wishing to stay longer in Turkey are advised to apply for a Residence Permit. They are available to yacht owners, their families and crew, on the condition that the yacht has a fully paid contract with an approved Turkish marina. They are valid for the duration of the marina contract, up to a maximum of two years on the first application. Costs for a one-year permit are around US$180, depending on your country's visa arrangements.

A foreign flag yacht without the owner aboard can enter Turkey and sail to another port to pick the owner up, but cannot change the complement of those on board.

Turkish coastguard out and about

Charter yachts entering Turkey (inevitably from Greece) must pay a charter fee (depending on LOA) to cruise around the Turkish coast.

Entry formalities A yacht entering Turkish waters for the first time must do so at a designated Port of Entry. A 'Q' flag and a Turkish courtesy flag should be flown. Here you will obtain a transit log valid for one year. You will have to visit the health office, passport police, customs, harbourmaster, and customs patrol, usually, but not always, in that order. You are then free to cruise on the itinerary detailed on the transit log which must be produced at any port or on demand from the *Sahil Guvenlik* (Coastguard).

Note Large fines are levied on yachts discharging waste into the sea, particularly in harbour. The maximum official fine is in the region of €235–310. However fines have been known to be as much as €620 and, in one case, €1,550. Ports strictly enforcing heavy penalties are Bozburun, Göcek, Kalkan and Kaş. Yacht skippers should never pump out holding tanks in harbour or at anchor whether threatened by a fine or not.

Note See the special regulations that apply for Skopea Limanı in Chapter 4.

Ports of entry in the eastern Aegean
Çeşme
Kuşadasi
Didim Marina
Turgutreis Marina
Bodrum
Datça
Marmaris
Fethiye
Kaş
Finike
Kemer

Special Environmental Protection Areas (SEPA)

There are established marine nature reserves at Foca, Ayvalik archipelago, Gököva Körfezi, Datça-Bodrum peninsula, Koycegiz-Dalyan coast, and Fethiye-Göcek Körfezi. Restrictions apply to waste water discharge and in Fethiye-Göcek there are additional restrictions on anchoring in some bays. Olü Deniz near Gocek has been closed to yachts for a number of years to try to curb pollution from diesel engines.

'Blue Card' (Mavikart)

In 2009 legislation was passed, effectively banning black and grey water discharge from yachts in the Mugla Province whose seaboard basically runs from Güllük to Fethiye. The area covered is considerably larger than existing SEPA areas and the restrictions somewhat more draconian. The restrictions are initially being introduced to the Fethiye Körfezi area and particularly to Skopea Liman. Not surprisingly all sorts of problems for the implementation of the scheme have surfaced. Most of these problems have been to do with the lack of infrastructure to implement the regulations: lack of pump-out points, inadequate resources to police the area, inadequately trained staff, and problems over how the scheme will be administered and processed on an individual basis. There have also been problems over the exact interpretation of the legislation and just how it should be implemented. This confusion over the scheme has resulted in rumours, misguided comment and not a little scaremongering, none of which has been helped by the fact that the authorities do not seem to understand what is going on and nor do those connected to yacht services in the area. There is plenty of room for confusion here.

TURMEPA, an NGO concerned with the environment and particularly with the sea areas around Turkey, has been instrumental in the call for greater regulation, but does not have the resources to administer or implement the rules. The mix of an NGO, local government and state government agencies has created not a little confusion.

The Blue Card scheme was first introduced in 2010, but an exception was made for yachts as the infrastructure was not in place. It seems that a revised scheme for yachts will be introduced into the Fethiye-Göcek SEPA in 2012 (but see the comments on the practical implementation in November 2011 in Chapter 4). Below I have outlined the basics of what is proposed, but it must be emphasized that this interpretation can easily change and in all likelihood will change given the confusion that has surrounded the introduction of the scheme.

1. **Blue Card** All boats in the area will need to purchase a 'Blue Card' on which will be recorded data about the boat and crew and importantly will record the dates and volume at designated pump-out stations. The card is valid for the duration of the stay in Turkey.

2. **Black water** All boats must have black water tanks which are discharged at registered waste disposal sites. Discharge is to be recorded on the Blue Card. No black water to be discharged within the SEPA.

3. **Grey water** All boats must have grey water tanks or for smaller yachts grey water outlets must be plumbed into the black water tank. Discharge is to be recorded on the Blue Card. No grey water to be discharged within the SEPA.

4. **Pump-out stations** Waste pump-out points are being established in marinas and harbours. A mobile pump-out boat (run by TURMEPA) is also in operation. It is planned to have 22 pump-out stations between Bodrum and Fethiye.

5. **Bilge water** No bilge water or oil waste to be discharged into the water.

6. **Garbage** No garbage to be disposed of in the water OR ashore except in designated areas.

7. **Mooring** Yachts are only able to moor to mooring buoys and bollards on the shore in designated areas. Boats can only stay for three days in one place and 11 days total in the SEPA. The plan is to restrict boat numbers to c.1,112 within the SEPA (this includes marina berths and moorings).

8. **Other prohibitions** See the publication by the Ministry of Environment & Forests in Chapter 4.

Pollution in the Mediterranean

The following is an excerpt from my *Mediterranean Cruising Handbook* (Imray)

Pollution and Sustainable Development

The following information is taken from a paper *Land-Based Pollution of the Mediterranean Sea: Present State and Prospects* by Dr Francesco Saverio Civili, Coordinator, MED POL Programme, UNEP/MAP, Athens 2010.

Back in the 1970's land-based sources (LBS) were identified as the origin of most marine pollution. In 1975 the United Nation Environment Program (UNEP) brought together the culturally and politically diverse countries of the Mediterranean and drew up the Mediterranean Action Plan (MAP), which was adopted by 21 Mediterranean states, and the EU. Later they adopted and signed the Protocol for the Protection of the Mediterranean Sea against Pollution from Land-Based Sources (LBS Protocol, 1980). By 1996 this was revised to prioritise the phasing out of substance 'toxic, persistent and liable to bio-accumulate' (PBTs). This protocol covers the Mediterranean Sea, and the entire watershed area within the territories draining into it, waters on landward side of territorial boundaries, and brackish waters, marshes, coastal lagoons and groundwater. In 2008 the latest version of the LBS was adopted, establishing a clearly targeted legal framework for the progressive elimination of land-based pollution. The Strategic Action Plan (SAP) is the basis under which the LBS Protocol will be implemented over the next 25 years.

Agricultural run-off, in the form of pesticides, has long been identified as a major pollutant, and with countries around the southern and eastern coastal regions set to increase agro-food production five-fold by 2025, the control of run-off is clearly an important target.

More than 200 petrochemical plants, energy installations and basic chemical plants are located along the Mediterranean coast and river catchment basins, including at least 40 major oil refineries, cement plants, steel mills, food processing plants, tanneries, textile mills, and pulp and paper mills. They are significant carriers of chemical pollutants discharged directly or indirectly into the sea. These harmful pollutants, PBTs, are regulated under the convention.

One third of the Mediterranean population, approximately 145 million people, are concentrated on a narrow coastal strip. This number is expected to double by 2025. As 50% of tourists arriving in the Mediterranean are based on the coast, and with an estimated doubling in tourism related development, visitor numbers could reach 350 million by 2025.

If we make a comparison of land and sea based numbers in Marmaris Bay we get the following figures.

• There are around 1,800 yacht berths in Marmaris with around 20% of berths occupied by charter boats. Of the balance of private yachts probably only 50% will be used at any one time. Lets say there will be an average of three people on an average yacht, probably an over-estimate. That means there will be something like 3,240 people on yachts assuming the charter fleet is full and half of the private boats are occupied.

• In Marmaris there are estimated to be 60,000 tourist beds. Lets assume a mean 75% occupancy in summer and we are talking about 45,000 people. Other figures suggest a total of 350,000 at the height of summer The resident population is around 30,000.

Whichever way you look at it the difference between the yacht population and the land-based population is huge. Moreover marina based yachts will be using the marina showers and toilets and hence the mains sewage system anyway. Given that the treated sewage is disposed of in the sea, that is it is not treated sufficiently to be recycled for use, that means that significant amounts of organic matter and bacteria are discharged and significant amounts of chlorine. None of these are helpful to the marine environment.

Cheese Local soft cheeses (feta types) are cheap and good. Locally made and pre-packed hard and processed cheeses are adequate and reasonably priced. Imported cheeses (usually Camembert and blue cheeses) are expensive.

Canned goods Reasonable choice of canned goods, although there are not a lot of meat-based stews and the like. Canned vegetables, beans and fruit are good and relatively cheap.

Coffee and tea Imported instant coffee is available, although comparatively expensive. Filter coffee is also available. Local coffee can be ground coarsely to make an acceptable cup. The packaged ground coffee is ground very fine for Turkish coffee and tends to clog filters if you are making filter coffee. Imported tea is available for the traditional 'cuppa'. Local tea doesn't make a British cuppa but is drinkable. Drink it Turkish-style: strong, black, and sweet.

Wines, beer and spirits Local wines are palatable, but on the whole they are neither cheap nor consistent. Try Angora, Villa Doluca, Dardanelles, and Kavaklidere for reds, and Angora, Kavaklidere, Villa Doluca, Sungurlu and Cankaya for whites.

Local beer (commonly Efes or Tuborg) is of the lager type, cheap, and eminently drinkable, although a bit gassy.

The local spirit, the aniseed-flavoured raki, is moderately priced and lethal. It is normally drunk half-and-half with water. Local brandy is hardly palatable. Imported spirits, if you can find them, are expensive, but local gin and vodka are reasonably priced and drinkable.

Banks

Major credit cards (Mastercard and Visa), debit cards and charge cards (American Express and Diners Club) are accepted in the larger towns and tourist resorts. You may need your passport for identification. All of the larger towns and tourist resorts have an ATM (automatic teller machine or 'hole-in-the-wall machine'), which will give you cash from the major credit and debit cards such as Visa or MasterCard with a pin number. Many UK debit and credit cards charge you for foreign purchases and cash withdrawals at anything up to 2% of the amount. The exchange rate set by the bank is also often loaded by up to 3%. See section in Greece on prepaid cards.

For smaller places carry cash. Banks are open 0800–1200 and 1330–1800 Monday to Friday.

Telecommunications

See the section on Telecommunications in Greece (on page 18), most of which applies equally to Turkey.

Notes

1. If you want to use a Turkish SIM card in a UK handset you will need to register your phone. Turkish authorities are clamping down on illegal/stolen mobile phones. You must register your mobile phone's IMEI number with customs officials when you enter Turkey. You are advised to carry proof of ownership. Failure to register it will mean your phone may cease to work after a few days. In practice this can be done at most Turkcell shops in major (tourist) towns where the procedure is well understood.

2. Call charges and data rates are considerably higher than the EU. Any packages you have for the EU do not apply here. In some places you may be able to pick up Greek telecommunication signals from the islands which will give you considerably lower charges.

Websites

Many websites are banned in Turkey, including my own! This is often to do with links to banned sites in Turkey – which includes YouTube and many of the social networking sites – although it can be for other more obscure reasons and at times for no apparent reason at all. There are ways around this, but don't assume because a website doesn't come up that the site is faulty. It will more likely be that the site is banned.

Sailing information

Navigation around the islands and along the coast is predominantly of the eyeball variety. The ancients navigated quite happily from island to island and between prominent features on the coast, and this is basically what yachtsmen still do in the eastern Aegean. Eyeball navigation is a much-maligned art, especially now that electronic position-finding equipment has arrived on the scene, but for the reasons outlined below, it is still essential to hone your pilotage skills.

For good eyeball navigation you need the facility to translate the two-dimensional world of the chart into the three-dimensional world around you. Pick out conspicuous features like a cape, an isolated house, a knoll or an islet, and visualise what these will look like in reality. Any dangers to navigation, such as a reef or shoal water, may need clearing bearings to ensure you stay well clear of them. Any eyeball navigation must always be backed up by dead reckoning and a few position fixes along the way.

Anyone with electronic position-finding should exercise caution when using it close to land or dangers to navigation. The paradox of the new equipment is that while you may know your position, often to an accuracy of 20m or less, the chart you are plotting your position on is not accurate in terms of its latitude and longitude. Most of the charts were surveyed in the 19th century using astronomical sights, and the position of a cape or a danger to navigation, while proportionally correct in relation to the land mass, may be incorrect in terms of its latitude and longitude. Some of the charts carry a warning, and corrections for latitude and longitude (usually the latter). Consequently you are in the anomalous position of knowing your position to perhaps within 20m, but in possession of a chart which may have inaccuracies much greater than this. Blind acceptance of the position from electronic position-finding equipment can lead, and has led, to disaster.

Navigation and piloting hazards

The comparatively tideless waters of the Mediterranean, a magnetic variation of around 4°E, and the relatively settled summer patterns remove many of the problems associated with sailing in other areas of the world. Just having no tidal streams of any consequence to worry about enhances your sailing a hundredfold. Despite this, there are hazards to navigation which, while not specific to the Mediterranean, should be mentioned here.

Haze

In the summer a heat haze can reduce visibility to a mile or two, which makes identification of a distant island or feature difficult until you are closer to it. Heavy rain in the spring and autumn cleanses the air and dramatically improves visibility.

Fog

In general fog is rare. In parts of the Aegean there may be a light radiation fog in the morning which can sometimes reduce visibility to a mile or less. Around Antalya there can be a radiation fog in the morning reducing visibility to a mile or less, but it has generally burned off by midday and by afternoon will invariably have disappeared.

Most of this coast is well marked using IALA system A

Fish farm off Salih Adası in Turkey

Reefs and rocks

The Dodecanese and adjacent Turkish coast have only a few isolated dangerous rocks and reefs and with care these are normally easily spotted. However, this absence of large areas of shoal water or extensive reefs can make the navigator lazy in his craft. The clarity of the water in the Mediterranean means you can easily spot rocks and shallows from the colour of the water. Basically, deep blue is good, deep green means it is getting shallow, lighter green means 'watch out', and brown lets you identify species of molluscs at first hand. However, with a bit of wind of any sort the whitecaps on the water can make identification of shallow water and reefs difficult and you should give any potential dangers a wide berth. In recent years some of these dangers have been buoyed, usually but not always using cardinal buoys or beacons, and this makes things somewhat easier. However, after winter storms buoys and beacons can be destroyed and will not always be replaced straight away.

Fishing nets

Care is needed around local fishing boats or in isolated bays where there may be surface nets laid. Vigilance is needed not to run over a net and incur not just the wrath of a fisherman but also, most likely, the net wrapped tightly around the propeller.

Fish farms

In a number of bays, coves and bights there are floating rafts of fish farms. In some places the fish farms restrict the space for anchoring and in others care is needed to avoid the raft anchors on the bottom. In a few places yachts are turned away by fish farm managers. Fish farms are frequently moved so the positions given in the plans and notes may change.

Lights

Although the islands and coast are quite well lit, the sheer extent of coastline means that it is impossible to light any but the most common routes used by ships and commercial fishermen. Navigation at night out of the common routes should be avoided unless you are familiar with the area.

Winds

The winds in this area are remarkably consistent in the summer. Details of the winds specific to the area are given at the beginning of each chapter, but in general the area comes under the influence of the *meltemi*.

The prevailing wind over the Dodecanese and along the Turkish coast is the *meltemi* blowing from the NW to W. It can blow up to Force 7 or even 8 at times, though normally it is around Force 4–6. It generally starts to blow in late June/early July and blows through until October. It can at times blow solidly day and night for a week or it may just blow for a couple of days. Along the Turkish coast and to a lesser extent in the Dodecanese there is a thermal component which reinforces the breeze during the day and lessens it at night and early morning. This thermal factor cannot always be relied on, but when it does occur is useful for making progress north.

Along the stretch of coast between Kekova and Antalya the dominant breeze is a land breeze blowing off the land in the morning and a sea breeze blowing onshore in the afternoon.

In the evening there may a katabatic wind off the high mountains of the Turkish coast, though there are only a few places (the eastern end of Gökova Körfezi and around Ölü Deniz are two) where you are likely to be affected by such a wind. On occasion the wind can get up to 30–35 knots, though it is usually less and it generally lasts only a few hours before dying down. In the summer there may be isolated thunderstorms with an associated squall, but these seldom last for more than a few hours and are normally over in less than an hour.

In the spring and autumn, depressions passing east either N or S of this sea area can give rise to strong southerlies or northerlies.

For more detail on the prevailing winds see the section at the beginning of each chapter.

The prevailing winds are from a constant direction in the summer, as you can see from these pines bent to the wind

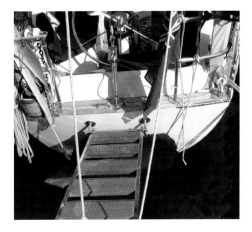

Stern-to is the normal method for berthing in Greece and Turkey

Berthing

Berthing Mediterranean-style with the stern or bows to the quay can give rise to immense problems for those doing it for the first time, or even the second or third time. Describing the technique is easy: the boat is berthed with the stern or bows to the quay with an anchor out from the bows or stern respectively to hold the boat off the quay. It is carrying out the manoeuvre which causes problems and here a few words of advice may be useful, but will not replace actually doing it.

Everything should be ready before you actually start the manoeuvre. Have all the fenders tied on, have two warps coiled and ready to throw ashore with one end cleated off,

Anchoring with a long line ashore

In many of the bays around the Greek and Turkish coasts you will be anchoring with a long line ashore. The prevailing winds in the summer are generally from a constant direction and you will be taking your long line to the shore where the prevailing wind is blowing off the land. The long line will be taking the strain.

Pick your spot, drop the anchor and then reverse in to your chosen rock or bollard and row a line ashore from the stern and tie it off. In most places the water is clear enough for you to gauge when you are close enough in. When you have let out enough chain on the bower anchor most boats will hold their stern into the wind with the engine in tick-over and in gear going astern, so you don't get wafted out into the bay taking the person who is rowing or swimming the line ashore with you. Just make sure the line doesn't go anywhere near the propeller. Usually a line of around 30m or so will be ample, but it's useful to have an additional length made up and tied on in the cockpit just in case.

In some places new bollards have been cemented onto the rocks to save the trees and your lines from chafe. In Skopea Liman in Turkey it is prohibited to tie lines around a tree and in other places this should be avoided if possible as a matter of principle. A rope tied around a tree can easily ring-bark the tree and kill it.

If you are swimming a line ashore wear some sort of footwear as there can be spiky sea urchins along the shore and getting the spines out is painful – I know.

The prevailing winds in the summer are from a pretty constant direction and in many coves there just is not room to swing to an anchor. I often get letters telling me the practice is unseamanlike, unnecessary and damned dangerous. It is none of these and given that the sea bottom drops off quickly in places, it is more seamanlike than swinging to an anchor, where if the anchor drags you are likely to drift out into deep water with no chance of the anchor digging in again.

If the wind should happen to suddenly blow violently into a bay putting you into a dangerous situation, I just let the stern line go and get the anchor up and then return in the dinghy to retrieve the line. At worst it's better to lose a line than the boat.

In many of the anchorages you anchor and take a long line ashore

and have the anchor ready to run. Where a windlass is fitted it is better to release the clutch and let the chain run out under gravity rather than under power, and to use the clutch as a brake when necessary. If you use the down button and the motor lets the chain out it will not run fast enough to keep pace with the speed of the boat, and you will end up with less chain out than you really need. When going bows-to with a stern anchor have the warp flaked out so it does not tie itself into knots as you are berthing. The manoeuvre should be carried out slowly using the anchor to take the way off the boat about half a boat length off the quay. The anchor should be dropped about three or four boat lengths from the quay and ensure you have sufficient chain or warp beforehand to actually get there. Many boats have a permanent set-up for going bows-to so there is not too much scrabbling around in lockers to extract an anchor, chain and warp. This can be quite simple: a bucket tied to the pushpit to hold the chain and warp and an arrangement for stowing the anchor on the pushpit. Boats going stern-to must have someone who knows what they are doing letting the anchor chain go. It should run freely until the boat is half a boat length off the quay. The important thing is to try to let the anchor go in line with the berth you are aiming to go into, and not at an angle. Many people insist it is better to lay the anchor at an angle upwind of your berth, which is all very well, but necessarily dictates that everyone else must do likewise. Accepted practice in the Mediterranean is to lay your anchor straight out. Laying your anchor out at an angle to the quay just means it is much more likely that someone will lay their anchor over yours, no matter how much you might jump up and down and object. It also becomes less than helpful should the wind change direction, such that your anchor is now to leeward. If your anchor is laid straight, dug in and tensioned, it will hold you off the quay. Provided of course that the same applies to your neighbours! A snubber should be fitted on the bower chain to take the weight off the windlass. When leaving a berth haul yourself out with the chain or warp using the engine only sparingly until the anchor is up – it is all too easy to get the anchor warp caught around the propeller otherwise.

For more information see *Adlard Coles Book of Mediterranean Cruising*.

The good tourist

However much we hate being tagged with the label, we all are tourists, some longer-term than others. If you like you can be the good holidaymaker, visitor, yachtsman, or whatever name is not offensive to your sensibilities. What is required of those of us who travel on the water around the Aegean or anywhere else in the world is that we do not stain the waters we travel on or the land we come to. Regrettably, some tourists seem not to have any understanding of the delicate relationship between tourist and locals, and there are a number of substantial local complaints about us.

Rubbish

Many of the smaller islands and mainland villages are just not geared up to disposing of the rubbish brought in by tourists, and on the water you will be visiting some small villages or deserted bays where there are literally no facilities at all. You should take your rubbish with you to a larger island and dispose of it there. Even the larger islands have questionable methods of disposing of rubbish, and there is nothing wrong with trying to keep the number of convenience-wrapped goods you buy to a minimum. My particular *bête noire* is bottled drinking water, as the discarded plastic containers can be found everywhere and when burnt (the normal method of disposal on the islands) produce noxious gases and dangerous compounds.

It hardly needs to be said that non-biodegradable rubbish should not be thrown into the sea. Even biodegradable rubbish such as vegetable peelings or melon rind should not be thrown into the water, except when you are three or more miles from land, as it ends up blowing back onto the shore before it has decayed or been eaten by scavengers. Toilets should not be used in harbour if there is one ashore, or they should be used with a holding tank. In Turkey you face a substantial fine for pumping toilets in a harbour or anchorage and the authorities are rightfully vigilant about enforcing this. Holding tanks should not be emptied until you are well offshore or pumped out at pump-out stations in harbours and marinas. There are more and more pump-out stations being installed around the coast of Turkey and in some places in Greece.

Many of the smaller islands and villages cannot cope with piles of rubbish from summer visitors, some of whom cannot read. Underneath this sign were bags of rubbish left by visiting yachts

Consciousness of pollution and individual responsibility for it is spreading through the villages and towns, and as tourists we also have a responsibility to keep the wilder parts of Europe free from pollution. Moreover, many of the sources of pollution are there to service the tourist trade and if there were no tourists then there would be less pollution.

Noise pollution

This comes in various forms, from the simple banality of making your presence known in an anchorage with the CD player or plugged-in MP3 turned up full blast, to inconsiderate motorboat owners with loud exhausts. Those who play loud music in deserted bays should reflect whether they would not be more comfortable in a noisy urban disco, preferably in their own country. Another annoying noise in an anchorage is the puttering of generators, and those who need to run their generator all day and night might consider whether they may not be more comfortable in a marina along the French or Italian Riviera where they can hook up to shore-power. Motorboaters with noisy outboards and inboards, and water-bikes (which have the most irritating whine in their exhaust note, as well as the most irritating people driving them) should keep well clear of boats at anchor and keep noise levels to a minimum in any anchorage or harbour.

Safety and seamanship

In some places powerboats and inflatables roar around an anchorage without regard for those swimming in the water. This is not just irritating but potentially lethal. If you have ever seen the injuries sustained by someone who has been hit by a propeller, you will immediately understand my concern. Accidents such as these frequently result in death, or for the lucky, horrible mutilation. Those on large craft should also keep a good lookout when entering an anchorage where people are out and about on the water or swimming off the back of the boat.

Remember when picking up someone who has fallen overboard to engage neutral, or you may replace death by drowning with death by propeller injuries. Although water-bikes do not have a propeller they are just as lethal if they hit someone at speed and injure them – it doesn't take long to drown.

In many bays swimming areas are now cordoned off with a line of small yellow, usually conical, buoys. Although this restricts the area you can anchor in, the swimming areas should be avoided, and in fact you can be fined for anchoring in one of these areas. Certainly the locals will let you know in no uncertain terms that you should not be there.

'Homo moronicus' at 10–12 knots in a crowded anchorage

Weather forecasts

Because of the high and large land masses in the Mediterranean it is extremely difficult to predict what local winds and wind strengths will be. The Greek meteorological services do their best, but nonetheless face an almost impossible task. Fortunately the wind direction and strength in the Aegean is remarkably consistent in the summer. For those who really want to listen to a weather forecast try the following sources, but remember to interpret them leniently.

Note I will give Turkish sources for weather at the very end of this section, but in general the Greek service is more accurate, comprehensive, and covers the Turkish coast anyway.

Greek Weather Forecasts

VHF Olympia Radio forecasts

A forecast for all Greek waters in Greek and English is given at 0600, 1000, 1600, 2200 UTC. For local time add two hours in the winter and three hours in the summer. The forecast begins with a synopsis of surface pressure systems, then covers all Greek waters for Z+24 hours with an outlook for a further 12 hours. Gale warnings are given at the beginning of the broadcast.

A *sécurité* warning on Ch 16 gives all the VHF channels for the different shore stations and you will need to choose whichever shore station is closest to you. In fact the advice notice on shore stations is often mumbled and at such a speed that it can be difficult to hear, but is worth listening to in case VHF frequencies for the different shore stations are changed from time to time.

Eastern Aegean shore station list

Khios	Ch 85
Rodhos	Ch 63
Knossus	Ch 83
Síros	Ch 04

Navtex

Navtex is part of GMDSS and sets automatically receive MSI (Maritime Safety Information). The data for Navtex stations in this part of the eastern Mediterranean is shown in the table below.

There has been some discussion in the past over message errors and non-recording of messages. In 2011 I experienced no problems with any of the stations listed below.

In areas where there is high ground surrounding the harbour or anchorage some problems can be experienced getting a clear signal, though less than might be expected.

Old-fashioned observations of cloud type and direction can still give you a good steer for what might happen on the morrow

For more details on obtaining weather forecasts refer to *Mediterranean Cruising Handbook* by Rod Heikell (Imray)

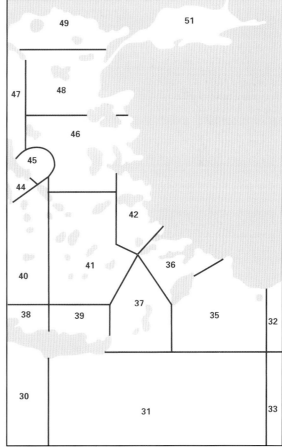

GREEK AEGEAN FORECAST AREAS

GREEK AEGEAN FORECAST AREAS

30	SW Kritiko	42	Samos Sea
31	SE Kritiko	43	Saronikos
32	Taurus	44	South Evvoikos
33	Delta	45	Kafireas Strait
34	Crusade	46	Central Aegean
35	Kastellorizo Sea	47	NW Aegean
36	Rhodos Sea	48	NE Aegean
37	Karpathio	49	Thrakiko
38	West Kritiko	50	Thermaicos
39	East Kritiko	51	Marmara
40	SW Aegean	52	W Black Sea
41	SE Aegean Ikario	53	E Black Sea

Navtex (N4) transmissions

Country	Transmitter identification character	Freq kHz	Times	Range M	Status of implementation character
Greece					
Limnos	L	518	0150, **0550**, **0950**, 1350, **1750**, **2150**	280	Operational
Iraklion	H	518	0110, **0510**, **0910**, 1310, **1710**, **2110**	280	Operational
Turkey					
Izmir	I	518	0120, 0520, 0920, 1320, 1720, 2120	300	Operational
Antalya	F	518	0050, 0450, 0850, 1250, 1650, 2050	300	Operational
Cyprus					
Peras	M	518	**0200, 0600, 1000, 1400, 1800, 2200**	200	Operational

Weather forecast times shown in **bold**

PHONE FORECAST

Call 108 for the Hellenic coastguard. Give your forecast area for a weather bulletin in Greek or English. (Greek phones only.)

SMS TEXT MESSAGE FORECAST

Poseidon provide a website weather forecast and can now send a basic forecast by text message to your Greek mobile phone. Text W GPS (co-ordinates of position for forecast) and send to 54546.

e.g. W GPS 38 50 20 43 requests a forecast for the area around Levkas.

The message gives wind strength and direction for 24 hours in three 6-hour intervals.

e.g. 24/9 15 4B (NW) indicates Force 4 NW wind at 1500hrs UTC on 24 September

The service costs around 25 cents per message (only available when using a Greek Sim card).

Television

On several of the television channels a weather forecast in Greek with satellite photos and wind forces and directions shown on the map is given after the news around 2100 local time. Many cafés and bars will have a television somewhere and you should ask for *o kairós parakaló*.

Port police and marinas

The port police get a weather forecast faxed to them several times a day. Depending on the inclination of the port police it is worthwhile asking them for a forecast.

Most of the marinas in Greece post a forecast, often taken from the internet.

GRIB files

Grib files are highly compressed weather data files which may be downloaded or received as emails and viewed on certain plotters.

Most of the internet weather and some email weather resources use Grib files. Grib (GRidded Information in Binary) files are computer-generated predictions of wind strength and direction and wave height and period. Basically two different models are widely used (because they are free) – GFS (General Forecast System) and NOGAPS (Navy Operational Global Atmospheric Prediction System) – although some agencies will fine-tune the models for specific regions.

Gribs are computer generated and rely principally on models using pressure differences to predict wind speed and direction. They do not have any input from a forecaster's grey matter that will assess the effects of land masses, frontal activity and squalls, and local geographical anomalies. They are not good at modelling thermal effects and the topographical effects of land masses and localised sea temperature differences.

In the Mediterranean it's not surprising that with large land masses around which heat up and cool at different rates depending on their orientation to the sun, there are significant thermal effects that gribs do not get right. Add to that the effects of channelling and funnelling from land masses and you must not expect accurate forecasts. Gribs are useful for getting an idea of wind speed and direction: over the open sea they work well, but do not rely on them in the Mediterranean. Probably the most accurate forecasts in the East Aegean are those on VHF and Navtex from the Hellenic National Meteorological Service.

Weather on the internet

A mix of graphic, text and satellite forecasts are widely available. As smartphones and tablets replace laptops, many of these services are also available as Apps on the Apple and Android platforms.

UGRIB
Grib files from www.grib.us where you download the UGRIB viewer and can then select areas for up to a 5-day forecast. Easy to use.

Windfinder
www.windfinder.com Originally a windsurfing forecast site that has expanded. 7-day forecasts.

Wind Guru
www.windguru.cz/int Another windsurfing forecast site. Remember forecasts are for spots close to the land.

Passage Weather
www.passageweather.com Gives weather world-wide.

Poseidon weather for Greece
www.poseidon.ncmr.gr/weather.forecast.html
Up to 72-hour surface wind forecasts for Greece. The best source of weather for Greek waters and adjacent Turkish waters.

Hellenic Meteo
www.meteo.gr/sailingmapf.asp
Detailed wind charts for all Greek waters for up to 72 hours.

Skiron
//forecast.uoa.gr
University of Athens site with good grib and synoptic charts.

Turkish State Meteorological Service
www.mgm.gov.tr
Marine forecasts for up to 72 hours, surface wind and wave heights for the eastern Mediterranean

DWD Mediterranean forecast
www.dwd.de
3-day text forecasts for a number of Mediterranean areas including the eastern Mediterranean. In German and English.

Weather Apps
In addition to Apps of some of the above websites I also use mobileGRIB and Weatherpro

Turkish weather forecasts

As mentioned previously, the best sources for weather along the Turkish coast originate in Greece. Any of the VHF, HF, Navtex, SMS or internet sources from Greece will provide weather information for Turkey. Weather forecasts originating in Turkey are as follows.

VHF Radio

Weather forecasts are broadcast on Ch 67 from most coast radios. These are in Turkish and English. They use powerful transmitters and repeaters which can be heard over most of the sea area covered in this book. Transmissions are at 0700 and 1900 UTC.

Istanbul Announce Ch 16. Broadcast on Ch 67 for sea area covering the Aegean coast and W. Med coast.

Antalya Announce Ch 16. Broadcast on Ch 67 for sea area covering Med coast.

These forecasts are not as comprehensive or as detailed as the Greek forecasts.

Television

On several of the television channels a weather forecast in Turkish with some very general wind force and direction is given after the news, at around 2130–2200 local time.

Harbourmaster and marinas

Most marinas will post a forecast for the day and sometimes up to three days. In most cases this is a print off of an internet forecast from one of the Greek sources.

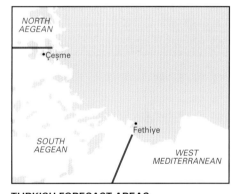

TURKISH FORECAST AREAS

TURKISH AEGEAN FORECAST AREAS

NORTH AEGEAN
(Canakkale-Cesme)

SOUTH AEGEAN
(Cesme-Fethiye)

WEST MED
(Fethiye-Anamur)

About the plans

The plans which accompany the text are designed to help those cruising in the area to get in and out of the various harbours and anchorages and to give an idea of where facilities are to be found. It is stressed that many of these plans are based on the author's sketches and therefore should only be used in conjunction with the official charts. They are not to be used for navigation.

Waypoints

Waypoints are given for all harbours and anchorages. The origins of the waypoints vary and in a large number of cases the datum source of the waypoint is not known. Where I have taken waypoints for a harbour or anchorage it has a note after it reading WGS84. All these waypoints are to World Geodetic Survey 1984 datum which, it is intended, will be the datum source used throughout the world. Most GPS receivers automatically default to WGS84.

It is important to note that plotting a waypoint onto a chart will not necessarily put it in the position shown. There are a number of reasons for this:

1. The chart may have been drawn using another datum source. There are many other datum sources that have been used to draw charts so check to see what datum is given.
2. All charts, including those using WGS84, have errors of various types. Most were drawn in the 19th century and have been fudged to conform to WGS84 (the term 'fuzzy logic' could aptly be used).
3. Even when a harbour plan is drawn there is still a significant human element at work and mistakes easily creep in, as I know to my cost.

The upshot of all this is that it is important to eyeball your way into an anchorage or harbour and not just sit back and assume that all those digits on the GPS display will look after you. In the case of waypoints I have taken and which are appended WGS84, the waypoint is indeed in the place shown. In the case of other waypoints it can be derived from the light position, from reports in my files, or from other sources.

I have also included useful waypoints which are listed at the beginning of the relevant chapter and included on the location maps. As above, any that are appended WGS84 are from my own observations, using the radar for distance off and a compass bearing for the direction. Given that some radar distance off readouts can be a bit of a guesstimate, these should be used with every caution. In most cases I have endeavoured to keep a reasonable distance off so that an error of, say, 50m, should be unimportant when the waypoint is 0·5M from the land. There are other occasions when I have shaved a cape or islet and the distance off is considerably less.

All waypoints are given in the notation:

degrees   minutes   decimal place of a minute

It is important not to confuse the decimal place of a minute with the older 60-second notation.

KEY TO SYMBOLS USED ON PLANS

 depths in METRES

 shallow water with a depth of 1m or less

 rocks with less than 2 metres depth over them

 rock just below or on the surface

 a shoal or reef with the least depth shown

 wreck partially above water

 wreck

 dangerous wreck with depth over it

 eddies

 rock ballasting on a mole or breakwater

 above-water rocks

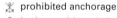 cliffs

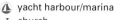 anchorage

prohibited anchorage

harbour with yacht berths

yacht harbour/marina

church

mosque

windmill

 chimney

castle

airport

ruins

houses

port police

port of entry

customs

waypoint

travel-hoist

shower

water

electricity

fuel

post office

tourist information

pine

trees other than pine

visitors' berths

fish farm

 yacht berth

local boats (usually shallow or reserved)

beacon

port hand buoy

starboard hand buoy

mooring buoy

Characteristics

light

lighthouse

F   fixed

Fl.   flash

Fl(2) group flash

Oc.   occulting

R   red

G   green

W   white

M   miles

s   sand

m   mud

w   weed

r   rock

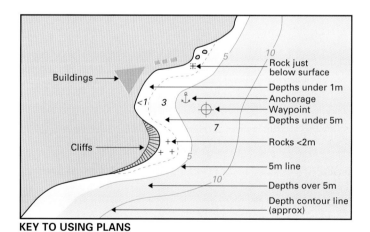

KEY TO USING PLANS

1

Northern Dodecanese
Pithagorion to Kós

Pandeli waterfront on Leros

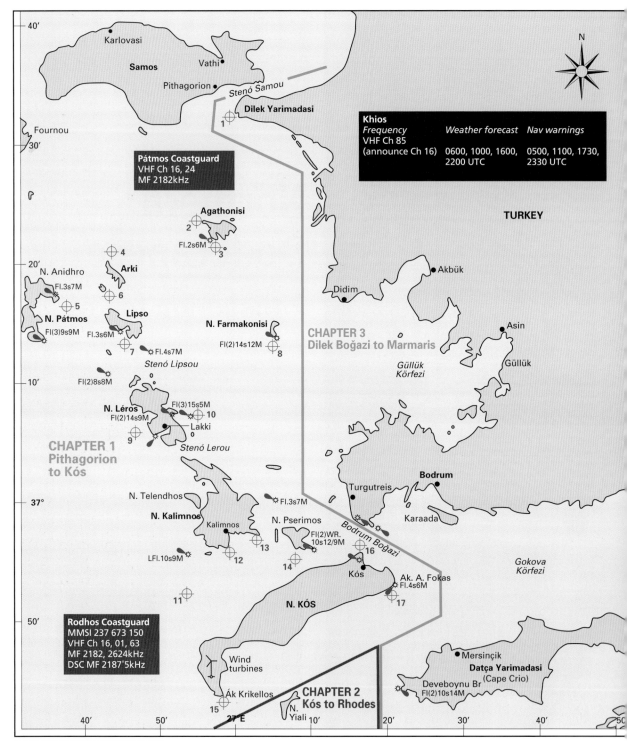

THE NORTHERN DODECANESE

USEFUL WAYPOINTS

⊕1 Stenó Samou W end
  (mid-channel Bayrak Adası N side)
  37°41'·86N 27°00'·80E WGS84
⊕2 0·4M W of Ák Nera (Agathonisi)
  37°28'·53N 26°54'·96E WGS84
⊕3 0·25M S of Ák Stifí (Agathonisi)
  37°26'·35N 26°57'·65E WGS84
⊕4 0·5M N of Ák Koumaro (Arki)
  37°25'·30N 26°43'·13E WGS84
⊕5 0·5M SE of Ák Yeranós (Pátmos)
  37°20'·01N 26°37'·31E WGS84
⊕6 0·25M S of N. Grilousa (Arki)
  37°21'·12N 26°42'·39E WGS84
⊕7 Mid-channel Frangonisi – Makronisi (Lipso)
  37°15'·64N 26°43'·95E WGS84
⊕8 1M S of Ák Petronkopis (Farmakonisi)
  37°15'·5N 27°05'·3E
⊕9 1M W of Ák Lakki (Léros)
  37°06'·86N 26°48'·14E WGS84
⊕10 1M E of Vrak Áy Kiriakí (Léros)
  37°08'·8N 26°54'·4E
⊕11 3M S of Vrak Safonídhi (Kalimnos-Kós Channel)
  36°50'·27N 26°54'·49E WGS84
⊕12 0·5M S of Áy Yeóryios (Kalimnos)
  36°54'·97N 26°59'·21E WGS84
⊕13 0·75M S of Ák Khali (Kalimnos)
  36°55'·95N 27°02'·97E WGS84
⊕14 0·25M S of Vrak Krevvatio (Psérimos)
  36°54'·82N 27°09'·39E WGS84
⊕15 0·5M S of Ák Krikellos (Kós)
  36°39'·80N 26°58'·43E WGS84
⊕16 0·75M N of Ák Ammóglossa (Kós)
  36°55'·70N 27°16'·42E WGS84
⊕17 0·25M E of Ák Áy Fokas (Kós)
  36°51'·67N 27°21'·69E WGS84

Castle of the Knights by the old harbour of Kós

Quick reference guide

	Shelter	Mooring	Fuel	Water	Provisions	Eating out	Plan
Samos							
Pithagorion	A	AC	A	A	A	A	•
Samos Marina	A	A	A	A	C	C	•
Agathonisi							
Áy Yeoryios	B	AC	O	B	C	C	•
O. Poros & O. Palos	B	C	O	O	O	O	•
Nisís Nero	C	C	O	O	O	O	•
Pátmos							
Skála Pátmos	B	AC	B	B	B	A	•
Órmos Meloyi, Livadhi & Kambos	B	C	O	O	C	C	•
Órmos Grikou & Dhiakoftou	B	C	O	O	C	C	•
Órmos Stavros	B	C	O	O	C	C	•
Arki							
Port Augusta	A	AC	O	B	C	C	•
N. Marathos	B	C	O	O	O	C	•
Port Stretto	B	C	O	O	O	C	•
Farmakonisi							
Órmos Tholou	C	C	O	O	O	O	•
Lipso							
Órmos Lipso	B	A	B	A	C	B	•
Lera Lipso	B	C	O	O	O	C	•
Léros							
Lakki Marina	AB	AC	B	A	B	B	•
Leros Marina	AB	A	B	AB	B	B	•
Partheni	A	C	B	B	C	C	•
Nisís Arkhangelos	C	C	O	O	O	O	•
Órmos Plakhoudi	C	C	O	B	C	C	•
Alinda	C	AC	B	A	B	A	•
Pandeli	B	AC	B	A	C	A	•
Xerokambos	B	AC	O	B	C	C	•
Kalimnos							
Limın Kalimnou	A	A	B	A	A	A	•
Vlikadhia	B	C	O	O	O	C	•
Órmos Linarias	O	C	O	O	C	C	
Mirties	C	C	O	B	C	B	•
Telendhos	C	C	O	O	C	C	•
Emborios	B	C	O	B	C	C	•
Órmos Palaionisou	B	C	O	O	O	C	•
Órmos Sikati	C	C	O	O	O	O	•
Órmos Pezonta	C	C	O	O	O	O	•
Órmos Akti	C	C	O	O	O	C	
Vathi	B	A	O	B	C	C	•
Pserimos							
Órmos Pserimou	C	AC	O	C	C	C	•
N. Plati	C	C	O	O	O	O	•
Órmos Marathos	C	C	O	O	O	O	•
Órmos Vathi	B	C	O	O	O	O	•
Kós							
Kós old harbour	A	A	A	A	A	A	•
Kós Marina	A	A	A	A	A	A	•
Kardamena	A	AB	B	A	C	A	•
Kamares	B	AC	O	B	C	C	•
Órmos Skinou	C	C	O	O	O	O	
Limnionas	AC	B	O	B	O	C	
Mastikhari	B	AB	O	B	C	B	•

PREVAILING WINDS

For the islands in this northern group the prevailing wind in the summer is the *meltemi* blowing from the northwest. From around mid-June until late September the *meltemi* blows at anything from Force 4–6 (11–27 knots) though at times it can get up to Force 7 (28–33 knots) or so and where the wind gusts down off high land it can be anything up to Force 1–3 more than the wind over the open sea.

The *meltemi* is generally lighter in early and late summer and blows most strongly in July and August. There is also something of a thermal component from the land mass of Asia Minor nearby, though not as demarcated as along the Turkish coast itself. Generally the wind will die down in the evening when the sun goes down and will be lighter in the morning before the wind gets up again around midday. This is not an infallible rule and it happens more in the spring and autumn than in the peak summer months of July and August. If you are heading north through the islands it can be advantageous to get up early in the morning and motorsail to make some northing before the wind kicks in again. Going south you have pretty much a sleigh-ride down through the islands. In spring and autumn winds are generally lighter, although depressions passing through the eastern Aegean can cause strong winds from the north or south for several days.

As with all the islands through the Aegean, you need to be careful of gusts off the high land in the lee of the land. Gusts down off the lee side can be ferocious and anything up to 10–15 knots over the wind on the open sea. Areas where these gusts are particulary severe are:

1 *Samos Strait and south coast* With the *meltemi* there are strong gusts in the lee of Samos especially around the western end. The *meltemi* is also channelled down through the Samos Strait.
2. *Agathonisi* Gusts down into Ayios Yeoryiou and along the southern side of the island.
3. *Órmos Pátmou* Anywhere in the approaches to Pátmos there can be severe gusts anywhere from north to west off the land.
4. *Lipso* Severe gusts in the approaches and in Lipso itself. Also gusts off the eastern end of the island.
5. *Léros* Severe gusts down into Alinda. Gusts into Lakki and around the southern end of the island.
6. *Kalimnos* Severe gusts in the approaches to Limın Kalimnos and along the south coast of the island to Vathi.
7. *Kós* Severe gusts off the south side of the island. Also gusts around the northern end and in the sea area from Ák Fouka across to Cape Krio.

THE DODECANESE

The Dodecanese (the 'Twelve Islands') lie in a crescent chain down the Asiatic Turkish coast before curving west towards Crete. The name 'Dodecanese' is of comparatively recent origin. It came into use in 1908 when 12 islands of this group, excluding Lipso, Kós and Rhodes, but including an outsider, Ikaria, protested about their deprivation of the special privileges and tax exemptions they had been granted in the 16th century by the Turks. Since then the name has come to include Lipso, Kós and Rhodes, but to exclude Ikaria. The group is also known as the Southern Sporades.

Like most of the Greek Islands, the Dodecanese are the tops of mountains that stood on the plain of the Aegean, long since flooded. The islands are for the most part bare of vegetation, although not to such an extent as the Cyclades. Several of the islands with abundant natural springs, notably Kós and Rhodes, are relatively green and wooded.

The history of the Dodecanese has largely revolved around the fortunes of Rhodes which dominated trade in this corner of the Aegean from ancient times until the 19th century. Today Rhodes dominates the new trade in tourists in the Dodecanese with over a million tourists in the summer. In the early Middle Ages the Knights of St John, based in their fortress in Rhodes, stamped the area with their military signatures. Most of the military architecture is not the ubiquitous Venetian and Genoese architecture so prevalent in other parts of Greece, but that of the Knights. The occupation of the Knights nonetheless ensured the Venetians and Genoese access to the trade in this part of the world. After the Knights finally capitulated to the Turks in 1522, the Dodecanese were to remain under Turkish rule until 1912.

Despite such a long period of unbroken occupation the islands have

Courtyard in the Castle of the Knights in Kós town

remained intrinsically Greek, and there is as little here to remind you of the long years under Turkish rule as elsewhere in Greece. After the Italo-Turkish war (1911–12) the islands were awarded to Italy, although they were to be passed on in due course to Greece. This promise was later conveniently forgotten and the Dodecanese remained under the Italians until the Second World War. Finally in 1947 they officially became part of Greece. For those not familiar with modern Greek history it comes as quite a shock to learn that these islands have been a part of Greece for such a short time, when visually and culturally they appear to be as much a part of Greece as any of the other islands.

Samos

Samos sits tight into the Turkish coast: in fact, less than a mile separates Greece and Turkey across the Samos Strait and this makes it the closest Greek island to the Turkish mainland. In this edition I only include Pithagorion and not the other harbours and anchorages on Samos. Pithagorion and nearby Samos marina has become the northern hub of the Dodecanese, though the island is part of the Eastern Sporades, so it makes sense to include it in this edition as a base from which to explore the islands to the south.

In the immediate approaches to Pithagorion and the Samos strait the *meltemi* usually gusts off the slopes behind. In lighter northerlies the pattern is that the wind will creep around the eastern end of Samos and blow from the east out of the Samos Strait. Later in the day it will sometimes blow off the slopes behind or may just continue to blow from the east. In southerlies a considerable swell is pushed onto the southern side of Samos, but once behind the outer breakwater at Pithagorion it is calm.

For details on Samos and the rest of the Eastern Sporades refer to *Greek Waters Pilot*.

Pithagorion

The town harbour and Samos Marina sit near the SE corner of Samos in the western approaches to the Samos Strait.

Pilotage

Approach The town and harbour at Pithagorion and the wind turbines on the slope above are easily identified from the distance. The approaches are clear of dangers although there can be strong gusts off the land and through the Samos Strait when the *meltemi* is blowing. Closer in the church and monastery of Metamorfosis, a solid monolith of a building, will be seen and you need to head just east of it for the harbour entrance. The outer breakwater of Pithagorion will be seen and although the entrance is wide care needs to be taken of ferries, tripper boats and fishing boats coming and going.

If you are going on the town quay make sure you leave the beacon in the town basin to port.

Mooring Go stern or bows-to the town quay where shown. Tripper boats occupy part of the quay to the south so leave these berths clear. The

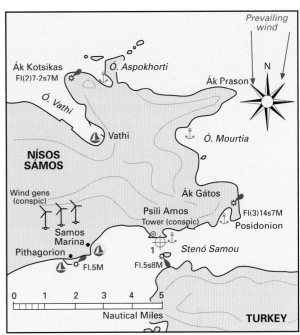

APPROACHES TO SAMOS STRAIT AND PITHAGORION
⊕1 Stenó Samou W end (mid channel Bayrak Adasi N side)
37°41'·86N 27°00'·80E WGS84

bottom is mud and good holding. Good shelter from the prevailing northerlies and the lighter easterlies out of the Samos Strait. In strong southerlies there is a surge in the harbour and you will need to pull well off the town quay. Charge band 2.

Yachts can anchor under the outer breakwater clear of the channel into the inner harbour. A number of small buoys mark a swimming area off the 'beach'. In general try to anchor no further south than the end of the stubby mole protecting the inner harbour. The bottom is mud and weed, good holding. Good shelter from the prevailing northerlies although the wind swirls around a bit.

Facilities

Services Water and electricity on the quay. The fuel quay in Samos Marina is the easiest place to get fuel.

Provisions Good shopping for provisions in the High Street where there are small supermarkets and bakers. Larger supermarkets on the road out of town but you really need a car.

Eating out Lots of tavernas and cafés on the waterfront and these are as good a place as any to take a cappuccino or breakfast. On the first street on the left going up the High Street is the

Aphrodite which has good Greek fare in a wonderful courtyard setting. Opposite is another taverna which has good food.

Other Ferries to Kuşadasi in Turkey and to Patmos. Ferries run to other Greek islands and to Piraeus from Vathi on the northern side of Samos. Flights to Pithagorion from European airports and internal flights to other islands and to Athens. Hire cars and motorbikes. Banks. ATMs. PO. Internet cafés.

General

When you sail into Pithagorion you are sailing into a harbour that dates from the time of Polykrates the Tyrant, around the 6th century BC. The meaning of 'tyrant' here is somewhat more benign than its later meanings and Polykrates instituted some civic reforms, surrounded himself with artists, writers, poets and musicians, and ordered the building of what Herodotus called three of the greatest engineering feats of the age. One of these was the building of the harbour, which was basically the same shape as the present harbour. There are still huge stone blocks used in the original construction of the harbour incorporated into the present harbour, though the recent works on the outer breakwater will likely cover much of this up. The harbour used to be called 'Tigani', the frying pan, and it is readily apparent why if you look at the shape of it on the plan, with the inner harbour forming the pan and the outer breakwater the handle.

The two other wonders of the age that Polykrates built were the Temple of Hera near Ireon around the bay to the west and the tunnel hewn through the slopes behind Pithagorion to bring water to the city. The Temple of Hera is now much destroyed, but the tunnel still remains and you can take a tour of a part of it. The tunnel was built starting on either side of the mountain and is over a kilometre long. Incredibly, where the two tunnels joined in the middle was less than a metre out; that's ancient engineering for you.

Pithagorion today plays the tune of a resort and not the harmonics of Pythagoras. The small town fairly hums with tourists, though not unsympathetically. The actual town is quite small, hemmed in by the steep slopes around it, and only on the river flat to the west is there a bit of sprawl and the airport. It's the sort of place you settle into: a morning cappuccino on the front, a bit of shopping for lunch and an amble around the streets in the evening to look for a taverna for dinner.

Pythagoras

The town was renamed Pithagorion relatively recently in 1955. Pythagoras was born on Samos but in fact spent little time here, travelling widely in his youth and then settling in Croton, modern Crotone on the heel of Italy. At an early age he visited Miletus on the mainland opposite and it is likely that he was influenced by the elderly Thales and his disciple Anaximander. Anaximander produced one of the earliest maps of the world and was a proponent for a scientific view of the world, a view that Pythagoras eagerly adopted. He lived for a while in Egypt and then returned to Samos before leaving to settle in Italy.

Pythagoras was an oddity who is known for his mathematical theorems but less well known for his religious cult which espoused a form of communal living, vegetarianism, reincarnation and the power of music. He constructed a mathematical theory of musical harmonics. He strived always for the pure, in science and in life, and believed that mathematics would one day explain the world and the cosmos. In this he was not far wrong.

In Pithagorion a statue commemorating the man stands prominently on the stubby mole protecting the inner harbour, where he is shown pointing up to what looks like a lop-sided cross (which I guess is meant to represent his theorem on a right-angled triangle). Or he could be sighting skywards as Pythagoras was an accomplished astronomer as well.

Pythagoras seemed able to do most things, to excel in complex abstract problems, to play the lyre well, to live a good if somewhat ascetic life, but if there was one thing he was not good at it was being politic. He was exiled from Crotone for allegedly meddling in the local politics and lived his final years out in Metapontium, a bit further around the Taranto Gulf from Crotone. He never returned to Samos.

Pythagoras surveying the harbour named after him

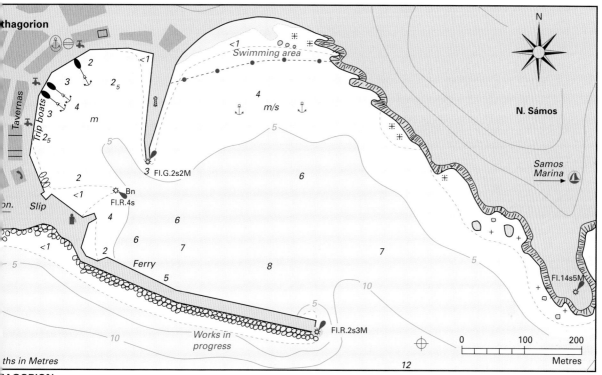

thagorion

Swimming area

<1

N

N. Sámos

Samos Marina

2

3

4

3

2_5

m

2_5

2

5

<1

4

m/s

5

3 Fl.G.2s2M

6

Tavernas

Trip boats

2

<1

Bn
Fl.R.4s

4

6

6

7

8

7

5

on.

Slip

2

Ferry

5

5

Fl.14s5M

Fl.R.2s3M

10

Works in progress

5

12

ths in Metres

0   100   200
Metres

AGORION
°41′·25N 26°56′·96E WGS84

agorion looking west over the anchorage into the harbour

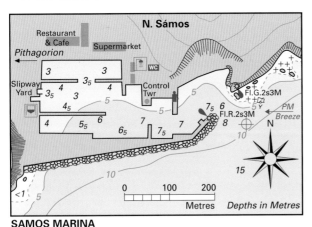

SAMOS MARINA
⊕37°41'·39N 26°57'·53E WGS84

Samos Marina

Pilotage

Approach Samos Marina lies just 1,000m east of the entrance to Pithagorion harbour. The entrance is difficult to make out but you will see the masts of the yachts inside. Just keep heading to the east of these yachts and the entrance will be seen. It is quite narrow getting through the entrance and if the *meltemi* is blowing through the Samos strait from the east there is a bit of slop rebounding off the shore. Care is also needed of yachts coming out of the narrow entrance. Inside the marina space is quite tight so manoeuvring into a berth can be difficult. Call up Samos Marina on VHF Ch 09 when approaching the entrance.

Mooring One of the marina staff will meet you in a RIB and guide you into your berth. Space inside

is confined so you will need to have everything ready before you berth. Berthing can also be a little complicated with the easterly wind beam-on going into many of the berths. Laid moorings tailed to the quay. Good all-round shelter. Charge band 4.

Facilities

Services Water and electricity at all berths. Showers and toilets. Laundry. Fuel quay at the entrance. Wi-Fi.

Provisions Supermarket in the marina. Otherwise in Pithagorion.

Eating out Taverna and café at the marina. Otherwise in Pithagorion.

Other Hire cars and motorbikes.

General

Samos Marina is a convenient base for exploring the Dodecanese to the south or heading north into the eastern Sporades. It is around 20 minutes' walk around the coast to Pithagorion town where you will find a bit more life than that in the marina.

ⓘ 22730 61600
www.samosmarina.gr

Agathonisi (Gáïdharos)

Agathonisi sits out on its own close to the Turkish coast, exiled by windswept sea and the fact that it is not really on the way to anywhere. In fact, the island probably gets as many visitors by yacht as it gets from land-based tourism, and for this reason the place is to be treasured. It is a gentle step back in time and although there are a 150 or so inhabitants, they seem happy to do a little subsistence farming, fish the surrounding waters, and in the summer make a few euros off the visitors. And of course, as on every island near the Turkish coast there is a military garrison housing a few homesick soldiers.

In earlier editions of my books I used the older name of the island, Gáïdharos, and was severely rapped over the knuckles by the local council for doing so. Gáïdharos means an 'ass' or a 'donkey', which the islanders tell me was the name inflicted by the Italians, intimating that the population was stupid and somewhat ass-like. In fact this name was used from medieval times to describe the shape of the island which, if you look at it, does resemble a donkey facing eastwards. In ancient

Samos Marina looking east into Stenon Samon

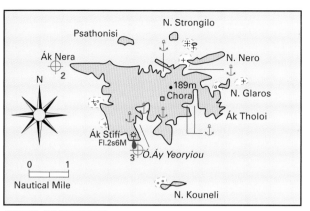

NISOS AGATHONISI

⊕2 0·4M W of Ák Nera (Agathonisi)
37°28'·53N 26°54'·96E WGS84
⊕3 0·25M S of Ák Stifí (Agathonisi)
37°26'·35N 26°57'·65E WGS84

times the island was called Yetousa and then Tragea, though it was of little consequence and there are no ancient ruins to indicate it was ever used by the Greeks or the Romans. In the 13th century the island was ceded to the monastery on Pátmos and it reverted to them when the Turks were expelled after the First World War. On the southeastern corner there is a Byzantine structure of indeterminate use (perhaps part of a warehouse or monastery) which is just about the only site on the island. Only in 1954 were the links with the monastery severed and since 1959 it has been autonomous.

The modern name of the island is said to have been bestowed by a priest from Fourni who was sent here sometime before the Second World War.

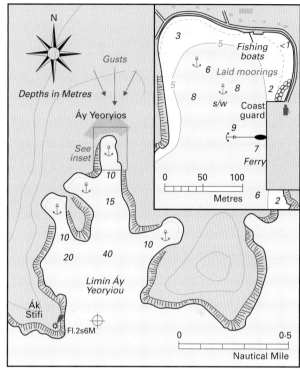

LIMIN AY YEORYIOU
⊕37°26'·65N 26°57'·91E WGS84

Agathonisi means the 'good-hearted' or 'worthy' island, referring to the apparent good nature of the inhabitants. The name was not really used until well after the Second World War had finished and the Italians had left. Whatever the merits of the name, the inhabitants are probably descended from monks and workers sent over

Looking E to the hamlet at Áy Yeoryios on Agathonisi

from Pátmos and possibly the odd pirate or two, as the pirates who captured Julius Caesar and held him ransom on Farmakonisi were said to be from Tragea.

ÁY YEORYIOS

Pilotage

Approach From the west the approach is straightforward and clear of dangers. As you close the southwest end of the island you will eventually see the light structure on the western side of the entrance to Limin Áy Yeoryiou. Closer in the entrance to the bay and a few buildings in the hamlet at the head will be seen.

Mooring Anchor off in the bay in 6–12m on mud, sand and weed – good holding. Alternatively you can go stern or bows-to on the quay leaving the southern end free for the ferry and the northern end clear for the coastguard launch. The ferry is scheduled to call three times or so a week, but in the summer seems to be daily, so if you know it is not due you can also use the rest of the quay, but check with the locals to be on the safe side. Good shelter from the *meltemi* but open to the south. Yachts can also anchor in any of the three coves around the bay where shown on the plan. In the coves it makes sense to try and get a long line ashore if you can.

Facilities

The island has no natural water so it is all collected in cisterns from rainwater. There is a fuel station by the quay. There are four tavernas dotted around the waterfront: George's is popular and has good fish, but I suggest you just wander around at dusk and pick one at random. Small minimarket. The ferry runs to Pithagorion and Pátmos.

General

Áy Yeoryios on Agathonisi

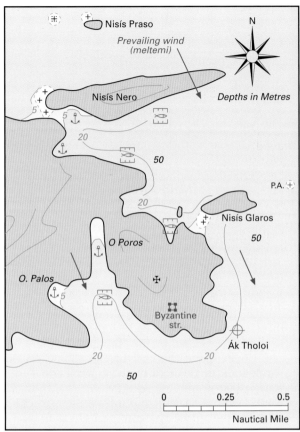

AGATHONISI EASTERN ANCHORAGES
⊕37°27'·25N 27°00'·5E

This bay and the small hamlet of Áy Yeoryios is a special place, geographically and spiritually removed from the larger islands. There is nothing to do here except contemplate when to go for a swim, a walk up to Megalo Khorio, and (importantly) when and where to have drinks and dinner. The bay is all clean turquoise water where you can dive off the boat for a swim safe in the knowledge that you are secure here even when the *meltemi* is blowing strongly.

Megalo Khorio, the 'capital' of the island, is built in a valley just over the ridge from Áy Yeoryios and hidden from the eyes of the pirates that used to prowl these waters. It has around a hundred inhabitants and is worth a walk although there is really nothing special to see. The old houses have few if any windows on the ground floor, presumably a defensive design should the house and village need to be defended in older, more piratical, days.

In Áy Yeoryios a number of villas are being

constructed around the slopes above the bay, but as yet there is nothing disastrous and this is still a friendly place where competition for the tourist euro does not extend to touting and has not yet set brother against brother.

ÓRMOS POROS AND ÓRMOS PALOS

To the east of Áy Yeoryios there is another large indented bay with two coves in it. These provide good shelter from the *meltemi*, although it does gust strongly into the bay. On the west side of the bay there is a fish farm and unfortunately also a fair amount of detritus from the business of fish farming. Anchor in either of the two coves where possible. The holding in here is not the best and you need to make sure your anchor is in and holding. If in doubt set a second anchor.

Prominent on the slopes on the east side of the bay is a large vaulted structure, most likely of Byzantine origin. It's difficult to know exactly what its purpose is, it may have been part of a grain store, though it is unlikely much grain was ever grown on this barren island without abundant water.

Agathonisi eastern side

Proceeding up the eastern side of Agathonisi you come to Nisís Glaros. Care is needed when passing between Glaros and Agathonisi as a reef and shoal water extend across much of the channel from Glaros. Keep closer to Agathonisi where there is reported to be 2·5–3·5m depths and have someone up forward conning you through. Alternatively go all the way around Glaros. If going around the E side of Glaros care is needed of the isolated reef lying approximately 500m ENE of Glaros.

Much of the eastern side is beset with fish farms, but a useful anchorage is under the western end of Nisís Nero where you can find reasonable shelter from the *meltemi*. Do not attempt to pass through the gap between Nero and Agathonisi as it has a reef running across it.

If you are navigating around this area two other reefs you need to look out for are the isolated reef just west of Nisís Praso and the isolated reef ENE of Nisís Glaros.

Pátmos

Pátmos sits out on the northwestern edge of the Dodecanese and in many ways is removed from the rest of the islands in appearance and its focus. It looks much like one of the Cyclades, with its bare rocky slopes dusted over with the white cube houses of the *chora*. It could be a Serifos or a Kithnos except for the grey monolith that sits at the very top. The monastery sets it apart and bestows on it the lucrative trade in cruise ships and visitors arriving by ferry that is the lifeblood of the island. Not much grows on the barren slopes and there are few souls around who would exchange working in a bar or a motorbike hire shop for tilling the rocky soil. And yet the island has a surprising calm to it when the cruise ships are not in, almost as if the monastery casts a shadowy air of reverence over the place and tones down all the gaudy and untidy tourism.

In ancient times it was of little importance, although there was an acropolis at Kastelli on the west coast. During the Roman period its fortunes declined and it became a place of political exile. St John was exiled here and this random event gave to the island its focus right up to the present. It started with the wild poetry of the Apocalypse that St John dictated in the cave on the island, and continued with the establishment of the fortified monastery which has become the second most holy site for the Orthodox church after Mount Athos. Although the monastery no longer rules the island and the surrounding islands, in Pátmos you get the feeling that you should behave properly or a monk will pop out from behind a rock and admonish you for unbecoming behaviour. You see few lager louts or hooray henry's around and topless sunbathing is confined to the more remote beaches. In the Cave of the Apocalypse and in the monastery a sign asks you to dress modestly, and the monks scowl at anyone showing a bit of midriff or too much thigh. I

suggest you dress appropriately and if the monks are a bit grumpy-looking, think how you would feel if thousands of idle sightseers wandered through a place you lived and worked in, not to mention loved.

Looking down over Skála Pátmos from the monastery

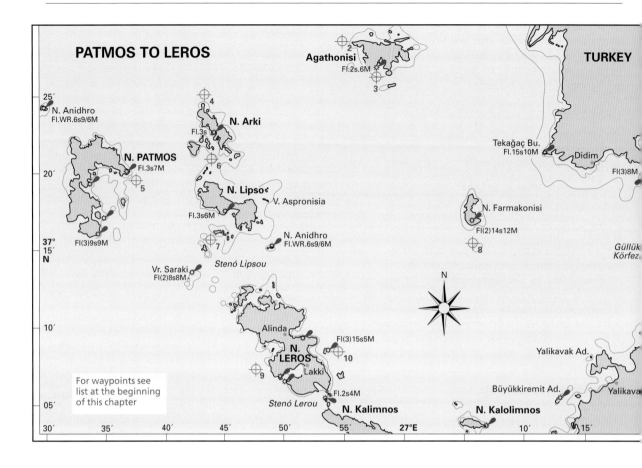

PATMOS TO LEROS

SKÁLA PÁTMOS

Although the approaches to Skála Pátmos are dotted with islets and reefs, with a little care the approach is straightforward.

Pilotage

Approach The grey stone fortified monastery atop the white houses of the *chora* of Pátmos is easily identified from some distance off. From the east if you head slightly to starboard of the *chora* you will be pointed pretty much towards the inlet of Skála Pátmos. From the northeast the approach is relatively clear of dangers as you head for Ák Yeranos, but from the east or southeast there are numerous islets and reefs in the approach.

Closer in the islets and rocks in the eastern approaches will be seen and if you aim for the channel between Khelia islet and Sklavaki reef things are pretty straightforward once you have identified Sklavaki reef, which shows up well as a brown smudge in the water. From here the houses of Skála will be seen and the entrance is straightforward.

Care is needed of ferries coming and going (which they do at speed) and there may also be cruise ships anchored in the bay. If you are sailing up towards Skála there can be gusts off the land with the *meltemi* so watch the water for any squally gusts.

Mooring The harbour gets crowded in high season so either arrive early or be prepared to anchor off in one of the bays around Ormos Patmou and potter in in the morning when some of the yachts have left. Go stern-to the quay north of the ferry quay and the basin. The wind tends to blow partly beam-on so it worth laying your anchor a long way out. The bottom is mud and weed, good holding. There may also be room to go on the new pontoon at the head of the bay. It is possible to anchor off in the bay, although swinging room is limited by laid moorings. Good shelter from the *meltemi*. Strong southerlies can make it untenable in here.

Note The new concrete quay around the head of the bay is mostly occupied by local boats and there is little room to be found. There are sometimes berths on the end of the pontoon running out from the quay.

Facilities

Services Water by tanker: he will come by the yacht quay and ask you if you need water. There have been reports that the water can be brackish. A mini-tanker does the rounds of the quay with diesel.

Provisions Good shopping for provisions near the quay although prices are a bit higher than average. In the old part of Skála are several minimarkets with most things.

Eating out Although you are near the old part of Skála the food here can be disappointing, with a preponderance of fast food joints. It's well worth going to sit in the buzz and excitement of the place and have a drink in the Café Arion near the waterfront which has been around for years. In the street just behind the Arion is

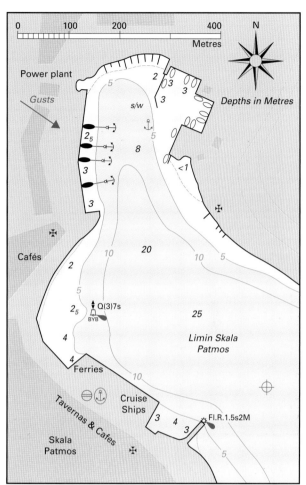

SKALA PATMOS
⊕37°19'·37N 26°32'·95E WGS84

Looking W across Patmos harbour to the yacht quay

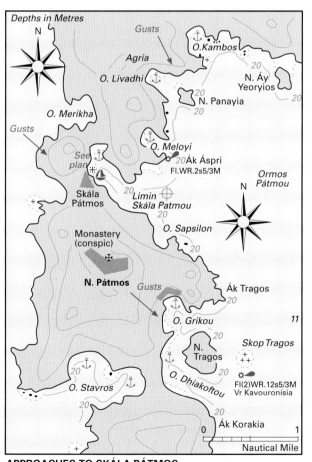

APPROACHES TO SKÁLA PÁTMOS
⊕37°19'·2N 26°33'·7E

Patmos looking north over N. Tragos and Ormos Grikou towards Skala Patmou
Airphoto

Pandeli Taverna which serves good Greek food and is popular with the locals. There are also some interesting looking tavernas further back in the old part of Skala. Behind the yacht quay is the Pirofani with good upmarket food, and around the beach at the head of the bay at Netia are a couple of more upmarket restaurants which are good value with a bit of peace and quiet.

Other Ferries to the other Dodecanese islands and through the Aegean to Piraeus. Local ferries to Lipso and Agathonisi. Bus to the *chora*. Banks. ATMs. PO. Internet cafés. Hire cars and motorbikes. You don't need much more than a scooter to get around as the island is small. The hire shops opposite the yacht quay are as good as any.

General

Skála is where everyone comes through on the way to the *chora* and the monastery. It hustles and bustles and when the cruise boats and a ferry are in, it positively heaves. Strangely enough, the yacht quay end of town remains fairly tranquil and you get only a few puzzled passers-by from the ships peering into the cockpit. When the cruise boats and ferries are not around Skála is a peaceful and quite likeable spot to settle back in.

To get to the chora and the monastery of St John you can take one of the infrequent buses from the ferry quay or a taxi. There is a footpath leading up the winding road that cuts across some of the corners, but arguably the easiest way is to hire a motorbike and persuade it to make the ascent. Then you can take it to Meloyi over the saddle on the northeast corner of the harbour for a cooling swim.

Anchorages around the coast of Pátmos

Órmos Meloyi The bay on the N side of Ák Aspri. Anchor in 4–7m on sand and weed, poor holding in places. Good shelter from the *meltemi*. Several tavernas ashore, including the amiable *Meloi* on the beach. This is a pleasant spot, although popular in the day with the locals who come here for a swim during siesta hours.

Órmos Livadhi (Agriolivadhi) The next bay N of Meloyi with the islet of Nisís Panayia in the entrance. Enter on the south side of the islet where there are good depths in the fairway. On the north side of the islet there is some shoal water off the northern end of the islet and around 3–5m depths through the channel, though care is needed. Anchor near the head of the bay in 4–6m keeping clear of the buoyed-off swimming area. Good shelter from the *meltemi*, although there are gusts into the bay. A couple of tavernas open in the summer.

Órmos Kambos Immediately northeast of Livadhi lies the bay of Kambos with a small hamlet. Anchor in 3–8m off the beach. Good shelter from the *meltemi* although again there are fierce gusts into the bay. A couple of tavernas ashore. You are getting towards the limit of Patmian tourism here

MONASTERY OF ST JOHN

The fortified monastery perched above the harbour is physically and figuratively the centre of Pátmos. It attracts cruise ships crammed to the gunnels with sightseers. It attracts the devout from all sides of the Christian faith. And it attracts the odd academic to its library, and a few idle yachties. If you are intent on visiting, time your visit for when the cruise ships are not in port or you will find the *chora* and the monastery impossibly crowded.

The monastery was founded in 1088 by Ioannis Khristodhoulos, an abbot from Bythnia, who obtained permission from the Byzantine emperor Commenus to build a monastery here. It is said to be built on the site where St John dictated the Apocalypse (or Book of Revelation). Khristodhoulos was a canny man and apart from permission to build a monastery, he also obtained tax concessions from the emperor and rights on trade. The latter were put to good use and over the years the monastery acquired much wealth and property. Surprisingly, through all the different occupying forces including the Venetians and Turks, these rights were by and large observed and the wealth of the monastery was left intact, including its large library which rivalled that of the Holy Mountain on the Athos peninsula.

St John is a bit of an enigma and there is a lot of scholarly discussion about whether he wrote the Apocalypse at all, whether he wrote it on Pátmos, and whether it has been so edited that the standard book in the Bible is a stripped-down version of St John's fiery poetry. Before you get to the monastery proper there is the Monastery of Apokalypsis over the cave where St John lived and where he dictated the Apocalypse to his disciple Prochorus. There is another mystery here as Prochorus is recorded as living a couple of centuries after St John. The saint himself had been exiled from Ephesus across the water around AD95 by the Roman Emperor Domitan. This puts John at well over a century old on his arrival on Pátmos, but he still had all his powers intact. Prochorus relates a story of how he took on the Priest of Apollo, a wizard by the name of Kynops. Kynops was fond of bringing up effigies of the dead from the bottom of the harbour and while he was on the seabed one day John turned the wizard into a rock – the same rock marked by the yellow buoy in the harbour. Local folklore has it that the rock is impossible to move and that fish caught around it smell bad.

Looking up to the *chora* and fortified monastery on Pátmos

Wherever the Apocalypse has come from, its wild poetry with vivid descriptions of the end of the world, the dead rising from their graves, of the battle between good and the Antichrist has influenced our ideas of the battle between good and evil from early medieval times to the present day. All the great artists have had a bash at representing it, from monks in their illustrations and frescoes through Fra Angelico, Michelangelo, Dürer and Hieronymous Bosch to William Blake. In art, literature and the cultural fabric of western civilisation we are imbued with these images and even now are sometimes pursued by religious fanatics who believe the battle is just around the corner and the Antichrist is living next door.

Further up from the cave is the Monastery of Ayiou Ioannou Theologou (St John the Divine) sitting on a rocky outcrop. It was built with defence in mind in those piratical times and the outer walls are heavily fortified and crenellated, and the roads inside narrow and winding. All around it the *chora* has grown up reliant on the shelter to be found inside these thick walls. The monastery and the cave are a UNESCO world heritage site and you do get a special feeling of what the times and life were like when you wander around the place, which is probably the best way to see it although a visit to the Treasury Museum is worth the effort. You cannot see the library unless you are a bona fide academic or theology student, but the treasury houses a number of illuminated manuscripts including the 11th-century parchment granting Khristodhoulos the island. There are enough cafés and snack bars to sit in and of course a number of shops selling guides to the monastery. And those quite spectacular views over the water to Arki and Lipso.

and Kambos is a wonderful place with some agriculture going on in the hinterland.

Nisís Áy Yeoryios/Koudros In calm weather there is a wonderful anchorage between Nisís Áy Yeoryios and Koudros just east of Kambos. Some care is needed of reefs and shoal water connecting the islets to Pátmos, but with care you can anchor between the two islets or to the east of the islet of Koudros.

Órmos Grikou Lies under Ák Tragos to the south of Skála Pátmos. Anchor in 8–10m off the resort. The bottom is thick weed and it can be difficult to get your anchor to hold, but persevere. The jetty off the beach is reported to have 2m depths off it. Good shelter from the *meltemi* although there are gusts into the bay. Ashore things have been much developed in recent years and there are lots of villas and apartments for the summer tourist trade. Several tavernas of variable quality. At the southern end of the bay is the strange volcanic lump of Kalikatsou which was formerly used by Christian hermits. The caves of the hermits pepper the sides and local lore tells of a tunnel running from the monastery to here in order to spirit away the valuables in the monastery in the event of a pirate attack.

Órmos Dhiakoftou (Petras) The bay south of Grikou. It affords reasonable shelter from the *meltemi*. Anchor where convenient off the coast keeping well clear of the wrecked coaster off the beach.

Órmos Stavros The large bay on the western side of Pátmos more or less opposite Dhiakoftou. Anchor off the beach at Psili Ammos on the north side in 3–10m on sand and weed. Reasonable shelter from the *meltemi*, although if it blows strongly swell is pushed up into here. In calm weather you can anchor off Alikes beach in the eastern corner. A simple taverna opens at Psili Ammos in the summer. The beach at Psili Ammos is the best on the island, though it is rarely overcrowded because of the relatively difficult access.

Note Around the southern end of Pátmos the *meltemi* tends to gust down with some force and there can be confused seas with the *meltemi* blowing across the current flowing northwards around Pátmos.

Órmos Merikha A calm-weather anchorage in the bay on the west coast more or less opposite the end of the natural harbour of Skála Pátmou.

Arki

Arki and the group of islands around it are situated east of Pátmos and north of Lipso. The islands are little inhabited, with Arki (the biggest island) populated by just forty or so inhabitants. The attraction for yachts is that few people visit here and while there may be a tripper boat or two around in the daytime, by night they have all disappeared back to Pátmos.

Note There are extensive reefs and shoal water around Arki and nearby islets that cannot be clearly shown on these plans. Navigation around the island and islets should be made in daylight only and with someone up front conning you in.

Historically the islands have been outposts of power centres on the larger islands around them and the mainland coast of Asia Minor. On the summit of Arki above Port Augusta are a few

ARKI AND LIPSO

⊕4 0·5M N of Ák Koumaro (Arki)
      37°25'·30N 26°43'·13E WGS84
⊕6 0·25M S of N. Grilousa (Arki)
      37°21'·12N 26°42'·39E WGS84
⊕7 Mid-channel Frangonisi – Makronisi (Lipso)
      37°15'·64N 26°43'·95E WGS84

remains of a Hellenistic fort which was partially rebuilt by the Romans and later by the Byzantines. Apart from this fort the islands are little mentioned by anyone, although I'd be surprised if they were not used by local traders and the odd pirate for shelter from the *meltemi*. The relative unimportance of the islands has meant that manmade influences have been kept to a minimum, and this has prompted the environmental organisation Archipelagos and the local government to establish a wildlife reserve here.

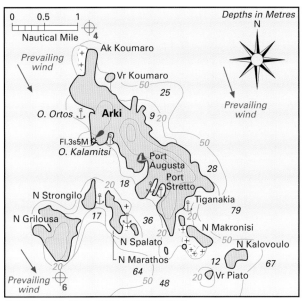

NISOS ARKI AND ADJACENT ISLETS

⊕4 0·5M N of Ák Koumaro (Arki)
37°25'·30N 26°43'·13E WGS84
⊕6 0·25M S of N. Grilousa (Arki)
37°21'·12N 26°42'·39E WGS84

PORT AUGUSTA (Avgousta)

Pilotage

Approach A dog-leg inlet on the west side of Arki. The approach through the islands is straightforward, although with the *meltemi* blowing there are strong gusts through the channels between the islands and off Arki itself. Care is needed when coming from the south to avoid the reef in the passage between Marathos and the islet off it (see separate entry). Although

Yachts on the quay at Port Augusta, Arki

the entrance is lit a night approach is not advised. In the closer approaches it is difficult to see exactly where the entrance is and it is easy to mistake Port Stretto for Augusta. When closing the coast you will eventually see the light structure and this positively identifies the inlet.

Mooring There is limited room to berth in Arki and in the high season it is frequently crowded. The inlet is narrow with little room to manoeuvre, so have everything ready before you turn the corner of the dogleg. Go stern or bows-to the quay at the head of the inlet. An alternative is to anchor off on the southeast side of the inlet and take a long line ashore. The bottom is mud and weed with a few rocks and generally good holding. Shelter from the

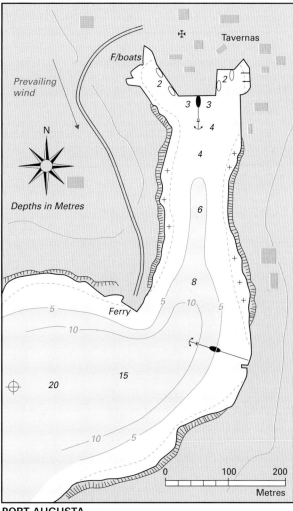

PORT AUGUSTA
⊕37°22'·59N 26°43'·88E WGS84

prevailing northerlies is good at the head of the inlet and also in the southeast corner. With strong southerlies I suspect a bit of a surge could develop in here. Yachts should not use the ferry quay on the west side of the entrance. If there is no room on the quay, yachts can either anchor with a long line ashore in the SE corner or try Port Stretto.

Facilities

There are two real tavernas in the hamlet in the square near the water's edge and most of their trade comes from yachts. There is also a café/taverna as well. They serve fairly typical fare although they will often have good fresh fish.

General

Augusta is one of those low key places where yachts usually dally for a few days. There are pleasant walks around the *garrigue*-covered slopes above the hamlet where just about the only inhabitants you will meet are the local goats. The water in the harbour is clean enough to swim in although in most places you will have to clamber down the rocky foreshore to get in the water.

Anchorages around Arki

Depending on the strength of the *meltemi* there are a few other anchorages which can be used with care around Arki.

Port Stretto (Limani) A double-headed bay where it is possible to anchor with reasonable shelter from the *meltemi*. Yachts normally head for the

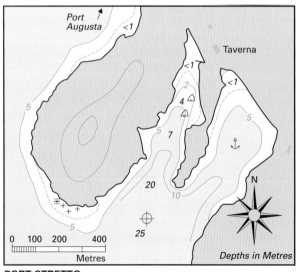

PORT STRETTO
⊕37°22'·31N 26°44'·23E WGS84

NORTHERN DODECANESE NATIONAL PARK

There are few nature reserves in Greece and the National Park being established at Arki and the archipelago around it is to be welcomed. In 2004 the Greek government began the process to establish the Northern Dodecanese National Park and it is being organised by Archipelagos, The Institute of Marine Conservation. This refuge encompasses the islands and islets extending from Agathonisi, Arki and Lipsi to Kalolimnos and Imia. Within the refuge it is forbidden to:
- hunt or capture game animals and other fauna
- remove sand or stone from the coastline
- pollute the surrounding waters
- destroy any of the natural flora
- build structures without taking into account the impact of buildings on the refuge.

How this will impact on yachtsmen using the area is not really detailed, although reference is made to the undersea littoral, especially to seagrass beds (*Posidonia oceanica*) which are an important breeding area for some fish, and to the protection of marine mammals, dolphins and the monk seal, which live in the surrounding waters. It may be that moorings will be laid in some areas to stop yacht's anchors ploughing furrows through the seagrass and disturbing the marine life there.

The islands are home to a variety of seabirds, including the rare Audouin's gull and Bonelli's eagle, which are protected species. The area will be monitored by Archipelagos which works with the local prefecture and has established research bases on Arki, Patmos and Fournoi. The Northern Dodecanese National Park is being viewed as a model for future parks and it is likely that more will be established around Greek waters in the coming years, though there is a whiff of politics here with the specific inclusion of the disputed rock of Imia in the plan (see section in Kalimnos).

The headquarters of Archipelagos is in Vathi on Samos. www.archipelago.gr

western arm where there are a number of mooring buoys near the head of the arm. Further in depths get variable and shallow. Yachts can also anchor and take a line ashore to the western side. The bottom is mud and weed, generally good holding once the anchor is in. Good shelter from the *meltemi*, but open south. Taverna ashore opens in the summer.

The eastern arm also affords good shelter from the *meltemi*. Like the western arm depths get shallow at the very head of the bay. Anchor off where convenient. Good shelter from the *meltemi* but open south.

Órmos Tiganakia The large open bay on the southeastern end of Arki. This has a good sandy beach and is sometimes visited by tripper boats. Make the approach around the eastern side of Kalovoulo and Makronisi to avoid the reefs around these islets. Depths become shoal towards the shore so edge in slowly and anchor in convenient depths. When the *meltemi* is blowing some swell works its way around into here and it is best to leave for better shelter.

In calm weather there are several other bays and coves around Arki that can be used, with Ortos and Kalamitsi on the east side of Arki and to the north of Port Augusta the most popular. With the *meltemi* these bays are not tenable. In calm weather yachts also anchor in the channel between Strongili and Marathos and off Kalavoulo at the southern end of Arki.

NISÍS MARATHOS

Marathos is the only other populated islet around Arki, though with just the families of the tavernas here it rarely amounts to more than half a dozen or so.

Pilotage

Approach The anchorage is on the east side of Marathos, partially sheltered by Spalato islet. In the channel between Marathos and Spalato there is an isolated reef with 5–7m in the channel on either side. With care and someone conning from upfront, you can come up through this channel, but the prudent approach is from the east, which means going around Spalato if you are coming from the south. When the *meltemi* is blowing there can be strong gusts down through the channel and as the reef is unmarked it can be difficult to see when there are whitecaps all around.

Mooring There are mooring buoys in the anchorage belonging to the tavernas here and if you pick one up then you should dine in the taverna which laid it. If you are anchoring the bottom has a covering of thick weed in places and the holding is patchy, so make sure your anchor is

Looking E into the bay on Nisis Marathos. Moorings have been laid by the taverna owners *Toni Font*

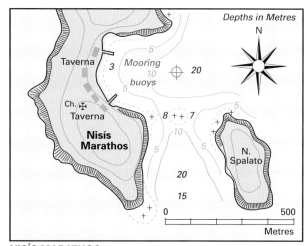

NISÍS MARATHOS
⊕37°21'·99N 26°43'·70E WGS84

well in. There are stakes on the N shore to take long lines ashore. Good shelter from the *meltemi* but open to the south unless you are tucked right up into the bay.

Facilities

There are three tavernas here. Marathi is run by the piratical-looking Mikhalis and is the place usually frequented by yachties. The other tavernas are more frequented by the tripper boats from Pátmos and only open for the summer.

Farmakonisi

This low-lying island sits on its own out to the east of the other islands and less than five miles from the Turkish coast. This has made it the obvious target for illegal immigrants to head for out of Turkey and into the EU. As I sit writing this some 70 illegal immigrants have been rescued from a sinking boat just off Farmakonisi and returned to Turkey. The island has a permanent military presence on it to guard Greek waters and to detain illegal immigrants who try to cross over

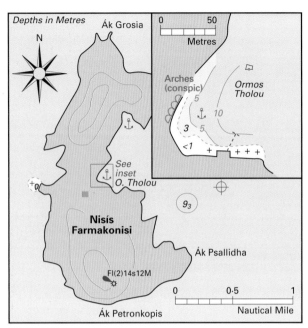

FARMAKONISI
⊕37°17'·7N 27°06'·5E

from Turkey. There is tragedy and a little black humour involved here, with several immigrants recently arrested having floated over on blow-up beach toys including a shark and a blow-up island complete with palm tree.

The permanent military presence on the island means that it can no longer be visited by yachts. Recent visitors have been waved away in no uncertain terms, and given that the smuggling boats have warning shots fired across the bows, it is best to keep clear of the place. I include the plan in case the rules are relaxed at some future date, as they have been in the past, and then yachts and the Greek fishermen who used to poach in Turkish waters from here will again be able to visit the island.

The only sheltered bay on the island is Órmos Tholou on the eastern side of the island. Here there are the remains of a Roman villa and nearby are a few other ruins dating from Roman and Byzantine times. It was here that Julius Caesar was captured by pirates and held for ransom for 38 days. It is related that he kept in good spirits and exercised and jested with his captors. Once the ransom was paid and he was released, he gathered together an expedition and returned to capture his kidnappers. They didn't get the chance to be ransomed and were all sentenced to death by crucifixion.

Lipso

Lipso sits just under Arki, the last piece of the jigsaw puzzle of islands around Pátmos. Like Arki it sits in a stretch of water where the *meltemi* can blow strongly at times and around Lipso it tends to gust fiercely through the channels and off the high land. In fact, most of my memories of the sea around here involve lots of white horses and spray over the deck. Like Arki it also has a dogleg harbour on the southwest side, though it tends to be more gusty than Port Augusta on Arki.

To a large extent its fortunes have been intertwined with its larger cousin across the water though it does claim an earlier association through its name. Lipso is said (mostly by brochure writers) to be a bastardised version of Calypso, the island that Odysseus was cast up on after his ship has been wrecked by a storm after surviving Scylla and Charybdis – still called by the same names – in the Strait of Messina. That association is highly unlikely as the island in the *Odyssey* is properly called Ogygia and the fair Calypso is the enchantress on the island who detains Odysseus for seven years. Ogygia is more likely to be one of the Maltese islands given the locations of Odysseus' long voyage home around the Italian islands and the fact that he reaches Ogygia after drifting for nine days (from a location near the Strait of Messina). Still, who knows in the end, and if Homer was from nearby Khios, then maybe he knew something about Lipso that we don't.

The island has had a reputation for producing good wine and used to produce the sweet red communion wine for Pátmos. Often this sort of recommendation ends in disappointment after you taste the stuff, but surprisingly this rocky little island produces a passable dry white which can be bought in Lipso village.

ÓRMOS LIPSO (Sokora)

The main port on the southwest side of the island.

Pilotage

Approach The islets of Nisídhes Khalava lie southwest of the entrance, with safe passage around either side and into the bay that shelters the port. The light structure on the northern entrance point will be seen when closer in and also a white chapel on the northern side of the bay. Once into the bay the houses of the village will be seen.

With the *meltemi* there are severe gusts down into the bay off the northern slopes and it is best to get the sails off in the approaches rather than in the bay itself.

Mooring Yachts can go stern or bows-to the new pier in the inner harbour. If going outside the pier go stern-to with plenty of chain out as the wind tends to gust down onto the beam. Alternatively there may be some room to go alongside the pontoon in the northwest corner.

Anchorage can be found off the north side of the outer bay to the west of the village where shown on the plan. Although there are strong gusts down off the slopes here, the holding is good and the location is a quieter one compared with the centre of Lipso itself.

Facilities

Services Water and electricity boxes on the pier. The harbourmaster will come down to connect you up and make a one-off charge. He also collects the rubbish in the morning and asks visitors to sort it for recycling. Fuel on the southeast side of the harbour and a mini-tanker does the rounds.

Provisions Minimarkets around the harbour. Lipso wine can be bought here.

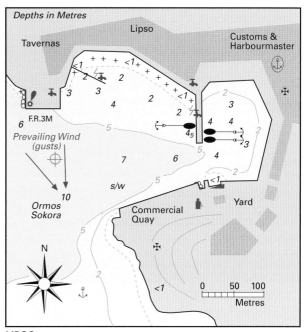

LIPSO
⊕37°17′·67N 26°45′·86E WGS84

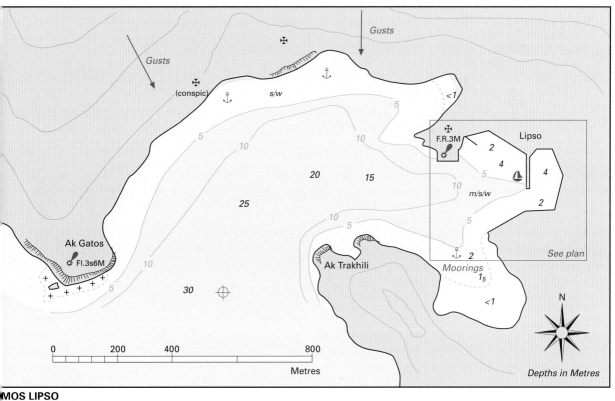

ÓRMOS LIPSO
37°17′·1N 26°45′·25E

Lipso harbour

Eating out Cafés and *ouzeri* around the harbour. It is worth starting off in one of the little *ouzeri* near the root of the pier. Then wander up the hill towards the church where there are a couple of good tavernas. Alternatively there are tavernas around the harbour.

Other PO. ATM. Internet café. Hire scooters. Ferries to Kós and Pátmos.

General

In common with some of the other smaller islands in the Dodecanese, Lipso has recently acquired a following by those 'in the know' and so has a surprising number of regular tourists who visit every year and stay in village rooms (most of them built recently) around the island. This means the island is a little more crowded than you might expect in the summer and downtown Lipso is quite a buzzing place of an evening. The locals all seem to take it in their stride and there is an interesting eclectic mix of backpackers and more genteel folk strolling around to choose a café or taverna for the evening meal.

In the village there is a small museum, called the Ecclesiastical Museum, though it houses a wide range of objects. Dominating the village is the Church of St John the Theologian, mostly constructed in the 1930s from donations from ex-pats in America. Inside is an icon showing the Virgin Mary cradling the dead Christ, the only known depiction of this. Every year on the festival of the Panayia (15 August) it is said that dead flowers in the church miraculously rejuvenate. The icon is originally from a small chapel south of Lipso and on the day of the festival it is carried back to the little church of Panayia Harou.

LERA LIPSO

A three-headed bay at the southern end of Lipso. Care is needed of the reef of Ák Acerba on the western side, but otherwise the approach is straightforward and yachts can proceed around

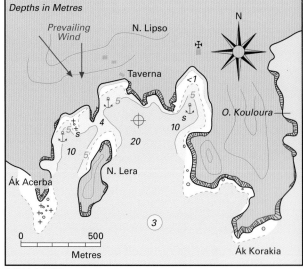

LERA LIPSO
⊕37°16′·5N 26°46′·5E

either side of Nisís Lera in the middle of the bay. Anchor in convenient depths in any of the coves around the bay and take a long line ashore. The bottom is sand, rock and weed and not everywhere good holding. The solitary taverna in the middle cove has laid moorings which you can pick up and for which a charge is made. With the *meltemi* howling through the anchorage and the uncertain holding it is not a bad idea to pick up one of the moorings.

The bay is an idyllic place, mostly visited by yachts. The Dilaila taverna ashore has good local fare and is well worth a visit of an evening.

Anchorages around Lipso

Makronisi On the south side of Makronisi and the islets around it there is a bay under the cliffs with suitable depths for anchoring and reasonable shelter from the *meltemi*. The turquoise water and wild location make it popular with tripper boats, but there is plenty of room for everyone to anchor here. Better thought of as a lunch stop though in settled weather it could be used as an overnighter.

Órmos Kouloura The bay immediately east of Lera Lipso. Reasonable shelter from the *meltemi* although it is more exposed than Lera Lipso.

Órmos Plati Yialos 37°18′·95N 26°44′·6E An inlet on the northeast side of Lipso. Anchor off the beach with a long line ashore to the north side of the cove. Limited shelter from the *meltemi* and not a place to stay when it starts blowing. Taverna ashore in the summer.

Órmos Moskathou 37°19′·4N 26°43′·1E An indented bay on the north of Lipso. The *meltemi* blows straight into here so it is only really tenable in calm weather or southerlies. A fish farm in the east cove restricts anchoring room.

Léros

Léros has always made a case for being a misunderstood island. In earlier versions of my *Greek Waters Pilot* I had numerous letters from Leriots in high places complaining about me mentioning that the island's name sounds like the demotic *lera* meaning 'grubby' or 'roguish', despite the fact that I also mention that I have always liked the island, visit it often, and find the islanders warm and welcoming. In ancient Greece it was called the Island of Artemis (the goddess of the hunt) probably an import from Miletus across the water as it was originally a colony of the city. Artemis is an interesting goddess, being almost certainly proto-Greek and a morphing of a much older goddess into a Greek deity. The Olympian version is that she was a daughter of Zeus and Leto and a sister of Apollo. She is also a bit of a contradiction in that she is generally held to be the virgin huntress, but is also associated with fertility. It can be no coincidence that one of the primary centres of worship was at Ephesus just across the water in Asia Minor where there was a celebrated Artemisium and a statue of Artemis covered in breasts, indicating her other role as a fertility goddess and perhaps an association with the original earth mother Eurynome. In the Hellenistic period this association was derided as Léros had a matriarchal system in place which was at odds with the resolutely patriarchal system in the rest of Greece.

The island has a lot of other unfortunate associations. It sided with Sparta during the Peloponnesian War although it was surrounded by islands on the Athenian side. During the Second World War it was captured by the British in 1943 after the Italian capitulation, only to have the

Léros Marina *Léros Marina*

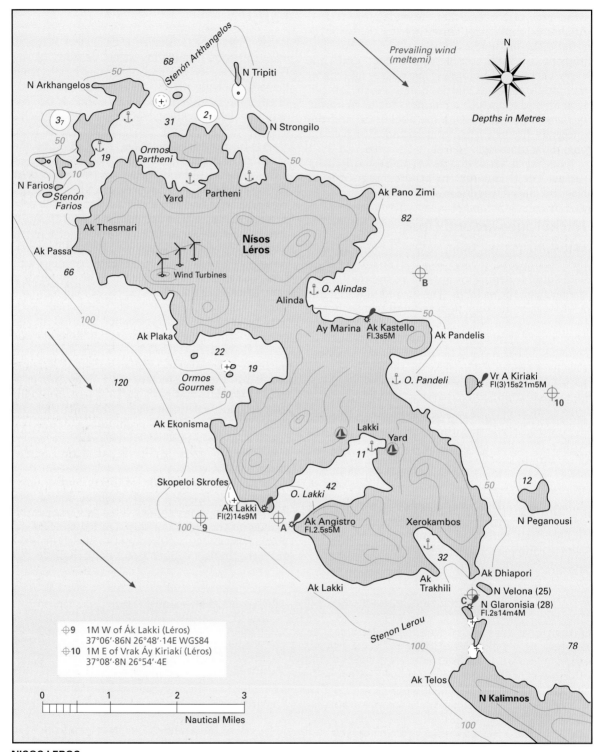

Prevailing wind
(meltemi)

N

Depths in Metres

68 *Stenón Arkhangelos*

N Tripiti

N Arkhangelos

3_7

31

2_1

N Strongilo

19

*Ormos
Partheni*

Ak Pano Zimi

N Farios

Yard

Partheni

82

*Stenón
Farios*

Ak Thesmari

**Nísos
Léros**

B

Ak Passa

66

Wind Turbines

O. Alindas

Alinda

Ay Marina   Ak Kastello
Fl.3s5M

Ak Pandelis

Ak Plaka

O. Pandeli

Vr A Kiriaki
Fl(3)15s21m5M

22

19

*Ormos
Gournes*

50

10

Ak Ekonisma

Lakki

Yard

11

12

Skopeloi Skrofes

42

O. Lakki

Ak Lakki
Fl(2)14s9M

9

A

Ak Angistro
Fl.2.5s5M

Xerokambos

N Peganousi

100

32

Ak Dhiapori

Ak Lakki

Ak
Trakhili

C

N Velona (25)

N Glaronisia (28)
Fl.2s14m4M

Stenon Lerou

100

78

Ak Telos

N Kalimnos

100

⊕9   1M W of Ák Lakki (Léros)
      37°06'·86N 26°48'·14E WGS84
⊕10 1M E of Vrak Áy Kiriakí (Léros)
      37°08'·8N 26°54'·4E

0   1   2   3

Nautical Miles

NISOS LEROS
⊕A 37°06'·72N 26°49'·78E WGS84
⊕B 37°10'·0N   26°52'·2E
⊕C 37°05'·63N 26°53'·26E WGS84

Germans mount a massive air and sea attack to take it back, causing much damage and suffering on the island. During the reign of the colonels in the late 1960s there was a notorious prison for dissidents at Partheni. And then there are the mental hospitals which caused a furore in the 1990s when Channel 4 and the tabloids exposed the awful conditions in the hospitals on the island. At Lakki I well remember the screams and shrieks emanating from the large hospitals around the harbour.

I mention all this because Léros has always had odd associations, and in a way this all adds to the mystery and attractions of the place. It is an enchanting island and from my first visit here in 1980 up to the present I always make a bee-line for the place. It is a much-indented island, cut with an unsteady hand by the gods, and there are excellent anchorages all around it. The people are friendly and although it cannot now be described as undiscovered, it is not overpopulated by tourists in the summer and thankfully has little of the crassness of Faliraki or Kardamena. Conditions in the mental hospitals have been radically reformed and new practices introduced for the care of patients. It is quite simply one of my favourite islands in the Dodecanese and there are few who do not like the place.

For getting around the island, this is one of those places where it is hardly worthwhile taking a scooter or hire car: you can get to more places by boat than you can by road and you are much better off sailing around Léros than chancing it on the roads.

PORT LAKKI

The main ferry port on the southwest side of the island.

Pilotage

Approach You would think the entrance to the large bay would be easy to identify, but it is not and it can be difficult to work out just where the entrance proper is. To the north there are a number of wind turbines on the hill north of Órmos Gournes and closer in the group of rocks off the coast to the northwest of the entrance will be seen. Close in the two light structures on either side of the entrance can be picked out. With the *meltemi* or strong southerlies there is always something of a reflected swell off this west coast and there can be lumpy confused seas. Once you are inside the entrance to the bay the sea dies

ART DECO AND THE FASCISTS

In 1922 Benito Mussolini and his Fascist Party came to power and in 1923 the Treaty of Lausanne formally ceded the Dodecanese to Italy (although they had already occupied the islands since the First World War). Mussolini had grandiose plans for a Mediterranean Empire stretching from Italy east to the Dodecanese and including large chunks of North Africa. He wanted to build a neo-Roman empire and in the Dodecanese he set about it with a passion. Lakki was chosen as the main naval base for the Dodecanese and a new town was built on the shores around the head of the bay.

The architectural style was Art Deco and the town was modelled to produce wonderfully clean, rounded buildings with a minimum of decoration. There are wide boulevards, a superb market and shopping arcade with covered walkways and a circular atrium, a cinema built with a fine curved façade, the old Léros Palace Hotel, and in the streets behind large Art Deco villas are scattered amongst the newer 'pour-and-fill' buildings so prevalent in Greece. Inside, the buildings are light and airy and in direct contrast to local houses where the object is to keep the sun out so they remain cool.

For years this whole Art Deco town was crumbling away and a number of the larger buildings were used as mental hospitals. In recent years the value of this singular town has been recognised and some of the buildings are now being repaired. I can think of only one other place that compares with Lakki, and that is Napier in New Zealand, where in 1931 an earthquake measuring 7.8 on the Richter Scale flattened the town and pushed the earth up to such an extent that the harbour is now inland. My mother was in this earthquake and she described it as one of the most frightening things she had ever experienced. It was decided to rebuild the town in Art Deco style and it now titles itself the Art Deco capital of the world. Lakki has many similarities and it is to be hoped that this fantastic architecture will be preserved from further decay despite its associations with the repressive rule of the Fascists between the two world wars.

Art Deco cinema

Art Deco building near the harbour, formerly one of the old mental hospitals

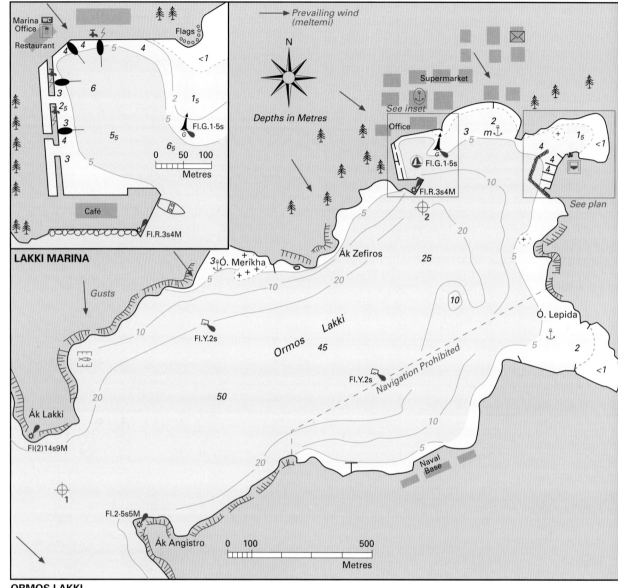

LAKKI MARINA

ORMOS LAKKI
⊕1 37°06'·72N 26°49'·78E WGS84
⊕2 37°07'·52N 26°50'·95E WGS84

away, but with the *meltemi* you will have gusts from different directions off the high land on the north side of the bay. Once up to Lakki Marina there is a green buoy marking the shallows off the town proper which you need to leave to starboard if you going to Lakki Marina. If you are headed for Leros Marina then stay in the middle of the fairway and call up the marina for details of the final approach.

Note There is a Greek naval base on the south side of the bay and yachts should make sure they keep clear of the prohibited zone shown on the plan.

Mooring

Lakki Marina Situated on the NW side at the head of the bay. Go stern or bows-to in the small marina at Lakki. There are laid moorings tailed to the quay and someone will usually be there to wave you into a berth and help you tie up. It's best

Lakki Marina in Órmos Lakki

to call up in advance on VHF Ch 11 although the high land around the harbour limits VHF range. Good all-round shelter. Charge band 2.

Léros Marina Situated at the eastern end at the head of the bay. The entrance is at the N end of the breakwater. Call up on VHF Ch 10 for instructions. Berth where directed in the marina.

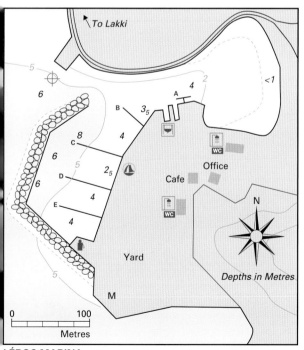

LÉROS MARINA
⊕37°07′·75N 26°51′·3E

There are laid moorings tailed to the pontoons. Good all-round shelter. Charge band 2.

Anchorage Yachts also anchor off the town to the east of Lakki Marina in 3–8m. The bottom is mud and good holding once the anchor is in. The prevailing wind gusts into the end of the bay from the northwest so shelter is good here. Alternatively anchor in Órmos Merikha in 4–5m taking care of the reef in the bay. Good shelter from the *meltemi* and you can take the dinghy around to Lakki town. In calm weather or light northerlies a few yachts also anchor at Lepida in the southeast corner of the bay, and even though it is technically in the prohibited zone, the authorities don't seem to mind most of the time. With southerly gales there are severe gusts off the south side of the bay and a considerable sea heaps up at the head. In this case the only really safe place to be is tucked up into the west side of Lakki Marina or in Léros Marina.

Facilities

Services

Lakki Marina Water (not potable) and electricity at every berth. Potable water by mini-tanker. Toilets and showers. Laundry facilities. Fuel by mini-tanker. Wi-Fi.
① 22470 26009
www.lakki-marina.gr

Léros Marina Water (not potable) and electricity at every berth. Potable water by mini-tanker. Toilets and showers. Laundry can be arranged. Fuel by mini-tanker. Wifi. Full service boatyard with 20-/50-/160-ton travel-hoists and all yacht service facilities.
① 22470 26600
www.lerosmarina.gr

Provisions Good shopping nearby in the town. Large supermarket a short distance up the main road out of town. It's worth a walk around the colonnaded shops in town just for the experience.

Eating out In town the Petrino near the post office is the best bet with outdoor tables under the Art Deco clock tower. It serves the usual fare but cooked well. Good Italian pizzeria Fontana di Trevi on the waterfront with wonderful 'front of house'. At Lakki Marina and at Leros Marina there is a café/taverna. Along the waterfront there are a number of pizza/snack bars and cafés. At Merikha a taverna in the bay opens in the summer.

Other PO. ATMs. Hire scooters and cars. Bus to Platanos and Alinda and taxis. Ferries to Piraeus and Rhodes with stops along the way.

General

Lakki is an odd place, surrounded by the monumental Art Deco buildings from the 1930s. Wandering around the deserted boulevards of the town is like being on a decaying film set, maybe something like an old black and white horror movie or a bit of *film noir*. It is hardly the most populated place on Léros and the most the tourists arriving by ferry see is the café at the dock and the road out of town. This adds to the melancholy of the place – though I for one find that a bonus.

The bay immediately west of Lakki Marina houses the Leros Yacht Club in what has to be one of the most idyllic locations for a yacht club. Apart from the teaching side in opis and lasers, the club hosts a number of races that cruising boats can participate in including the Goran Schildt (a Finnish writer who lived on the island) Memorial Race in September. *Skylax* did OK in the race in 2011 and the party afterwards is stupendous.

ÓRMOS GOURNES

37°08'·5N 26°48'·0E

This deep-indented bay to the north of Lakki looks like it should afford some shelter, but in fact any swell running outside tends to rebound into here and if the *meltemi* is blowing the bay is a bit like being in a washing machine with swell coming from all directions. In calm weather it is possible to anchor off the beach in the northeast corner to the east of the islet (Áy Isadora) with a small white chapel on it. If the *meltemi* gets up you should up anchor and head for Lakki. There is a taverna on the beach and on the south side of the bay there is a small shallow fishing harbour.

ORMOS PARTHENI

Pilotage

Approach Partheni is fringed by rocky islets and a reef, although in practice the approach is straightforward. The only real danger in the approach is the reef in Stenon Arkhangelis between Nisís Arkhangelos and Vrak Petalidha. Once under the lee of Nisís Arkhangelos you lose

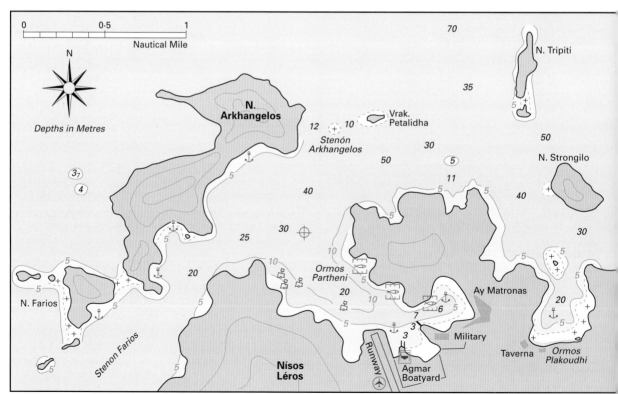

ORMOS PARTHENI AND APPROACHES
⊕37°12'·0N 26°47'·5E

the swell from the *meltemi* blowing down on the top of Léros and the entry to Partheni becomes apparent. On the southwest side of the entrance there are some big-ship mooring buoys and you will see the boatyard on the south side of the bay.

Mooring The anchorage off Áy Matronas in the southeastern arm of the bay is pretty much taken up by fishing boats and they don't always take kindly to you anchoring here. A small yacht should be able to squeeze in, but larger yachts will have to anchor further out in the bay. The bottom is mud and weed, good holding. Shelter here is nearly all-round, even anchored out from the entrance.

Note Agmar Marine have plans to build a marina in the bay, although at the time of writing no details were available on the planned final form or on when work will start. There are mooring buoys off the travel hoist bay that yachts waiting to be hauled can pick up.

Facilities

Some provisions and several tavernas ashore in Áy Matronas. On the south side of the bay next to the airport is the boatyard run by Agmar Marine from Lakki Marina. The yard has become popular as a place to leave yachts for the winter even though it is a bit off the beaten track. At least you are close to the airport if you are flying out.

Agmar Marine 70-ton travel-hoist. 350 berths ashore. Chandlers. Most yacht repairs can be arranged. Electricity and water. Showers and toilets. Taverna just outside the yard near the entrance to the airport.
www.lakki-marina.gr

General

When I first visited here most of Partheni was under the military, who have now downsized to the buildings between the boatyard and Áy Matronas. Under the colonels political dissidents (read 'communists') were sent here and the place acquired a sinister reputation for torture and the 'accidental' deaths of inmates. Áy Matronas itself is a wonderfully scrappy little village which remains pretty much outside any mainstream tourism and is mostly made up of a few fishermen and smallholders.

Partheni could refer to a number of goddesses. Parthenos ('virgin') is a title given to Athena, hence the Parthenon in Athens. Parthenos was worshipped in Carian times on the mainland opposite and it is likely that this goddess was merged with Artemis at a later date. There is said to be a temple to Artemis somewhere around Partheni, although the signpost near the airport leads to a few ruins of a fort. Other sources say the temple was at the present-day church of Áy Kyras – or the ruins may lie somewhere under the airport or the boatyard.

Anchorages around Partheni

Arkhangelos Yachts can anchor off under the lee side of Nisís Arkhangelos, although depths come up quickly and it may be best to anchor with a long line ashore. There is also an attractive anchorage under Nisís Farios in calm weather with wonderful turquoise water all around.

Órmos Plakoudhi The bay to the east of Partheni. Care is needed of the above-water rocks and reef around them lying in the middle of the entrance to the bay, although it is easily spotted and the reef shows up well. Try to creep as far around into the southwest corner of the bay as possible although a number of moorings restrict space to some extent. Good shelter in here from the *meltemi* as long as you are tucked into the southwest corner. At weekends the beach here is very popular and crowded so try to time your visit for a weekday. A taverna opens in the summer.

ALINDA (Alinta)

The deep bay and alternative ferry port on the east side of Léros.

Pilotage

Approach From the distance the castle and four windmills on the saddle of the hill above the southern entrance of Alinda can be seen from some distance off. The bay is steep-sided and the entrance clear of dangers apart from a 5m patch off the northern entrance. When the *meltemi* is blowing the wind literally screams down off the slopes around and in Alinda. You should have the sails off before entering the bay as it can come as a nasty surprise to find you have more wind in the bay than outside it.

Mooring With the *meltemi* the only safe place to be is anchored off in the northwest corner of the bay. In lighter weather or southerlies you can anchor off the quay in the southeast corner or there may be space to go alongside or stern-to on the southwest side of the ferry quay. The short mole northwest of the ferry quay is usually full of fishing boats. Care is needed in Alinda as the bottom throughout is hard sand and rock and not

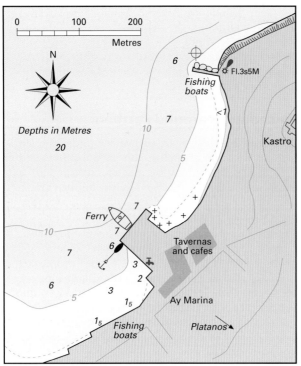

AY MARINA
⊕37°09'·62N 26°51'·23E WGS84

Alinda looking down over the bay from the Kastro

The Battle of Leros

Alinda was the focus of the German attack after a
British division occupied the island when the Italians
capitulated in 1943. In a similar situation to
Cephalonia, the Italians either wanted to fight on the
side of the Allies or return to Italy. The British took
most of the Dodecanese Islands including Leros,
though they were severely under-resourced and had
virtually no air cover. The latter was to be the undoing
of the British occupation of the islands.

German troops landed to the north and south of
Alinda after the airforce had pounded the British
garrison, then paratroopers caught the hopelessly
outnumbered Allied troops in a pincer movement. The
Greek battleship *Queen Olga* and the British *Intrepid*
were sunk in Port Lakki in the attack.

The defeat at Leros led to the collapse of the Allied
war effort in the Dodecanese and the rest of the
islands surrendered after Leros had fallen. There is an
interesting account of the Small Boat Squadron around
the Dodecanese and adjacent Turkish coast in
Improvise and Dare by Johnny Guard. At Alinda there
is the Allied War Graves Cemetery and the Historical
and Ethnographic Museum in Alinda has a whole
section devoted to the Battle of Léros.

Near Lakki there are a number of tunnels used during
the war which are now open to the public.

good holding. Make sure your anchor is holding
before leaving the yacht to go ashore.

Facilities

Services Water near the quay in Áy Marina. You
may be able to get a mini-tanker to deliver fuel
to the quay.

Provisions Minimarkets near the quay in Áy
Marina and ashore in Alinda at the head of the
bay.

Eating out Tavernas on the waterfront in Alinda
and in Áy Marina. Around the quay at Áy
Marina the area has been sympathetically
redeveloped and there are a number of good, if
slightly more expensive, restaurants situated
close to the sea. A good place to treat yourself
to a special meal.

Other PO. ATMs in Áy Marina. Internet cafés.
Hire scooters and cars. Bus to Platanos.

General

At the head of the bay, the old port of Alinda has
all but been engulfed by modern tourist facilities
around the beach. The gem of the bay is Áy
Marina which zigzags up the hill to meld into

Platanos at some undefined point. The architecture is a mix of styles although much of Platanos dates from the 20th century when the capital was moved to here. There are wonderful lanes winding up the hill and most of the startling white houses are clothed in bougainvillaea.

Above the town the castle can be reached by steps from the town square in Platanos. It is probably Byzantine in origin and was then re-modelled by the Knights of St John, the Venetians and the Turks. It's worth a visit as much for the view and for the medieval church of Panayia tou Kastro (the Virgin of the Castle) just inside the gates as for the Kastro itself.

PANDELI (Panteli)

A small harbour and anchorage just over the hill to the south of Alinda.

Pilotage

Approach The islet of Áy Kiriakis lying in the approaches to the bay of Pandeli is easily identified. The harbour and anchorage at Pandeli are in the northwest corner of the bay and there are no dangers in the approaches. Although there are some gusts into the bay they are nothing like the ferocious gusts into Alinda.

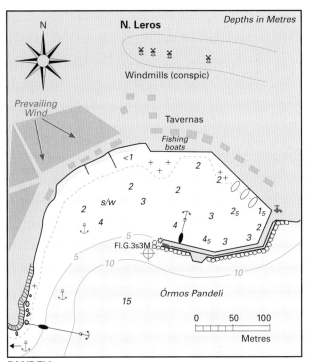

PANDELI
⊕37°09'·00N 26°51'·80E WGS84

Pandeli, the small fishing harbour and anchorage just around the corner from Alinda

Pandeli waterfront

Mooring Yachts can go stern or bows-to the end of the outer breakwater if there is room. Most of the other berths inside are occupied by fishing boats and you should not take their berths. In the past it used to be that from September to May yachts could not use the harbour when the fishing season was in full swing, but the prohibition seems to be something of a variable feast so play it by ear. Good shelter from the *meltemi* in here but southerlies cause a surge and you should seek shelter elsewhere.

The alternative to the harbour is to anchor off the beach in 4–8m. The bottom here is sand and weed and good holding. You may be able to take a long line ashore, which makes sense as the *meltemi* tends to blow off the shore here. Just south-west of the harbour and anchorage off the beach at Pandeli there is a small cove that can also be used, although it is not quite as sheltered as the anchorage of Pandeli village.

The anchorage here is exposed to southerlies and in the event of a blow from the south the best policy is to go around the corner to Alinda.

Facilities

Water on the quay and diesel can be delivered by mini-tanker if you are in the harbour. Minimarkets in the village and a whole array of tavernas and bars. Two of the original tavernas here, Psarapoula and the *ouzeri* Tzouma, have reasonable fare amongst the now extensive line-up of tavernas.

Hire cars and motorbikes at Pandeli, and most other things can be found up the hill in Platanos.

General

The place has been 'discovered' and a rash of rooms and small hotels have been built around the original waterside fishing village. It is still an attractive place, with whitewashed houses covered in bougainvillaea, and tamarisk trees around the port with nets and the odd octopus hung out to dry.

For yachts this is a popular spot because it is a lot less gusty here when the *meltemi* is blowing and it is also a bit more intimate than Alinda. Yachtsmen may protest at fishing boats using the harbour, but it is after all a fishing village and this lends some veracity to the place, in contrast to other harbours where the fishermen have been forced out by RIBS and runabouts owned by holidaymakers.

XEROKAMBOS

Pilotage

Approach Coming from the west the approach is straightforward with good depths everywhere. From the east you need to pass between N. Velona and Mikro Glaronisi where there are good depths. Do not attempt to pass between Mikro Glaronisi and Megalo Glaroniso off the top of Kalimnos as a reef connects the two islets and a swell heaps up through the gap. The bay can be a bit difficult to identify from the west as the low rocky cliffs don't give much indication of where the entrance is, but closer in there is little room for confusion. Coming through the gap between the islets in the channel you will see the houses at the head of the bay.

Mooring Yachts normally anchor off in the bay in 5–10m on sand and weed, good holding. Alternatively there may be a mooring free that you can pick up. The small harbour in the northwest corner is used by fishing boats, but there is sometimes space on the end where you can go stern or bows-to. Don't stray too far towards the short pier off the hamlet where there are shallows and rocks.

The bay affords good shelter and is only open south. Even with moderate winds from the south the bay is tenable.

Facilities

Several tavernas ashore serving the usual fare, with good fresh fish often available. A diving school operates from the hamlet and will organise dives around the nearby coast. A *caique* ferry runs daily in the summer to Mirties on Kalimnos.

General

Xerokambos is a relatively quiet place after the hustle and bustle of Alinda and Pandeli, with just a few 'village' rooms and a hotel ashore. You don't even get that many people coming here on a weekend as the beach is pretty scrappy. There is also a dive school ashore.

Built into a crevice in the rocks is a picturesque little chapel devoted to Panayia Kavourodena – the 'Virgin of the crabs', which refers to the icon of the Virgin that a fisherman found amongst the rocks here and which instantly cured him of a crab bite. He took the icon home, but that night had a dream about a woman in black who asked him to return the icon to where he found it. The chapel is built on the very same spot. Up the hill near the village of Lepidha there is a small castle with wonderful views over to Lakki and across to Kalimnos. It is built on the site of an ancient fortification from around the 3rd century BC.

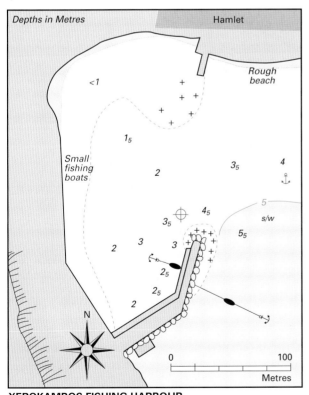

XEROKAMBOS
⊕37°05'·94N 26°52'·86E WGS84

XEROKAMBOS FISHING HARBOUR
⊕37°06'·47N 26°52'·18E WGS84

Xerokambos looking NW from Ak Dhiapori

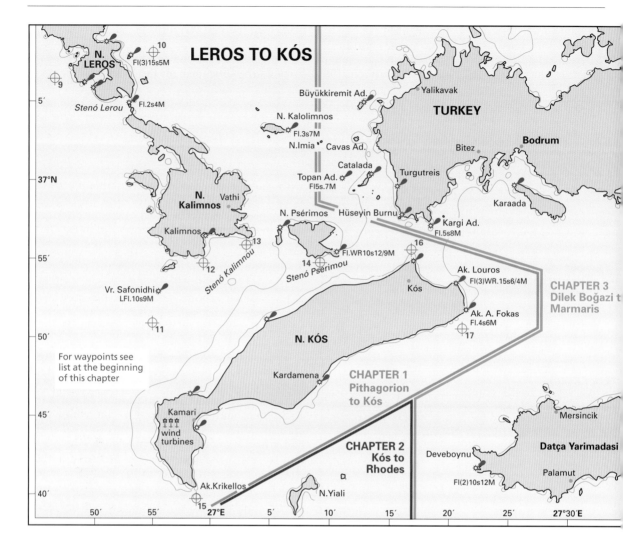

Kalimnos

Kalimnos is a great craggy lump of rock that grows out of the sea like some prehistoric monster. In ancient times it was associated with Léros and the two islands were referred to as one, the Kalydnian Islands mentioned in the *Iliad*. In fact it has been settled since Neolithic times, as remains found at Dhaskalio Cave near Vathi show. It is likely that the main settlement in Classical times was on the coast near Pothia, although some reckon it may have been on the isthmus connecting Telendhos to Kalimnos which was submerged in the AD554 earthquake.

Kalimnos was evidently important during the Byzantine era, with a number of forts and chapels scattered around the island. In the Middle Ages the island was raided by the Seljuk Turks and the island was virtually abandoned until the Venetians and then the Knights of St John arrived on the scene. When the Knights were forced to abandon Rhodes they also abandoned their other settlements and Kalimnos came under the governance of the Ottoman Turks who remained here until the First World War despite the Greek War of Independence. In common with the rest of the Dodecanese it was occupied by the Italians after the First World War and only became Greek after the Second World War.

Kalimnos has long been regarded as the centre of sponge fishing in Greece, though it is difficult to know when this happened. Why it happened is somewhat more apparent. The island is basically two valleys sandwiched between barren limestone ridges unsuited to agriculture and not well endowed with natural springs. At some point in

Lepidha
N Peganousi

Nisós
Léros
• **Xerokambos**

50

56
Fl.2s14m4M
N Velona
N Glaronisia

Stenón
Lerou
71

Ak Telos

150

100

⊕**12** 0·5M S of Áy Yeóryios (Kalimnos)
36°54'·97N 26°59'·21E WGS84
⊕**13** 0·75M S of Ák Khali (Kalimnos)
36°55'·95N 27°02'·97E WGS84

N

Depths in Metres

97

O. Petronda
Ak Mirties
O. Sikari
Ak Khondri Miti

96

94

122
O. Apitiki
See plan
Emborios

50

See plan

Ak Kefala
Ak Poundha
O. Palionisou

N Kalavros

100

O. Argano
O. Pezonda
Ak Pezonda

Ak
Kastelli

50

N Telendhos

Vr Apano

Ak Karapsili

Stenon Telendou
Mirties

**Nísos
Kalimnos**

N A Kiriaki

Or Profitis Ilias
.679

Platanos
See plan
Vathi
Ormos Vathi

Panormos
Ak Katsouni

O. Linarias
84

O. Akti

127

100

Ak Trakhilas

Ak Khali

O. Pithan

See plan

**Kalimnos
(Pothia)**

O. Kalimnou

50

⊕
13

Vr A Andreas

Ak Tolmi

55

Ak A Yeóryios

Stenón Kalimnou

O. Vlikadhia

0.5   1   2   3

50

N Nera

⊕
12

Nautical Miles

63

S KALIMNOS

time the fishermen turned their attention to gathering sponges and the tradition established deep roots on the island. By the beginning of the 19th century sponges were much sought after in Europe and most Kalymniot sponges went to England. By the end of the 19th century Kalimniots were exporting sponges all over the world and the sponge fleet numbered hundreds of boats. The principal merchants acquired considerable wealth, as evidenced in some of the grand villas around Pothia. Even after the Second World War there were still 140-odd boats in the sponge fleet, though these gradually decreased and by the time I first visited the island in 1980 the numbers were down to 25 or so. In 1986 disaster overtook the industry as a strange disease afflicted Mediterranean sponges causing them to get strange white patches and, worse, to become brittle. It appears that abnormally warm currents circulated around the Aegean basin, and the proximity of this event to the explosion at Chernobyl gave rise to a lot of conspiracy theories. It appears more likely that increased

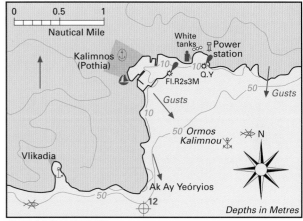

ORMOS KALIMNOU

⊕12   0·5M S of Ak Ay Yeóryios
         36°54'·97N 26°59'·21E WGS84

Port Kalimnos looking SW along the recently widened NW quay

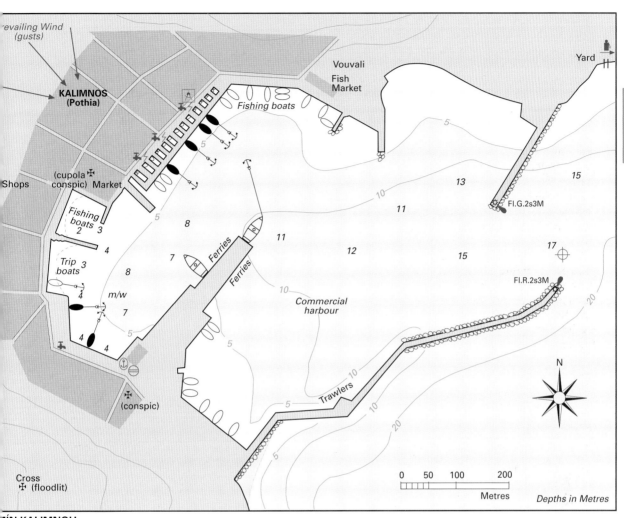

Prevailing Wind (gusts)

KALIMNOS (Pothia)

Shops

(cupola conspic) Market

Fishing boats 3 2

Trip boats 3

m/w

(conspic)

Cross (floodlit)

Vouvali Fish Market

Fishing boats

Yard

5

13

11

Fl.G.2s3M

15

15

8

11

Ferries

Ferries

12

15

17

Fl.R.2s3M

7

8

7

Commercial harbour

Trawlers

N

10

20

0   50   100   200

Metres

Depths in Metres

LIMÍN KALIMNOU
36°56′·84N 26°59′·69E WGS84

water temperatures from global warming affected the sponges as has happened in other parts of the world. The sponge fleet fell apart and today only a few boats leave every year.

The decline of the sponge fleet in the 20th century led to Kalimniots emigrating in large numbers to Australia and America. The island has few natural resources to sustain a large population and even today it is said that the main income on Kalimnos is in remittances from those who emigrated. After the 1986 disaster efforts have been made to foster tourism on an island which until then had pretty much turned its back on the tourist industry, and although there is some package tourism on the west coast, it is nothing like that on Kós and Rhodes.

LIMIN KALIMNOU (Pothia)

The main harbour and capital on the southern end of Nísos Kalimnos.

Pilotage

Approach Coming across from Kós and the east the town and harbour are easily identified in the large bay of Kalimnos. If you are coming from the west you won't see the town and harbour until you are right up into the bay and around Ák Áy Yeoryios. When the *meltemi* is blowing there are severe gusts down into the bay and off the high land to the east of Órmos Kalimnou. It can be a real struggle getting up into the bay with the gusts and it is often better to get the jib off and motorsail up to Kalimnos harbour.

Mooring Most yachts go stern or bows-to the new quay in the NW corner of the inner harbour. You will see it ahead of you as you pass through the entrance of the inner harbour. Go stern or bows-to where there is room. A bit of care is needed in places if you have a deep rudder where underwater balasting extends out reducing depths to 1·6–1·8m though there are mostly 2m depths. Good shelter from the *meltemi* which blows off the quay here though there is a bit of wash when the tripper boats and ferries go by. Open to southerlies which blow straight in.

Alternatively head into the inner harbour in the SW corner and go stern or bows-to the quay. Make sure you drop the anchor a fair way out as the *meltemi* tends to blow beam-on. Good shelter once your anchor is in and better shelter from southerlies here than in the NW corner.

The holding on mud is generally good although there are a few places in the SW corner where the holding is suspect. Some care is needed in the SW corner of crossed anchors between yachts on the south and west sides of the basin, though there is little you can do about it.

Kalimnos Marina The project to build a marina in the southern basin of the outer harbour appears to have been shelved for the foreseeable future.

Facilities

Services Water and electricity on the quay in the NW and SW of the inner harbour. In the NW corner one of the taverna owners will wander over to connect you. In the SW corner a 'man' will come around to connect you. Fuel by mini-tanker who does the rounds of the yacht berths.

Provisions Good shopping for provisions nearby with a with a couple of largish supermarkets on the waterfront near the cathedral. There are also some wonderful old-fashioned shops with sacks of beans and grains, and large bottles with preserves and other mysterious things inside.

Eating out The waterfront is ringed by tavernas and *ouzeri* although some have become more tourist-orientated with awful photo-menus and mediocre food. In the square near the cathedral on the waterfront there are two taverna/ouzeries, the *Kafenes* and the *Manias* which have good food and a convivial atmosphere.

Other PO. ATMs. Internet cafés. Hire cars and scooters. Ferries to Piraeus and Rhodes and islands in between. Small airport for internal flights on prop planes.

General

Kalimnos, or more properly Pothia, is a bustling noisy town: motorbikes and cars roar around the narrow streets, the waterfront is all of a hubbub as *caiques* unload and tripper boats tout for business, the Muses *caféineion* is full of men gesturing and shouting at each other, and somewhere in the middle of this mêlée a few bemused yachties wander around. The town is built around a natural valley and is a jumble of buildings that all look as if they have been washed down the valley from the old capital at Khorio inland. It is a very Greek place, much removed from Kós town or the sanitised precincts of the castle at Rhodes, and once you get used to the dust and noise and confusion, most people end up with a sneaking affection for the place.

Pothia is the new capital and was only established in 1850. Prior to this the capital was Khorio, further up the valley and strategically close to the castle on the slopes nearby so the inhabitants could take shelter from the pirates that ravaged this coast. With the decline in piracy towards the end of the 19th century the inhabitants moved down to the coast to be closer to the natural harbour of Órmos Kalimnou and the burgeoning inter-island trade that was developing. It is likely that the harbour has long been used, although there are few references or remains to tell us so. On the road to Pothia there are the ruins of the Church of Christ of Jerusalem built by the Byzantine emperor Arcadius in thanks for surviving a storm when he sheltered here while en route from Jerusalem.

The Italian occupation of the Dodecanese was not a happy time for the island and the inhabitants of Pothia responded to the occupation by painting their houses white and the shutters and doorways blue to remind the Italians both of the Greek flag and that it was to Greece that this island really belonged. In recent years other colours have crept in but a lot of the houses still use the blue and white colour scheme. Down on the waterfront there is the idiosyncratic 18th-century Christos cathedral with a melange of frescoes and icons and a marble iconostasis from the tortured imagination of the Tiniot sculptor Yiannoulis Halepas. Not that you really have to dwell on any of this because the attraction of Pothia is just wandering around the back streets (and dodging the mopeds), looking into the shops and artisanal workshops until you decide you have had enough and it's time to settle in on the front with a coffee or a cold drink.

Sponge fishing

It may come as a surprise to some that the bath sponges you use to work up a lather are, or were, a colony of animals, albeit sessile ones belonging to the phylum *porifera*. This phylum of simple invertebrates is probably related to other simple multicellular organisms like coral and jellyfish. They occurred early on in the evolution of multicellular organisms, around half a billion years ago, and have diversified to fit most marine environments, although they are most prolific in tropical waters around coral. Although a simple organism, they can live for up to 200 years. Around six species of sponge are considered worth gathering for the commercial market and of these the Mediterranean sponges have been the most prized.

The sponge that comes up from the bottom looks and smells nothing like the honey-coloured articles tourists buy in the shops. It is a brown, sometimes nearly black, animal, often with bits of seaweed and other marine growth encrusted on it, and after a couple of hours in the sun it smells abominable. After the sponges have been left in the sun to dry they are squashed to break up the fibres and the marine growth on them and then washed in seawater for a day or so. The sponges don't yet look like the finished article, but they are beginning to smell better. To get them looking as we know them they are bleached to remove the pigmentation and then washed again. It seems the real thing will never be out of favour because despite the development of artificial sponges, chemistry cannot imitate nature and only the real thing has that almost creamy feel to it.

The sponge-fishing boats leave for their annual voyage in May or June and slowly cruise the coast until October. Aboard one of these small boats, often only 12 or 14m (about 38–46ft) long, will be five or six men, living and sleeping sponges until the winter. The sponges are found in anything from 10–70m (30–230ft) of water and a diver will spend about an hour underwater doing his stint. The equipment is often antiquated and makeshift and would give a professional diver the horrors. A wetsuit is worn to keep warm and air is supplied along a long hose to a simple mask and regulator. The sponges are cut off their rocky beds and loaded into nets to be hauled on board where they are washed.

Given the antiquated equipment and the depths to which divers were going it is not surprising that fatalities occurred and the 'bends', nitrogen narcosis, was common. When a diver surfaces too quickly nitrogen bubbles are trapped in the blood and interfere with the nervous system and the circulation of the blood. Those who survived were often crippled for life, unable to straighten their limbs (hence the term 'bends') and often in great pain from the effects on their nervous system and circulation.

Kalimnos has long been known as the home of sponge fishing and the present-day factory is on the north side of the harbour. These days only a handful of boats leave Kalimnos to go diving for sponges as stocks in the Mediterranean have been severely depleted. Recently an agreement was reached with Libya to dive for the sponges in Libyan waters where there are still beds of the Mediterranean sponge. Most of the sponges you see

on sale these days do not come from Greece, but are shipped in from the Philippines, the Red Sea and the Caribbean. In Tarpon Springs near Tampa on the west coast of Florida there is a modern-day colony of Greeks, mostly from Kalimnos, who emigrated to the USA after the

Sponges on sale in Port Kalimnos

second world war and settled there to dive for sponges and fish the rich tropical waters. Today they make a good living out of being a Greek mini-republic complete with tavernas and a good export industry sending sponges back to Greece. During the 2004 Olympics in Greece the organisers wanted all the athletes and their support staff to have a Greek sponge each, which ironically were all imported from outside Greece.

The humble sponge has been celebrated from Homer onwards and even today no synthetic creation can match the soft, creamy, almost sensuous feel of a natural sponge. In the *Odyssey* the sponge was used to wipe down tables much as its synthetic imitators are used today. There are also references to it being used to drink wine (though given the plentiful evidence of cups that sounds somewhat fanciful to me). It has been used by artists to apply paint and as an ancient form of contraception. And of course it has always been used to wash the face and body, from Homer's *Iliad* to the present-day.

If you are browsing in the shops around Pothia I can recommend Faith Warn's *Bitter Sea* (published by Guardian Angel and available locally), a book detailing the lives of the Kalimniot sponge divers and the rise and fall of the sponge diving industry. And you can of course buy sponges all around the waterfront on Kalimnos and in the other islands, though the chances are they come from outside the Mediterranean.

European advertisement (1880) for Kalimniot sponges

ÓRMOS VLIKADHIA

A narrow inlet around one mile west of Ák Áy Yeoryios, the western entrance point to Órmos Kalimnos. Care is needed of Asproniktis, a rock and reef off the western entrance to the bay, but otherwise the approach is straightforward. Anchor off where convenient keeping clear of the buoyed swimming area at the head of the bay. There are a number of laid moorings in the bay which reduce the space available, so you will often have to anchor some way out from the head of the bay. The bottom is rocky with weed and the holding is not the best in here. With the *meltemi* gusting down off the slopes make sure your anchor is well in. Good shelter from the *meltemi* but open south, and if it blows from the south, you will need to get out as a large swell is pushed into the bay.

Ashore there are a couple of tavernas and a pretty scrappy beach. There is also a small Museum of Submarine Finds housing an eclectic collection of finds, sponges and shells and a reconstructed wreck. In recent years the locals here have not been helpful to visiting yachts, in some cases getting them to move on, so you need to play it by ear on arrival in the bay and if the locals are unhelpful there is not really much to detain you here.

Looking N into Vlikadhia

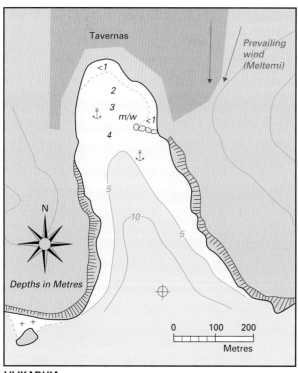

VLIKADHIA
⊕36°55′·6N 26°58′·0E

WEST COAST OF KALIMNOS
⊕36°59′·4N 26°55′·25E

Nisís Nera

⊕35°55'·5N 26°56'·6E

The islet lying off the southwest corner of Kalimnos which can be identified by the white chapel on it. Local boats sometimes anchor off in the cove on the southeast side where there is some shelter from the *meltemi*, although there always seems to be some swell curling around into the anchorage. It is probably best used as a lunch stop in calm weather.

Órmos Linarias

⊕35°58'·3N 26°55'·7E

The open bay on the west side of Kalimnos. The bay is virtually untenable except in a flat calm. With the *meltemi* there are strong gusts down the channel between Telendhos and Kalimnos and with southerlies a swell is pushed up into the bay. The bay is ringed with some pretty awful hotels and holiday apartments so there is little loss in not stopping here.

Mirties

⊕36°59'·7N 26°55'·8E

Mirties is another of those holiday areas like Linaria, though a little more sympathetic. In the southeast corner there is a small *caique* harbour and also the pier used by the local *caique* ferries running across to Telendhos. Although there are adequate depths in the entrance to the harbour, it is mostly shallow inside and is in any case full of local boats, so even small yachts stand little chance of finding a berth in here.

In calm weather yachts used to anchor off here, but recent reports indicate that the port police prohibit anchoring in the bay now. There are petty local politics involved here between the local fishermen and tripper boat owners running across to Telendhos and other parts of the community that would like to see yachts in Mirties. At the moment yachtsmen are caught in the middle of this squabble and it is best to steer clear of the area – literally.

Telendhos

In good weather the anchorage off the island is well worth visiting, though it should be treated as a lunch stop rather than an overnight anchorage. From the channel nose in towards the beach and anchor in 5–8m. The water is wonderfully clear here and for the most part it looks as if depths shelve gradually towards the coast. With a light *meltemi* there is a bit of a lee here but not enough

if moderate northerlies blow. A few years ago mooring buoys were laid in the bay, but as at Mirties there was some local disagreement and yachts were discouraged from stopping here. Again, you will have to play it by ear.

The small harbour off the hamlet has 2m depths in the outer part, but further in shallows quickly and is in any case full of local boats with little room for visitors.

Telendhos is great lump of rock that looks as though it has been cleaved clean off a mountain in Kalimnos – and so it has in a way. It was joined to the main island until a massive earthquake in AD554 submerged the isthmus connecting it to Kalimnos. There are accounts of an ancient city under the water, although I haven't seen anything I would positively identify as buildings. It did cause the evacuation of the Byzantine town of Áy Konstandinos high up in the middle of the island and some ruins still survive here as well as the church of Áy Konstandinos. It is a rugged hike up to the site, which gives you some idea of what the pirates that plagued this area were up against if they wanted to raid the town. Down on the shore in the hamlet of Telendhos there are over half a dozen tavernas catering for the tourists who come across from Mirties on day trips.

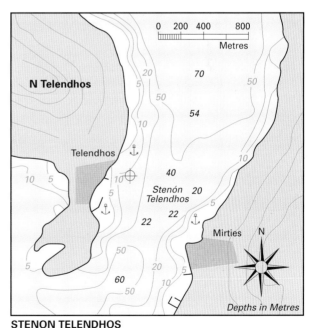

STENON TELENDHOS
⊕36°59'·87N 26°55'·47E WGS84

EMBORIOS

Pilotage

Approach It can be difficult to identify where things are in the approach to Emborios. Kalavros islet is difficult to identify against the land behind it and you will not see the buildings around the bay until you are closer in. With the *meltemi* there are strong gusts down off the land and it can be a bit of a battle getting up into the bay.

Mooring In the bay there are numerous moorings you can pick up, depending on where you are going to eat for the night. The moorings are laid by one or other of the tavernas and have the name of the taverna marked on the buoy. Alternatively anchor clear of the moorings off the village or in the cove on the west side. There is a fish farm in here but there is still room to anchor clear of it. You need to make sure your anchor is well in as the holding is poor here, with thick weed over mud and sand, and it may make sense to take a long line ashore if you can. There is a pier off the village with 4m depths off the end, but it is used by local boats.

Emborios on the northwest corner of Kalimnos

Facilities

A minimarket and tavernas ashore. The tavernas around the village have the usual fare. On the slopes above the first cove to the west there is Baba Nikólaos sitting on the slopes above the beach and, as well as a fine view, his food is not bad at all.

General

Emborios is a useful stop on the way north and a pleasant enough place with some village rooms and the tavernas. The coast and Kalavros are ringed with fish farms and as always these seem to have mini-rubbish tips next to them for old drums of chemicals and other detritus generated by the farms: not always the most pleasing environment to be around. At one stage Emborio and Argano in the bay to the southeast were used by *caiques* trading around the islands until the construction of the port at Kalimnos town.

Órmos Palionisou (Baia Isolavecchia)

This deep fjord-like bay is seldom frequented except by the occasional tripper boat, and even they don't usually stay too long. It is a spectacular place with steep limestone cliffs going straight up from the bay and if there was access it would be something of a rock-climbers' paradise. You can anchor off at the end of the bay and take a long line ashore. The holding is bad on rock and some sand and weed so it is best to take a long line ashore. There are gusts with the *meltemi*, although at the head of the bay these are not too bad. There is a primitive taverna and tables and chairs ashore, though I have never seen it open.

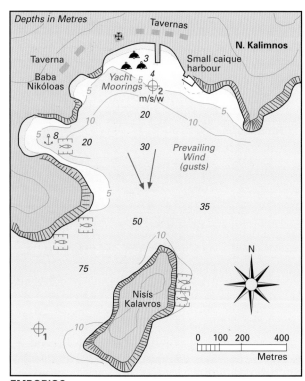

EMBORIOS
⊕₁ 37°01'·91N 26°55'·43E WGS84
⊕₂ 37°02'·71N 26°55'·70E WGS84

Órmos Palionisou on the east coast of Kalimnos

Órmos Pezonda

The deep bay to the south of Palaionisou. It is also quite spectacular, with steep cliffs dropping straight down into the water. With the *meltemi* some swell rolls around into the bay so it should really be used in calm weather, although again care is needed over anchoring here. There is said

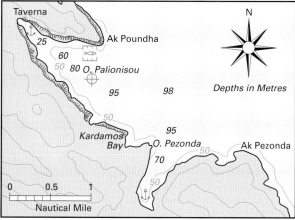

PALIONISOU TO PEZONTA
⊕37°01'·92N 26°59'·63E WGS84

to be all sorts of debris from the Second World War on the bottom so perhaps some care is needed in case you snag the odd unexploded bomb.

VATHI (Rina)

Pilotage

Approach It is difficult to see just where the entrance is to this mini-fjord, although there are no real dangers as you close this steep-to coast so just keep chugging in until you locate it. At the entrance you will see the houses at the head of the inlet and probably the masts of other yachts in here.

Mooring Go stern or bows-to on the quay just in from the short pier, leaving the end of the pier clear for the tripper boats that frequent the place. Care is needed of underwater rubble along this stretch of quay so proceed with caution. It is always crowded in here and space is at a premium, so don't rely on always getting a berth. Alternatives are to go alongside the north side where rings and posts have been cemented into the cliff. There is no quay as such but the cliffs drop abruptly into the water. Not my cup-of-tea but judicious use of fenders should make it work in calm weather. Alternatively try anchoring and taking a long line ashore in one of the coves beyond the buoyed swimming area. You may also be able to anchor further in with a long line ashore although there are a lot of moorings here that get in the way. Shelter is good in here with the *meltemi*, although there are strong gusts off the high land and down the valley. One thing to watch out for is wash from the high-speed ferries passing by. Yachts have been thrown against the quay and badly damaged so keep pulled well off and make sure your anchor is holding.

Facilities

Water on the quay, though it is often turned off in the summer. Minimarkets and tavernas in the village at the head of the bay. There is nothing much to choose between the tavernas in the village. The 'yacht club' on the pier is a sporadic enterprise and may or may not be open.

General

At one time this little gem of a place existed on a bit of fishing, the citrus orchards growing in the valley leading down to the sea, and the occasional yacht that visited. That was a while ago and now tripper boats bring in herds of people to the tavernas, most of the land in the valley is for sale

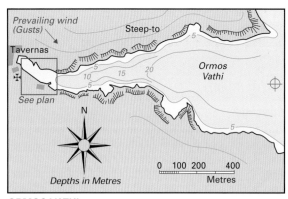

ORMOS VATHI
⊕36°58′·32N 27°02′·83E WGS84

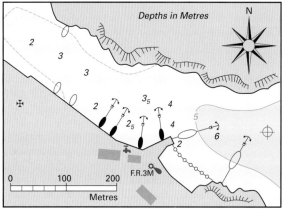

VATHI
⊕36°58′·42N 27°02′·12E WGS84

and villas are sprouting everywhere, and the locals are creaming it in. You can see why. The steep fjord is dramatically beautiful and the valley where the citrus grows is one of the few places on the

Vathi looking down onto the yacht quay from the opposite side of the fjord *Toni Font*

island that has abundant water. The green swathe of orchards drops down to the blue Aegean between the steep cliffs to provide one of those panoramas that tour organisers drool over. If you can't find a space in here or it all becomes a bit claustrophobic I suggest you head for Palaionisou where the scenery is just as grand, but there are no roads into the bay and the silence is deafening.

Órmos Akti (Áy Nikolaou, Katsouni)

⊕36°57′·7N 27°02′·8E

The large bay south of Vathi and situated just around the corner from Ák Kahli, the southeastern extremity of Kalimnos. Much of the bay is obstructed by fish farms, but you can still get into the head of the bay and anchor there. With the *meltemi* there are fierce gusts down into the bay and it is advisable to get sail off before you enter. Care is needed of an underwater rock

---

Imia or Cardak

In 1995 Papandreou's PASOK government decided to look at its territorial interests and disputes with Turkey. There had always been arguments in the northern Aegean over territorial limits, but these had never come to anything. Papandreou pinpointed an islet, really a large lump of rock, called Imia by the Greeks and Cardak by the Turks, lying to the east of Kalimnos. The Greek government offered to subsidise anyone who wanted to live on this flyspeck and the Mayor of Kalimnos decided to plant a Greek flag on the rock. A few days later the Greek flag was replaced by a Turkish flag and then all hell broke loose. The Greek and Turkish navies hovered on either side of the rock in a face-off that fortunately didn't explode into a full-scale firefight. Eventually the Americans put pressure on both sides to back down and allow the fate of the rock to be decided by future negotiations.

I was involved in this whole debacle because in my pilots and the chart series I edit, I show a border between Greece and Turkey. High level deputations from both countries, replete with admirals and diplomatic staff, visited Imray's offices and quizzed us all over just how the boundary between the two countries had been arrived at. It didn't go down too well when we told both of them that we simply drew a line midway between the two countries and that there was no deep historical reason for the exact position of the line. Readers of the books and users of the charts were surprised to find that all borders between Greece and Turkey disappeared in subsequent editions, a decision we made to avoid future involvement in this territorial squabble.

Note It's interesting to see that the Northern Dodecanese Wildlife Refuge includes Imia as part of it: you can't help thinking that some politics are being introduced into environmental concerns that need to be kept clear of politicians' ambitions.

reported near the head of the bay and sometimes marked by a white buoy. Anchor off the beach to the south of the underwater rock. With a strong *meltemi* some swell enters the bay though it is still usually tenable.

Tavernas ashore.

Psérimos

The bare rocky island between Kalimnos and Kós.

ÓRMOS PSÉRIMOU

The only harbour and the only settlement of any size on the island. While you might think this cove on the W side would be an ideal spot to stop at for lunch or overnight, that is not the case. Every day tripper boats head out from Kós and Kalimnos and meet in Psérimos in a riot of frayed tempers, loud music and heaving bodies. The sandy beach is covered in day-trippers and the locals get more and more surly as the day wears on. The only sane policy is to arrive late in the afternoon or early evening when the tripper boats are heading home and there is some room on the quay. Around this time the locals also experience a sea change and become somewhat more friendly to visitors.

Pilotage

The small hamlet of white houses around the beach on Psérimos is easily recognised and if you are unsure then watch the tripper boats homing in on the harbour. Care is needed of the reef and rocks off Ák Sphuri, but otherwise the approach is clear of dangers. Once up to the harbour try to find a berth and go stern or bows-to the quay tucked in behind the rough stone mole, bearing in mind the comments above. The bottom is sand and weed with some rocky ledges, generally good holding once you get the anchor in. The *meltemi* tends to send some swell into the bay, but once you are tucked in here the shelter is good.

Tavernas and bars ashore.

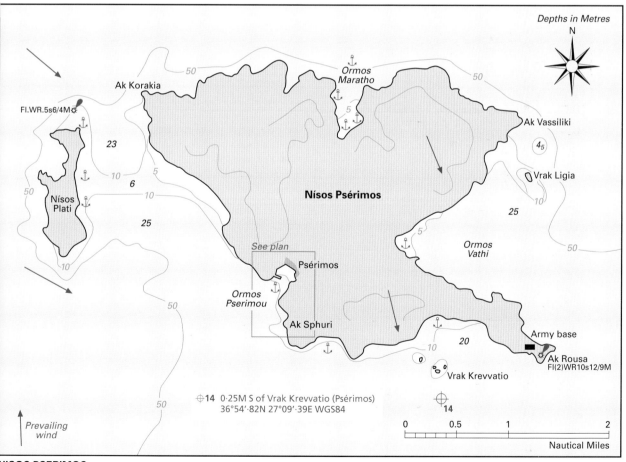

⊕14 0·25M S of Vrak Krevvatio (Psérimos)
36°54'·82N 27°09'·39E WGS84

NISOS PSERIMOS

Psérimos *Toni Font*

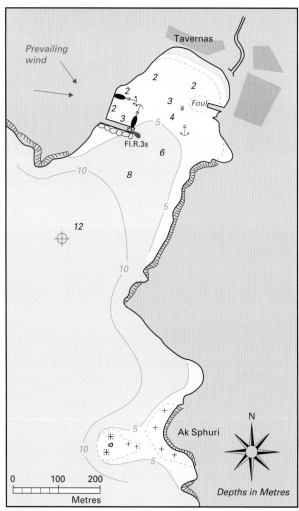

PSERIMOS
⊕36°55′·7N 27°07′·7E

Other anchorages around Psérimos

Nisís Plati The skinny, relatively low-lying island lying off the west side of Psérimos. Tripper boats anchor on the lee side of the island, off the chapel near the southern end or at the northern end between N. Nekrothikes and Plati. With the *meltemi* the southerly anchorage is to be preferred although some ground swell creeps around into here. At the northern end the anchorage is tenable with a light *meltemi*, but when it starts blowing you should vacate here. Both anchorages have suitable depths for anchoring (3–6m) over a sandy bottom and brilliantly clear water.

Órmos Maratho The bay on the north side of Psérimos approximately halfway along. With the *meltemi* a swell is pushed into the bay and it is not really usable. With light northerlies or any winds with a southerly component in them the bay is a useful stop.

Órmos Vathi The large bay on the eastern side of Psérimos. Good shelter from the *meltemi* here with just a military post nearby to keep you company. A large Greek flag is painted onto the rock on the southeast corner of Psérimos. Anchor in 5–10m as it shallows up quickly further in. The bottom is sand and weed, not everywhere good holding.

Psérimos southern anchorages There is reasonable shelter from the *meltemi* in the two bays on the south side of Psérimos, although it is a bit bleak here and some swell works its way around into the anchorages.

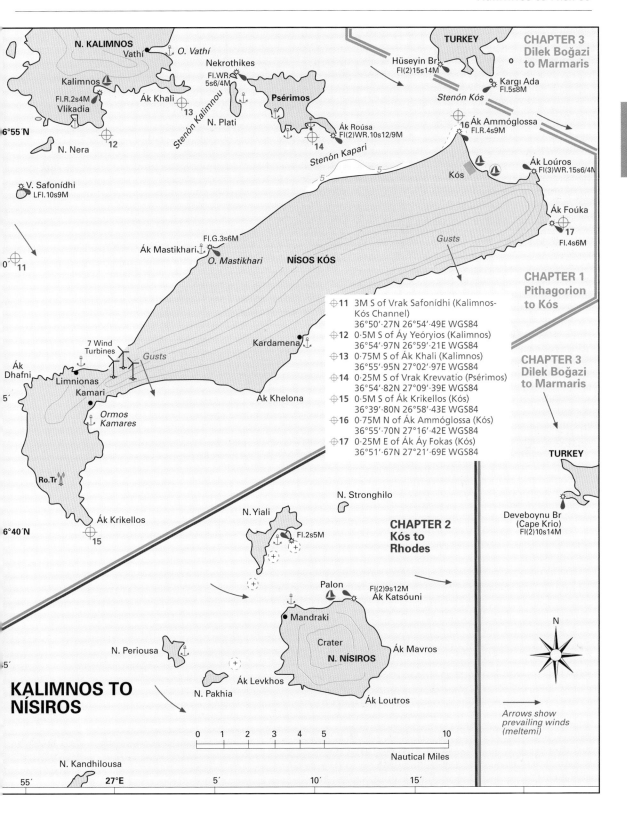

N. KALIMNOS
Vathí • · *O. Vathí*
Nekrothikes
Kalimnos ⚓ Fl.WR.
Fl.R.2s4M 5s6/4M
Vlikadia ☀ Ák Khali
6°55′N Stenón Kalimnou **13** N. Plati **Psérimos**
☀ N. Nera **12**
Ák Roúsa
Fl(2)WR.10s12/9M
14
Stenón Kapari

TURKEY
Hüseyin Br ☀
Fl(2)15s14M
☀ Kargı Ada
Fl.5s8M
Stenón Kós
16 Ák Ammóglossa
Fl.R.4s9M

CHAPTER 3
Dilek Boğazi
to Marmaris

Kós ⛵ ⛵ Ák Loúros
Fl(3)WR.15s6/4M

☀ V. Safonídhi
LFl.10s9M

Ák Foúka
17
Fl.4s6M

Fl.G.3s6M
Ák Mastikhari ⚓
O. Mastikhari **NÍSOS KÓS**

Gusts

0
11

CHAPTER 1
Pithagorion
to Kós

⊕**11** 3M S of Vrak Safonídhi (Kalimnos-
Kós Channel)
36°50′·27N 26°54′·49E WGS84
⊕**12** 0·5M S of Áy Yeóryios (Kalimnos)
36°54′·97N 26°59′·21E WGS84
⊕**13** 0·75M S of Ák Khali (Kalimnos)
36°55′·95N 27°02′·97E WGS84
⊕**14** 0·25M S of Vrak Krevvatio (Psérimos)
36°54′·82N 27°09′·39E WGS84
⊕**15** 0·5M S of Ák Krikellos (Kós)
36°39′·80N 26°58′·43E WGS84
⊕**16** 0·75M N of Ák Ammóglossa (Kós)
36°55′·70N 27°16′·42E WGS84
⊕**17** 0·25M E of Ák Áy Fokas (Kós)
36°51′·67N 27°21′·69E WGS84

Kardamena ⚓

CHAPTER 3
Dilek Boğazi
to Marmaris

7 Wind
Turbines
Gusts
Ák
Dhafni
Limnionas
Kamari
Ák Khelona

TURKEY

Ormos
Kamares

Ro.Tr ♨

N. Stronghilo

Deveboynu Br
(Cape Krio)
Fl(2)10s14M

Ák Krikellos
6°40′N **15**

N. Yiali
Fl.2s5M

CHAPTER 2
Kós to
Rhodes

Palon ⛵
Fl(2)9s12M
Ák Katsóuni

• Mandraki

N. Periousa ⚓

Crater
N. NÍSIROS Ák Mavros

5′

Ák Levkhos

N. Pakhia

Ák Loutros

KALIMNOS TO
NÍSIROS

N

Arrows show
prevailing winds
(meltemi)

0 1 2 3 4 5   10

Nautical Miles

N. Kandhilousa

55′ **27°E**   **5′**   **10′**   **15′**

Kós

Of all the islands covered so far, Kós is the one that most people know of, with the possible exception of Pátmos. It has levered itself into the mass tourist market, chasing hard on the coat-tails of market leader Rhodes. Consequently this island is well served by European charter flights and well populated with tourists in the summer. It also has a large marina which consistently gets good reports from those who use it. Unfortunately the arrival of mass tourism here has accelerated what centuries of wind and weather failed to do. Large areas of the island, in fact almost anywhere there is anything vaguely resembling a beach, have been turned into some of the tackiest resorts in Greece, replete with a heaving mass of beer-swilling inhabitants who thankfully rarely leave the reinforced concrete barracks and pubs and clubs they have come for. The nominal population of Kós is around 22,000 but in the summer this increases by some 50,000 tourists, many of them British. To like this place you need to work hard, to love it is difficult. Fortunately in a yacht you can, with care, avoid the naff resorts and their inhabitants.

Geographically Kós is somewhat like Kalimnos, a great hump-back whale of an island, though somehow it manages a more benign aspect from seawards. The ancient city was an important and prosperous one with Minoan and Mycenean roots. The ancient capital of Astipalaia was at the western end of the island above Kamari and it prospered under the Ionian period centred on the mainland opposite.

The island seems to have had something of an identity crisis down through the ages. It has variously been called Meropis after a mythical king; Nymphaeon after the numerous nymphs said to inhabit the place; Karis; and finally Kós which probably refers to a crab, an early symbol of the ancient city. The ancient city of Kós, exposed amongst the modern town, was founded around 366BC and was part of the Dorian Hexapolis that included cities on the adjacent mainland coast and Rhodes. The old harbour at Kós is probably pretty much where the ancient harbour was. Scattered around Kós town are the ruins of ancient Kós emerging like some ancient god shrugging off his long burial, and it's a pleasing place to wander around in the morning before the clubbers wake up and start drinking again.

The island has a mountain running down it, though on its western side the land flattens out and there is fertile soil for agriculture. In ancient times it was praised for its fertility and Kós did not need to concentrate on seafaring in the way some of its neighbours needed to do. The Kós variety of lettuce was introduced to Europe from here and it was once famous for its silk, so much so that it gave its name to the *Coae vestes*, the diaphanous silk dresses prized by Roman women. Kós also gave us Hippocrates, the father of modern medicine, and the Asclepion built in his honour just outside Kós town is a wonderfully tranquil place, a marble homage to the great physician.

The ancient city declined during Byzantine times and a couple of earthquakes in AD142 and 469 helped things along. (In fact, the bones of the ancient city were not really recognisable until an earthquake in 1933 exposed them and the Italians decided to excavate.) In 1431 the Knights of St John started work on the fort that now stands at the entrance to the old harbour and it is something of a palimpsest, with all sorts of ancient masonry incorporated into its walls including a statue or two. The Knights gave it up after they were forced out of Rhodes by Suleiman in 1522 and Kós came under Ottoman sway. In the old town there are still a couple of minarets to remind us of the Turkish occupation which lasted until the First World War when the Dodecanese was occupied by the Italians. They built a graceful town centre with arcaded shops and wide streets and much of this still remains, sandwiched in between the graceless reinforced concrete around it. Kós reverted to Greece after the Second World War and was an important military outpost looking out into the jaws of the ancient Ceramic Gulf (Gökova Körfezi) until mass tourism arrived in the 1970s.

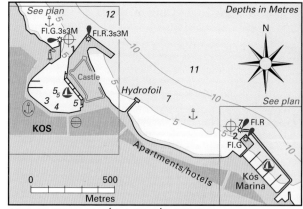

APPROACHES TO KÓS AND KÓS MARINA
⊕1 36°53´·88N 27°17´·34E WGS84
⊕2 36°53´·84N 27°17´·97E WGS84

It is easy to decry this tourism, and I do, but if you stay clear of the environs of Kós town, Kardamena and nearby resorts, and some of the resorts on the northwest side of the island, you avoid the worst of it and some of us can end up acquiring an affection for the island that was not immediately apparent on first acquaintance.

KÓS

Note I give details of the old harbour here first, but most yachts will head for the marina just southeast of the old harbour. The approach to the marina is pretty much the same as for the old harbour so will not be repeated there.

Pilotage

Approach From the west care is needed of the shoal water off Ák Ammoglossa. The shoals extend some distance off and the temptation is always to cut the corner until you suddenly find yourself looking at the sea bottom. Keep at least one mile off and don't turn the corner until you are sure you are well clear of them. As you approach the old harbour there will often be speedboats and jet-skis around as well as the odd ferry and tripper boat, so keep a careful eye out for other craft. A large brown hotel on Ák Ammoglossa is conspicuous and once into the lee of Kós the harbour and Castle of the Knights will be seen. From the east the approach is more straightforward with no real dangers and the castle and the town of Kós are easily identified. The marina lies ¾ mile southeast of the old harbour.

Mooring Don't go on the town quay unless you want a flea in your ear from the local tripper boat

Yacht berths under the Castle of the Knights in Kós harbour

operators. Yacht berths along the quay running around the east side of the harbour are now administered by Kós Marina. Berth stern or bows-to wherever you can fit in. Yachts can also go stern or bows-to the outer end of the north quay clear of the local boats. At present there is room for half a dozen yachts here although it may be that local boats colonise this area in the future. The bottom is gooey mud and good holding though it is also littered with laid moorings. Good shelter although a strong *meltemi* can cause a bit of a surge though the new commercial pier at the entrance has improved things. There is also a bit of wash when the tripper boats return. Charge band 2 on the eastern side.

Facilities

Services Water and electricity boxes along the east quay. Water tap on the N side but you will need a long hose.

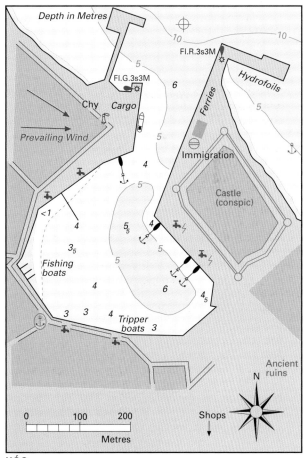

KÓS
⊕36°53′·93N 27°17′·38E WGS84

Provisions Good shopping for provisions nearby and a small daily covered market in Eleftherias Platia near the cinema.

Eating out Kós old town is replete with more fast-food joints than most places. I'd avoid anywhere on the waterfront and anywhere around Bar Street. They are generally awful and overpriced. To find somewhere good to eat in Kós you need to go well inland to the market square and then head for the old Turkish quarter where you will find Petrinos and the Kriti near the church of Theologou. The Kriti faces the church and Petrinos is tucked up the steps behind. Alternatively try some of the Italian restaurants halfway between the old harbour and the marina.

Other Banks and ATMs. Internet cafés. Hire bicycles, motorbikes and cars. Taxis. Ferries to the other Dodecanese islands, Cyclades, Piraeus and to Rhodes. Ferries to Bodrum in Turkey. Internal flights and lots of charter flights and budget flights to European countries.

General

Kós town is well worth a visit despite my comments in the introduction to the island. Visit it in the morning before the revellers arise unless you yourself want to roister. Most of the old town was rebuilt by the Italians after the 1933 earthquake and a fine job they did. The colonnaded front and streets running off it are in a sort of monumental style with some Art Deco additions.

Sprinkled through the town are remnants of other occupiers: a couple of minarets and a Hamam; a Jewish synagogue; the Castle of the Knights; and the ruins of the ancient city which were exposed in the 1933 earthquake. These are not far from the port and you can wander through them at will; in fact they are used as shortcuts by the locals. In this Kós has a rather magical appeal, with the old and the new jumbled up together and some often incongruous places next to one another. The Italianate 'Bar Street' with its thumping woofers and crowds spilling out onto the street rubs shoulders with the ancient agora nearby. The Castle of the Knights, replete with a jumbled collection of statuary and coats of arms, sits next to the ferry quay and overlooks Tripper Boat quay on the other side. The old Turkish quarter is adjacent to the Western Excavations where the old Acropolis was and which was first built over by the Romans and then had an early church on the site.

Hippocrates' plane tree, a venerable old and gnarled tree with scaffolding holding the branches up, is said to be the tree under which Hippocrates taught. It's said to be 700 years old, so obviously is not the same one that Hippocrates sat under, and even the 700 years may be questionable although this tree is probably one of the largest in Europe. The ancient Greek herbalist Dioscorides (1st century AD) said that the little hairs from the leaves and seeds falling off the tree in the summer affect the hearing and sight. The leaves have also been used for their astringent and ophthalmic properties to treat eye inflammations and wounds, so perhaps it's appropriate that Hippocrates sat under such a tree.

If you are in the marina it would be silly not to wander up to the old town and around its streets, though I suggest you stick to the south side of the harbour rather than heading for the tangle of modern Kós on the north side. While it is not really possible to love Kós in the summer, you may end up with a sneaky affection for it and if you want a rowdy night out then this is the place.

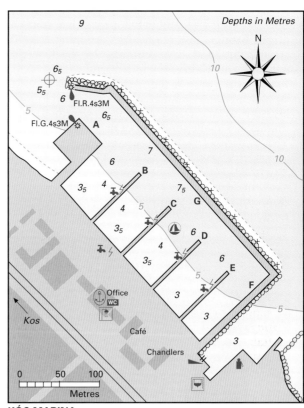

KÓS MARINA
⊕36°53′·84N 27°17′·97E WGS84

Kós Marina looking NW towards Kós town   *Kós Marina*

KÓS MARINA

Pilotage

Mooring Yachts approaching the marina should call up on VHF Ch 77 (callsign *Kós Marina*) and wait until the marina RIB comes out to guide them into the harbour and to a berth. Do not enter the marina until the RIB comes out. The RIB will help manoeuvre the yacht into place and staff on the pontoon will help with lines. Berthing is stern or bows-to with laid moorings tailed to the pontoon. Good all-round shelter. Charge band 2/3.

Facilities

Services Water and electricity at every berth. Showers and toilets ashore. Laundry services. Chandlers.

Provisions Minimarket in the marina. Better shopping outside the marina.

Eating out Café in the marina. Tavernas and some Italian restaurants nearby on the waterfront or just back from it on the road to Kós town.

Other Wi-Fi. Otherwise see Kós town above.

General

The marina gets a lot of kudos from those that use it and sets the standard for many other Greek marinas. It is somewhat out of things here, but to some extent that is a blessing and it is something of a peaceful oasis away from the large hotels elsewhere. In the future there are plans to extend the facilities and hopefully a taverna or two will decide to open inside the marina.

① 22420 57500

www.kosmarina.gr

KARDAMENA

Pilotage

Note Care is needed of very strong gusts blowing off the high coastline along the SE coast when the *meltemi* is blowing. At times there may be 40–45 knot gusts when the wind over the open sea is 30–35 knots. The worst places seem to be off the three prominent capes: Krikellos, Khelona and Fouka.

Approach The harbour lies pretty much halfway along the SE coast of Kós. The long sprawling line of breeze-block hotels and bars and clubs betrays its presence and closer in the harbour will be seen.

Hippocrates

Hippocrates was born on Kós in 460BC and probably died on the island in 370BC. His name is honoured in Kós to this day and the Asclepion built in his honour after he died is a must to visit. Like the Asclepion at Epidavros, it has an almost mystical quality about it, though this is easily shattered when the tour buses disgorge hordes of tourists intent on doing a 10-minute tour before heading off for lunch. Although Hippocrates is always associated with Kós, it is likely he travelled widely around the Aegean teaching his holistic medicine and no-one is really sure how much time he spent in Kós itself. Still he is remembered to this day by the Hippocratic Oath that doctors take when they qualify and it is worth remembering what the original oath says (the modern oath has been much modified):

'I swear by Apollo Physician and Asclepius and Hygieia and Panaceia and all the gods and goddesses, making them my witnesses, that I will fulfil according to my ability and judgement this oath and this covenant: To hold him who has taught me this art as equal to my parents and to live my life in partnership with him, and if he is in need of money to give him a share of mine, and to regard his offspring as equal to my brothers in male lineage and to teach them this art – if they desire to learn it – without fee and covenant; to give a share of precepts and oral instruction and all the other learning to my sons and to the sons of him who has instructed me and to pupils who have signed the covenant and have taken an oath according to the medical law, but no one else. I will apply dietetic measures for the benefit of the sick according to my ability and judgement; I will keep them from harm and injustice. I will neither give a deadly drug to anybody who asked for it, nor will I make a suggestion to this effect. Similarly I will not give to a woman an abortive remedy. In purity and holiness I will guard my life and my art. I will not use the knife, not even on sufferers from stone, but will withdraw in favour of such men as are engaged in this work. Whatever houses I may visit, I will come for the benefit of the sick, remaining free of all intentional injustice, of all mischief and in particular of sexual relations with both female and male persons, be they free or slaves. What I may see or hear in the course of the treatment or even outside of the treatment in regard to the life of men, which on no account one must spread abroad, I will keep to myself, holding such things shameful to be spoken about. If I fulfil this oath and do not violate it, may it be granted to me to enjoy life and art, being honoured with fame among all men for all time to come; if I transgress it and swear falsely, may the opposite of all this be my lot.'   Transl. Ludwig Edelstein

Patients travelled to the Asclepion from all over the Aegean seeking a cure for what ailed them. Some of the medical practices can sound surprisingly modern, echoing the advances in sanitation in the Victorian era where supplying clean drinking water, improved sewerage and attention to hygiene in hospitals did far more to keep disease at bay than the new drugs and treatments that were being discovered. The ancient Greeks also used alternative methods of treating disease

Asclepion just outside Kós town

which have recently been rehabilitated into the western mould of medical thinking. In the Asclepion empirical techniques involved frequent washing of the body; drinking clean water (all Asclepions were built near a reliable source of good water); keeping the local environment clean by disposing of old clothes and bandages, and cleaning cooking and other implements properly; and making sure patients get plenty of rest. Ritual healing included inducing a sleep-like trance, possibly by burning drugs in a vessel, and then leaving the patient until the sleep therapy (encoemesis) had done its job. It is possible that some form of mesmerism or hypnotism was used similar to that practised at Hemithea on the mainland coast opposite where a form of hypnotism was used to reduce pain during childbirth. This sort of holistic medicine has a resonance in our own 21st century where we now recognise that the power of the mind over the body can stimulate the immune

Temple of Asclepius

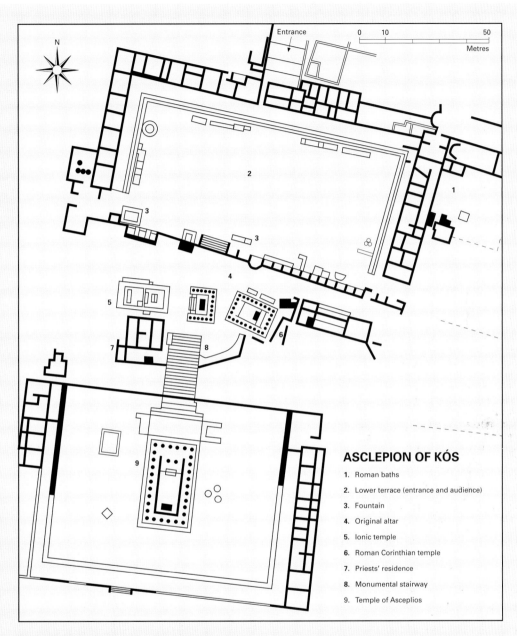

ASCLEPION OF KÓS

1. Roman baths
2. Lower terrace (entrance and audience)
3. Fountain
4. Original altar
5. Ionic temple
6. Roman Corinthian temple
7. Priests' residence
8. Monumental stairway
9. Temple of Asceplios

system and produce some surprising results without the need to resort to some of the heavy-handed drug regimes that characterise mainstream medical practice.

The Asclepion was built a short time after Hippocrates' death in tribute to his teachings. You ascend onto the lower terrace through the entrance to a large area used for celebrations and games. In front of you is a lower stairway leading to several temples and the priests' house, above which rises a monumental stairway leading to the Temple of Asclepius. The site was largely excavated and partially rebuilt by the Italians, a renovation that has been criticised by some, though to my eyes it is sympathetic enough as it provides just enough material detail while still allowing room for the mind to imagine the rest.

The Asclepion is open Tuesday to Sunday 0800–1900 in the summer and a few euros are charged for entrance. To get there from Kós town there is a local bus, or hire a bicycle or scooter. The village of Platani on the way back to Kós is a good spot to stop for lunch.

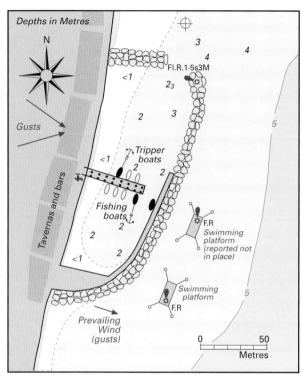

KARDAMENA
⊕36°46′·95N 27°08′·8E

General

Some 30 or 35 years ago Kardamena was a small fishing village. Today it is a sprawling resort catering for bottom-line package holidays promoting cheap booze, loud music, bars and pubs with pseudo-English names complete with karaoke nights, bingo and darts. This place is so un-Greek it has to advertise a 'real Greek night with real Greek dancing' which would in any case fail any investigation by an advertising standards regulator. That said, it is a handily placed overnight stop along this coast, though don't bank on getting a good night's sleep as there are clubs here licensed to broadcast dance and techno until deep into the wee small hours.

KAMARES

Pilotage

Approach Kamares sits tucked in under the SW end of Kós where the island hooks to the south. The bay is being developed at a steady rate and it is a little hard to pick out exactly where the harbour is until closer in. At least the gusts tend to die off some as you get into the bay compared to further up the coast. The small harbour is on the west side of the bay and it is here you should head for.

Mooring There is usually room for a few yachts to go stern or bows-to on the pier or in the small

Care is needed of several swimming platforms lying off the breakwater in the summer (recently reported not in place) but otherwise the approach is fairly straightforward as long as you make the approach from seawards.

Mooring Go stern or bows-to off the central pier or alongside the quayed section of the outer breakwater. It is really a matter of finding space amongst the tripper boats and watersports boats berthed in here and there is not always a lot of room. The prevailing wind gusts off the slopes, which can make berthing difficult at times. Good shelter inside.

Facilities

Services Water at the root of the pier.
Provisions Minimarkets ashore.
Eating out A few tavernas, none of which I can recommend, and a lot of fast food of all types nearby, including fish and chips if that is what you want. (You could be forgiven for thinking that pizza and burger and chips was normal Greek cuisine here.)
Other ATM. Hire motorbikes and cars. Kós airport is about 5km away.

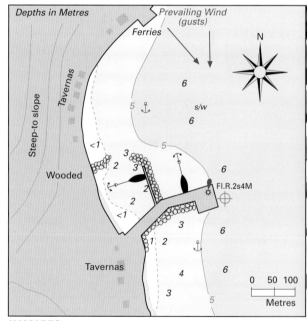

KAMARES
⊕36°44′·2N 26°58′·4E

fishing harbour, but don't rely on it. Alternatively anchor off to the north of the harbour. The bottom is sand and weed, good holding. Good shelter from the *meltemi* which tends to be lighter in this corner of the bay.

Facilities

Services Water at the root of the pier.
Provisions Limited.
Eating out Several tavernas nearby and also a very noisy disco.

General

Kamares used to be a small fishing village but no longer. The rash of hotels and rooms-for-rent along the rest of this coast has inexorably spread to this bay and there are now hotels and clubs around the bay and more in the building – though as yet nothing like the development further east. The arrival of hotels and self-catering apartments has introduced those other species that go with them, the water-bike and para-sailing boats, and these zoom irritatingly around the bay.

Above Kamares are the few ruins left of ancient Astipalaia, the original ancient capital of Kós. There is not a lot here to see, just the remains of a temple and an amphitheatre, but is a relatively peaceful spot with fine views over the sea.

ÓRMOS SKINOU

Just round the corner from Kamares on the west side of Ák Pelli is the large bay of Skinou. In settled weather this is a pleasant anchorage removed from all the hubbub elsewhere around this coast. When the *meltemi* is blowing some swell creeps around into the bay. The water shallows up some way out and you can anchor in 3–4m on a sandy bottom by carefully creeping in over the shallows. The water is a wonderful turquoise here and the surroundings relatively peaceful.

Neolithic man evidently thought it a good place to live c.3500BC, as evidence found in the Cave of Aspri Petra on the slopes above shows.

LIMNIONAS

⊕36°46'·5N 26°58'·0E
A small fishing harbour on the north side of the SW end of Kós. The harbour has 1·5–2·5m depths in the outer part, although much of it is shallow and rockbound. When the *meltemi* is blowing the harbour should not be approached as a large swell is pushed down onto the coast. In calm weather small yachts might want to take a look in here. Care is needed of rocks around the entrance and

on the north and south side of the harbour. The small quayed area in the NW corner of the harbour is usually full of local boats.

Ashore there are a couple of tavernas and in the summer the scrappy beach is popular with the locals.

MASTIKHARI

A small harbour about halfway along the NW coast of Kós. Care is needed in the approach when the *meltemi* is blowing as a heavy swell sets down onto this coast. Once around the breakwater try to go stern or bows-to in the NW corner of the harbour. The end of the quay is used by the small ferry to Kalimnos and most of the rest of the NW quay by tripper boats. On the south side of the harbour and along much of the west quay depths decrease quickly to less than a metre. Good shelter from the *meltemi* in here, although there is a bit of a surge when it blows strongly. The bottom is soft mud and dead weed, mostly poor holding.

Ashore there are numerous tavernas and cafés and bars catering for the apartments and small hotels around this bit of coast. Although it has its share of tourists, Mastikhari is altogether a quieter and really quite likeable place with enough going on in the harbour and the agricultural hinterland relating to things Greek to make it quite different to the coast on the south side.

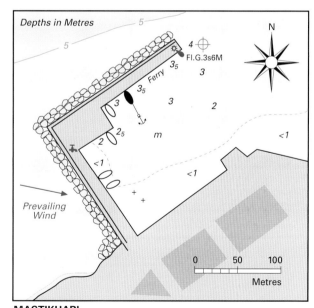

MASTIKHARI
⊕36°51'·2N 27°04'·6E

2
Southern Dodecanese
Kós to Rhodes (and Kastellórizon)

Panormitis looking over the monastery to the entrance
Toni Font

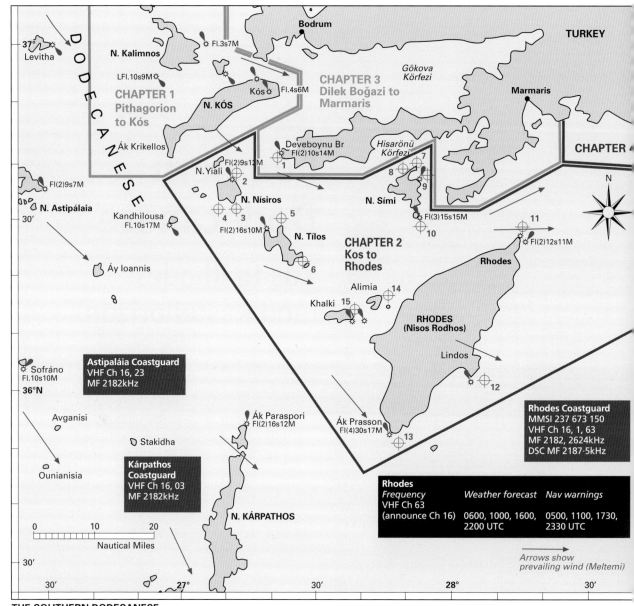

THE SOUTHERN DODECANESE

Kastellórizon looking down to
the yacht quay

USEFUL WAYPOINTS

⊕**1** 0·75M W of Deveboynu Bükü (Knidos/Turkey)
36°41'·45N 27°20'·90E WGS84
⊕**2** 0·5M N of Ák Katsouni (Nísiros)
36°37'·70N 27°11'·36E WGS84
⊕**3** 0·5M S of Ák Loutros (Nísiros)
36°32'·92N 27°11'·66E WGS84
⊕**4** 1M S of Ák Levkhos (Nísiros)
36°32'·72N 27°08'·28E WGS84
⊕**5** 0·5M N of Ák Angistrou (Tílos)
36°29'·58N 27°21'·10E WGS84
⊕**6** Mid-channel between Tílos and Andítilos
36°22'·6N 27°26'·9E
⊕**7** 1·5M N of Ák Makria (Sími)
36°41'·68N 27°51'·70E WGS84
⊕**8** W entrance of Nímos Passage (Sími)
36°38'·72N 27°49'·76E WGS84
⊕**9** 0·25M N of Ák Koutsoumba (Sími)
36°38'·17N 27°52'·35E WGS84
⊕**10** 0·38M S of Vrak Kouloundros (Sími)
36°30'·43N 27°52'·17E WGS84
⊕**11** 1M N of Ák Milon (Rhodes)
36°28'·45N 28°13'·25E WGS84
⊕**12** 0·4M E of Ák Lindos (Rhodes)
36°03'·20N 28°05'·78E WGS84
⊕**13** 1M S of Ák Prasso (Rhodes)
35°51'·53N 27°45'·24E WGS84
⊕**14** 1M E of Ak Katsouni (N. Alimia)
36°16'·84N 27°44'·89E WGS84
⊕**15** Mid-channel N. Khalkis-N. Mallonisi
36°14'·92N 27°37'·67E WGS84

PREVAILING WINDS

For the islands in the southern Dodecanese the prevailing wind in the summer is still the *meltemi* blowing from the northwest, except that towards Sími and Rhodes the wind curves to blow from the west. From around mid-June until late September the *meltemi* blows at anything from Force 4–6 (11–27 knots) though at times it can get up to Force 7 (28–33 knots) or so and where the wind gusts down off high land it can be anything up to Force 1–3 more than the wind over the open sea.

The *meltemi* is generally lighter in early and late summer and blows most strongly in July and August. There is also something of a thermal component from the land mass of Asia Minor nearby, though not as demarcated as along the Turkish coast itself. Generally the wind will die down in the evening when the sun goes and will be lighter in the morning before the wind gets up again around midday. This is not an infallible rule and happens more in the spring and autumn than in the peak summer months of July and August. If you are heading north through the islands it can be advantageous to get up early in the morning and motorsail to make some northing before the wind kicks in again. Going south you have pretty much a sleigh-ride down through the islands. In spring and autumn winds are generally lighter although depressions passing through the eastern Aegean can cause strong winds from the north or south for several days.

Quick reference guide

	Shelter	Mooring	Fuel	Water	Provisions	Eating out	Plan
Yialí							
Órmos Yialí	B	C	O	O	O	O	•
Nísiros							
Mandráki	C	AB	B	B	B	B	•
Palon	B	A	B	A	C	B	•
Tílos							
Livádhi	AC	AC	B	A	B	B	•
Áy Stefanos	B	A	O	O	O	O	
Áy Antonios	B	AB	B	B	O	C	•
Plaka	C	C	O	O	O	O	•
O. Eristou	C	C	O	O	O	O	•
Sími							
Sími Limanı	B	A	B	A	B	A	•
Pethi	A	AC	O	B	C	C	•
Áy Marina	B	C	O	O	O	C	•
O. Thessalona	B	C	O	O	O	C	•
O. Nanou	B	C	O	O	O	C	•
O. Marathouda	B	C	O	O	O	C	•
O. Faneromeri	B	C	O	O	O	C	•
N. Seskli	C	C	O	O	O	O	•
Panormitis	A	C	O	O	C	C	•
Áy Emilianos	C	C	O	O	O	O	•
O. Emborios	B	C	O	B	C	C	•
Rhodes							
Rhodes Mandráki	A	A	A	A	A	A	•
Rhodes Emborikos	A	A	B	A	A	A	•
Rhodes Marina	A	A	B	A	A	B	•
Faliraki	B	AB	O	A	C	B	
Lardhikos	B	C	O	B	C	C	•
Órmos Kalathos	B	C	O	O	O	C	•
Lindos	B	C	O	B	B	B	•
Áy Apostoli	B	C	O	O	O	C	•
Órmos Lardhos	C	C	O	O	C	C	•
Plimiri (Ák Istros)	C	C	O	O		C	
Ák Vigli	C	C	O	O	O	C	
Ák Prasso	C	C	O	O	C	C	•
Skala Kamiros	O	AC	B	A	C	C	•
Fanai	A	A	B	A	O	C	
Khálki							
Emborios	B	AC	B	A	C	B	•
Órmos Potamos	B	C	O	O	O	C	•
Alimia							
Órmos Alimia	B	C	O	O	O	O	•
Eastern anchorages	C	C	O	O	O	O	•
Kastellórizon							
Limín Kastellorizou	B	AB	B	B	C	B	•
Mandráki	B	C	O	B	O	C	•
Navlakas	C	C	O	O	O	O	
Frangolimani (Áy Yeoryios)	B	C	O	O	O	O	

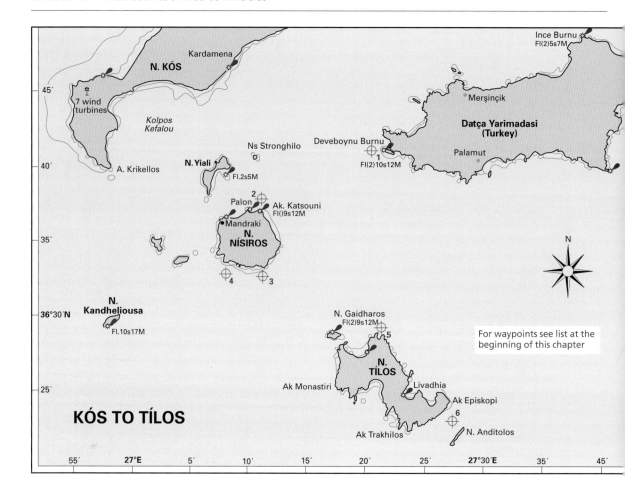

KÓS TO TÍLOS

Yialí

The island of Yialí, two humps joined by an isthmus, lies off the SW side of Kós before you get to Nísiros. This is a windswept part of the world and when the *meltemi* is blowing you will frequently find it heaves down over his stretch of sea between Kós and Nísiros. Yialí is not really the sort of place you would want to head for as it is intensively mined for pumice and the mining and loading operations mean the sea area south of the island is covered in a cloud of dust and bits of pumice for miles. Pumice is used as an abrasive in everything from toothpaste to grinding compounds and this whole island seems to be composed of the stuff.

It is useful as a safe haven from the *meltemi* and some have even expressed a liking for the usually deserted anchorage of Órmos Yialí – deserted, that is, apart from ships loading pumice

off the chute that extends out from the dock. Care is needed of the numerous reefs in the approaches and in the bay. Make the approach on a NW course leaving Nisís Áy Antonios to starboard. The reef off the southern end of N. Áy Antonios is easy to identify as the rocks break the surface in places, although the chop from the *meltemi* can disguise it to some extent. Anchor in 3–5m off the NE end of the beach fringing the isthmus on sand and weed, good holding. Alternatively anchor on the NE side of Áy Antonios in 6–10m. With a strong *meltemi* the first anchorage is best.

Note In Órmos Yialí it is reported that a large concrete block was accidentally dropped in the N of the bay and is a danger to navigation. Best reports suggest it lies between Nisís Áy Antonios and Yialí. It is not possible to navigate through this passage, and caution is advised in the vicinity.

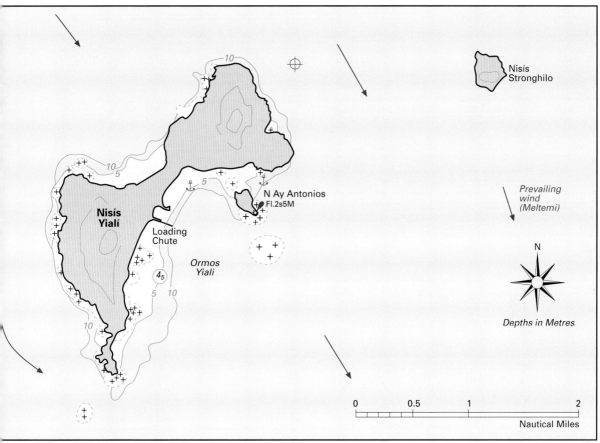

YIALI AND NISIS STRONGHILO
40'·79N 27°08'·61E WGS84

Nísiros

Nísiros is a volcano rising above the sea floor to the crater (actually two craters) at the top. Compared with Kós it is a green island, for the most part dropping straight into the sea, and it is populated by under a thousand souls. Everywhere there is evidence of subterranean volcanic activity with hot springs bubbling up all around the island, one of which has been turned into the spa centre at Loutra on the north coast, and there have been attempts to utilise geothermal energy to drive turbines to produce electricity for the island, though these have so far come to nothing. On the rich volcanic soil trees and crops grow well on the steep slopes, giving the island an unlikely green aspect from seawards compared with other islands in this group.

The volcano erupted as recently as 1933 and there are records of eruptions in 1422, 1873 and 1888. When you go up to the volcano there is a diabolical sulphurous smell hanging around the crater, and the sight of the moonscape with sulphurous vents and hissing noises only reinforces the perception from the smell. The crater is a must to visit and I'm not sure whether it is my imagination, but it feels like something is brewing underneath. As you wend your way down into the crater along a path encrusted with sulphur crystals you get the feeling from the fumaroles and the vibration underfoot that although the volcano is deemed inactive, there is something going on below the surface. In any other country you wouldn't be allowed within a couple of hundred metres of the crater, but here you get to walk around on a crust, said to be just 15cm thick and even if it's more it doesn't feel like it, with superheated water and gas below trying to find a way out. It's really quite scary.

Volcanoes in the Aegean

Nísiros sits at the eastern edge of a chain of volcanoes stretching across the Aegean. Probably the best known of these is the simmering volcano at Thíra where you sail straight into the submerged caldera and can tie up to the smoking plug of Néa Kammeni in the middle. Thíra is well known because it is surmised that this was the island of Atlantis that Plato described disappearing below the sea. It is known that a catastrophic eruption occurred at Thíra around 1400BC and that the Minoan inhabitants had to flee the island. The caldera at Thíra is around three times the size of the caldera of Krakatoa and an eruption here would be roughly five times as big as that at Krakatoa in 1883. This event would have devastated the whole region and some think it was this natural catastrophe which abruptly terminated the Minoan civilisation and left the way open for the Myceneans to expand and re-colonise the Aegean.

Although Thíra is the largest volcano in the Aegean – in fact it is the largest volcano in the Mediterranean – it is by no means the only one. To the west of Thíra lies Mílos and here again you sail into a vast caldera. To the north at Methana there is another volcano and scattered around Nísiros there are several submarine volcanoes.

These volcanoes all sit on the Aegean tectonic plate which is pushed from the south by the African plate, from the north by the Eurasian plate, and from the east by the Turkish plate. The volcanic activity and the numerous earthquakes which rock this region are caused by the African plate sinking under the Aegean plate to the south of Crete. The plate is creeping northwest at 4–5cm a year and the buckling of the Aegean plate allows molten magma to find its way to the surface through weaknesses in the earth's crust along the Aegean volcanic arc.

Although Nísiros might look like a midget alongside Thíra and Mílos, it is in fact a large volcano. Nísiros and the sister islands around it did not exist 160,000 years ago. Around this time a huge submarine volcano

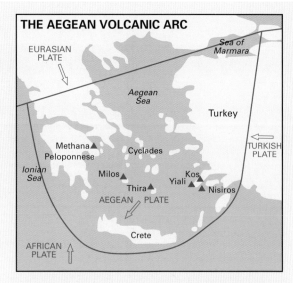

THE AEGEAN VOLCANIC ARC

erupted somewhere around present-day Yialí and formed the island of Nísiros and Yialí. Kós was covered with a thick deposit of ash and pumice and Nísiros itself slowly emerged from the depths over the next ten thousand years. Yialí is mostly composed of pumice which is excavated from the south side and loaded onto ships on the southeast side of the island.

The Aegean arc is still active, with the most recent eruptions occurring at Thíra in 1925–26 when Néa Kammeni and Mikro Kammeni were joined together. It is worth remembering that this island is the plug of the caldera. At Nísiros the most recent eruptions were in 1933, 1888 and 1873. One other event related to the Aegean arc was the huge earthquake in 1956 centred off the north coast of Amorgós which caused a *tsunami* up to 17m high. At the moment geologists believe there is no risk of a catastrophic eruption and the likelihood is that Thíra will have a minor eruption to release pressure as might Nísiros also.

In 1996–98 a 'volcano-seismic crisis' occurred on Nísiros. During this period 1,600 earthquakes were recorded, with a maximum force of 5.3. The area experienced a 14cm uplift and in 2001 a large fissure appeared in the caldera floor. Scientists concluded that the volcano had entered a period of 'unrest'. They put this down to 'shallow intrusion of a magma body', and not seismic activity. Either way, it certainly adds to the frisson when walking into the crater.

Surprisingly, the main crater at Stefanos, that everyone visits, is not the most active crater. That is Polyvotis, a smaller crater to the NE, named after the eponymous founder of the island who was a Titan who Poseidon imprisoned by ripping off a chunk of Kós and pinning him underneath.

That chunk of rock is Nísiros and the groaning from within is said to be Polyvotis attempting to escape. Like many myths there is a kernel of truth in here, as it is likely that a catastrophic eruption along the lines of Thíra or Krakatoa separated the island from Kós some 25,000 years ago.

If you are visiting the crater the best thing to do is hire a scooter or take a car early in the morning or in the late afternoon to avoid the midday rush hour when the tripper boats from Kós disgorge hordes of visitors who are shunted onto buses for the trip to the crater.

Note The island is pretty much dependent on rainwater stored in cisterns. There is a reverse osmosis plant but for some reason it is not always functioning.

Nísiros (complete with smoking volcano) and offlying islands. From a copper engraving by Piacenza 1688

MANDRÁKI

Pilotage

Approach The main ferry harbour for Nísiros on the NE corner of the island. The buildings around the harbour and the stubby mole are easily identified.

Mooring Go stern-to in the SW corner wherever there is room. It is not very comfortable in here when the *meltemi* is blowing and may be untenable when it really blows up, so it should only really be used in light weather. There is even a surge with any winds from the west and it is open north through east. The tripper boats from Kós use this harbour and you need to leave room for them. The ferry also calls here and uses the end of the mole. It does not usually drop an anchor but ties stern-to and uses its propeller wash to keep it off the quay; this wash also affects any yachts tied up here so care is needed.

Facilities

Most provisions and numerous tavernas ashore. Avoid the tavernas around the harbour which mostly cater for the trippers arriving from Kós.

General

It's a pity Mandráki does not have a better harbour as the village itself is a pleasing place, little-frequented apart from the dockside. The village proper is arranged around a public orchard and is a warren of lanes with brightly

With bubbling pools and the persistent hiss of escaping gases, a walk into the crater isn't for the faint-hearted

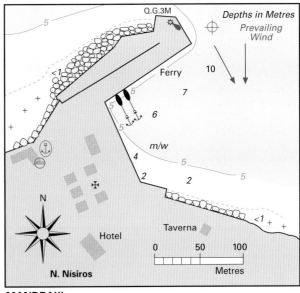

MANDRAKI
⊕ 36°36′·9N 27°08′·5E

Mandráki on Nísiros

painted houses on either side. A local who has done well owns the Vitex Paint Company and you can't help thinking he gives a discount to other locals to keep appearances up on the island. He has also funded the new Ethnography Museum. The village itself is hemmed in by a castle, known as the Knights (of St John) Castle, within which there is the monastery of Panayia Spillani. Outside the village on the west coast is Palaiokastro, the ruins of a 7th-century BC citadel with much of it still intact.

If you are in the harbour at Palon it is well worth making the effort to visit Mandráki. It remains a pleasing place with a minimal amount of tourism intruding on it, unlike its sister island across the water.

PALON (Paloi, Palli)

Pilotage

Approach From the east the most obvious feature is the abandoned building of the old spa centre, a cluster of stone buildings with red roofs, standing on the foreshore immediately east of Palon harbour. From the west the harbour will not be seen until you are around the rocky headland (Ák Akrotiri) sheltering it. Some care is needed when

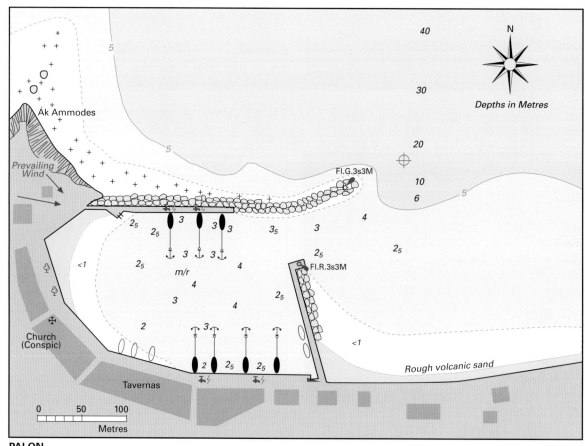

PALON
⊕36°37'·24N 27°10'·44E WGS84

Palon harbour looking E towards Ák Katsouni

approaching from the west (and when leaving Palon and heading west) to keep well clear of the Akrotiri headland and the rocky reef running out for at least 100m from it.

When approaching the extended breakwater you will be turning side on to the swell from the *meltemi* so care is needed as you make the turn into the entrance. Depths shallow up towards the shore so don't stray too far towards the beach. Once under the breakwater the water is relatively flat.

Mooring Proceed into the harbour and go stern or bows-to the outer breakwater or the south quay. Berths off the east quay can be used if the harbour is full – go alongside. The harbour has been dredged and there are currently minimum depths of 2·5m at most berths. The bottom is mud and weed, good holding. Good all-round shelter.

Facilities

Services Water and electricity on both quays – a fixed daily charge (€10 2011) is made. The water is not for washing down the boat but for filling tanks only. Fuel by mini-tanker.

Provisions Small minimarkets and a bakers.

Eating out Several tavernas on the waterfront which are all pretty convivial places with views over the harbour. They are all much of a muchness so use your nose to sniff one out.

Other Irregular bus to Mandráki. Hire cars and scooters.

General

Once you are safely inside and tied up there are few people who fail to fall under the spell of this little harbour. The old spa centre to the east is the Pantelidhi spa, once renowned for its warm thermal waters. Behind it are the ruins of some old Roman baths and a small chapel built into the rock.

Tílos

Sitting on the western edges of the other islands, Tílos has always been something of a poor cousin to the other islands. In fact, many have no idea where the island is and yachts sailing around the Dodecanese will often pass it by in favour of the better known islands. From seawards the brown rocky slopes might lead you to think this was yet another parched island, but venture inland and you come to greener hinterland where groves of trees are interspersed amongst the fields. Around the fields, mostly now fallow, are stands of oaks and cultivated olives, figs, pomegranates and almonds. Tílos has numerous springs and significant artesian reserves which account for the surprisingly green interior. Up until recent years the island was an important source of grain for the surrounding islands, but now it is shipped in from northern Europe and agriculture has declined. As a consequence the population has also dwindled as the young leave for the larger islands and mainland cities and although there has been an increase in tourism in recent years, there are nothing like the numbers that go to nearby islands.

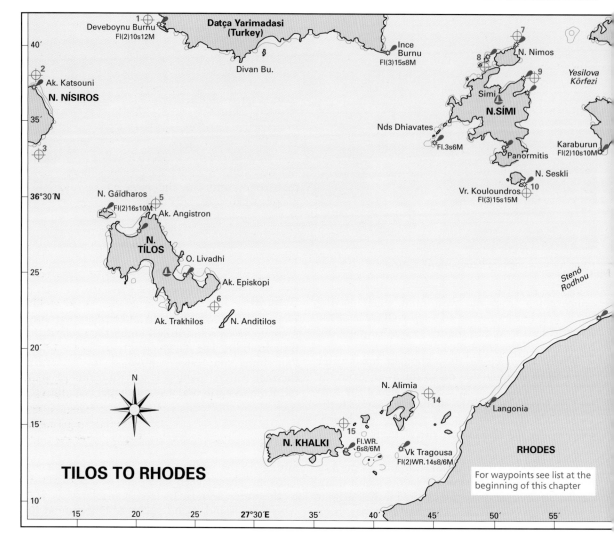

The history of the island is somewhat nondescript except for a significant event that happened in prehistory. During the Late Quaternary period when Tílos separated from what is now mainland Asia Minor, a group of elephants were trapped on the island. Remains of dwarf elephants, loosely belonging to extinct European elephants, have been found in a cave at Kharkhadio inland and have been given the name *Palaeoloxodon antiquus Falconeri*. The dwarf elephants are tiny by comparison to the African or Indian elephant, with the partial reconstruction of a juvenile in the local museum putting it at around 50cm high by 70cm long, so a mature elephant may have been around 1·25m (4ft) high. It is still something of a mystery how they died out. Human remains from this period indicate that prehistoric

man may have co-existed with the elephants and hunted them to extinction. Or they may have just run out of food, or some catastrophic natural event like a huge volcanic eruption may have finished them off. Interestingly, at Áy Antonios there are said to be the remains of humans encased in lava Pompeii-style, so it is possible that the pachyderms of Tílos became extinct after a similar cataclysmic event.

The mythopoeic origins of Tílos are a by-product of the cataclysmic eruption that formed Nísiros when debris from the epic battle between Poseidon and Polyvotis rained down in this part of the sea. Later it had associations with the sun-god Helios, though this is not surprising given the proximity of Rhodes and the adoration of Helios Apollo that existed there. The island was

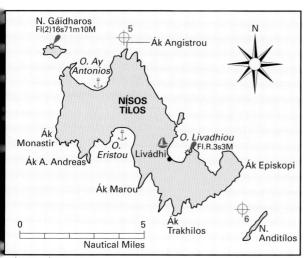

NÍSOS TÍLOS

⊕5 0·5M N of Ák Angistrou (Tílos)
36°29'·58N 27°21'·10E WGS84
⊕6 Mid-channel between Tílos and Andítilos
36°22'·6N 27°26'·9E

sufficiently prosperous to found the colony of Gela on the southern coast of Sicily in the 7th century BC and in later years there is mention of temples and cities, though little remains today. After the Roman period the island declined almost to nothing until the Knights of St John arrived and built seven small forts across the island. After the Knights left things declined again and the island suffered a whole catalogue of disasters: the Venetians razed the island as part of their campaign against the Turks; pirates from the Barbary coast raided the island, followed by raids by local Greek pirates; the Italians virtually ignored the place and the Germans took all the livestock for their troops towards the end of the Second World War.

Tílos elephant: Reconstruction of the pygmy elephant of Tílos in the museum

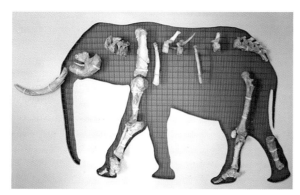

Today the island is popular with Brits looking for a little more than burgers and beer. The visitors managed to persuade the local mayor to declare the island a 'no hunting' zone and there are various rules in place to try to develop the island in a sympathetic way. This may be about to change as locals look to tourism as the only real source of revenue in the future and local Greek hunters see the British influence as interfering in their natural rights. Hopefully Tílos will not go the way of Kós or Rhodes, even halfway down that road, and for the moment it remains a pleasantly low-key sort of place.

LIVADHI

Pilotage

Approach Livadhi lies on the west side of the large bay of Órmos Livadhiou on the north side of Tílos. Once you are into the bay the village will be seen and you can then proceed to the small harbour or the anchorage. The only real thing to watch out for here is the shoal water just south of the harbour entrance.

Mooring Inside the harbour go stern or bows-to the outer breakwater or stern or bows-to the west side of the harbour. Laid moorings tailed to the quay on the west side. Large yachts can go stern-to on the outside of the breakwater after the ferry

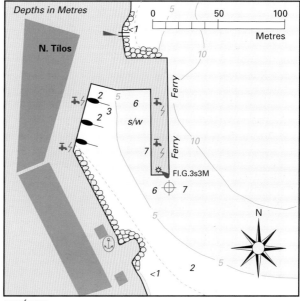

LIVÁDHI
⊕36°25'·02N 27°23'·18E WGS84

has left. Good shelter inside and adequate shelter outside, although some swell creeps around into the bay causing yachts on the outside to roll.

Yachts can also anchor in the bay in 4–10m off the beach on sand and weed, good holding. The anchorage can be uncomfortable with the *meltemi* as the swell curves around into the bay. There can also be gusts in here.

Facilities

Services Water and electricity boxes in the harbour.

Provisions Most things can be found in the minimarkets in the village. Also bakers and butchers.

Eating out Livadhi has a surprising number of tavernas for such a small place, most of them reliant on summer trade. In the harbour itself Blue Sky is an authentic fish restaurant and in the village there are several other likely looking spots. Even along the front you will find reasonable food, though some are better than others: try Niko's or any of the others that look like they are there for more than just one summer.

Other Ferry to Rhodes. ATM. Internet café. Car and scooter hire. Irregular minibus to Megalo Chora.

General

Even just a few years ago this place looked quite different, with none of the rambling development that has extended around the shoreline (not that it's really that bad). Livadhi is still a very likeable place and the harbour area and the old village centre exude charm even though visitors far outnumber the locals. The capital of the island, Megalo Chora, is inland to the northwest and it's worth a visit just to wander around, although it has its attractions. A new museum has been built to house remains such as the dwarf elephants and you can visit the cave of Kharkhadio en route to Megalo Chora if you have your own transport. Above the *chora* one of the castles built by the Knights of St John hovers over the village like a Medieval mirage.

ÁY STEFANOS

⊕36°24'·8N 27°24'·0N

This small fishing harbour lies on the east side of Órmos Livadhiou. Although there are 3m depths in the entrance, these rapidly shoal to 1·5m and less in the middle. In addition the harbour is usually full of fishing boats so there is little to interest a yacht here, especially now the harbour at Livadhi has yacht berths.

Livadhi harbour on Tílos

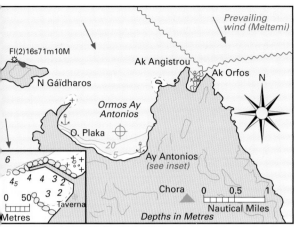

ORMOS AY ANTONIOS (PLAGIO)
⊕36°28'·0N 27°19'·8E

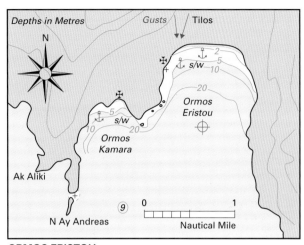

ORMOS ERISTOU
⊕36°25'·12N 27°20'·8E

ORMOS ÁY ANTONIOS

The large bay on the north of the island. The approach is straightforward and clear of dangers. When the *meltemi* is blowing it sets large seas down into this bay and you should head for Livadhi. In light winds the anchorage at Plaka on the NW side of the bay provides some lee from the *meltemi*. Anchor off the beach, which is little frequented apart from a few campers in the summer.

At Áy Stefanos there is a small harbour that can be used in light weather. With any wind from the north a heavy swell sets down onto the entrance. If there is room go stern or bows-to on the outer end of the quayed section of the harbour. Reasonable shelter from the *meltemi*, although there is a surge. Taverna on the shore. It is about half an hour's walk to Megalo Chora.

ÓRMOS ERISTOU

⊕36°26'·0N 27°21'·0E

The large bay on the west side of Tílos. There is good shelter from the *meltemi* here, but very strong gusts which come straight down the middle of the island across the central plateau and exit in Eristos. The bottom gradually slopes into the shore so you can potter in and anchor in 3–5m on sand and weed. Don't go too far in as a rocky strip borders the beach. Although there is good holding here you need to let out a good scope and ensure the anchor is well in to cope with the gusts. Good beach ashore and a taverna close to the beach.

Sími

Sími is the Rorschach blob of an island lying tucked in under the Turkish coast. It is a barren rocky island with little in the way of fresh water, so very little grows here, and not surprisingly this has meant it has had to look to the sea to survive. Simiot shipwrights built galleys for the Knights of St John and later for the Turks, enjoying a special relationship with the Ottomans who granted generous tax concessions to the Simiots. Later Simiot sponge-fishing boats worked all over the Mediterranean and Sími along with Kalimnos was the centre of sponge fishing. After the First World War when the Italians occupied the islands the tax concessions which the Simiots had enjoyed were dispensed with and Sími's golden age was on the wane. Kalimnos took over the sponge fishing industry (see the section on sponge fishing under Kalimnos) and many Simiots emigrated to the USA and Australia.

There is some confusion over where the name of the island comes from. One derivation, etymologically linked to English, is that Prometheus modelled a man from clay on the island and taught him the arts and gave him the gift of fire. Zeus, angry at the Titans impudence, turned him into a monkey, hence the word 'simian'. The only problem with the monkey story is the more common myth of 'Prometheus bound' in which, an angry Zeus punished the Titan by chaining him to a rock on Mount Caucasus where an eagle pecked at his liver for eternity. An alternative, but more

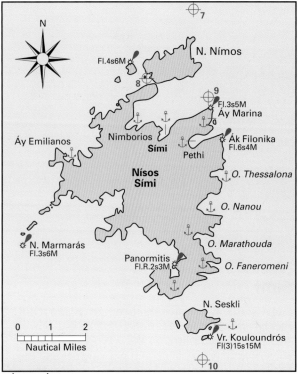

NÍSOS SÍMI

⊕7 1·5M N of Ák Makria (Sími)
36°41'·68N 27°51'·70E WGS84
⊕8 W entrance of Nímos Passage (Sími)
36°38'·72N 27°49'·76E WGS84
⊕9 0·25M N of Ák Koutsoumba (Sími)
36°38'·17N 27°52'·35E WGS84
⊕10 0·38M S of Vrak Kouloundrós (Sími)
36°30'·43N 27°52'·17E WGS84

mundane mythic origin, is that the island is named after a daughter of King Ialysos of Rhodes, called Sími, who was abducted by a sea-god called Glaucos and brought to the island.

For most of its history Sími has been dominated by its big brother Rhodes. It was part of the Dorian Hexapolis, with the main city and acropolis at the *chora* on the top of the ridge on the south side of the harbour. It was occupied in turn by the Romans, Byzantines, the Knights of St John and the Turks. Under the Turks and a favourable tax regime the island prospered and for once in its history eclipsed Rhodes. From the 17th to the 19th centuries Sími prospered as never before in the sponge trade and building swift galleys for the Ottomans. It's said that its annual taxes were paid in the biggest and softest sponges

which went straight to the Sultan's harem. At this time the large neo-classical villas that grace Sími town were built around the *chora* and down to the water's edge and this gives the harbour an aspect like nowhere else in the Dodecanese.

After the Italian occupation the island declined and emigration reduced its population from some 25,000 at the beginning of the 20th century to less than a thousand. Today with tourism some have returned and it also has a significant permanent population of Brits and others.

SÍMI

Pilotage

Approach The exact location of the harbour can be a bit of mystery from the west or east. From the west it is reasonably easy to work out where it is once you are through the Nímos Passage and the houses at the entrance to Sími harbour can be seen. From the east the exact location is more difficult and some yachts head into Pethi in the mistaken belief it is Sími. Even once around Ák Koutsoumba you will not see the houses around the harbour until you are right up into the bay. Once the houses around the harbour can be seen the approach is straightforward, with deep water right up into the harbour.

Some care is needed in the blind approaches as the tripper boats from Rhodes tend to cut the corner around Ák Koutsoumba at full speed. Likewise *gulets* and other craft using the Nímos Passage as a shortcut tend to charge through at speed so some care is needed.

Mooring Go stern or bows-to on the north or south quay where directed by the harbour attendant who will usually whistle and wave you into a spot and take your lines. He makes a small charge on behalf of the town council for which you get a receipt. The outer part of the N quay is reserved for the large tripper boats and ferries, and given the amount of propeller wash they cause you are better off further down the quay if you can manage it.

Remember when dropping your anchor that the harbour is very deep, usually some 12–20m where you drop the anchor, so you will need to let out plenty of scope. The bottom is mud and rock, poor holding in places. Good shelter from the *meltemi* in the harbour, although there can be gusts. The tripper boats and ferries also cause a fair amount of wash when they arrive. With

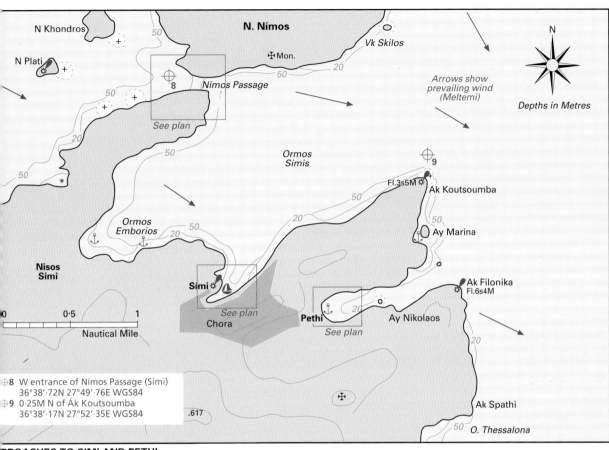

N Khondros

N. Nímos

Vk Skilos

✠ Mon.

N Plati

50

Nimos Passage

⊕
8

See plan

20

50

50

Ormos
Simis

⊕
9

Fl.3s5M ✿ Ak Koutsoumba

50

20

50

Ay Marina

Ormos
Emborios

50

20

Nisos
Simi

Sími ✿

⚓

Ak Filonika
Fl.6s4M

See plan
Chora

Pethi
See plan

Ay Nikolaos

20

20

0   0·5   1

Nautical Mile

Ak Spathi

.617

50   O. Thessalona

N

Arrows show
prevailing wind
(Meltemi)

Depths in Metres

⊕8 W entrance of Nímos Passage (Sími)
    36°38'·72N 27°49'·76E WGS84
⊕9 0·25M N of Ák Koutsoumba
    36°38'·17N 27°52'·35E WGS84

PROACHES TO SIMI AND PETHI

Sími harbour

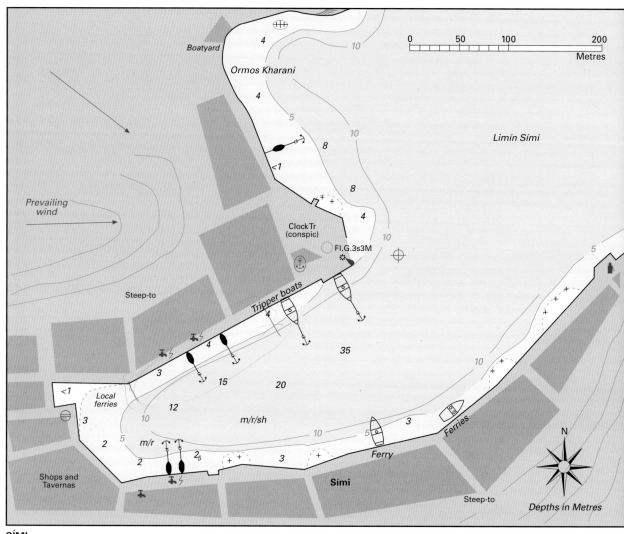

SÍMI
⊕36°37'·09N 27°50'·40E WGS84

southerlies a surprising amount of surge develops in the harbour and this could be dangerous with strong southerlies, in which case Pethi is probably the best place to head for.

Facilities

Services Water on the quay. The harbour attendant will open it up for you. Electricity can be connected on request. Fuel by mini-tanker: ask the attendant.

Provisions Reasonable shopping around the harbour. A bakery and butcher's near the west end of the harbour.

Eating out It is best to head for the south side of the harbour where there is a little clutch of tavernas close to a small square. Try the Trata ('Trawler') which offers pork with honey and coriander seeds amongst other things; the Dhimitris that does good fish; or around the main square try the Ellinikon.

Other ATM. Internet café. Bus between Sími harbour and Pethi. Taxis. Hire scooters. Ferries to Rhodes.

General

Few people fail to fall in love with Sími. The large neo-classical mansions in various hues of ochre, powder blue, cream and rose climb up the steep slopes around the harbour to create an amphitheatre of fine architecture with the deep blue of the harbour underneath. Climb up the paths and stairs on the *chora* side of the harbour and you will see what I mean: laid out below is just one of the most pleasing views around, and one that has changed little since the 19th century. Thankfully the town has had an historic preservation order on it from the early 1970s so there is little in the way of square blankety-blank concrete buildings to intrude on the view.

Even all the day-trippers who are ferried into Sími from Rhodes and Turkey every day have departed by late afternoon and you can almost hear a collective sigh of relief in Sími as they count the day's takings and life gets back to normal. If you have to do tourism then this is the way to do it. Apart from gazing around the pleasing vista from your cockpit and attending to your lines when the tripper boats charge in, there is not much more to do apart from taking a stroll around town to decide where you will have an evening drink and where to have supper.

PETHI

Pilotage

Approach This long inlet lies just over the hill from Sími harbour. The entrance is reasonably easy to see and is distinguished by a large above-water rock in the mouth of the entrance. Leave it to starboard, although there is deep water on either side. From the entrance you proceed down the steep-sided inlet which has a popular little beach at Áy Nikólaos on the south side. At the end you will see the houses of Pethi with a large hotel conspicuous at the head of the inlet.

Mooring There may be room to go stern or bows-to on the south side of either of the piers keeping clear of local boats and water taxis. Most boats will have to anchor out in 6–12m. The bottom in Pethi is sand, mud and weed, notoriously bad holding and you need to make sure your anchor is well in and if necessary lay a second anchor. When the *meltemi* is blowing there are strong gusts into the anchorage and even when you think your anchor is in, it is still a good policy to lay a second. The last time I was in here my anchor dragged at 0300 in the morning and we had to spend another hour and a half re-laying it.

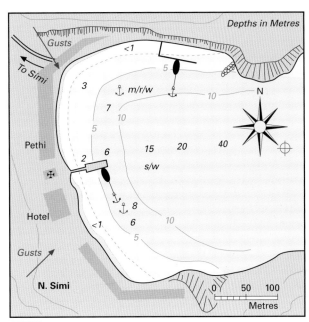

PETHI
⊕36°36′·95N 27°51′·70E WGS84

Facilities

Several tavernas on the waterfront and a minimarket nearby. It is a long hike up to the *chora* and down into Sími town or you can take the minibus which leaves from in front of the hotel.

General

Pethi is a pleasant enough place and many of the yachts here in the day will leave to go elsewhere for the night. If it were not for the poor holding it would be an idyllic little spot. A few villas are

Pethi from the anchorage

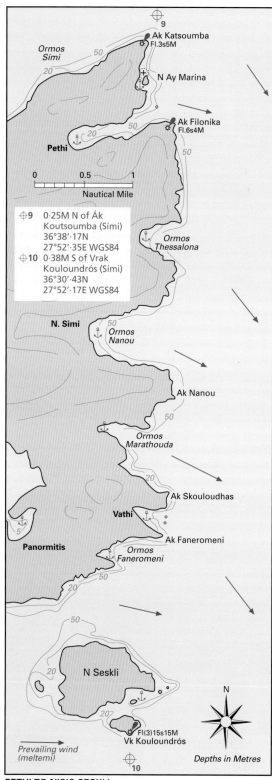

⊕9 0·25M N of Ák
Koutsoumba (Sími)
36°38'·17N
27°52'·35E WGS84

⊕10 0·38M S of Vrak
Kouloundrós (Sími)
36°30'·43N
27°52'·17E WGS84

PETHI TO NISIS SESKLI

being built around the slopes, but despite the hotel it retains enough character to make a ramble ashore worthwhile.

ÁY MARINA

On the north entrance to Pethi is the islet of Áy Marina with a miniature monastery, really more of a hermitage, on it. Under the islet there is a small cove with good shelter from the *meltemi*. A reef connects the islet to the shore on the north side of the cove, so make the approach from the south side. Anchor in 4–6m on a sandy bottom.

Ashore there is a small beach that is frequented by day, but usually empties by dusk. A simple bar/café ashore.

ÓRMOS THESSALONA

⊕36°35'·83N 27°52'·78E WGS84

This cliff-girt bay lies a short distance south of Pethi. It is a magnificent place with precipitous cliffs dropping straight down to the sea. You will need to potter in to the head of the bay to anchor in 5–8m off the beach at the head. With the *meltemi* there are strong gusts down into the bay so make sure your anchor is well in. Good shelter, although a swell sometimes creeps around into the bay when a strong *meltemi* is blowing.

ÓRMOS NANOU

⊕36°34'·97N 27°52'·56E WGS84

A large bay just south of Thessalona. Potter into the beach and anchor off the beach in convenient depths. It is very deep in here and there are strong gusts with the *meltemi* so make sure the anchor is well in. Like Thessalona this bay is a wonderfully wild and savage place with pine trees bordering the steep-sided valley that runs down to the shore. A café/bar on the beach opens sometimes in the summer.

ÓRMOS MARATHOUDA

⊕36°33'·89N 27°52'·30E WGS84

A fjord-like bay just south of Nanou. Anchor in 4–8m at the head of the bay. With the *meltemi* there are strong gusts so make sure your anchor is well in. This is a remote and wonderful place little frequented by anyone.

ÓRMOS FANEROMENI

⊕36°33'·0N 27°52'·5E

The last of these magnificent bays on the west coast of Sími. Like Marathouda it is a fjord-like bay with deep water until near the head of it. Anchor off the head of the bay. With the *meltemi* there are strong gusts into the bay.

NISÍS SESKLI

The islet off the southeast corner of Sími has a small cove on the southeast side that affords some shelter from the *meltemi* in idyllic surroundings. Make the approach from the southeast and proceed cautiously into the cove between the tiny islet (Artikonisi) towards several above-water rocks. Anchor in 5–7m tucked in as far as you can. The bottom is sand and weed. When the *meltemi* gets up some swell works its way around into the anchorage so it is best regarded as a morning swim and lunch stop, although in calm or light weather it is possible to overnight here. The cove is also used by some of the tripper boats working around Sími, but they usually only stay for an hour or so.

In antiquity the islet was known as Teftlousa and there are the remains of an ancient wall on the summit and a small harbour in the cove. The chapel here is to the Apostle Paul (Pavlos) who is said to have put in here to wait out bad weather. Today it is a dependency of the Panormittis monastery and it used to support a small farm with fruit trees and crops as, unlike most of Sími, it has a natural spring.

PANORMITIS

Pilotage

Approach It can be difficult to determine just where the enclosed bay is, especially coming from the south. Once you are around into Órmos Panormitou a white windmill on the east side of the entrance and the large white buildings of the monastery will be seen. When the *meltemi* is blowing it will be right behind you and some sea piles up in the narrow entrance. Once inside it the seas disappear and there is flat water.

Mooring Anchor towards the northeast end of the bay in 3–6m. Alternatively anchor in the SW corner clear of the pier. The bottom is sand and weed with some rocks and good holding once you have got the anchor in through the weed. The pier in the bay is used by local tripper boats, although there may be some room after they have left in the afternoon as long as you leave before they arrive again next morning. The bay offers good all-round shelter and although the *meltemi* blows over the land into the anchorage, the gusts are not too bad as the wind lifts to get over the high land.

Facilities

Limited provisions ashore in a shop, and several tavernas which mostly cater for the day-trippers that arrive daily. Bread from the monastery.

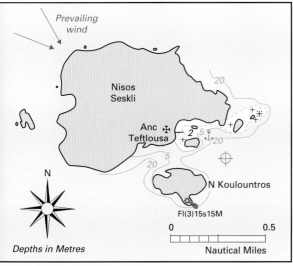

NISOS SESKLI ANCHORAGE
⊕36°31'·1N 27°52'·45E

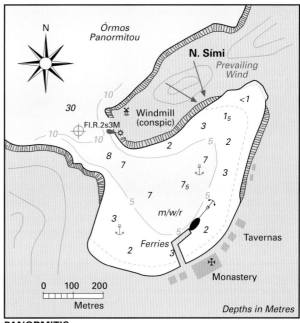

PANORMITIS
⊕36°33'·12N 27°50'·53E WGS84

Panormitis looking over the monastery to the entrance   *Toni Font*

General

The Monastery of St Michael ashore, a two-storey, fairly bland-looking complex apart from the rococo wedding-cake bell tower, is of comparatively recent origin (1740), although it has bits of earlier structures incorporated into it. There are several marble columns incorporated into the church and a Venetian winged lion over the main entrance. The monastery itself is rather nicer to wander around than it looks from the anchorage, with a shaded colonnaded walkway and a peaceful air to it, as long as you are there before or after the tripper boats disgorge the day-trippers.

The monastery is said to have been founded when a local farmer's wife was digging in the fields and found an icon of St Michael the Archangel under a mastic tree. She took the icon home, but in the morning it had disappeared and she found it again under the tree in Panormos. This happened three times, after which she realised that it wanted to be in Panormos and so a church was built. This particular story, where an icon or a statue is removed and it then mysteriously returns to where it was found, is a common mythopoeic tradition around the Mediterranean. Although St Nicholas is the patron saint of sailors in Greece, somehow St Michael has been dragged in here at Panormittis and the monastery has become something of a shrine for sailors. There are models of sailing boats in the small museum and these are said to have floated here and by some mysterious means ended up in the bay. Others are votive offerings along the lines of those in Tiniotissa in Tinos in the Cyclades. On St Michael's day (8th November in the Gregorian calendar) the monastery is crowded with visitors from all over Greece. Visitors can stay in the monastery and although a charge is not made, a tip is expected (currently €10–15).

ÁY EMILIANOS

An anchorage on the west coast of Sími, tucked under the headland on which the monastery of Áy Emilianos stands. With the *meltemi* heavy seas set onto this coast and you need to take care in the

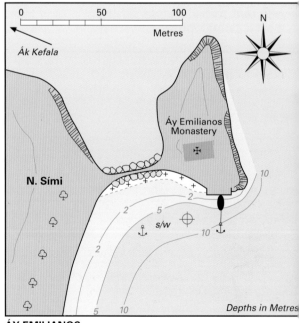

ÁY EMILIANOS
⊕36°36'·4N 27°46'·5E

approaches to the bay. From seawards you will see the monastery on the headland as well as the monastery of Áy Filimonas on the slopes further inland. Anchor off behind the headland and take a long line ashore if possible. Tripper boats tend to use the stubby quay. There is some shelter from the *meltemi* here, but a swell does creep around into the anchorage causing yachts to roll at anchor.

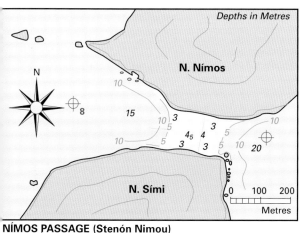

⊕8 W entrance of Nímos Passage (Sími)
36°38'·72N 27°49'·76E WGS84

NÍMOS PASSAGE (Stenón Nimou)
⊕36°38'·66N 27°50'·30E WGS84

Nímos Passage. It is deep enough – really!

Nisís Nímos

Nímos is the barren sister island to Sími separated by a narrow and quite shallow passage. The island is all rock and scrubby vegetation and has virtually no habitation. On the south side, once you are through the passage from the west, there is a startling white monastery on the shore, but that is about the sum total of what goes on on Nímos.

Nímos Passage is a convenient shortcut that avoids going all the way around the top of Nímos and it is much used, even by some quite large *gulets* and trawlers. The passage looks daunting the first time as the water comes up to a startling turquoise where you could swear the keel is going to cut a groove through the sandy bottom. In fact there are 4m least depths in the middle of the passage. From either direction approach the passage cautiously as it is difficult to see if anyone is coming from the opposite direction at the east end of the passage and you may turn the corner to find someone else barrelling through from the other direction.

ÓRMOS EMBORIOS

This large bay north of Sími is not as useful as it might appear on the chart. In the bay depths are considerable until you are nearly on the beach at the end. You will need to anchor in 15m or so at the head of the bay and often it is in use by tripper boats. An alternative is to anchor off on a shoal patch off Áy Spiridion on the south side of the bay. As long as the *meltemi* is not blowing too strongly this is quite OK as a lunch stop and you will be anchoring in a more civilised 6–7m. There are tavernas at the head of the bay and also in Áy Spiridion on the south side.

Rhodes

Rhodes is the biggest island in the Dodecanese and one that most people will have heard about. It has more people arriving on holiday than anywhere else in the Dodecanese: over a million in the summer, more than any other Greek island with the exception of nearby Crete. The number of tourists arriving has inevitably changed the character of the island, with some of the package holiday destinations, like Faliraki, making the headlines for the libidinous alcohol-fuelled behaviour of the sort of tourist, many of them British, that you would sail a hundred miles to avoid.

The island can also be something of a nightmare for those arriving by yacht. It does not have an abundance of good harbours, the main town has the sort of tourist haunts that you would really rather forget, the locals and the authorities are not always the most friendly around, and everywhere there seems to be noise and confusion after quieter places around the Dodecanese. You need to persevere with Rhodes to get the best out of it and while not everyone will fall in love with the place, some retain a sneaky affection for it.

Part of the problem with present-day Rhodes is that it has always been a favoured isle. Throughout history it has been praised for its benign climate, for its gentle aspect and green valleys, its clear water and its sandy beaches. It's almost as if the gods turned against the island because it is so blessed with natural beauty and what the gods started, 21st century man has connived to carry on in pursuit of Mammon, without regard for all that is around him.

The origin of the island's name is something of a mystery. It may come from the Greek word *rhodon* for rose, although the hardy rock-rose

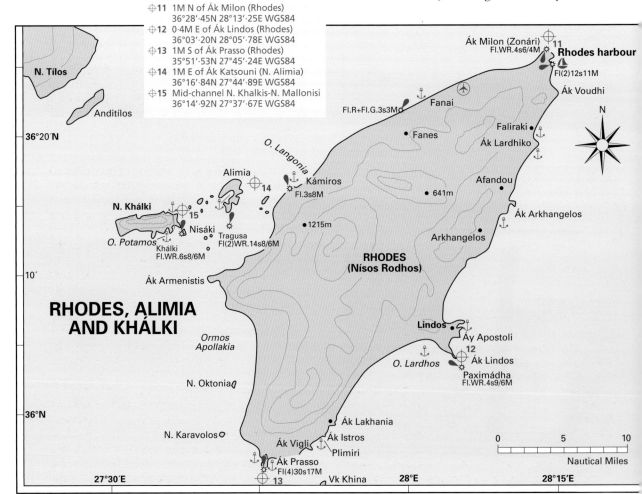

⊕**11** 1M N of Ák Milon (Rhodes)
36°28'·45N 28°13'·25E WGS84
⊕**12** 0·4M E of Ák Lindos (Rhodes)
36°03'·20N 28°05'·78E WGS84
⊕**13** 1M S of Ák Prasso (Rhodes)
35°51'·53N 27°45'·24E WGS84
⊕**14** 1M E of Ák Katsouni (N. Alimia)
36°16'·84N 27°44'·89E WGS84
⊕**15** Mid-channel N. Khalkis–N. Mallonisi
36°14'·92N 27°37'·67E WGS84

RHODES, ALIMIA AND KHÁLKI

Mandráki harbour looking SSW *Peter Kleinoth/MareTeam*

common in other parts of the Mediterranean is not native here. Other suggestions are Rodon, the daughter of Poseidon and Amphitrite, from the mythical ancestry of the island, or the Greek word roidi for pomegranate. In antiquity it had other names: Stadia, referring to its ellipsoid shape; Ophioussa from the many snakes on the island; Poeissia for its fertility; Olyessa because it is earthquake prone; and Makaria the 'blessed isle' referring to its beauty.

The fertile island has been inhabited since prehistoric times. Carians from mainland Asia Minor opposite lived here and the Phoenicians established a colony here as a stepping stone along their Aegean trade routes. In turn the Minoans and then the Dorians established colonies here. Homer mentions three cities on Rhodes: Lindos with its enclosed bay forming a natural harbour; Ialysos in the northwest; and Kamiros about 20 miles down the coast from Ák Milon. These three cities prospered and established numerous colonies around the

Mediterranean. In 408BC the cities decided to pool resources and founded the city of Rhodes on the present-day site.

Rhodes, with its harbour and advantageous site, soon eclipsed the other cities. There was ample flat land to build the city on and the inhabitants utilised the natural lie of the land to build three great harbours. Trading ships could now skim across to the top of Rhodes with the prevailing etesians and then continue on along the coast of Asia Minor, a much easier task than getting down to Lindos or braving the lee shore on the west coast. Rhodes quickly became the most important city in the southwestern Aegean and the Rhodians built up a large merchant fleet.

Rhodes managed to avoid much of the conflict that racked the Aegean until the death of Alexander the Great. In the conflict that followed the city was besieged for a year but managed to hold out against the superior forces of Polioketes. Rhodes continued to prosper after the siege and built up a merchant fleet that rivalled any in the

Aegean. Rhodes drew up a code of maritime law (though some say it originally came from Lindos) and this was adopted by the Romans and can even be detected in present-day maritime law. The city became a centre for learning and the arts and attracted artists and philosophers from around the Mediterranean. For a while Rhodes co-existed peacefully with the Romans until the assassination of Julius Caesar. Rhodes had backed Caesar and a year after his death (43BC) Cassius sacked the city and left it in ruins. Rhodes staggered on and Pliny records that even in the 1st century AD, it still had over 2,000 statues, despite the fact that many had been destroyed or carted away.

After the Romans Rhodes came under Byzantine rule and drifted along with whoever was in power: the Byzantines used it as a useful port; it was sacked by the Saracens; it enjoyed a brief renaissance under the Venetians who used the port to ferry crusaders to the Holy Land; and the Genoese took over from their rivals the Venetians. In 1306 the Genoese gave shelter to the battered remnants of the Knights of St John who had finally abandoned hope of taking and holding Jerusalem. By 1309 the Knights were in charge of Rhodes and so began the construction of the fortified city we see today.

The fortifications built by the Knights allowed the city to prosper again and for that prosperity to spread to nearby islands and across to the coast of Asia Minor. The Knights built castles and watch-towers from Tílos to Kós and on the mainland coast at Bodrum and Marmaris. They were ferocious fighters and on the water their slim galleys were renowned for their speed and manoeuvrability.

For over a century the Knights ruled this corner of the Aegean, but a showdown was inevitable as the world order changed around them. In 1444 the Sultan of Egypt besieged Rhodes and in 1480 Mehmet II tried again, but on both occasions the Knights successfully defended the city. This was to change and in 1522 Suleiman I besieged Rhodes with a force said to number 100,000 men against 650 Knights and 1,200 supporters. For five months the Turkish forces besieged the city and eventually the Grand Master, Villiers de L'Isle Adam, was forced to seek terms and safe conduct for his much depleted forces. The story goes that Suleiman, impressed by the valour of the small force defending the city, remarked 'It is not

without some regret that I oblige this old Christian to leave his home'. The Knights sailed off to Malta where they started all over again to fortify their new home in Valletta.

Rhodes remained under Turkish rule until the First World War and the defeat of the Axis forces led by Germany. The Italians occupied the Dodecanese and ruled until 1947 when the islands were given back to Greece. The Italians, intent on recreating the glories of the old Roman Empire, set about rebuilding Rhodes with gusto. There has been much criticism of this rebuilding, but in truth it bears up well against the modern buildings thrown up after Greece regained the island. The old fortified town and castle were rebuilt and over time the rebuilding and the original have melded into a whole that is, by and large, faithful to the original without being too Disney-esque.

RHODES HARBOUR

Pilotage

Approach Rhodes sits on the flat land behind Ák Milon and from the west and north the large hotels around the beach and other buildings will be seen from some distance off. Care is needed to give the shoal water off Ák Milon a good offing as it is all to easy to cut the corner once you can see where you are going. Some sea piles up on this corner as the current normally runs west and then southwest so the westerly *meltemi* is blowing against the current and sets up awkward steep seas. Once you are around Ák Milon there is a bit of a lee from the seas and the wind, although it can still be gusty.

From the south and east the harbour complex at Rhodes is easily identified and you will often see cruise ships and ferries in the harbour. There are often ships at anchor in the roadstead as well.

Closer in the various basins will be seen. Mandráki is easily identified by the small fort with a lighthouse (Áy Nikólaos) and the three windmills along the eastern breakwater. Likewise Emborikos can be identified by the windmills along the breakwater of Mandráki. The marina is easy to identify as it sits all alone in something of an industrial wasteland until the foreshore is developed.

Some care is needed of the ferries, cruise boats and tripper boats coming and going and you need to keep a careful eye out when closer in.

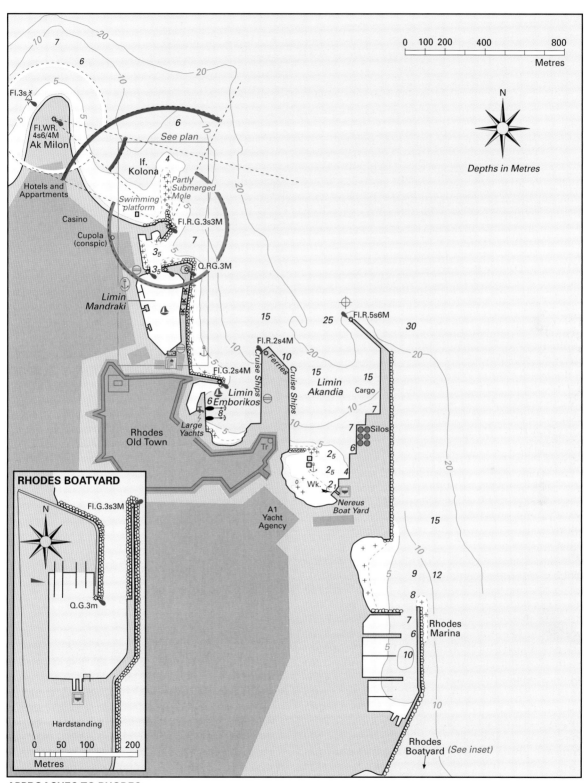

RHODES BOATYARD

Fl.G.3s3M
Q.G.3m
Hardstanding

0 50 100 200
Metres

N

Depths in Metres

0 100 200 400 800
Metres

Fl.3s

Fl.WR.
4s6/4M
Ak Milon

Hotels and
Appartments

Casino

Cupola
(conspic)

If.
Kolona

See plan

Partly
Submerged
Mole

Swimming
platform

Fl.R.G.3s3M

Q.RG.3M

Limin
Mandraki

Fl.R.5s6M

25

30

Fl.R.2s4M

Cruise Ships

Ferries

Cruise Ships

15

Limin
Akandia

Cargo

15

Fl.G.2s4M

Limin
Emborikos

Large
Yachts

Rhodes
Old Town

Silos

Tr

Wk.

Nereus
Boat Yard

A1
Yacht
Agency

Rhodes
Marina

Rhodes
Boatyard *(See inset)*

Mooring

Mandráki The harbour is hopelessly crowded and berths are jealously guarded. Most of the berths along the east quay are reserved for charter yachts, and to get one you will either have to negotiate with a charter company or one of the yacht agents here. There are a few laid moorings, but mostly you will have to use your own anchor, and crossed anchors and frayed tempers are commonplace. The bottom in here is gooey mud and good holding, though you should lay your anchor a long way out to avoid the permanent mooring chain that runs parallel to the east quay. If you do get a berth in here there is all-round protection and it has the advantage of being right in the middle of town.

Emborikos Most of the berths here are reserved for large yachts, but you may be able to squeeze in somewhere. Berths are handled by the yacht agents and you will frequently find someone on the quay waving you into a space if one is available. You may also find that you have to move later on because a large yacht is going to berth here and the port police will come down to tell yachts to move. The bottom here is mud with a few rocks and generally good holding. Shelter is good, although there is always some wash from ferries and work boats coming and going. As at Mandráki you are close to town and right under the bastions of the fortified old town.

Anchorage Yachts are sometimes allowed to anchor off just N of Emborikos basin. At times the port police will come and tell you to leave here so it's not a guaranteed option. If you do anchor here make sure you are not obstructing the access for the cruise ships and attendant tugs.

Rhodes Marina Work is in progress on the marina with a projected completion date at the end of 2012. In late 2011 work was going on building the shoreside infrastructure and the pontoons were in place. Yachts were not allowed entry at this time. The timescale for this marina has been off and on over more than 10 years so it's difficult to predict what will happen in the near future. No one in Rhodes really knows. When it does open it is likely there will be the usual facilities like water and electricity, fuel, showers and toilets and security. There have been suggestions that with gale force southerlies there is a surge in the harbour, but I haven't noticed any significant surge with the *meltemi* in here. At the moment it is pretty much out of the way in an industrial

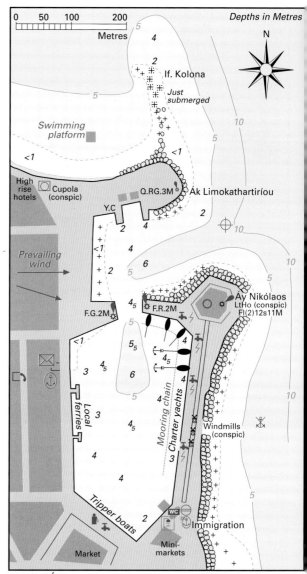

MANDRÁKI
⊕36°27′·12N 28°13′·67E WGS84

wasteland. The completion of the marina will certainly be welcomed by anyone visiting here.

Facilities

Services Water and electricity on the quay at Mandráki and Emborikos. At Mandráki you buy pre-paid cards in the office. A mini-tanker does the rounds delivering diesel fuel. Showers and toilets at Mandráki. Laundry in the town.

Provisions Good shopping nearby in the town and fresh fruit and vegetables in the market

Mandráki harbour in Rhodes. If you can get a berth here you are right in the middle of town

nearby. Many of the minimarkets will deliver to your yacht.

Eating out There are some excellent tavernas and restaurants in Rhodes, but you do need to exercise some care about where you go. I'd suggest walking up through the old town in a west-southwest direction where there are better tavernas than down on the bottom-feeding tourist streets. Sea Star on the corner of Sofokleous Square has some of the best seafood around. The Mandala Restaurant nearby has interesting food and for good Greek go to the Nereus. Nearby are other good tavernas you can sniff out around the warren of streets and it is pleasant walking around this area compared to the crowded streets down the bottom. Continuing on to Ippodamou St on the west side there is an excellent Italian restaurant called Palermo. Around the market at Mandráki there are some truly awful tavernas, but try Indigo which has good *mezes* and mains.

Other ATMs. Internet cafés. Hire cars and scooters. Buses to most places on the island (most leave from near the market at Mandráki). Ferries to most of the Dodecanese and through the Cyclades to Piraeus. Ferries to Marmaris in Turkey. Flights to many European destinations and internal flights to Athens.

General

Rhodes explodes on the senses with a cacophony of noise and activity: cars and scooters flying around the road that skirts the old castle walls; people everywhere touring the sites, shopping, or just mooching around until the cruise boats leave; tavernas and bars and cafés with waiters touting for business or busy serving; streets of shops with

Limın Emborikos under the walls of the castle

walled city is a UNESCO world heritage site and despite the tat and fast food shops in the lower levels, it really is an extraordinary place and quite possibly the best-preserved medieval fortified city in the world. There are numerous guides to places of interest in the city, but really this is a place you can just wander around in musing on what life was like here on a good day and during the last great siege when the Knights were finally forced to abandon the city. You cannot get up to the top of the walls except on a guided tour, although there is a small section near the harbour where you wander around part of the lower defensive structure. If nothing else impresses you, think about these walls which are up to 12m (nearly 40 ft) thick in places. Even a goodly amount of bombardment in the Second World War only dented parts of the city.

Outside the walled city most people will wander around the newer Rhodes, largely built by the Italians. Here fashionable boutiques have taken over the high street and souvenir shops and fast-food outlets occupy the waterfront area. Unless you are determined to buy some Gucci or Bulgari, the best thing to do is settle down in one

fashionable labels and some tat as well; everywhere this place just hums to the hymn of the summer tourist season. It comes as something of a shock to the senses and you will need a bit of time to adjust. Once you have settled in and planned visits to avoid the crowds, then you will find Rhodes does reward you.

The mighty walled city built by the Knights is an obvious must-see and you are best visiting it either early in the morning or early evening. The

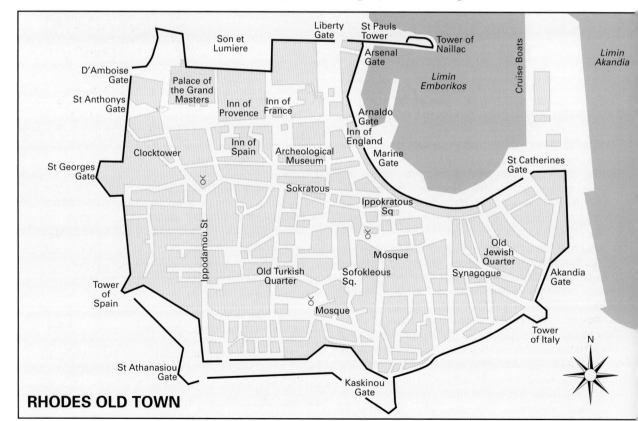

RHODES OLD TOWN

The Colossus of Rhodes

The Colossus of Rhodes, the bronze statue of Helios the sun god and one of the Seven Wonders of the Ancient World, may or may not have stood over the harbour at Mandráki as often depicted. The statue was immense and by any standards a spectacular landmark, standing some 35m high and weighing over a hundred tons, though it probably looked nothing like the 'jolly green giant' depicted on local postcards. Apart from satisfying the vanity of the city and commemorating its victory over Demetrios Polioketes during the first great siege of the city, it is likely it was a lighthouse to guide ships in, or at the very least, a tall 'conspic' glinting in the sun to guide mariners who were not quite sure where Rhodes was.

The origins of the statue begin with the first great siege of Rhodes. After the death of Alexander the Great there was political chaos as his generals and appointed governors squabbled amongst themselves over the greatest empire the ancient world had seen. One of Alexander's successors, Antigonus, ordered the Rhodians to help him take on another would-be successor, Ptolemy in Egypt. The Rhodians refused to do so: Egypt was, after all, one of their major trading partners and it would have been commercial suicide for them to stir up trouble in Egypt. The Rhodians' decision upset Antigonus and to punish them he sent his son, Demetrios Polioketes, to take the island in 305BC. Polioketes arrived flushed with success from taking Salamis in Cyprus and he arrived with a formidable force. He had some 200 ships, 40,000 soldiers and a war chest full of funds to draw on. In Rhodes there were just 8,000 soldiers and some 2,000 mercenaries, as well as 10,000 or so slaves who were promised their freedom if they fought alongside the Rhodians.

Polioketes seemed to have a fascination with novel and ingenious war machinery. He started the war with a catapult slung between two ships, that heaved huge stones into the town. When this didn't do the job he had his mega-machine Heliopolis, the 'Overthrower of Cities', constructed on the land and it is surprising the

Rhodians didn't give up at the sight of it. This machine was a 125-ton behemoth that stood nine storeys high, a combination of siege tower, catapult, drawbridges that could be dropped down, and a nest on top for archers. It was shielded by thick ox-hide against enemy archers and it trundled along on great oak wheels. Around Rhodes you can see piles of the stone balls that the catapults hurled into the city and yet still the Rhodians held out. For a year the siege went on until finally Polioketes' father ordered him to stop the siege and sign a treaty with the Rhodians. Polioketes did so and charitably gifted all his war machinery to the Rhodians so that it might be sold off and the proceeds used to build a commemorative statue to the siege.

That's where the funds for the Colossus of Rhodes came from, and the job of building the statue was given to the sculptor Chares of Lindos who designed the huge bronze statue of Helios the sun god. It took 12 years to build. Where it stood is something of a mystery, but there is no reason why it could not have stood astride the harbour. Ancient trading ships were really large boats and not big ships. A trading ship of the time was usually anything between 12 and 20m with a short stubby mast, around 10m tall on a 12m boat, on which a squaresail was rigged. Using the same sort of ratio a 20m boat would have a mast a tad under 17m, though likely less given the limits of the technology of the day for rigging and sail handling. Would a 17m mast pass under a 35m high statue without scraping his nether regions? It would be tight, but given that masts on larger ships were likely to have a smaller mast height to LOA ratio compared to the 12m boat, because of the limits of the technology involved, then just maybe the bronze giant could have straddled the harbour.

The colossus stood for 65 years until an earthquake in 227BC toppled it. The remains were piled up and not until nearly nine centuries later, in AD654, was it sold off for scrap. One apocryphal story has it that the bronze was melted down into cannonballs that were then fired into the city in the second great siege of Rhodes.

of the waterfront cafés with an overpriced coffee and watch all this frenetic life go by.

EAST COAST NOTE

When the *meltemi* is blowing there are gusts off the lee side of Rhodes, though generally these are not as fierce as those off the lee side of Kós and some of the other islands in the Dodecanese. Nonetheless some prudence is needed and it is best to tuck a reef or two in until you have gauged the strength of the gusts on any particular day. As a general rule the gusts are strongest at the northern and southern ends of the island, though even around Lindos you can get some fierce gusts.

FALIRAKI

⊕36°20'·7N 28°13'·2E

The small harbour of Faliraki is situated off the resort area of the same name some eight miles south of Rhodes harbour. The small harbour is rockbound with above and below-water rocks fringing the entrance and off the harbour itself. Small yachts may be able to creep into it on a westerly to southwesterly course with someone up front conning you in. There are 2–3m depths in the immediate approaches and in the entrance, but once inside depths shoal to less than 2m and in places less than 1m. Much of the room inside is in any case taken up with tripper and watersports boats for the hotels ashore.

Close to the harbour there are numerous restaurants and bars and along the beach there is a carbuncle of a resort that has at times featured in the tabloid press for the orgiastic behaviour exhibited here. This place has little to do with Greece and a lot to do with cheap booze, sun and sex. Even if you are interested in all those things, there are far far better places to go than Faliraki, or as it has been named in the press, 'Feely F***y'.

ÓRMISKOS LARDHIKO

Just around the corner from Faliraki is a miniature cove encircled by cliffs. Coming from the north you need to make the approach on a northwesterly bearing to avoid the shoal water and reefs off the coast to the north. In the entrance to Lardhikos there is a shoal patch with 2m minimum depth and you should creep in around the western entrance point to avoid it. Once inside there is very little room and you need

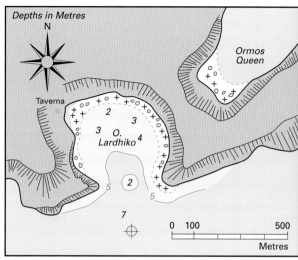

ORMISKOS LARDHIKO
⊕36°19'·3N 28°12'·8E

Geminos and the Anti-Kithera 'computer'

In 1901 some sponge divers sheltering under the lee of Anti-Kithera off the bottom of the Peloponnese found an ancient wreck on one of their dives. Amongst the statues and other artefacts found was a corroded mass of metal that was painstakingly restored at the National Archaeological Museum in Athens. Once the corrosion of some 2,000 years (the wreck is from the 1st century BC to the 1st century AD) was removed the device was found to be some sort of precursor to the clock, with a box with dials and inscribed plates on the outside and a complex system of gear wheels within. It is in effect similar to a 17th- or 18th-century clock. This is no simple mechanism as part of the system has been shown to consist of around 20 gear wheels that probably operated as a differential geared system.

From inscriptions on some of the plates this was obviously an astronomical device. It uses an astronomical calendar similar to one written by Geminos of Rhodes with inscriptions relating to the sun and to Venus and possibly to other planets as well. Its purpose is uncertain, although certainly astronomical, and the best conclusion is that it is like an analogue computer to work out the positions of the sun, moon and stars, a sort of clock of the heavens. Whether it was used on board the ship to calculate astronomical positions or was just being transported somewhere is uncertain, though it had been repaired several times so was evidently in use.

Geminos of Rhodes was likely a Greek, even though he has a Latinised name, who lived in Rhodes around this period (c.10BC to AD60). His book on astronomy, the *Isagoges*, draws on the work of other great Rhodian astronomers, notably Posidonius, and has much material pertinent to the Anti-Kithera 'computer'. He describes

the movement of the constellations and even the possibility that stars are at different distances from the earth; the variation of the length of days and nights at different latitudes; the phases of the moon and the basis of a lunar calendar; and the rising of the zodiac signs at night and the movement of the planets. Geminos also wrote a history of mathematics which has been lost, but in relation to the Anti-Kithera 'computer' it is his work on astronomy and particularly his writings on the astronomical calendar that mark him out as the likely source of the information used in the Anti-Kithera device. It is impossible to know whether he had it constructed, but at least the theoretical input for the practical device seems to be his.

It is the only known mechanism of its kind from this period and its importance is like somebody 2,000 years hence finding the only surviving remains of a digital computer, signifying that our society was skilled enough to build such things. From the Anti-Kithera 'computer' we know the ancient Greeks could build a complex analogue 'computer' to plot positions in the heavens and it is unlikely that it is the only device ever built at this time. Cicero mentioned a device constructed by Posidonius of Rhodes that reproduced the motion of the sun, moon and five planets, and Archimedes much earlier on is said to have constructed a small planetarium. It is a pity we don't know exactly how it worked, but that it is an important link to the clock-making tradition in Europe and the calculation of latitude is certain and some historical rethinking of the practical skills of Greek and Roman navigation techniques needs to be made in the light of the Anti-Kithera 'computer'.

to anchor and take a long line ashore in the northeast corner, avoiding the popular little beach in the northwest corner. The cove is so small that if there are several tripper boats in here it is difficult to find a spot to anchor and get a line ashore.

There is a taverna on the beach and also up the top, along with a minimarket. The cove is a pleasant spot though popular in the summer. Immediately northeast of Lardhikos is Antony Queen Bay (the mis-spelt name has even made it onto local maps), where *The Guns of Navarone* was filmed in 1961 and where Quinn apparently had property. I do know he had a wonderful old wooden motorsailer, around 45ft long, that friends of mine bought in the late 1970s and lived on for many years while cruising between Rhodes and Cyprus.

ORMOS KALATHOS

This long sandy beach north of Lindos provides some shelter in the southwest corner. Anchor in 5–6m off the beach. If the *meltemi* blows strongly some swell rolls down into the anchorage and you are better off going to Lindos or around the corner to Lardhos. Ashore several tavernas open in the summer.

LINDOS

Pilotage

Approach As you close Ák Áy Amilianos from the north or coast up past Ák Lindos from the south, you will see the buildings of Lindos crowned by the castle. Some care is needed from the south (and from the north when leaving Lindos to head south) of Nisáki Pendeli and the shoal water joining it to the coast. Otherwise the approach to Lindos is straightforward in deep water.

Mooring Anchor outside of the buoyed area near the pier or in the northern part of the bay. The northern anchorage has some large boulders on the bottom (which you can usually see) so it may be prudent to rig a trip line. Tripper boats will often anchor and take a long line ashore on the west side of the bay clear of the buoyed area. The bottom is mostly sand with some rocks and generally good holding. Shelter in here is good, although with the *meltemi* there can be strong gusts so make sure your anchor is well in.

In calm weather some yachts anchor on a sandy patch just north of the entrance. This is a

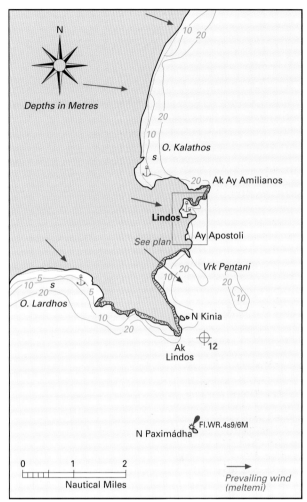

O. KALATHOS TO O. LARDHOS
⊕0.4M E of Ak Lindos 36°03′·20N 28°05′·78E WGS84

spectacular spot with clearer water than Lindos. It is more of a lunch stop than an overnight anchorage and it is probably best to tuck up inside Lindos Bay for the night.

Facilities

Provisions There are several minimarkets in Lindos town. Dinghy over to the jetty to get up to the town.

Eating out Tavernas and fast food outlets in Lindos serving fairly sub-standard fare for the masses bussed in daily.

Other ATM. Hire cars and scooters. Bus to Rhodes.

General

Much of what I have written about the sort of mass tourism in Rhodes town applies here, although in the case of Lindos, this spectacularly beautiful place seems to have lost its soul, or perhaps it has sold it, as unlike in Rhodes town there does not seem to be a beating heart here after the buses leave. It is a gem of a place, a shimmering white cluster of almost Cyclades-style houses looking out over the natural amphitheatre of a bay and topped off by the castle on a crag behind the town. If you go ashore the town is all black and white mosaic lanes and courtyards with bougainvillaea and hibiscus adorning everything. It is a picture postcard sort of place and that is its curse.

Lindos gets an estimated half a million visitors every year and by late morning the road into Lindos is lined with tour coaches disgorging tourists. Locals and tourists alike seem to interact in a weary waltz where cash is exchanged for the sights of Lindos and no-one seems very happy. The tourists, having done their duty, slump into a bar or taverna or descend to the crowded beach before catching the coach home.

Lindos was one of the original big three cities on the island until Rhodes city itself was built and the ancient town declined. It's well worth the walk up to the castle of the Knights on the summit inside which are extensive remains of the ancient city of Lindos. It's an evocative place atop the craggy lump of rock with wonderful views down over the town of Lindos and over the sea. Much of the ancient city was quarried by the Knights to build the castle, but enough remains to give you a good idea of what the acropolis was like. The town of Lindos itself was built on seafaring and

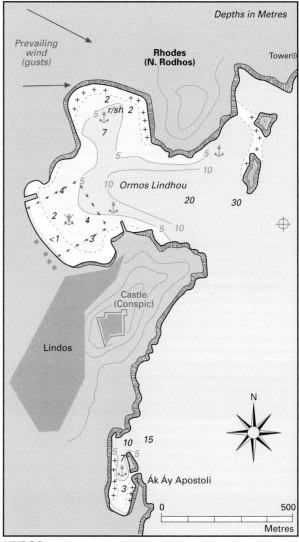

Lindos anchorage *Nigel Patten*

LINDOS
⊕36°05′·73N 28°05′·82E WGS84

Lindos looking up to the castle from the anchorage

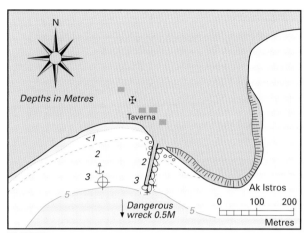

PLIMIRI
⊕35°55′·6N 27°51′·4E

continued through medieval times to the 18th century when the fortunes of the town declined to almost nothing. Visit the town early in the morning or in the early evening when the coach parties are not tramping through the town, and it will seem a lot more benign than at midday.

ÁY APOSTOLI (St Paul's Bay)

A narrow cove lying just south of Lindos Bay. The steep-sided inlet sitting under the castle appears to offer nearly all-round shelter, but any swell outside rebounds into here, making it a less comfortable spot than Lindos Bay. Once inside anchor and take a long line ashore as there is limited swinging room.

The bay takes it name from St Paul who is said to have found refuge in here when the boat carrying him was caught in a storm. The story goes that St Paul prayed for deliverance and the narrow inlet was miraculously revealed to him. There are a surprising number of inlets and bays that bear his name around the Mediterranean, a tribute to the tireless proselytiser who made many voyages around the coast of Asia Minor and the offlying islands spreading the new religion.

ÓRMOS LARDHOS

The large bay tucked under Ák Lindos with a long gravelly beach running around it. There is reasonable shelter from the *meltemi* tucked into the northeast corner of the bay, although any swell around rolls into here so it is best used as a lunch stop. Anchor in 4–8m off the beach. This area has become something of an extension to the Lindos strip and there are numerous self-catering apartments and small hotels on the waterfront with associated tavernas on the beach.

PLIMIRI

Under Ák Istros there is something of a lee from the *meltemi* and a yacht can anchor off the short mole tucked under the south side of the cape. Care is needed in the approaches of a dangerous wreck situated approximately half a mile south of the cape. Anchor in 3–5m on sand. Some swell rolls into here but overall the shelter is adequate. Taverna ashore near the root of the mole. The small church here is interesting in that it has some ancient bits and pieces incorporated into it, including Corinthian columns.

There has been talk of building a marina here, but given the stop-and-start progress of Rhodes Marina, this would seem to be a distant dream.

Ak Vigli

⊕35°54′·15N 27°49′·1E

A knobbly headland lying around one mile south of Istros. It is easily distinguished by a tower on the extremity. Some shelter from the *meltemi* can be found in the anchorage on the south side of the headland, though care is needed of reefs fringing the cape and the coast. Anchor in 5–6m off the beach.

Note Care is needed of reefs and shoal water SW of Ak Vigli which extend for up to half a mile off the coast. From the anchorage at Ak Vigli you need to head SSE before shaping a course for the bottom of Rhodes. Coming north keep a prudent distance off before turning in towards Ak Vigli.

Ak Prasso

⊕**13** 1M S of Ak Prasso 35°51'·53N 27°45'·24E WGS84

The southernmost tip of Rhodes is a very windy place indeed, so much so that it has become a mecca for windsurfers and kite-surfers. The island of Prasonisi with the light on it is connected to Rhodes by a low sandy bar and from the distance looks like an island. On the south side you can anchor off the sandy strip in 3–5m, taking care to avoid the underwater cable running from the northwest end of the sandy strip. The anchorage is subject to severe gusts and a swell tends to creep around the end so it is not comfortable in here. The north side of the strip is in continuous use by the wind and kite-surfers and in any case it is a lee shore. The anchorage is not a secure one and I don't really recommend it, even for a lunch stop.

On the north side nylon primary colours zoom up and down in the gusty winds which are accelerated around this end of the island. Ashore there is a minimarket and several tavernas to cater for the surfers who congregate here when the *meltemi* blows.

SKÁLA KAMIROS (Órmos Langonia)

The ferry port for Khálki just across the water. A short quay is tucked into the corner of the bay and here there is some shelter from the *meltemi* and from southerlies. The ferry uses the end of the quay and local boats occupy much of the rest of it, so there is little room for a yacht to tuck in here. You will most likely have to anchor out and that is not only uncomfortable but also not a good place to be if it blows up. You should not leave the yacht unattended.

Ashore there are numerous fish tavernas and cafés. Tour parties often stop here for lunch after visiting other sites on Rhodes, so it is not exactly peaceful.

On a craggy rock under Órmos Ak. Kopria in the southern approaches to Langonia is the impressive Kastello Kritinias built by the Knights. It looks a bit like a fairytale castle and commands the western approaches through the offlying islands of Khalkia and Alimnia to Rhodes.

Note Between Órmos Langonia and Fanai there are several wrecks just off the coast marked on the chart. While coasting up here I thought I would try to see if they were still there as many are so old they have deteriorated to a pile of scrap metal on the bottom. To my surprise I glided over the top of one complete with derricks and communication masts sticking up to just under the surface and was lucky not to impale the boat on it. So the wrecks are there and they are dangerous to navigation: give them a wide berth.

FANAI

A small harbour on the northwest side of Rhodes. The harbour is prone to silting and at present the entrance has less than 1m in the entrance. Only shallow-draught yachts should close the entrance and then only in calm weather as the *meltemi* heaps up at the entrance and there can be

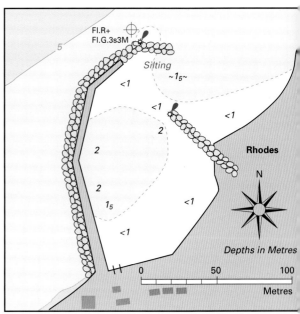

FANAI
⊕36°21'·9N 27°58'·6E

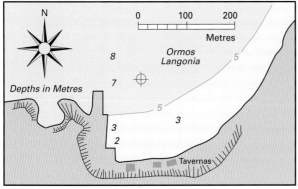

SKALA KAMIROS
⊕36°16'·4N 27°49'·6E

breaking waves. Once inside depths are a little more at 1·5–2m and you can go stern or bows-to or alongside the quay on the breakwater if there room. Local boats take up much of the quay space and it can be difficult to find a berth here. Good shelter once inside, although there is a bit of a surge with the *meltemi*.

Ashore there is a taverna by the harbour and Fanai village is about a kilometre inland. With the *meltemi* constantly blowing onto this coast it is likely the harbour will continue to silt at the entrance and so any approach to the harbour should be in calm weather and with an alternative harbour in mind.

Khálki and Alimia

The approaches to these islands and navigation between them look a nightmare maze of islets, rocks and reefs. In practice it is a lot easier than it looks on the chart, though you still need to exercise some care and make sure you positively identify what is what with the Mk 1 eyeball. The following is worth noting when navigating in the area.

1. When the *meltemi* is blowing identification of the rocks and reefs is confused by all the white horses around. The *meltemi* gusts down through the channel between Khálki and Alimia so you can expect to find more wind than over the open sea. For a first-time approach through the channel it is helpful if you can do it in relatively calm weather.
2. Xera rock is difficult to spot although it is above water.
3. The reef ESE of Nisáki is also difficult to pick out.
4. Most of the other rocks and the islets are relatively easy to identify.

The two islands of Khálki and Alimia have always been dependent on big brother Rhodes just across the water. The islands here are parched lumps of limestone, rocky sea-gates to the bigger island with an impressive array of underwater teeth waiting to snap up the unwary mariner. I'm sure there must be more than a few ancient ships lying on the seabed around the channel between these islands.

Khálki used to support a sizeable population numbered in the thousands, many of them

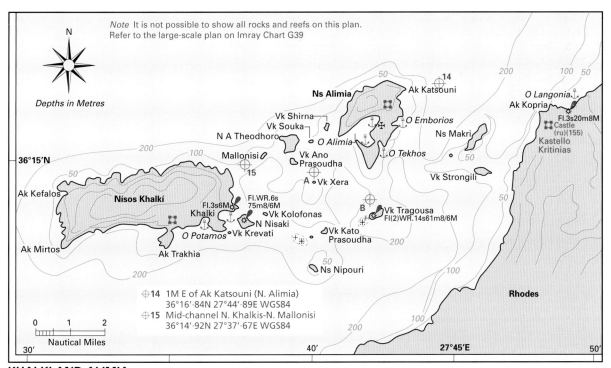

KHALKI AND ALIMIA

⊕A 0.5m N of Vk Xera 36°14'·82N 27°40'·19E WGS84
⊕B 0.5m N of Vk Tragousa 36°13'·99N 27°42'·41E WGS84

engaged in fishing and particularly sponge fishing. As at Kalimnos and Sími, when sponges became scarce the inhabitants emigrated to Rhodes and Athens and across the water to the USA and Australia. Today there is a population of just 300 or so on Khálki who are outnumbered by tourists in the summer, and no-one at all on Alimia.

The islands are peaceful places after Rhodes and although Khálki now has some tourism, it is an affable and mostly unobtrusive intrusion on the island. There is nothing much to do here, nothing you must see. There is the castle that the Knights built to defend the island and you should wander around just to look at the town, but after that the main interest is what the local fishermen have caught for dinner and who has arrived on the ferry from Langonia. And maybe a swim before dinner.

KHÁLKI

Pilotage

Approach From the south and east the three windmills on the ridge above the bay are easily identified and once into the bay the houses around the harbour will be seen. When approaching from the north the northern channel (18m in the fairway) between Nisís Nisaki and Khálki is difficult to make out, but closer in will be seen. The power station in the bay to the north of Emborios is conspicuous. From the south or north and west the approach is straightforward with few dangers in the way, but from the east the approach is through the channel peppered with rocks and reefs. As mentioned above, some attention is needed when navigating through the channel between Khálki and Alimia, but with care

it is easier than it looks on paper. A night approach is not recommended.

Mooring Head for the T-pontoon and go stern or bows-to where directed or where there is a space. The 'pontoon man' will normally be around to direct you to a space and help you tie up. You will be dropping anchor in fairly deep water, 20m if going on the end of the pontoon, so have plenty of scope ready. The pontoon is removed in the winter, normally November to April.

If the pontoon is full there may be a space on the ferry pier. The only other alternative is to anchor off. Good shelter from the prevailing wind which blows in from the WNW. In unsettled weather head for the anchorage in Alimia. Charge band 2 on the pontoon.

Anchorage You can anchor off to the east of the pontoon though depths are considerable and you will be dropping anchor in 10–20m depending on how close you go to the coast. It is deep until close to. You may also be able to find a space to anchor on the south side though the bottom is littered with moorings. Alternatively there is Órmos Potamos around the corner or Alimia.

Facilities

Services Water from a tap at the pontoon though water is a scarce commodity and it may be turned off. The only petrol station is at Kania north of Emborios.

Provisions Minimarkets and bakery in Emborios.

Eating out Around the harbour square there are numerous tavernas, mostly offering honest Greek food, and you should use your nose to sniff out one you like. The Minori near the pontoon is very friendly, and further round the Kai Ftais does good mezes.

Other ATM. Wi-Fi at some of the cafés. Ferries to Skála Kamiros and Rhodes town.

Looking E out of Emborios. The yacht pontoon is partially obscured by the tallest clock tower in the Dodecanese!

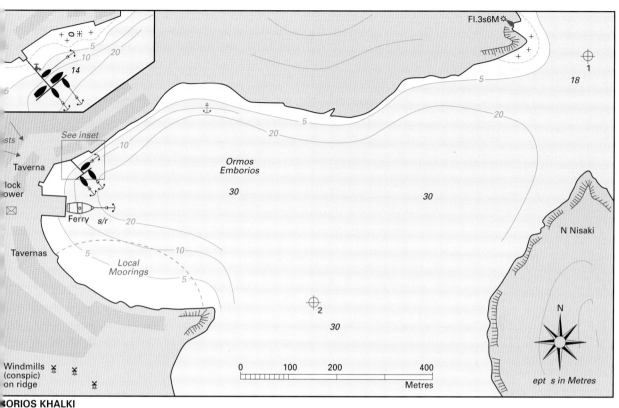

▶ORIOS KHALKI
36°13′·51N 27°37′·61E WGS84
36°13′·26N 27°37′·08E WGS84

General

When I first visited this island in 1980 it was a ruin of a place and I commented then that, like Sími, it would one day rise from a half-ruined town of once pleasing architecture in a style not dissimilar to Sími to become a desirable place to escape to. Not surprisingly that has happened: most of the houses have been sympathetically restored and Khálki looks somewhat like a mini-Sími, though not without some hiccups along the way. In 1983 UNESCO put together a program to restore the houses around the harbour, but after five years little had been done. It seemed much of the money and most of the goodwill had evaporated without the islanders getting much out of it. UNESCO was kicked out and the town council got together with a number of tour operators to restore the houses for summer lets. Thankfully no-one suggested a Faliraki-like development and today Khálki is the acceptable face of tourism.

The harbour and central square have been prettified and cars are banned in the summer. It all works wonderfully well and the water in the harbour is so clear the houses have swimming ladders down into the water and bonito hunt smaller fish around the pontoon. The tavernas and bars here are good local places serving honest Greek food without the pretension of *kultura* restaurants elsewhere. And the locals and tourists all seem to get on quite happily in a symbiotic relationship where neither is harming the other. In fact, the place has an uncanny calm to it that takes a bit of getting used to after the hustle and bustle of Rhodes.

ÓRMOS POTAMOS

A bay on the south side of Khálki just around the corner from Órmos Emborios. The approach is straightforward although there are gusts with the *meltemi*. Anchor in 3–6m off the scrappy beach. Good shelter even with the gusts.

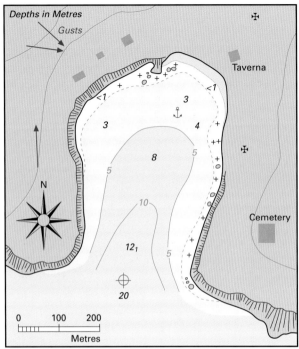

ORMOS POTAMOS
⊕36°13'·0N 27°36'·35E

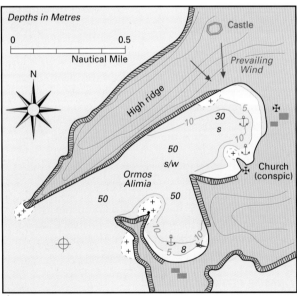

ÓRMOS ALIMIA
⊕36°15'·8N 27°41'·5E

The bay is popular with tourists, though again it is not a rowdy place. A taverna on the shore opens in the summer. You can walk along the coast here to the castle of the Knights to the west or just do what most people do and swim in the wonderful clear water of the bay.

ÓRMOS ALIMIA

Pilotage

Approach Once through the maze of islets, rocks and reefs (see above), the entrance to Alimia is straightforward with deep water up to the edges. There are strong gusts with the *meltemi* so it's best to get your sails down before entering the bay. The only danger to be aware of is the reef jutting out from the southern entrance to the bay just inside the entrance proper.

Mooring Anchor in the south bay or at the head of the bay in the north. With the *meltemi* either the south or north bay affords good protection. In unsettled weather including southerlies head for the south bay. You can also anchor tucked in as far as possible behind the spit with a church on it in the north bay, although the tripper boats from Khálki tend to monopolise this spot. The bottom is mostly sand with some weed, good holding once the anchor is in. Good shelter from the *meltemi*, although there are gusts.

General

The island has no permanent population and no facilities. A few fishermen from Khálki have houses here and goats and sheep are grazed on the island, but you rarely see anyone here apart from the tripper boat tourists who usually disappear around mid-afternoon. On the summit is a castle built by the Knights which is a steep hot climb to get to, though when you do there are wonderful views across to Rhodes.

Near the shores of the bay are some buildings used by the Italians and Germans during the Second World War and in one of these some nostalgic cartoons depicting what life might be like back home or on a tropical island somewhere other than Alimia. The bay was sporadically used during the war as a naval base and there are some remains of moorings and other wartime detritus scattered around. The villagers were deported to make way for soldiers, and never returned after the war. There are remains of German submarine pens in the outer part of the bay.

East coast anchorages

On the east side of Alimia there are two bays that can be used in settled weather. Órmos Tekhos lies on the other side of the thin waist at the southern end of the island and Órmos Emborios is less than a mile north of it. Órmos Emborios is the best of the two and there are reasonable depths for anchoring. Reasonable shelter from the *meltemi* and wonderfully remote surroundings with crystal clear water. Explore them in calm weather and then chug around into Órmos Alimia for the night.

Kastellórizon (Megisti)

Kastellórizon is the easternmost outpost of Greece, lying some 70 miles east of Rhodes, its nearest Greek neighbour, but only a mile or so off the Turkish coast opposite. It is a barren lump of rock with steep-to cliffs around much of it and in

summer it is lashed by the *meltemi* and in winter by savage southerly storms. With a population of just 300 it is something of an anomaly, a remote outpost of things Greek marooned off the Turkish coast. Strange, then, to think that this small island with a diminutive population was a thriving metropolis with a population of some 10,000 a hundred years ago. In Kastellórizon town you can buy postcards and posters showing the port in its heyday, the harbour full of trading schooners anchored off or unloading cargo around the docks. The harbour is often described as the best natural harbour between Rhodes and Beirut, an observation repeated verbatim by guide books; but you only need to look at a map to see that this is patently not true, and anyone who has sailed the coast opposite could name half a dozen natural harbours that are better than Kastellórizon. (In fact, Büçak Deniz at Kaş a mile away is a better natural harbour than Kastellórizon.)

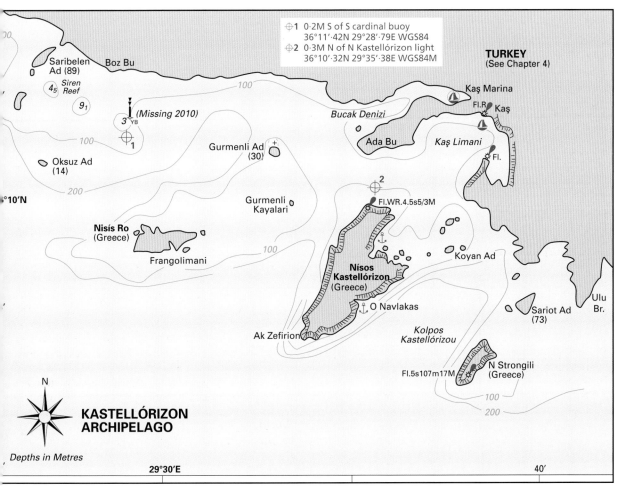

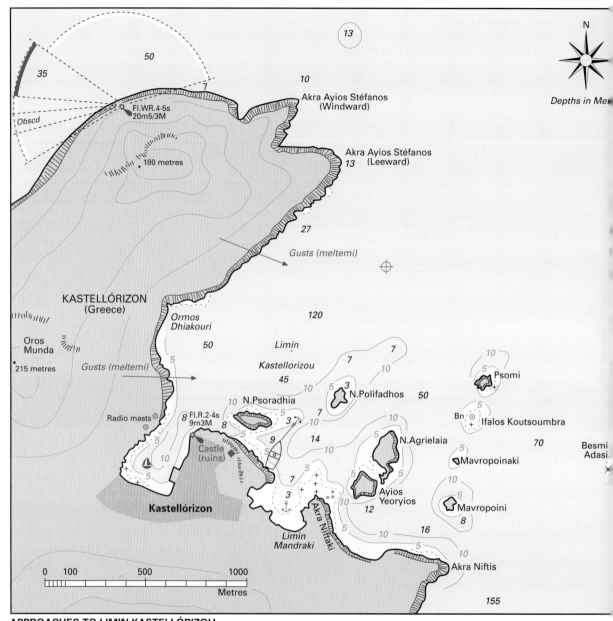

APPROACHES TO LIMIN KASTELLÓRIZOU
⊕36°09′·58N 29°36′·20E WGS84

The reversal in fortune for the island derives from a number of factors. At the end of the 19th century the rich shipowners in Kastellórizon struggled on with sail when much of the world was converting to steam power. Most of their trade depended on the coast opposite and this dried up after Turkey joined the Axis forces in the First World War. After the war the islanders overthrew the Turkish authorities and elected to join the Dodecanese under the Italians. For a while it was ruled from Samos by a Greek governor and then in 1915 the French, fighting their corner in the Hatay, took over Kastellórizon until 1921, when it finally became part of the Dodecanese under the Italians. In the Second World War when the Italians finally surrendered to the Allies in 1943, it was occupied by the British until 1944. Just before the British left a fuel dump caught fire and exploded, destroying half of the town. There was also some looting that went on before the British left and although the British blamed the Greeks and the Greeks the British, there still remains some ill will towards the British. Effectively this once grand town had been reduced to rubble and those who returned found not only their houses but their possessions gone as well. Not surprisingly this was the last straw for the inhabitants and most of them emigrated to Australia and the USA.

Today the recent sad history of the island and its geographical isolation bestow a bittersweet atmosphere to the island. It now has a ferry service once a week to Rhodes and the airport built in 1986 lessens its apparent isolation. You might think that the islanders' dependence on their Turkish neighbours in Kaş for everyday essentials – a *caique* ferry does a regular run across to the town, usually on the Friday market day, so the islanders can shop for fruit and vegetables, clothes, pots and pans, in fact just about anything you can think of – would engender a spirit of mutuality between the islanders and the Turks opposite. Instead it seems to foster a brooding resentment about their plight, and a rancorous nationalism that is often sadly evident to visitors to the island. A few tourists arrive on the ferry or by plane and yachts visit the island from Kaş. It should be noted that this is an informal arrangement, usually welcomed by the islanders as the yachts bring additional revenue to the place. Non-EU flagged yachts arriving cannot clear into Greece here and their details must be faxed to Rhodes where they will need to go to formally clear in. A not inconsiderable charge is made for this. For EU-flagged yachts the situation is somewhat better and although harbour fees will sometimes be charged, they do not have to pay the 'administration fee' that is made on non-EU yachts.

LIMIN KASTELLÓRIZOU
⊕36°09′·17N 29°35′·59E WGS84

Kastellórizon harbour looking from the yacht quay

Kastellórizon

In recent years some of the émigrés, mostly Australian, have begun to return in the summer and some of the grand old shipowners' houses have been restored.

LIMIN KASTELLÓRIZOU

Pilotage

Approach From the west there are few dangers that are not easily identified, and the great bulk of Ak. Áy Stefanos is easily identified. From the east there are numerous islets and reefs in the approaches and some accurate eyeball navigation is required. The islets are reasonably easy to identify and establish your position from, although care is needed of the reef south of Besmi islet. The best policy for a first time approach from the east is to head for the western tip of Koyan Adası taking care of the fringing reef around it and then head for Nisís Psomi (Bread Islet) before turning westwards towards Nisís Polifadhos and around into the harbour. If you are crossing from Kaş just head towards Ák Stefanos and avoid all the islets in the eastern approaches.

The approach would be a good deal more straightforward but for the fact that the *meltemi* can howl down into the approaches, whipping up white horses that make it difficult to identify rocks and reefs, not to mention the distraction caused by the howling wind itself.

Mooring Yachts normally go stern or bows-to the quay in the southeast corner. Care is needed of the ballasting which runs out a short distance underwater. The holding here is not always the best on mud and rocks, so you need good scope and make sure the anchor is in and holding. At times you may be able to go alongside the ferry quay, but enquire at the port police first. Shelter here is adequate in the summer when the *meltemi* is blowing, but there can be a surge with a prolonged blow. Southerlies also tend to cause a surge in here.

Note
Yachts coming across from Kaş are in something of a no-man's land here. You can check into Kastellórizon from Kaş, but you cannot obtain a transit log here. Non-EU flagged boats will have their details faxed to Rhodes and must pay a fairly hefty 'processing' fee. EU-flagged yachts may also have to pay harbour fees which sometimes appear to be negotiable. Given that you are in an isolated little entrepot away from the mainstream and that most yachts will return to Turkey from here, I suggest you go with the flow even if you don't like it. Happily for most of the summer season the port police ignore yachts visiting here from Turkey and usually you will not see a soul.

Facilities

Kastellórizon is dependent on importing most things from Greece or Kaş across the water, so there are few facilities. Some fuel may be available in jerry cans. Water is scarce. Basic shopping, though fresh produce is poor. On the waterfront there are a number of tavernas and you should choose with care. Try Ipomoni or the Kaz Bar.

General

Kastellórizon is really just a place to wander around in and look at the bones of a once thriving town. Many of the villas have been restored, mostly by Australian Greeks, who come here in the summer, so it is not unusual to hear a 'gidday – alright mite' when wandering around. Above the town there are the remains of a castle built by the Knights and now housing a small and really quite interesting museum. Nearby is the only Lycian rock tomb in Greece, though if you have come across from Turkey it is likely you have seen quite enough of these already.

MANDRÁKI

Close east of Kastellórizon harbour there is the bay of Mandráki. The approach to the bay is littered with rocks and reefs and if you are coming from the harbour (as is likely) then go outside Psoradhia and then into the bay, taking care of the reef running out from the eastern side of the bay. You can also pass between Psoradhia and Kastellórizon, though the channel is narrow and the water so clear you could swear the keel is going to dredge a channel across the bottom. There are around 4m least depth in the middle of the channel but it shallows rapidly to the sides.

Much of Mandráki is fringed by shoal water so you need to anchor some way out in 3–5m on sand and rock, indifferent holding in places so make sure the anchor is well in. There is a good lee from the *meltemi* here and good swimming and snorkelling in the bay and around the reef. A taverna ashore serves good fresh fish and it is a short walk into Kastellórizon town.

ÓRMOS NAVLAKAS

⊕36°08'·0N 29°35'·2E

A fjord-like inlet on the east coast of Kastellórizon, reported to give good shelter from the *meltemi*. It is quite deep in places so you will probably have to take a long line ashore.

Nisís Ro (Áy Yeoryios)

The largish island lying off the west side of Kastellórizon. Until 1982 it was inhabited by the celebrated 'Lady of Ro', Despina Achladioti, who lived here alone for some 40 years and religiously hoisted the Greek flag every morning. In her later years she was feted by the Greeks and had a stamp issued in her honour and appeared on television. She was buried on the island with full military honours in 1982 and today there is just a small army post who keep raising the flag every day. According to some on Kastellórizon she was something of a battleaxe who, sadly, in the end was mis-used by mainland Greek nationalists for their own ends; the view on Kastellórizon is that she was as pragmatic as anyone else on the island whose lifeline is across the water in Kaş.

FRANGOLIMANI

⊕36°09'·1N 29°30'·2E

An inlet on the south side of Nisís Ro that is reported to afford good shelter from the *meltemi*. It is uncertain whether you can or cannot use this anchorage. Recent reports suggest the military do not like you stopping here and at present it may be best to avoid it. There is nothing ashore except goats and the army post.

Mediterraneo

Mediterraneo is a 1991 film by Gabriele Salvatores and written by Enzo Monteleone. It was filmed on Kastellórizon in 1990 and magically encapsulates the spirit of place. This place is the Mediterranean: the people, the culture, the coast, the climate and life around this enclosed sea. There is a magic about it that transcends the tired supermarket cynicism of our globalised lifestyle. You could describe the plot and the film as 'naïvely sentimental' and I'd go with that. Naïvety is much under-valued. And sentiment is fine as long as it's not sloppy nostalgia for an imagined past.

Mediterraneo follows a disparate group of Italian soldiers sent to a remote Greek island to scout and hold it against the British. The island in the film is Kastellórizon, which is about as remote a Greek island as you can get even now. Amongst the group are an artist, a farmer and a dedicated army sergeant. All of them are romantics and dreamers of a sort. When they arrive the island seems deserted and not long after there is an explosion on the horizon which is their relief ship being blown up. In the confusion of occupying the island one of them destroys the radio and most of them abandon hope of rescue.

The island then comes to life. It has not been depopulated after all – the islanders have been hiding, and when they realise the Italian soldiers are not going to harm them, they reappear. They are mostly women and the very young and very old. The Italians settle down to a life that could loosely be called 'paradise with a hard edge'. They have everything they need to eat, drink and amuse themselves. One of them falls in love with the local prostitute; another two fall for the beautiful shepherdess who believes a *ménage à trois* is how it all works. The artist starts painting murals in the church while others fish and help out around the village. Life settles into a rhythm under a sunny Mediterranean sky surrounded by aquamarine water.

It might last forever except for the war over the horizon. And end it must. This is a variation on the lotus-eaters theme, on escaping from the harsh reality of war and embracing life and love. Of course it's naïve, it doesn't explore the anti-war and embracing life themes except in a marginal way, but this movie touches a chord that others can't reach. Watch it and see the sun come out. It is in Italian with sub-titles, but don't let that put you off.

3

Dilek Boğazi (Samos Strait) to Marmaris

Restaurant jetty in Okluk Köyü

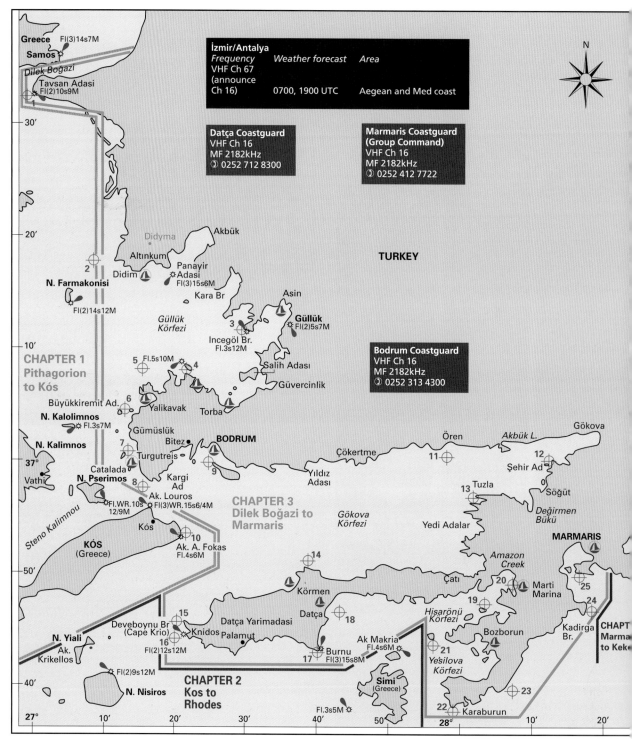

Greece Fl(3)14s7M
Samos
Dilek Boğazi
Tavsan Adası
Fl(2)10s9M

İzmir/Antalya
Frequency   Weather forecast   Area
VHF Ch 67
(announce
Ch 16)   0700, 1900 UTC   Aegean and Med coast

Datça Coastguard
VHF Ch 16
MF 2182kHz
☎ 0252 712 8300

Marmaris Coastguard
(Group Command)
VHF Ch 16
MF 2182kHz
☎ 0252 412 7722

30'

20'

Didyma
Akbük
Altınkum
Panayir
TURKEY
2
Didim Adası
N. Farmakonisi   Fl(3)15s6M
Kara Br
Asin
Fl(2)14s12M
Güllük   Güllük
Körfezi   Fl(2)5s7M
3
Incegöl Br.
Fl.3s12M
Salih Adası

Bodrum Coastguard
VHF Ch 16
MF 2182kHz
☎ 0252 313 4300

10'
CHAPTER 1
Pithagorion
to Kós

5 Fl.5s10M
4
Güvercinlik

Büyükkiremit Ad. 6
Yalikavak   Torba
N. Kalolimnos
Fl.3s7M
Gümüslük   Gökova
Bitez   Ören   Akbük L.
N. Kalimnos   **BODRUM**
37°   7   Çökertme   11   12
Turgutreis   Şehir Ad
Vathi   Catalada   Kargi   Yıldız   13 Tuzla
N. Pserimos 8   Ad   Adası   Söğüt
Fl.WR.10s Fl(3)WR.15s6/4M   **CHAPTER 3**   Değirmen
12/9M   Ak. Louros   **Dilek Boğazi to**   Gökova   Bükü
Kós   **Marmaris**   Körfezi   Yedi Adalar   **MARMARIS**
KÓS   10
(Greece)   Ak. A. Fokas   Amazon
Fl.4s6M   Creek
50'   14   Çatı   20   Marti 25
Marina
Körmen   19   24
15   Datça 18   Hisarönü
Deveboynu Br   Datça Yarimadasi   Körfezi   Bozborun   Kadirga   CHAPT
(Cape Krio) Knidos Palamut   Br.   Marma
N. Yiali   16   Ak Makria   21   to Keke
Ak.   Fl(2)12s12M   Fl.4s6M   Yeşilova
Krikellos   17 Burnu   Körfezi
Fl(2)9s12M   Fl(3)15s8M
40'   **CHAPTER 2**   Simi
N. Nisiros   **Kos to**   (Greece)   23
Rhodes   22 Karaburun
Fl.3s5M
27°   10'   20'   30'   40'   50'   28°   10'   20'

USEFUL WAYPOINTS

⊕**1** 0·25M W of Tavsan Adası
37°39'·01N 26°59'·63E WGS84

⊕**2** 2M SW of Tekağaç Burnu light
37°20'·03N 27°09'·73E WGS84

⊕**3** 0·5M W of Incegöl Burnu light
37°13'·75N 27°29'·65E

⊕**4** Mid-channel between Büyüktavşan and coast
37°09'·58N 27°21'·99E WGS84

⊕**5** 0·5M N of Gemitaşi
37°09'·4N 27°16'·5E

⊕**6** Mid-channel between Büyükkiremit Adası and Küçükkiremit Adası
37°05'·28N 27°13'·47E WGS84

⊕**7** 0·5M E of Çatalada light
37°00'·72N 27°13'·96E WGS84

⊕**8** 0·5M S of Hüseyin Burnu light
36°57'·33N 27°15'·85E WGS84

⊕**9** 0·25M W of Karaada (NW) light
36°59'·77N 27°25'·04E WGS84

⊕**10** 0·25M E of Ák Áy Fokas (Kós)
36°51'·67N 27°21'·69E WGS84

⊕**11** 0·3M S of Ören Burnu light
37°00'·86N 27°58'·07E WGS84

⊕**12** 1M W of Orta Ada (Şehir Adaları) light
36°59'·98N 28°11'·07E WGS84

⊕**13** 1M N of Koyun Burun light
36°56'·58N 28°01'·34E WGS84

⊕**14** 0·5M N of İnce Burun light
36°49'·19N 27°38'·45E WGS84

⊕**15** 0·5M W of İskandil Burnu (Knidos)
36°42'·75N 27°21'·17E WGS84

⊕**16** 0·75M W of Deveboynu Bükü (Knidos)
36°41'·45N 27°20'·90E WGS84

⊕**17** 0·75M S of İnce Burnu
36°38'·69N 27°40'·69E WGS84

⊕**18** 0·25M S of Uzunca Ada light (Datça)
36°43'·28N 27°42'·83E WGS84

⊕**19** 0·5M S of Tavşan Adası (Hisarönü Körfezi)
36°44'·99N 28°03'·38E WGS84

⊕**20** 0·5M N of Catalca Burnu (Keçi Bükü)
36°47'·31N 28°06'·69E WGS84

⊕**21** 1M W of Atabol Kayası
36°40'·33N 27°56'·31E WGS84

⊕**22** 1M SW of Karaburun light
36°32'·44N 27°57'·94E WGS84

⊕**23** 0·3M E of Kızılada Adası
36°35'·76N 28°08'·19E WGS84

⊕**24** 0·2M E of Kadirğa Burnu light
36°43'·81N 28°18'·47E WGS84

⊕**25** S entrance to Sark Boğazı (Marmarıs Limanı)
36°47'·83N 28°15'·84E WGS84

PREVAILING WINDS

The prevailing wind in the summer is the *meltemi* blowing down the coast from the northwest to west. Along this stretch of coast the wind tends to follow the contours of the coastline and blow into the gulfs. It follows the coast so closely that it blows right around Karaburun opposite Sími and southwest up the coast, though there are exceptions.

When the wind is lighter it tends to follow the coast a lot more closely than when it is stronger. With a stronger *meltemi* the wind eventually manages to get up over the geographical barriers in the way and blow more directly from the northwest. In the Gulf of Güllük the *meltemi* blows into the gulf from the west and west-northwest. On the northern side of the gulf there are gusts into some of the bays, but by and large the wind is funnelled into the gulf to blow from a westerly direction. Along the Gulf of Gökova the wind will gust down from the northwest along the north of the gulf as far as Çökertme or Ören. In the middle of the gulf the wind is channelled to blow from the west and WNW. Along the south side of the Datça peninsula the wind again gusts off the land from the northwest and across the isthmus at Datça itself it can fairly scream into the large bay with Datça at the head. Between Sími and Karaburun the wind is channelled to blow from the northwest. At Marmaris the wind again manages to get over the high land and is funnelled down into Marmaris Bay.

Generally the wind will blow at around Force 4–6 (11–27 knots), though at times it can get up to Force 7 (28–33 knots) or so, and where the wind gusts down off high land it can be anything up to Force 1–3 more than the wind over the open sea.

To temper all of this there is a thermal component from the large land mass of Asia Minor. Generally the wind will die down in the evening when the sun goes and will be lighter, in the morning, before the wind gets up again after midday. This is not an infallible rule and happens more in the spring and autumn than in the peak summer months of July and August. In spring and autumn winds are generally lighter, although depressions passing through the eastern Aegean can cause strong winds from the north or south for several days.

There are also katabatic winds to take into account and these are generally strongest in the autumn. Known areas for katabatic winds are at the eastern end of Gökova Körfezi and the eastern end of Hisarönü Körfezi. Generally the wind will blow from a north to northeasterly direction up to Force 7 or so for around 3–4 hours. Then all will be quiet again.

Fish farms

This part of the Turkish coast, and in particular the Gulf of Güllük, has long been populated with fish farms. Until recently they blighted many of the bays around this gulf, restricting anchoring space and turning the water to a murky green colour. A change in policy has led to fish farms being moved from many of these bays, out into the deeper waters off the islands in the gulf; around Ziraat Ada in the north part and Büyüktavşan and Salih Adası in the south. This welcome shift will hopefully allow the waters to recover, and bays to return to their natural state.

Please note that fish farms are frequently moved so the positions given on the plans and in the notes may change.

Quick reference guide

	Shelter	Mooring	Fuel	Water	Provisions	Eating out	Plan
Dip Burnu	C	C	O	O	O	O	•
St Paul's Bay	C	C	O	O	O	O	•
Port St Nikolao	B	C	O	O	O	O	•
Kovala Liman	B	A	B	A	O	C	
Güllük Körfezi							
Çukurcuk	B	C	O	O	O	O	•
Büyükturnali	C	C	O	O	O	O	
Didim Marina	A	A	A	A	B	B	•
Altınkum	B	C	B	B	B	A	•
Kuruerik Bükü	B	C	O	O	C	C	•
Akbük Limanı	C	C	O	B	C	C	
Kazıklı Limanı	B	C	O	O	O	C	•
Paradise Bay	B	C	O	O	O	O	
Çam Limanı	C	C	O	O	O	O	
Gök Limanı	C	C	O	O	O	O	•
Asin Limanı	A	AC	B	A	C	B	•
Isene Bükü	B	C	O	O	O	O	
Güllük	C	AB	O	B	B	B	•
Varvil Köyü	C	C	O	O	O	C	
Küyüçak	A	C	O	O	O	C	•
Salih Adası	C	C	O	O	O	O	•
Guvercinlik	C	C	O	B	C	B	•
Torba	B	A	O	B	C	B	•
Demir Limanı	C	C	O	O	O	O	
Ilica Bükü	B	C	O	O	O	C	•
Port Atami	B	A	O	A	O	C	•
Türk Bükü	B	AC	O	B	C	B	•
Gündoğan	B	AC	O	B	C	C	•
Agacbasi	C	C	O	O	O	C	
Yalikavak Limanı	B	C	O	O	O	C	•
Yalikavak Marina	A	A	A	A	B	B	•
Gümüslük	A	AC	O	B	C	B	•
Çatalada	C	C	O	O	O	O	
Turgutreis Marina	A	A	A	A	A	A	•
Gökova Körfezi							
Akyarlar	B	C	O	B	C	C	•
Aspat Köyü	C	C	O	B	O	C	
Karği Köyü	C	C	O	O	O	C	
Bağlar Köyü	C	C	O	O	O	C	
Ortakent	B	A	B	B	B	A	•
Bitez	B	C	O	B	C	B	•
Ada Boğazi	B	C	O	O	O	O	•
Gümbet	B	C	B	B	A	A	
Bodrum Marina	A	A	A	A	A	A	•
Kargiçik	C	C	O	O	O	C	•
Orak Adası	C	C	O	O	O	C	•
Alakisla	C	C	O	O	O	C	•
Çökertme	B	AC	O	B	C	C	•
Ören	O	C	B	B	C	C	
Akbük	C	AC	O	B	O	C	•
Gökova Iskelesi	C	C	O	B	C	C	•
Gelibolu	C	C	O	O	O	C	•
Şehir Adalari	B	C	O	O	O	C	•

	Shelter	Mooring	Fuel	Water	Provisions	Eating out	Plan
Söğüt	A	AC	O	A	C	C	•
Keşr	B	C	O	O	O	O	•
Değirmen Bükü	A	AC	O	A	O	C	•
Kargılıbük	A	C	O	O	O	C	•
Tuzla	B	C	O	O	O	O	•
Hirsiz Köyü	O	C	O	O	O	O	
Yedi Adalari	A	C	O	O	O	C	•
Catalca	C	C	O	O	O	O	
Amazon Creek	B	C	O	B	C	C	•
Velibükü	C	C	O	O	O	O	
Gökceler Bükü	B	C	O	O	O	O	•
Çati	B	C	O	O	O	O	•
Gölyeri	C	C	O	O	C	O	
Körmen	A	A	B	A	O	C	•
Mersinçik	C	C	O	O	C	C	•
Knidos to Datça							
Knidos	B	AC	O	O	O	C	•
Palamut	B	A	O	A	C	B	•
Mesudiye Bükü	B	AC	O	A	C	C	•
Parmak Bükü	C	C	O	O	O	C	
Karği Köyü	C	C	O	O	O	C	•
Datça	B	AC	B	A	B	A	•
Perili to Değirmen Bükü	B	C	O	O	O	C	•
Hisarönü Körfezi							
Çiftlik Limanı and Kuruca Bükü	B	C	O	B	C	C	•
Gönlücek	C	C	O	O	O	O	
Armak Bükü	C	C	O	O	O	O	•
Bençik	B	AC	O	A	O	C	•
Kuyulu Bükü	B	C	O	O	O	C	•
Marti Marina	A	A	A	A	C	C	•
Keçi Bükü	A	AC	O	A	C	B	•
Turgut	C	C	O	O	O	C	
Delikliyol Limanı	C	C	O	O	O	C	•
Selimiye	B	AC	O	A	C	B	•
Dirsek	B	AC	O	O	O	C	•
Yeşilova Körfezi							
Bozburun	A	A	A	A	B	B	•
Kiseli Adası	B	C	O	O	O	O	•
Söğüt Limanı	C	C	O	O	O	C	•
Bozuk Bükü to Marmaris							
Bozuk Bükü	B	AC	O	O	O	C	•
Serçe Limanı	B	C	O	O	O	C	•
Gerbekse	C	C	O	O	O	C	•
Çiftlik	C	C	O	O	C	C	•
Kadirğa	C	C	O	O	O	O	
Kumlu Bükü	C	C	O	B	C	C	
Turunç Bükü	C	C	O	B	C	C	•
Marmaris Netsel Marina	A	A	A	A	A	A	•
Albatros Marina	A	AC	B	A	C	C	•
Pupa Yat Hotel	B	AC	O	A	C	C	•
Marmaris Yacht Marine	A	A	A	A	C	C	•

ANCIENT CARIA

In ancient times the coast and the hinterland were divided into provinces that owed their origins to the indigenous population or to peoples who colonised it from other areas. In many cases it is difficult to determine whether an area was so named from the indigenous population or colonists or, as is often the case, a mixture of the two. Caria is one of those regions whose origins are unsure with conflicting evidence and ancient commentaries giving no definitive answer. Herodotus (484–425BC) tells us that the Carians were originally from the Greek Islands, subjects of King Minos of Crete, that they were great seafarers and fighters who manned the Minoan fleets. They were then called Lelagians and when the Dorian and Ionian Greeks spread from mainland Greece down through the islands, the Lelagians were forced across to the coast of Asia Minor. Thucydides, the Athenian historian (460–396BC), gives a variation of Herodotus' story. He claims the Carians were pirates throughout the Greek islands and that King Minos expelled them when their piracy got out of hand. Pausanias, that intrepid travel writer of the 2nd century AD, says that the Carians were a native race of Anatolia and that colonists from Crete had mixed with them and adopted their name.

Archaeological evidence tends to the opinion that the Carians were an indigenous race with a long history of their own. Colonists from across the water most certainly arrived here and were absorbed into the local population, along with new ideas and skills that were adopted by the native Carians. The brief mention Homer makes of the Carians in the 8th century BC is that they were 'barbarous of speech', and it is interesting that today the harshest dialect in western Turkey is still found in this region. Turks from Istanbul often comment that they cannot understand all that is said in Bodrum (and Turks from Bodrum say that is just as well).

Right through the Greek and Roman periods the Carians preserved their own identity. Greek and Roman architectural ideas were adopted and presumably so were matters of dress, diet, and religion. One thing the Carians were long famous for was their seafaring skill. As far back as the 6th century BC the Carian fighting fleet was a feared and respected force, though there is a curious tale told by Herodotus that rather confounds this apparent fame. When Xerxes was preparing his fleet for the invasion of Greece in 480BC, Artemisia, queen of Caria. not only contributed ships to the expedition but also joined the fleet in person. At the Battle of Salamis when the Persian fleet was routed by the numerically inferior Greek fleet, Artemisia managed to escape in an unusual way. While her own ship was being pursued by an Athenian ship, by design or accident she turned and bore down on a ship from her own side, a Calyndian vessel, and ramming it amidships sank it with all hands. The Athenian ship then left her alone presuming she must be fighting on the Greek side. Xerxes, watching from a distant hillside, assumed the Calyndian ship to be one of the enemy and was full of praise for Artemisia's bravery. Apparently none of the luckless Calyndians survived to tell the real story.

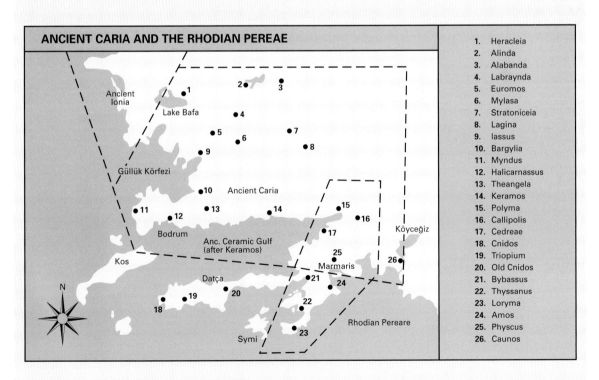

ANCIENT CARIA AND THE RHODIAN PEREAE

1. Heracleia
2. Alinda
3. Alabanda
4. Labraynda
5. Euromos
6. Mylasa
7. Stratoniceia
8. Lagina
9. Iassus
10. Bargylia
11. Myndus
12. Halicarnassus
13. Theangela
14. Keramos
15. Polyma
16. Callipolis
17. Cedreae
18. Cnidos
19. Triopium
20. Old Cnidos
21. Bybassus
22. Thyssanus
23. Loryma
24. Amos
25. Physcus
26. Caunos

ANCIENT CARIA (continued)

At its greatest Carian territory extended from what is now Lake Bafa in the north to Lake Köyceğiz east of Marmaris. In the north were the ancient cities of Heracleia, Alinda and Alabanda. In the south Caunos represented the most southerly Carian territory and overlapped into Lycia. The area corresponds almost exactly to the modern administrative province (*vilayet*) of Mugla. Caria remained intact through the great invasions that swept through Asia Minor without losing its identity, although that identity took a bit of a battering along the way. When the Persians dominated Asia Minor under Darius and Xerxes, Caria was part of the greater Persian Empire. However, with Xerxes' defeat by the Athenians and the formation of the Delian Confederacy, the Carian cities came under Athenian sway. With the Spartan victory over Athens in 405BC the Carian cities were under Spartan rule, though only for a brief 10 years until the Spartans were removed from power. The Persians now moved in again and divided their empire into satrapies, provinces ruled by a local governor who owed allegiance to Persia. In 377BC Mausolus became satrap of Caria and he craftily developed Caria into an independent power without upsetting his Persian masters. Alexander the Great stormed through the region in 334BC and with the aid of

Queen Ada, an exiled Carian queen, soon had the region firmly under his control. Queen Ada was installed as ruler and appears to have become something of a mother figure to the eccentrically talented Alexander. The death of Alexander in 323BC left a power vacuum and like much of the then civilised world, Caria was fought over by various groups, though none gained any lasting control.

The Romans finally sorted things out and with the defeat of the Macedonian King Phillip V in 197BC, order finally returned to the region. There were political hiccups with the arrival of Mithriadates in 88BC and Antony's orgiastic rule a little later, but the defeat of Antony by Octavius marked the beginning of an era of stable government and prosperity for Caria. Towards the end of the Roman Empire and the birth of the Byzantine, Caria began to decline, the population moved away, and the once great coastal cities lost their former power and some of their splendour. What happened in the interior is difficult to know: certainly Caria could no longer be considered a region but rather a collection of coastal towns. On the whole antiquity had been kind to Caria. The centuries that followed were to be less so as Caria became more and more a remote and forgotten region.

If you look at a map of Turkey and exercise a little imagination, in the southwest corner you will see what looks like a great gaping set of jaws snapping at the island of Kós just tantalisingly out of reach. To the north is another gulf with the island of Farmakonisi just offshore, and further south is another gulf enclosing the Greek island of Sími. To the east up a steep-to coast is the Bay of Marmaris just across from Rhodes. This region between the Gulf of Güllük and Marmaris encompasses the greater part of what was ancient Caria. For the inland sites in this area, excursions are best made from Bodrum or Marmaris where buses and *dolmuş* can get you to most of them. Alternatively, a hire car will let you cover more ground and offers greater flexibility so that you can spend as much or as little time at a site as you want. From Didim to Marmaris you can sail around the gulfs and coast spending as much or as little time as you wish looking at the ancient sites. At most of the sites there is a sheltered anchorage or a harbour nearby and even if you are not interested in ancient bits of rubble or have suffered from a surfeit of Graeco-Roman remains, only the most hard of heart can deny the romance of sitting on deck and watching dusk settle on the skeleton of a Cedreae or a Cnidos.

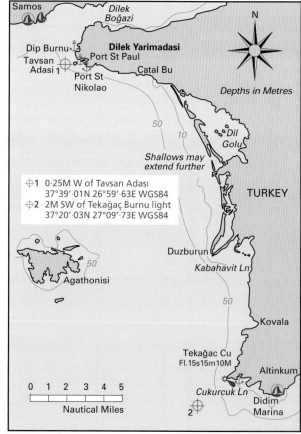

DILEK BOĞAZI (SAMOS STRAIT) TO THE GULF OF GÜLLÜK

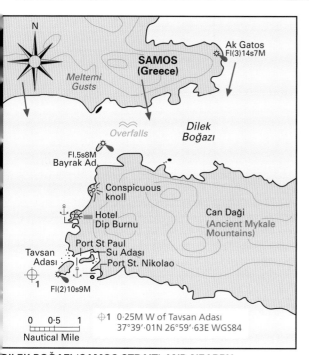

Port St Paul looking NE over Tavşan Adası

DILEK BOĞAZI (SAMOS STRAIT) AND NEARBY ANCHORAGES

Dilek Boğazi

In Greek, Diavlos Samou (Samos Strait). This chapter in this edition has been extended to cover Pithagorion on Samos and the adjacent Turkish coast from Dilek Boğazi. In truth this means just a clutch of anchorages around the mountainous divide of Dilek Yarimadasi, with no real anchorages after the peninsula until you get to Güllük Körfezi (the Gulf of Güllük). The ancient Gulf of Latmos provided refuge and sheltered anchorages in ancient times, but has now silted to the line of low brown water you will see along the coast. Care is needed as the silted areas extend further than shown on some charts. See the section below on *The Ancient Gulf of Latmos*.

Dip Burnu

A small bay on the western end of Dilek Yarimadasi that provides some shelter from the *meltemi*, but really should only be used in calm weather. Anchor in 4–5m off the shore. There is an army base here but little else. There is better shelter to be had in Port St Paul or Port St Nikolao on the south side of the peninsula.

Port St Paul

Off the SW corner of the peninsula lies Tavsan Adası with a conspicuous light structure on it.

Tavsan Adası partially shelters an anchorage tucked up under the peninsula that is also sheltered by another islet, Su Adası. Proceed on the east side of Tavsan Adası into the bay and anchor in 2–5m. The holding on sand and weed is bad and you need to make sure your anchor is well in. With the *meltemi* there are strong gusts down into the anchorage and, not surprisingly, some ground swell manages to work its way round into the bay.

There is a *jandarma* post nearby and there have been some reports of yachts being turned away from here. The bay is named after the irascible acolyte Paul, who is said to have put in here to rest his oarsmen after the task of rowing up the coast, presumably from somewhere like Miletus in the ancient Gulf of Latmos. Perhaps he was on his way to Ephesus where he lectured endlessly to the idolaters at the temple until eventually they tired of him and had him booted out. One thing for sure is that he was a tireless traveller who got around this end of the Mediterranean at a fair old rate given the means of travel available to him.

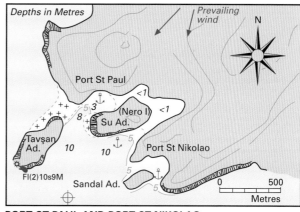

PORT ST PAUL AND PORT ST NIKOLAO
⊕ 37°38'·74N 26°59'·63E WGS84

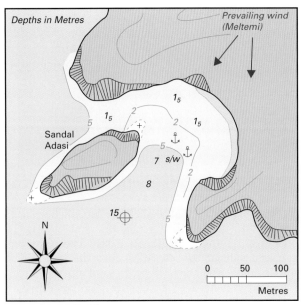

PORT ST NIKOLAO
⊕37°38'·80N 27°00'·95E WGS84

Port St Nikolao

The small bay, really a cove, on the east side of Port St Paul. A small islet, Sandal Adası, lies on the western side and the approach should be made leaving the islet to port. Proceed cautiously into the bay and anchor in 2–5m on a sandy bottom. There are some gusts down into the bay, but overall shelter is better than in Port St Paul. The only problem here is that it gets crowded if there are even four or five boats in here.

Port St Nikolao looking N

Off the islet there is said to be the wreck of a boat that you can dive over. Occasionally the soldiers from the *jandarma* post will wander around here, more out of boredom and in the hope of booze and cigarettes than for anything official.

Kovala Limanı

37°27'·12N 27°13'·14E WGS84

A shallow harbour near the outflow of the Menderes (ancient Meander) River. The harbour silts badly and at the time of writing a large part of the harbour on the eastern side has less than a metre and in places patches of mud at water level. Small trawlers and other fishing boats still get in here close to the outer breakwater, but only shallow-draught yachts or lifting keel yachts should attempt to get in here and then only in calm weather. In any case there is not a lot of room to berth.

There is a good fish restaurant nearby and the coast road runs into Altinkum.

GÜLLÜK KÖRFEZI (THE GULF OF GÜLLÜK, ANCIENT GULF OF MANDALYA)

Güllük Körfezi is a bite-sized gulf that is not nearly as deep or as wide as the other two gulfs to the south of it. That said, it is still a deeply indented gulf with a large number of anchorages around it and a couple of small harbours that offers an interesting and diverse cruising area, though some parts are more sympathetic than others. It also has the new Didim Marina on the northern side. It is the ancient Gulf of Mandalya and dotted around it are a number of important ancient cities and a few smaller ones with interesting connections. Today the gulf is pretty much ringed by modern towns in the shape of uniform holiday villages, though sadly they lack much in the way of amenities and there will be little mythology associated with them in the distant future.

On the north side of the gulf is Altınkum, a resort area run wild that in lots of ways resembles a wild west town, with unfinished roads, acres of identical villas in an alleged 'Mediterranean' style, and just inland from it the remains of the largest Ionic temple in the world ring-fenced from the burgeoning development all around it. In the far southeast corner of the gulf is Iassus, an altogether more gracious place where the ruins of the ancient city atop the slopes above the harbour are complemented by some small-scale tourism.

The Ancient Gulf of Latmos

From seaward it is impossible to visualise the coastline north of Altınkum as it was before the time of Christ. It appears uniformly flat and monotonous. Not until you take a trip inland, and survey from on high what is now a great plain crisscrossed with ditches to keep it drained, do you get any idea of what the ancient coastline was like. At the eastern end of the plain, Bafa Lake is all that remains of the Latmian Gulf, and even its salty waters are receding as more silt is brought down by the ancient Menderes or Meander river (Turkish: Menderes Nehri). At one time this river emptied into the sea some 15 miles further east.

Around the ancient gulf stood a number of great Ionian cities, including the greatest of them all, Miletus. Silting was taking place in ancient times and is not a modern phenomenon. Strabo tells us that the channel to the harbour at Priene had to be kept dredged. It should be remembered that the largest ships of this period drew little more than a metre or two. John Morrison gives the dimensions of a large trireme as: length 35m, breadth 4–6·5m, draught 1–2m. Trading vessels were appreciably smaller, and a typical 14m trader, such as the Uluburun wreck from the 14th–15th century BC would have had around 5m beam and would draw 1·5m, though when fully laden this could increase to 2m.

A tour around these ancient sites is much recommended, and I would say that you will get more out of these less visited sites than a visit to Ephesus, which although more complete, lacks some of the mystery of the Latmian sites.

Miletus Miletus was one of the birthplaces of western science and philosophy. Thales of Miletus, who lived in the late 7th century BC, was the first of the Ionian physical scientists. He attempted to determine the material basis of the world, finally determining it to be ultimately water. He is credited (by Herodotus) with

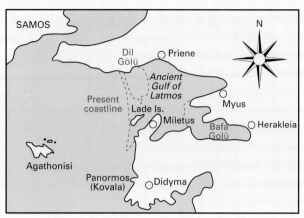

THE ANCIENT GULF OF LATMOS IN 500BC

having determined to within a year the solar eclipse of 585BC. He studied the cause of the Nile floods and devised a method to measure the height of the Pyramids. He is traditionally remembered as the archetypal absent-minded professor who fell down a well while mulling over a problem. Anaximander was a pupil of Thales who excelled in his studies of geography and astronomy and is credited with the first map of the world, a circular map showing the Mediterranean at the centre of the world and a great ocean surrounding Europe, Asia and Africa. Anaximenes, a contemporary of Anaximander, held that the material basis of the world was air, and not water as Thales had thought. What is extraordinary about this trio is that the basis for modern science and philosophy is established with their thinking and writing, and man had now moved from myth to logic (logos).

The ruins of Miletus are also extraordinary. As you approach them you will see the small museum on the left, and standing in a field on the right the Ilyas Bey Camii, a mosque built in 1404 with a huge domed centre, looking for all the world like a Byzantine church. Atop it there is usually a stork's nest. As you continue on all along the road there are the ruins of the city and in the distance the huge theatre built to seat fifteen thousand. It takes an effort of will to summon up what this great city, once the most powerful in the Greek world, was like, as now its four harbours have silted and all around are gently undulating plains. The only clue that this was once sea is the slightly boggy nature of the ground around here after rain.

The theatre at Miletus

The Temple of Athena at Priene

The ancient harbour at Herakleia under Latmos

Priene Occupies a spectacular site on a rocky shelf on the side of the ancient Mykale Mountains. The city was moved here from a site further inland when silting forced abandonment of the harbour. By Roman times the harbour at this new site had also silted. Consequently, Priene was never considered an important city during the Roman occupation, and its architecture was never adulterated by Roman modifications. It remains an excellent example of what an Ionian city was like, with few additions cluttering the site.

Myus Was situated on the banks of the Menderes in the NE of the ancient gulf. It was never a great city, and little of interest remains today. If you are going here the last bit is on a rough track and you will probably need to walk the final 500m unless you have a 4WD.

Herakleia (Herakleia-under-Latmos) You can get to the ancient city by hiring a boat from the campsite on the southern side of Bafa Lake, or you can drive there. Although it was never an important city, the ruins are picturesque on the stark slopes of Mount Latmos and it is

perhaps the most dramatic site around the gulf. The waters of the lake below help one to visualise what the city must once have looked like.

A legend associated with the site adds to its romance. Endymion, variously described as a king, a shepherd or mystic, was apparently a beautiful young man with whom the moon goddess, Selene, fell in love. She caused him to fall asleep forever so that she might look upon his beauty whenever she wished. The legend of Endymion endured into the Middle Age when the phrase 'the moon sleeps with Endymion' was commonly used to mean a mystical communion with God.

On an island nearby (Salih Adası) are a few remains of ancient Karyanda, a small provincial town in comparison with Iassus, remembered as the birthplace of Skylax. I confess to a special interest in Skylax, and indeed my latest yacht is called *Skylax*. Skylax of Karyanda is little known, but he is mentioned by Herodotus for his exploratory trip to India and he also wrote the first known pilot for sailors in Mediterranean waters, the *Periplus of Skylax* (or pseudo-Skylax), in which he says of Caria:

'And after Lydia is the nation Karia, and in it the following Hellenic cities: Herakleia; then Miletos; then Myndos with a harbour; Halikarnassos with an enclosed harbour and another harbour around the island and a river; Kalymna, an island; Karyanda, an island with a city and harbour (these people are Karians); an island, Kós, with a city and an enclosed harbour.'

(Transl. G. Shipley 2002)

So if you are sailing by Salih Adası, tip your hat to this early navigator and explorer who lived here some 2,500 years ago.

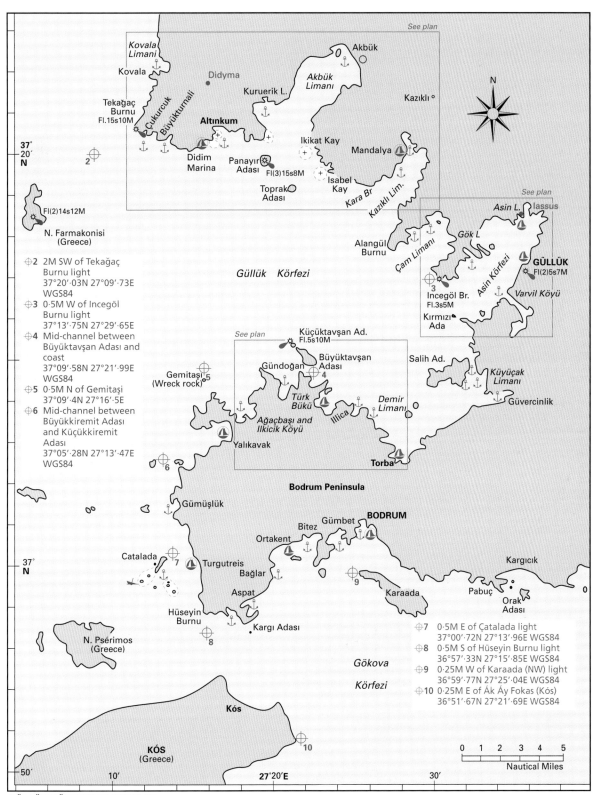

See plan

Kovala Limani
Kovala
Didyma
Kuruerik L.
Akbük
Akbük Limanı
Kazıklı °
Tekağaç Burnu
Fl.15s10M
Çukurcuk
Büyükturnali
Altınkum
Didim Marina
Panayır Adası
Fl(3)15s8M
Ikikat Kay
Mandalya
Isabel Kay
Toprak Adası
Kara Br
Kazıklı Lim.

N

Fl(2)14s12M
N. Farmakonisi
(Greece)

⊕2 2M SW of Tekağaç
Burnu light
37°20'·03N 27°09'·73E
WGS84
⊕3 0·5M W of Incegöl
Burnu light
37°13'·75N 27°29'·65E
⊕4 Mid-channel between
Büyüktavşan Adası and
coast
37°09'·58N 27°21'·99E
WGS84
⊕5 0·5M N of Gemitaşi
37°09'·4N 27°16'·5E
⊕6 Mid-channel between
Büyükkiremit Adası
and Küçükkiremit
Adası
37°05'·28N 27°13'·47E
WGS84

Güllük   Körfezi

See plan
Asin L.   Iassus
Alangül Burnu
Çam Limanı
Gök L
Asin Körfezi
GÜLLÜK
Fl(2)5s7M
Incegöl Br.
Fl.3s5M
Varvil Köyü
Kırmızı Ada

Küçüktavşan Ad.
Fl.5s10M
See plan
Gündoğan
Büyüktavşan Adası
Salih Ad.
Küyücak Limanı
Gemitaşi
(Wreck rock)
Türk Bükü
Demir Limanı
Güvercinlik
Ağaçbaşı and
Ilkicik Köyü
Illica
Yalıkavak
Torba

Bodrum Peninsula

Gümüşlük
Gümbet
BODRUM
Bitez
Ortakent
Kargıcık
Catalada
Turgutreis
Bağlar
Aspat
Karaada
Pabuç
Orak Adası
Hüseyin Burnu
Kargı Adası

N. Psérimos
(Greece)

Gökova
Körfezi

⊕7 0·5M E of Çatalada light
37°00'·72N 27°13'·96E WGS84
⊕8 0·5M S of Hüseyin Burnu light
36°57'·33N 27°15'·85E WGS84
⊕9 0·25M W of Karaada (NW) light
36°59'·77N 27°25'·04E WGS84
⊕10 0·25M E of Ák Áy Fokas (Kós)
36°51'·67N 27°21'·69E WGS84

Kós

KÓS
(Greece)

0 1 2 3 4 5
Nautical Miles

GÜLLÜK KÖRFEZI TO BODRUM

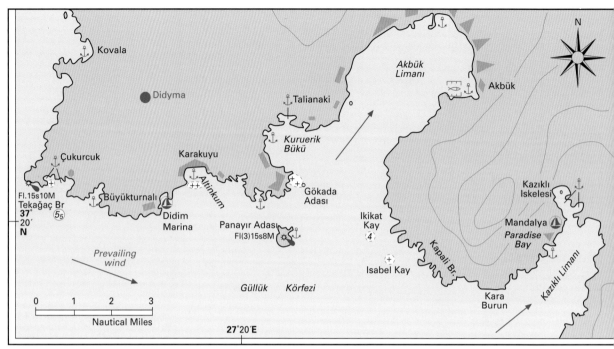

NORTHERN SIDE OF GÜLLÜK KÖRFEZI

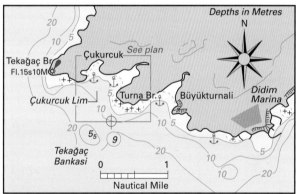

ANCHORAGES UNDER TEKAĞAÇ BURNU
⊕37°20′·6N 27°12′·7E

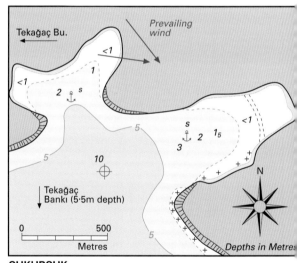

ÇUKURCUK
⊕37°20′·95N 27°12′·5E

ÇUKURCUK

At the northern entrance to Güllük Körfezi, Tekağaç Burnu is a low spit of land under which there are a number of anchorages. The lighthouse on the cape is easily seen from the distance. Closest to the cape is Çukurcuk where you can find good shelter from the *meltemi*. Care is needed in the approaches of Tekağaç Bankasi, a reef with 5·5m over lying approximately ¾ of a mile south of the anchorage. It is unlikely to bother most yachts, but the exceptional clarity of

the water makes it look a lot shallower and quickens the heartbeat for a bit.

The small west creek is no longer obstructed by a fish farm so motor in gently towards the east creek. The bottom shelves gently to the shore so you can potter in and drop anchor in 2–3m depths. The clarity of the water means that it looks a lot shallower than it is, but just edge in gently until you get to useful depths to anchor. The *meltemi* blows off the coast across the low-lying cape so you will be dropping back when you anchor. The bottom is sand and mud, good holding. The bay is open south so in unsettled weather this is not a place to be.

BÜYÜKTURNALI

Just east of Çukurcuk there is another bay which also affords reasonable shelter from the *meltemi*. Like Çukurcuk it is very clear and you should motor in gently to useful depths and drop anchor in 2–4m. The bottom is sand and mud, good holding.

Just over the brow of the hill further east the relentless development from Altınkum is spreading ever closer to these bays, so enjoy them while you can.

D-Marin Didim Marina looking W over the entrance
Didim Marina

D-MARIN DIDIM MARINA

A new marina, developed by the Dogus group, lying just west of Altinkum.

Pilotage

Approach The approaches are clear of dangers and the high outer breakwater is easily identified from the west and south. The masts of yachts inside will be seen and closer in the two mini-lighthouses at the entrance will be seen. There are good depths in the immediate approaches and inside the marina. Call up the marina on VHF Ch 72 (D-Marin Didim) when off the entrance and a RIB will come out to guide you in.

Mooring Berth stern or bows-to where directed. Laid moorings tailed to the pontoons or the quay. Marina staff will help you berth. Good all-round shelter and yachts are wintered afloat here. Charge band 3/4.

Anchorage At present yachts can anchor under the NE breakwater clear of the entrance where there is adequate shelter from the *meltemi,* which tends to blow from the WNW into the gulf. There is a buoyed swimming area off the beach and yachts should make sure they do not obstruct the area.

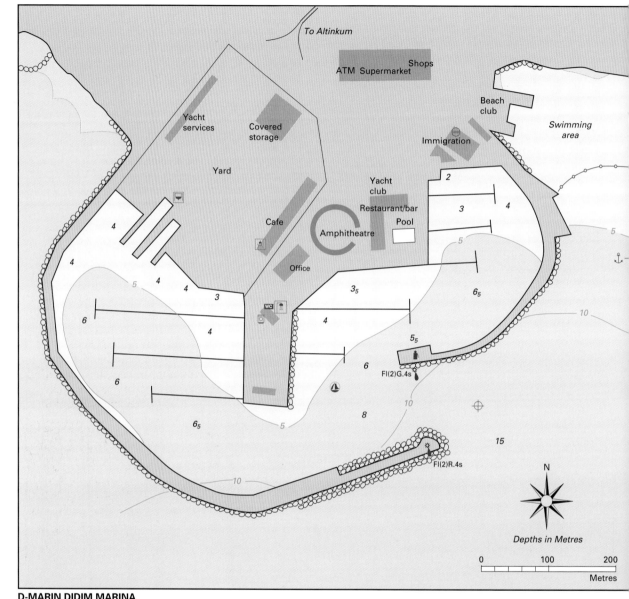

D-MARIN DIDIM MARINA
⊕37°20'·22N 27°16'·01E WGS84

Facilities

Services Water and electricity at all berths. Shower and toilet blocks. Laundry facilities. Wi-Fi. Fuel quay near the entrance. Electric golf cart service around the marina. Chandlers and full service boatyard.

Provisions Carrefour supermarket immediately behind the marina. Other shops in Altinkum.

Eating out Five-star restaurant at the Yacht Club. Snack bar/cafés behind the marina. Beach bar/café on the beach on the NE side of the marina. In the boatyard the workers' café has an excellent and cheap set menu for lunch. Otherwise walk into Altinkum where there are numerous restaurants.

Other Customs and immigration in the marina and yachts can clear in and out of here. ATMs. Hire cars and motorbikes. Regular *dolmuş* service to and from Altinkum. Bodrum Airport is around two hours away.

Didyma

Didyma was not one of the Ionian cities, but a religious sanctuary to Apollo, famed for its oracle long before that at Delphi became prominent. Oracles were issued as early as 600BC, and one of the earliest oracles inscribed here regarding piracy instructs the suppliant that 'It is right to do as your fathers did'.

Didyma was famed for its huge temple. The original temple to Apollo was destroyed by the Persian Darius in 494BC, and lay in ruins until Alexander the Great arrived. The remains of the huge temple that can be seen today date from 300BC, and although work continued on it for two hundred years, it was never finished. Some of the roughly hewn stonework and numerous unfluted columns can be seen. This is the largest Ionic temple in the world, measuring approximately 120m by 60m. It was largely destroyed by an earthquake in the 15th century, but sufficient columns remain in place to give an impression of its size.

If you come here expecting to find a wonderful isolated site you are in for a disappointment. The disaster area that is Altınkum means that resort apartments spread in a dusty straggling web around the site, taking away a lot of its mystery and power.

The temple at Didyma

General

D-Marin Didim Marina is a five-star oasis along this stretch of coast where the staff are welcoming, the manager goes out of his way to be helpful, and the Yacht Club is like a very luxurious second home where you can get a drink or a meal in convivial surroundings looking out over the pool and the marina. Within the marina is one of the largest yards I have seen attached to a marina, with a 400-ton travel-hoist and hard standing for hundreds of boats.

The marina is also conveniently situated for visits overland to the sites around the ancient Gulf of Latmos, to Miletus, Priene and Heracleia under Latmos, as well as to Ephesus. You can safely leave your boat here and hire a car or take an organised coach or mini-bus tour. My preference is to hire a car and drive yourself around the sites with the aid of a good guidebook. You can do a clockwise tour in a day starting with Didyma (get there early before the coach tours), Miletus, Priene and then back through Heracleia. If you

have overdosed on ancient bits of rock by the time you get to Priene, miss out Heracleia and retrace your route back to Didyma.

The marina is not cheap, but you do get five-star facilities so, go on, spoil yourself and grab a few days of luxury. The alternative is the hell-hole that is Altınkum immediately east and, trust me, you are better off cosseting yourself within the marina for trips ashore and to break up a passage in this part of the world.
☎ 0256 813 8081
www.dogusmarina.com.tr

ALTINKUM

Pilotage

Approach The coast here is fringed by rocks and reefs so make the approach from a little distance out. Altınkum itself is easily identified by the hotels and bars and restaurants surrounding the bay. What is not easily seen is the reef running across the entrance of the bay. You want to head for the eastern end of the bay and proceed in slowly with someone up front conning you as the reef obstructs much of the entrance. The end of the reef is sometimes marked by a pole or a small buoy, but do not rely on this. And don't be fooled by the local boats going around the western end of the reef. There is a passage here but for a first

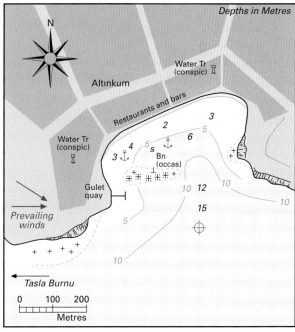

ALTINKUM (Skrophes Bay)
⚘ 37°20'·94N 27°16'·95E WGS84

Altınkum looking into the bay. Note the reef that just shows up off the *gulet* pier

time approach use the eastern end which is wider and deeper.

Mooring Once into the bay anchor in 3–6m on sand and mud keeping clear of the buoyed-off swimming area. Good holding and good shelter from the *meltemi*, although there are gusts into the bay.

Facilities

Provisions Good shopping for provisions in the town. Head out behind the town proper from the northwest corner of the bay to find minimarkets and fruit and veg.

Eating out There are more restaurants than you can shake a stick at around the bay, so just use your nose to sniff out somewhere you like. I have yet to find somewhere I would recommend.

Other Banks. ATMs. PO. Internet cafés. Hire cars and motorbikes.

General

What was once a small fishing village has mutated into a sprawling mass of look-alike reinforced concrete, a dusty unplanned resort that has spread to cover much of the nearby coast and extends inland for a fair distance as well. At night the bay resounds to over-amplified music from the clubs and bars so don't expect to get much sleep here. (If you get the feeling I don't much like this place you would be right.) It is not dissimilar to Faliraki on Rhodes or Kardamena on Kós in that it seems to exist solely for the sort of bad tourism that promotes sun, sex and cheap alcohol, so the whole place has little that is really Turkish about it.

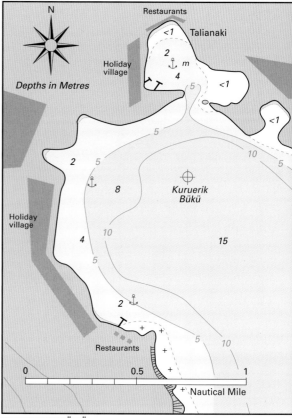

KURUERIK BÜKÜ
⊕37°22′·0N 27°20′·0E

KURUERIK BÜKÜ

Along the much built-upon coast from Altınkum is Kuruerik Bükü, an enclosed bay which affords good shelter but not solitude. As you coast around from Altınkum do not pass inside the low-lying Gökada Adası which is connected by a reef to the coast. Once into Kuruerik Bükü anchor on the west side of the bay in 2–4m on mud. Good shelter from the *meltemi*, although at times an annoying swell can creep around the cape, irritating rather than dangerous. Holiday villages and hotels line the shore and you will find restaurants and bars ashore.

In the north of Kuruerik Bükü is an enclosed lagoon, Talianaki, where you can anchor in 2–4m if there is room. Part of the bay is usually cordoned off with buoys as a swimming area. Again there are restaurants and bars ashore.

Kuruerik literally means 'dry plum', though whether that is a proper translation I'm not sure. Certainly there is not a lot of fresh water around

Akbük Limanı looking across to the spit in the north of the bay

on this stretch of coast so, who knows, perhaps the plums did shrivel under the hot Mediterranean sun in this part of the world.

AKBÜK LIMANI

This large bay in the northeast corner of Güllük Körfezi affords only limited shelter and while it was once a wilderness, those days are long gone. It is now almost entirely surrounded by holiday villages so that all you see are vast swathes of blank concrete.

There are several places you can anchor. At the very end there is an islet connected by a causeway to the coast. Anchor on either side of the islet or in a bight under a stubby headland just west of the islet. In both of these places there is adequate shelter from the *meltemi*, although a swell often works its way up into the large bay.

On the east side of the large bay there is a small harbour, at 37°23′·18N 27°25′·81E WGS84, used by local fishing boats and some tripper boats. A small yacht might find room behind the mole where there is good shelter. Ashore there are restaurants and minimarkets.

IKIKAT AND ISABEL KAYASI

As you proceed around from Akbük Limanı to Kazıklı Limanı, there are two reefs lying less than a mile offshore. Ikikat Kayası has depths of 4m over it, although the old Admiralty chart 1546 gives depths of just one fathom (2·2m) over it. To the southeast of Ikikat is Isabel Kayası with depths of 2·2m over it, although again Admiralty chart 1546 gives depths of just half a fathom (1·1m) over it. There are good depths inshore of the reefs or alternatively stay well offshore to avoid these two reefs.

KAZIKLI LIMANI

This large bay lies just around the corner from Akbük Limanı and as you start heading east from Akbük, the scenery changes from concrete to pine forest with just bits of development here and there. By the time you get to Kazıklı Limanı you are in a different world and for some of us, a better one. The entrance to the bay is relatively easy to identify as the low-lying land of the northern coast of the gulf rises up to higher land around the large bay.

There are several places a yacht can make for.

Paradise Bay An unnamed cove on the west side of the bay that has been given the moniker 'Paradise Bay' by some earlier cruising yachts. The mussel farms that were previously here have been removed and access to the bay is not now obstructed. Anchor near the head of the bay in 3–5m on mud, good holding. Good shelter from the prevailing wind in delightful surroundings.

Paradise Bay in Kazıklı Limanı

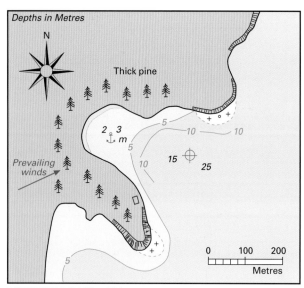

PARADISE BAY (Kazıklı)
⊕37°19´·1N 27°28´·1E

Just north of the bay a holiday village has been built and I suspect it is only a matter of time before development creeps down to this anchorage.

Mandalya Marina A new 'boutique' marina under construction on the west side of the entrance to Kazıklı Iskelesı.

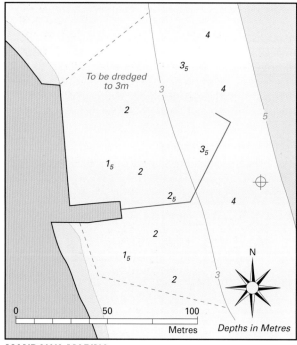

MANDALYA MARINA
⊕37°19´·9N 27°28´·6E

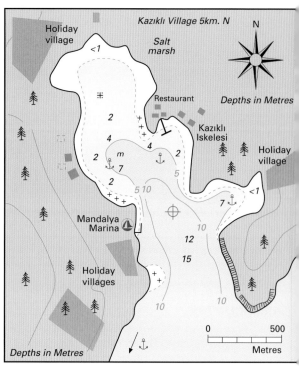

KAZIKLI ISKELESI
⊕37°20´·1N 27°28´·7E

Shore-side development is under way, with the jetty and pontoon installation to follow.

The project is aiming for completion in 2012.

Go stern or bows-to where directed. There will be laid moorings tailed to the pontoon. When complete there will be all the usual facilities including a restaurant.
ⓘ 0538 730 3700
www.mandalyamarina.com

Kazıklı Limanı looking NNE over Paradise Bay and Kazıklı Iskelesı

Kazıklı İskelesi At the head of the bay a yacht can anchor in several places depending on wind and sea. There is good shelter tucked into the west side of the bay or on the east side. Even when it is blowing outside it is usually calm in here. In the cove on the east side there is a jetty off a restaurant and yachts can go stern or bows-to with care. Not surprisingly there is good fish to be had on the menu.

At one time this was a small isolated enclave with just wild country ashore. No more. A number of holiday villages now surround the bay and it is a sound bet that more development will follow until the bay is ringed by concrete.

ÇAM LIMANI

The large bay on the west side of Incegöl Burnu before you head up into Asin Körfezi. There are several coves on the west side which provide some shelter from the *meltemi*, although some swell does tend to roll up into the bay. Inevitably fish farms have been sited along this more protected side of the bay and some care is needed manoeuvring around them. The cove about halfway up the west side of the bay affords the best shelter, although even here there can be some swell rolling in depending on the strength of the *meltemi* outside. The head of the bay can also be used although it affords less shelter than the coves on the west side.

Most of this bay is still wild country that has been little developed, except for the east side where holiday villages and villas are creeping down the coast.

ASIN KÖRFEZI

This small gulf at the southeastern end of Güllük Körfezi has a number of anchorages around it, as well as two harbours at Asin Limanı and Güllük. Of these, Asin Limanı is the only really usable harbour as Güllük has little room for yachts and is mainly used by small cargo ships and fishing boats. The gulf is free of dangers away from the coast and closer in most of the dangers are charted except for one: off Ince Burun there is an uncharted rock lying approximately 150m off the coast. See the relevant section for Ince Burun further on.

ASIN KÖRFEZI
⊕Incegöl Burnu light 37°12´·7N 27°31´·3E

Asin Körfezi looking SE across Ziraat Ada towards Güllük

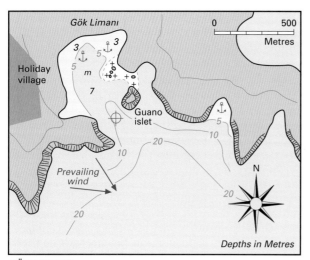

GÖK LIMANI
⊕37°14'·8N 27°32'·25E

GÖK LIMANI (NARLI BÜKÜ, SHIERO BAY)

Gök Limanı is the squiggly bay lying about halfway along the western side of Asin Körfezi. The exact location of the bay can be difficult to ascertain, but if you coast along here it will become obvious. Once you are heading up into the bay the islet in the approaches can be identified as it is white with guano. Care is needed of the reef off the islet and on the east side of the bay, but it is easily identified when closer in and there is plenty of room in the fairway.

Anchor in 3–6m on mud. Good shelter from the *meltemi* tucked into the northernmost bay. Development has spread around these slopes and inevitably a holiday village and villas are being built on the slopes.

On the other side of the long headland sheltering Gök Limanı there are several other coves that can be used. Fish farms are peppered around here and there, but you can still find room to anchor off. The exact location of the fish farms varies as they tend to be moved when too much detritus (uneaten food and fish poop) has been deposited on the bottom.

ASIN LIMANI
(Port Isene, Kurin, ancient Iassus)

Pilotage

Approach In the approaches the large abandoned hotel complex on the crown of the hill on the west side of the harbour is easily identified. As you close the inlet the castle on the eastern side of the inlet will be seen, and closer in the Byzantine tower on the east side of the entrance stands out well. Care is needed of the ancient breakwater just under the surface which extends from the western side of the entrance. It is not always easy to see, depending on the angle of the sun. At times the sunken breakwater is marked by some small red buoys, but don't rely on them. If you head for the Byzantine tower on a northerly course and aim to pass around 15–20m off it you will be in good depths and clear of the submerged breakwater. The end of the submerged breakwater is sometimes marked by a stick or a small buoy – in recent years an old ex-fish farm blue-grey 20-gallon drum has been used – but you should not rely on a mark being in place.

Mooring Go stern or bows-to the quay on the west side. The southern end of the quay is usually free. The bottom is mud and weed, good holding once the anchor is in. Good shelter from the *meltemi*. At night you may get a northeasterly land breeze, so make sure that you lay out a fair measure of chain and that the anchor is in and properly holding.

It is also possible to anchor with a long line ashore to the south of the jetty, though there is little benefit to be gained.

Asin Limanı looking NE over the harbour and the site of ancient Iassus

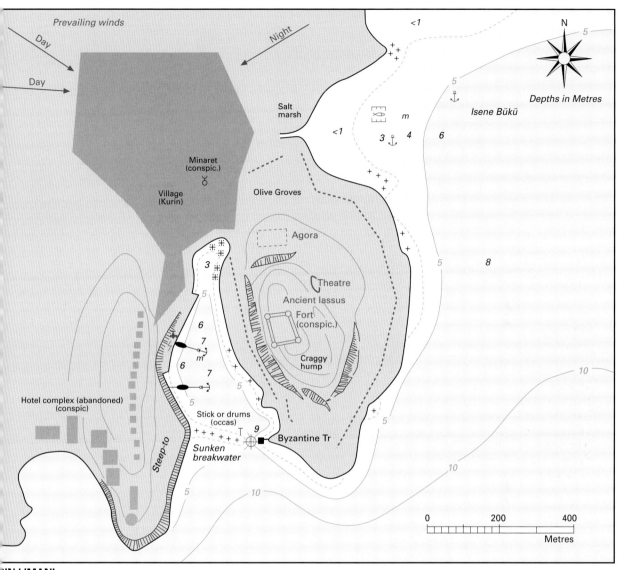

Prevailing winds
Day
Day
Night

Salt marsh
<1
<1
+ + +

Minaret (conspic.)
Village (Kurin)

Olive Groves

Agora

Isene Bükü

Depths in Metres

N
5
5
5
3 4 6

Theatre
Ancient Iassus
Fort (conspic.)
Craggy hump

3

5
6
7
m
6
7

5

5

Hotel complex (abandoned) (conspic)

Steep-to

Stick or drums (occas)
Sunken breakwater

9
Byzantine Tr

5
8

10

10

5

10

5

10

0   200   400
Metres

ƏIN LIMANI
37°16′·37N 27°34′·98E WGS84

Facilities

Services Water on the quay towards the north end. A mini-tanker may be able to deliver fuel to the quay. Electricity can also be connected.

Provisions Provisions in the village. You may be able to buy some mussels from the fishermen.

Eating out Restaurants around the harbour. These are friendly enough places and I'd suggest you just wander around and choose whichever one takes your fancy.

Other Taxi or *dolmuş* to Milas.

General

I like this place under the craggy slopes with the ruins of ancient Iassus atop the steep ridge, but many people seem to find it a bit of a mournful spot. The locals are friendly, it is rarely crowded, and the straggling village of Kurin is a delight to wander around with bits of ancient stone re-used in the village houses. On the eastern slopes the ruins of ancient Iassus are easily accessible and pleasantly informal. You will often find some of

Ancient Iassus

IASSUS (IASSOS)

The mythical origins of the city say that it was founded by Peloponnesians from Argos, and artefacts recovered from the site indicate that it was indeed occupied in Mycenean times, and later colonised from the Argive in about 900BC. It was also described as an island by ancient commentators, and it is entirely possible that the craggy hump connected by a low isthmus on which the Greek city sits was once an island: don't always doubt the myth-makers. Later it had a close association with the Milesians and became Carian in character. In the 5th century BC it became part of the Delian confederacy. It sided with Athens against the Spartans and Persians on numerous occasions, each time to its cost. It was sacked by the Spartans in 412BC, sacked again by Lysander a little later, and made a Persian satrapy in 387BC.

When Alexander arrived the people of Iassus fared better. Alexander was particularly moved by the story of the boy from Iassus who befriended a dolphin. Whenever the boy went to bathe in the sea the dolphin would come and let him ride upon his back. Coins of Iassus around this period bear the image of a boy riding on the back of a dolphin, so it evidently made an impact on the citizens of Iassus. The story relates that one day the dolphin attempted to follow the boy ashore and was stranded on the beach and died. The boy was inconsolable and soon afterwards dived into the sea and swam out until he drowned. Another story (with less melancholy measure) relates that Alexander appointed the boy as a priest in the Temple of Poseidon in Babylon because of his association with the dolphin and the sea.

George Bean relates another story, told by Strabo about the inhabitants: 'Most of the wealth of Iassus came from fish, particularly the export of salted fish. One day the inhabitants were watching a performance in the theatre when the gong signalling the start of the fish market was sounded and all but one of the audience rushed off to do business there. An actor came up to thank the old man who had remained behind and he, cupping his hand to his ear, exclaimed he had not heard the signal and promptly shuffled off to join his fellow citizens at the market.' In fact, at the head of the gulf much of the land has been reclaimed, including that on which Bodrum Airport sits, and was in antiquity a large inland sea rich in fish stocks. Iassus controlled the fishing industry in this sea and it is likely that, as at Caunos, fish farming is not a new phenomenon.

After siding with Athens, Iassus sided with Mithridates against the Romans, and so Sulla let pirates sack it to teach the inhabitants a lesson. They seem to have had an uncanny knack of teaming up with the losing side. Iassus declined after this, but was the seat of a bishopric during Byzantine rule. The fort on the top of the craggy hump was built by the Knights of St John.

To the west of the hummock with the ruins atop is a long irregular wall, over a mile in length before it turns towards the coast, which then apparently ran back along the coast around the unfinished hotel to form a large compound. This is a massive wall, over 2m thick in places, with watch-towers and fortified gates. Inside the foundations of numerous buildings have been found. It

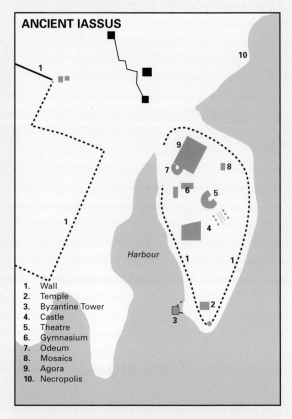

ANCIENT IASSUS

1. Wall
2. Temple
3. Byzantine Tower
4. Castle
5. Theatre
6. Gymnasium
7. Odeum
8. Mosaics
9. Agora
10. Necropolis

is thought to have been built around the 4th century BC, possibly by Mausolus from Halicarnassus, though for what reason is unknown.

The ruins of ancient Iassus on the hummock or 'island' have been partly excavated by the Italian school, who return each summer to continue the excavations. The Temple of Zeus, the city wall, the *agora* and a small theatre, the theatre proper, and parts of the land wall for the city can be seen today amid the olive groves. The site is enchanting.

Asin Liman looking out to the entrance

the village livestock grazing under the old olive trees in the *agora* at the foot of the slopes.

The uncompleted hotel complex on the top of the western side was abandoned because it didn't have planning permission and in any case is on the unexcavated remains of part of ancient Iassus. Given that it has not the slightest bit of architectural merit alongside the ancients' workings, lets hope it decays into something a little more attractive.

ISENE BÜKÜ

The large bay on the north side of the headland on which ancient Iassus sits is a useful anchorage with good shelter from the *meltemi*. There is a fish farm in the bay, but still plenty of room to anchor off the beach with wetlands behind. Anchor in 3–5m on mud and weed, good holding. You can also anchor with a long line ashore on the west side of the bay, taking care of the rocky patches off the coast.

The wetlands behind are rich in bird life. A number of masonry structures, possibly part of an ancient necropolis, are scattered about the marsh and the shore, although nearer the shore there may have been an old shipbuilding yard from Byzantine or Ottoman times.

GÜLLÜK (Küllük)

Güllük is a port lying pretty much opposite Asin Limanı. You will sometimes see ships anchored out in the gulf waiting to come into the harbour although most ships now use the new commercial harbour 1M north of Güllük.

Güllük

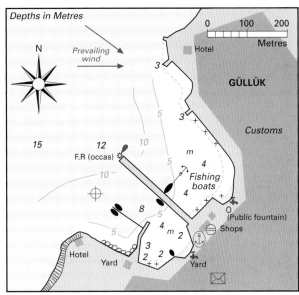

GÜLLÜK
⊕ 37°14′·4N 27°35′·8E

Pilotage

Approach The cluster of buildings around the coast and the central pier are easily identified. The approach is free of dangers, although the *meltemi* blows straight into here and you should have all sails down before you enter the harbour.

Mooring There are few places for a yacht to berth although it may be that the old cargo pier will be developed for yachts now the new commercial harbour is completed. You may find a berth under the stubby jetty in the southeast corner and this affords the best shelter. Alternatively try the new pontoon on the outside of the jetty. Do not rely on finding a berth here. In calm weather if you just want to do some shopping you may be able to tie up to the central pier, though the authorities are not always keen on this. Alternatively try anchoring out on the north side well clear of the pier for a short stay in calm weather. The berths on the pier and at anchor are not safe when the *meltemi* is blowing.

Facilities

Services Water on the quay in the southeast corner; a mini-tanker can deliver fuel by arrangement.
Provisions Good shopping for provisions with a Migros supermarket nearby.
Eating out Several restaurants around the harbour.
Other PO. ATM. *Dolmuş* to Milas and Bodrum.

General

Güllük is a hub for fishfarm boats, though a small sleepy one that seldom has too much activity going on. Emery ore is shipped out from the hinterland and incoming cargo varies from heavy machinery to bulk goods. The coast around Güllük has now been much developed and holiday villages and hotels stretch along the coast either side of it. The centre of Güllük around the harbour remains pleasantly low-key, with a small yard and fishing boats. At one time *gulets* used to be built here and some of these had more shapely hulls than the *gulets* built elsewhere. These hull shapes were reminiscent of old pilot cutters and really quite beautiful to look at.

VARVIL KÖYÜ (Ulelibük, ancient Bargylia)

⊕37°12'·8N 27°34'·35E WGS84

A large bay to the south of Güllük. A large holiday village lies on the south side of the marshy bay. Care is needed entering the bay as rocks fringe the sides and depths come up quickly to the marsh at the head. Anchor before you get to the fish farm in the bay in 5–6m on mud, good holding. Around the shores villas have been built,

and it is difficult to imagine what the place was like when the city of Bargylia stood on the southern shore.

Some of the ruins of ancient Bargylia remain, but much of the ancient stone has been carted off elsewhere and recycled into newer buildings. It is also likely that some of it has been lost in the rash of development now taking place. The present name Varvil preserves the ancient name ('b' is pretty much interchangeable with 'v' in Greek). The city was not of great importance and seems to have prospered from the 3rd to the 1st centuries BC. You can see some of the remains of the city on the southern side to the east of the holiday village.

Ince Burun

Uncharted rock 37°11'·30N 27°32'·11E WGS84

On the south side of Ince Burun (more a squiggly headland than a full blown cape) there is a small private harbour attached to a hotel and villa complex. Care is needed in the vicinity of the cape as there is an uncharted rock just under the surface in the position given above. The reported position lies approximately 150m due south of the breakwater head.

Küyüçak looking across to Salih Adası   *Kadir Kir*

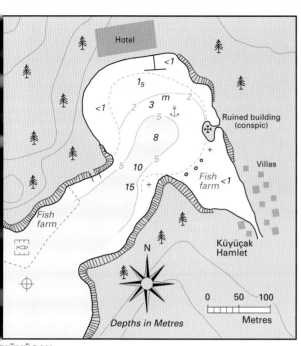

KÜYÜÇAK
⊕37°08′·83N 27°32′·74E WSG84

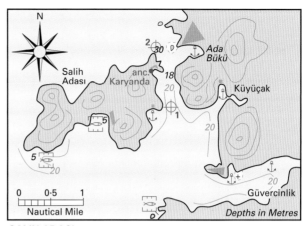

SALIH ADASI
⊕1 37°09′·58N 27°32′.30E WGS84
⊕2 37°09′·96N 27°32′.13E WGS84

Yachts are usually permitted, if there is room, to go into the small harbour where there is good shelter. Restaurant ashore in the hotel.

KÜYÜÇAK

An inlet on the east side of the channel between Salih Adası and the coast. There are fish farms all around this channel and in the entrance to Küyüçak. Once you are in the entrance you will see a stone building standing on a T-shaped projection into the head of the bay. Head into the anchorage on the north side of the bay. The south creek is shallow. Sunsail used to run a watersports club here but not any longer. The hotel is now a brash resort with loud music and it's fair share of Balkan and Russian tourism. If you are looking for peace and quiet this is not the place. A pier runs out from the hotel, but it is used by a watersports club.

Ashore there is a restaurant and minimarket in the hotel. Küyüçak village is down around the southern creek. The ruined building in the bay is a ghostly reminder that this was once a Greek village as much of this coast was populated by Greeks prior to the population exchanges in the 1920s.

Salih Adası

The island opposite Küyüçak. There are a number of anchorages around the island, though most of these are much encumbered by fish farms. The fish farms tend to be moved from time to time so the positions given may not be exact. Usually you can find somewhere to squeeze in around the fish farms, though shoreside there will often be a rubbish tip for the old containers of fish food and the surrounding water is rarely clear because of excess fish food and other detritus. The bay on the southeast side where the anchor is shown is usually free of fish farms and you can anchor in 3–5m. Good shelter from the *meltemi*.

That aside, the island is an attractive place with a cluster of villas around the bay on the south side and several anchorages on the east side as indicated on the plan.

GÜVERCINLIK

A large bay under Küyüçak running back east to the coast road between Milas and Bodrum. Once you are up to the entrance the houses around the head of the inlet and hotels and villas along the south side will be seen. A number of chalets on the northern headland also stand out.

The best shelter is in the cove under the northern headland. Otherwise anchor off the village. Although the *meltemi* blows straight into the bay, it lifts a little at the head and the swell coming in is rarely dangerous. The holding on mud and weed is reasonable. If the wind does kick in and push a bit of chop up into the bay then go

Skylax of Karyanda

On the northeast corner of Salih Adası there are a few overgrown ruins of ancient Karyanda. The site has not been excavated but I'm sure that under the terraces there would be plenty to find. There are enough ashlar blocks around and bits of a column, pottery sherds and other ancient bric-a-brac to suggest there was a sizeable town here. Unfortunately a fish farm processing plant is being built over part of the site on the isthmus and the manager was adamant he did not want me wandering around.

The city was never an important one, although Skylax does say it had a harbour, though he may have meant a sheltered anchorage – probably the bay on the east side in the channel. It was not a Lelegian town as many on the Bodrum peninsula were at the time, but appears to have been a Carian/Hellenic town from the early Classical period (7th to 6th century BC? although pottery found here is only dated to the 4th century BC). Skylax of Karyanda (c.5–6th century BC) mentions it as his home. At some time in its history, possibly in 300BC, the site of the city was moved to the shores of a lake on the mainland, usually identified as that at Golkoy on the coast opposite. Here there is evidence of a Byzantine settlement, under which may be the Mk II version of Karyanda.

I have a personal interest in all this as I have long been interested in Skylax of Karyanda, who probably wrote the first *Periplus* or pilot for the Mediterranean and was also appointed by the Persians to explore the eastern boundaries of their empire. Herodotus tells us a little about this extraordinary man after whom my boat is named, and for the rest we have to interpolate a bit. The map of his travels is my best guess at where he travelled, given that he was to explore the eastern boundaries of the Persian Empire a few decades before its expansion to the borders shown for 490BC.

Darius appointed Skylax to make the trip possibly in 519–512BC. He sailed up the Aegean coast to the Black Sea and then east to what is now Georgia, where he trekked overland to the head of the Indus River (Greek Sinthos), probably somewhere around present-day Islamabad. From here he travelled down the Indus to the Indian Ocean. It is likely he walked the initial stages as the river is difficult to navigate, but in the Indus

The site of ancient Karyanda – did Skylax live there?

Valley it slows and can be navigated. In 1857 the British constructed a 377ft steamer for the lower reaches of the Indus, although it only drew 2ft and was powered by paddle wheels for the shallower sections where propellers would foul the bottom. From here Skylax made his way round the Arabian peninsula and up the Red Sea to Egypt and then home to Karyanda. It is likely he used local craft to make the last part of the voyage as we know this was already a popular sea trading route.

No account of this expedition by Skylax remains and we only know of it from Herodotus and Aristotle. A *Periplus of the Mediterranean* survives, but this has later additions and so is usually known as the Periplus of Pseudo-Skylax. I and a number of others believe that this pilot is probably from Skylax with later additions, but that is all a matter of conjecture and for the time being Skylax is remembered by a few interested scholars, and in the name of my boat.

For more information on Skylax and Pseudo-Skylax see www.mediterraneansailing.info

Stump of a column used by local fishing boats to tie up to on Salih Adası

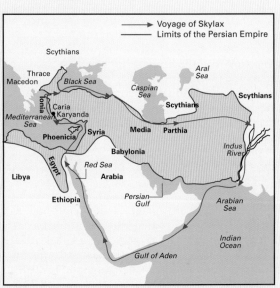

PERSIAN EMPIRE IN 490BC (Showing Skylax expedition)

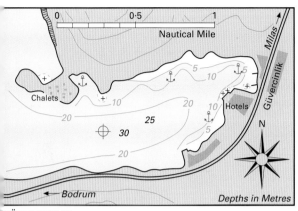

GÜVERCINLIK
⊕37°07´·88N 27°33´·77E WGS84

up into the cove in the NW corner where it is better sheltered.

At the head of the bay there are restaurants and cafés and several minimarkets. In the summer this is a popular place and fairly hums with people in the evenings. The main road runs around the head of the bay and you can get a bus or *dolmuş* to Bodrum from here.

The anchorage in the cove on the northern entrance to Güvercinlik *Kadir Kir*

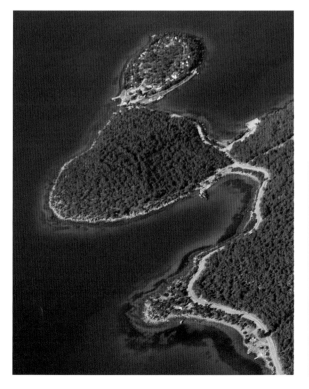

TORBA

Pilotage

Approach This small harbour lies in the southwest corner of Torba Limanı (Turfunda Bükü). If you are approaching from the west you won't see the harbour and village, but you will see several large hotel and apartment complexes spreading eastwards around the bay. There are no dangers in the approaches except for the shoal patch (3·7m) off Ilica, and once into the bay the harbour and entrance are easily identified.

Mooring You may be able to find a berth stern or bows-to on the inside of the outer breakwater, although in the summer this is a busy place and there may not be a berth. In settled weather you can go on the outside of the breakwater with a long line ashore to it. There is adequate shelter here as the *meltemi* tends not to blow into Torba Bay. Inside the harbour there is good all-round shelter.

To the east of Torba there are a number of jetties associated with the hotels or apartments ashore. These are usually busy in the summer with tripper and watersports boats.

Facilities

Provisions Several minimarkets in the village.

Eating out There are several restaurants around the edge of the harbour and others inland. Just go and sniff one out, although the Zeytin Dali has been recommended for its *gozleme* (crêpes) and *manti* (Turkish tortellini).

Other Dolmuş and taxi to Bodrum.

Torba Bay with Torba harbour top left *Kadir Kir*

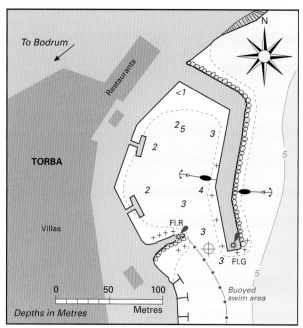

TORBA
⊕37°05′·3N 27°27′·5E

GÜLLÜK KÖRFEZI – SOUTH COAST

General

Torba is a fairly upmarket sort of place with villas and boutique hotels dotted around the slopes, and that means it has a pleasantly low-key atmosphere without excessive decibels. It is likely that Torba has long been used as a harbour because it has such a good lee from the *meltemi*. Few historical remains can be found apart from a Byzantine church on the slopes to the east. The little harbour is a pleasant spot with sympathetic restaurants around it and if you are anchored on the seaward side of the breakwater, there is the bonus of swimming straight off the boat in clear water.

Torba looking over the harbour to the entrance

DEMIR LIMANI

A small bay just over two miles northwest of Torba. The shoal patch off the entrance (least depth 3·7m) is easily spotted in good light. Anchor near the head of the bay. There is a jetty here used by *gulets* and you may be able to find a berth on here, though it would pay to reconnoitre first in the dinghy to see what depths there are. The shelter in here is good as the *meltemi* blows across the mouth of the bay, but some swell inevitably curves around into the bay, making it a bit uncomfortable.

There has been some development around the head of the bay in recent years.

ILICA BÜKÜ (Cennet Köyü)

A long inlet under wooded slopes just round the corner from Denir. The entrance is easily identified and there are considerable depths right on into the bay. Atami Hotel and Port Atami on the west side will be seen once into the entrance. The fish farms have been moved from the bay though this may be only for the summer as the buildings ashore are still there.

1. Anchor at the head of the bay in 5–8m and take a long line ashore. The bottom is mud and weed, good holding once the anchor is in. Good shelter from the *meltemi* although some

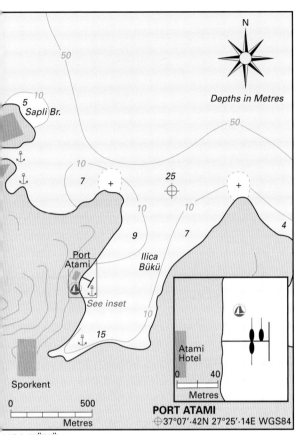

PORT ATAMI
⊕37°07'·42N 27°25'·14E WGS84

LICA BÜKÜ
⊕37°07'·75N 27°25'·33E WGS84

line ashore in either of the two coves. It is quite deep here so you will need a fair amount of chain. A holiday village has now been built on Sapli Burnu so the place is no longer the peaceful haven it used to be.

TÜRK BÜKÜ (Goltürkbükü)

Pilotage

Approach All around the west side and the head of the bay are holiday villages, apartments, villas and hotels, none of them much use in identifying exactly where you are. At Golkoy there are yet more houses and hotels. Thankfully the large islet (appropriately called Büyük Ada, 'big island') on the western side of the entrance is reasonably easy to identify, although it does tend to merge into the land behind from the distance. The approaches are free of dangers so even if you are not sure exactly what is where, you can sail into the bay and once inside things become clear. Like Ilica most of the fish farms are moved in the summer. If you are sailing into the bay there can be strong gusts off the high land on the west and especially through the channel between the islets and the coast. If a strong *meltemi* is blowing it is best to get sail off before you get into the bay.

swell does work its way down into the bay. Sporkent holiday village is nearby. Ilica means 'fresh- or hot-water spring' and apparently somewhere in the bay a spring bubbles up from the bottom.

2. ***Port Atami*** Off the hotel on the west side a T-pontoon has been laid. This is part of Atami Hotel on the slopes above. Go stern or bows-to where directed. Laid moorings tailed to the pontoons. Good shelter from the prevailing wind blowing into the gulf. Water and electricity on the pontoons. Security and shower and toilet facilities.

   The hotel has an excellent restaurant and serves Japanese food at lunch time. The hotel is run by a Turkish-Japanese couple and exhibits a certain flair for tasteful design. You can use the hotel facilities by negotiation. Charge band 4.

3. ***Sapli Burnu*** Under Sapli Burnu to the west of Ilica there are two coves that provide good shelter from the *meltemi* provided you are tucked right in close. Anchor and take a long

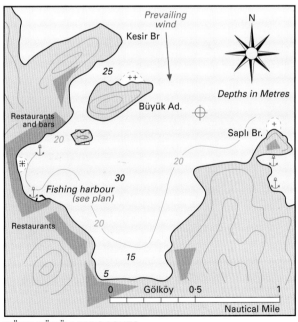

TÜRK BÜKÜ APPROACHES
⊕37°08'·14N 27°23'·78E WGS84

Mooring There are several places yachts can go inside this large bay.

1. On the west side of the bay yachts can anchor off in 10–15m. A reef runs out from the middle of the bay for about 100m and most yachts anchor to the north of this short reef where there is good shelter from the *meltemi*. The bottom is mud, sand and weed, patchy holding in places, so make sure your anchor is well in as the *meltemi* tends to gust down into the anchorage.

2. **West side piers** Most of the restaurant/bars on the west side have constructed wooden piers out into the water. Mostly these are for restaurant/bar customers to swim off, but you may be able to moor stern-to by negotiation. You would be expected to eat in the restaurant.

3. **Türk Büku fishing harbour** In the southern corner of the bay there is a fishing harbour. There is little room inside, although there may sometimes be a space. Yachts can also go stern-to the outside of the breakwater which has been fashioned into a quay. Care is needed of underwater rubble close to the quay. There are some laid moorings but usually you use your own anchor.

Fashionable Türk Büku

In the summer the bay can get very crowded with *gulets*, tripper boats and yachts kept more or less permanently here throughout the summer.

Facilities

Services Water and electricity on the quay in the fishing harbour and on some of the jetties by arrangement.

Provisions Numerous minimarkets in Türk Büku village or in Golkoy.

Restaurants There are some pretty upmarket restaurants around the west side of the bay, much frequented by the jet-set from Istanbul and Ankara. Yakamoz restaurant (also has a *pide* restaurant) and Guverte serve good food. Tiyatro and New Yorker are more upmarket places.

Other ATM. PO. *Dolmuş* and taxi to Bodrum.

General

At one time Türk Büku was a modest little fishing village, but that was 30 years ago and it bears no resemblance whatsoever to its former self. Türk Büku has become an upmarket resort where the inhabitants allegedly come to escape from the noise and chaos of Bodrum, but for anyone who has been here it soon becomes obvious that they have brought the noise and chaos with them. It is not a quiet place at night and it gets very, very crowded in the summer.

Golkoy on the eastern side is a somewhat more modest place, though it too has its fair share of tourism. Golkoy (Gol means lake) is thought to be where Karyanda was removed to from Salih Adası. Strabo tells us that Karyanda was moved to a position by a lake and this lake was called

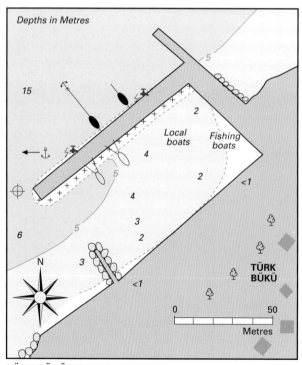

Depths in Metres

TÜRK BÜKÜ FISHING HARBOUR
⊕37°07′·74N 27°22′·72E WGS84

Türk Bükü looking onto the anchorage on the western side of the bay

Lake Karyanda. The 'lake' at Golkoy is now much diminished and little more than a marsh, but the name of the Turkish village probably recalls something more like a lake. There are the remains of a Byzantine town here and it is likely that somewhere underneath is the mainland site of Karyanda.

In recent years the two villages were merged into the one entity and re-titled Goltürkbükü. It is interesting that these names (including Türk Bükü) are all recent. When I first came here more than 30 years ago the bay was called Rum Bükü after the Greek village that had been here for centuries. Rum is a corruption of 'Rome', the word signifying that the inhabitants were non-Turkish and Christian, including Greek Orthodox. It was soon changed to Türk Bükü and has now become Goltürkbükü.

GÜNDOĞAN (Farilya, Phariah)

Pilotage

Approach The island of Büyüktavşan Adası is easily identified and Küçüktavşan Adası has a conspicuous white light structure on it. (Tavşan means 'rabbit', so they are 'Big Rabbit Island' and 'Little Rabbit Island' respectively.) An old Greek church will be seen on the summit of Büyüktavşan. The slopes around Gündoğan and the smaller bay to the east are now almost entirely encircled by holiday villages, though the extent of them makes identification of any one salient point

difficult. The entrance to the bay is free of dangers and once into it things become clearer.

Mooring There are several places a yacht can go.

1. **Gündoğan harbour** If there is room small yachts may find a berth in the harbour. Most of the space is taken up by local boats and tripper boats, so do not rely on finding a berth here. Good shelter inside. Yachts can also anchor with a long line to the outer breakwater in calm weather. With the *meltemi* blowing this is not the best option here.
2. **Southwest corner** There is a T-jetty here where there may be space, although it is usually full of tripper boats. You can also anchor off here, although shelter is only mediocre from the *meltemi* and some swell rolls in.
3. **West side** Anchor off the bight on the west side in 10–15m. Better shelter than in the southwest corner but still uncomfortable with the *meltemi*.

The bottom in the bay is mud, sand and thick weed, not everywhere good holding.

Facilities

Water from a tap in the harbour. Minimarkets in the village at the head of the bay. Numerous restaurants and cafés around the waterfront.

General

Gündoğan, like its neighbour Türk Bükü, is an attractive bay obliterated by the development of just about every square metre of land around it.

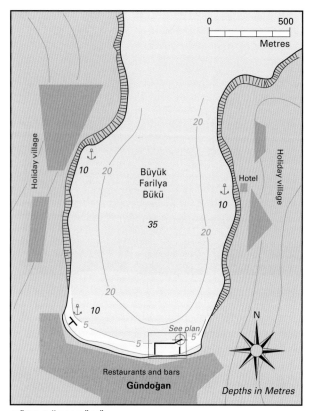

GÜNDOĞAN BÜKÜ
⊕37°07´·88N 27°20´·86E WGS84

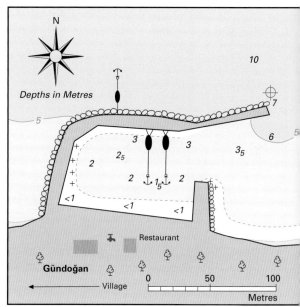

GÜNDOĞAN
⊕37°07´·88N 27°20´·86E WGS84

The holiday villages here, like many around the coast, have little architectural merit and look much like military barracks in their gridded formations. Gündoğan and Farilya mean 'sunset'

Gündoğan (Farilya) looking SW over Küçük Farilya Bükü to Büyük Farilya Bükü

and as long as you don't mind the sun setting over a sort of Surbiton-on-sea, by all accounts the sunsets here are spectacular.

Nearby there is the Peynir Çiçeği (Cheese Flower) cave where Bronze Age artefacts have been found, including ceramics and axes, so it is likely this area was inhabited from very early on (c. 2000BC). The Greek name for the bay (Farilya) I suspect relates to the Byzantine period. On Büyüktavşan Adası there are the remains of a monastery, including the church you can see in the approaches, and no doubt there was a shoreside cousin of the monastery in Gündoğan. On the hills behind are the ruins of ancient Madnasa, a Lelagian town of some importance on the Bodrum peninsula.

AĞACBAŞI LIMANI

⊕37°07´·60N 27°18´·90E

Two bays to the west of Gündoğan which are likewise encircled by holiday villages and hotels. There is a watersports centre here and the bay is often dotted with sails and watersports craft. With the *meltemi* this is not an ideal place to be and in any case has little to recommend it when the shelter on the other side of the Yalikavak peninsula is much better.

The rock off Yalikavak peninsula, Gemitasi (Wreck Rock), is more conspicuous than its modest height (6·4m) might suggest and makes a good landmark when rounding the peninsula.

YALIKAVAK

Pilotage

Approach Once round Yalikavak Yarimadasi the holiday villages around the slopes of the bay and the village itself at the head of the bay will be seen. When the *meltemi* is blowing there can be strong gusts into the bay off the high land on the northern side so it would be prudent to shorten sail coming into the bay. Care is also needed of the reef off Yalikavak Marina on the south side of the bay. Keep to the north side of the bay in the approaches and you will be well clear.

Mooring There are several places to go. Yalikavak Marina is dealt with in a separate entry.

1. **Piresun Köyü** The first usable bay on the north side as you come into Yalikavak Limanı. Anchor in 5–8m on mud and weed, good holding once the anchor is in. The *meltemi* gusts down into this bay, but the water is generally flat and no swell penetrates.
2. **Bahçe Köyü** The next bay in after Piresun. Again anchor in 5–8m on mud and weed clear of the underwater pipelines. Good shelter from the *meltemi*.
3. **Boatyard corner** In the northeast corner yachts sometimes anchor off the boatyard here.
4. **Yalikavak Harbour** The tiny harbour off Yalikavak village. The harbour is very small and generally crowded with local boats and *gulets*. Yachts are generally discouraged from berthing here now the new marina is open.

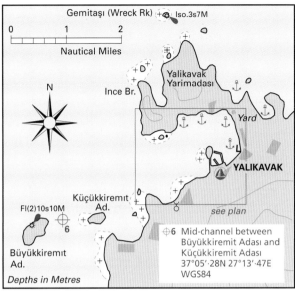

APPROACHES TO YALIKAVAK

Large *gulets* sometimes go stern-to on the village quay to the southwest of the harbour, but this is totally exposed to the *meltemi* and is not just uncomfortable, but can be downright dangerous.

Facilities

Services Water on the quay in Yalikavak harbour.

Provisions Good shopping in the village with minimarkets and bakers.

Eating out Numerous restaurants around the harbour and waterfront. There is a very good *pide* restaurant just near the stub mole of the old harbour.

Other ATMs. PO. Internet cafés. Hire cars and motorbikes. *Dolmuş* to Bodrum.

Yalikavak looking out over the bay and the new marina

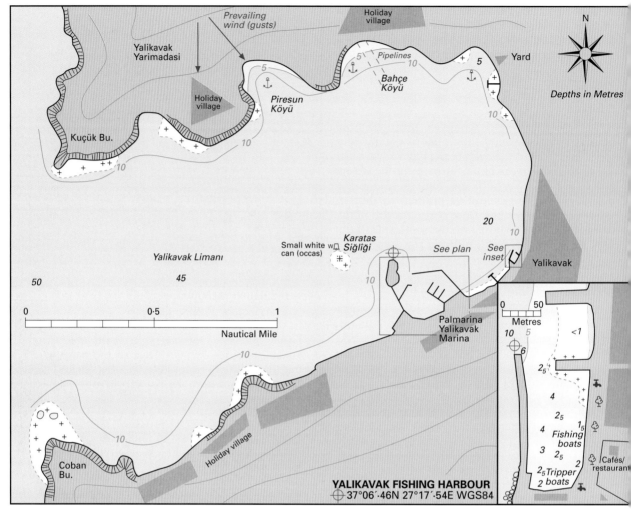

YALIKAVAK LIMANI
37°06′·41N 27°16′·92E WGS84

General

What was a small fishing village has, like others around the coast, expanded into a sizeable resort and holiday villages and hotels adorn the slopes of the bay. Yet Yalikavak retains some charm and the village centre around the old harbour and the waterfront is a pleasant place to wander around. Most yachts will now head for the new marina and if you are there, make an effort to walk around into town.

The bay is not known to have been used in ancient times, probably because it does not have a sheltered harbour and the *meltemi* howling into here would pin boats in for days. To the south are the ruins of ancient Uranium, a small Lelagian town populated by Lelagians who abandoned the island of Sími further south.

PALMARINA YALIKAVAK MARINA

Pilotage

Approach The marina is easily identified once you are into the bay. Care is needed of the western remnants of Karatas Siğliği to the west of the entrance. It is sometimes marked by a small white buoy, but don't rely on it being in place. The best policy is to stay more towards the north side of Yalikavak Limanı and then head for the entrance on a course of around due south. Once close to the marina the entrance is on the eastern side of the artificial island that has been created at the end of the western breakwater. Before you enter call up the marina on VHF Ch 72 (or if that doesn't work 06 or 16 callsign *Palmarina*) and follow instructions from the marina staff. They will usually come out to you in a RIB to guide you in.

Mooring Where directed. Most yachts will be directed to the 'Fishermen's Village' where there are laid moorings tailed to the quay. The *meltemi* blows straight into the marina, which can make berthing a bit tricky at times, though staff will assist you in berthing. Good shelter inside, although the *meltemi* does blow straight into the marina and cause a bit of a popple on the water. Charge band 5.

Facilities

Services Water and electricity at all berths. Telephone and TV connections. Wi-Fi. Showers and toilets. Self-service laundry. Waste pump-out Chandlers and all yacht services. 100-ton travel-hoist and yard. Port of entry with Customs and Immigration (planned).

Provisions Migros supermarket in the marina complex.

Eating out There is a café in the marina and other restaurants towards the village or further west around the coast. The Deniz to the west of the marina is long established and has excellent seafood.

Other ATM. Taxis and hire cars.

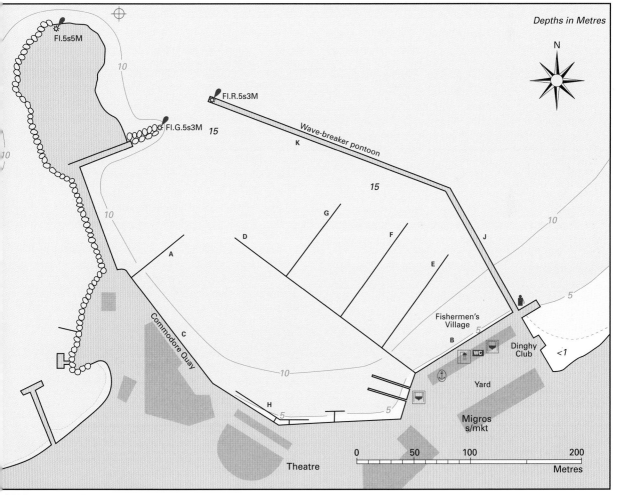

⌐MARINA YALIKAVAK MARINA
7°06′·41N 27°16′·92E WGS84

Yalikavak Marina looking out over the entrance   *Kadir Kir*

General

The marina is a wonderfully landscaped place, with green lawns and palms dotted around amongst the discreet architecture. There are boutiques, a chandlers, a fitness centre and health spa and a restaurant or two. An open-air theatre has been built and concerts have already been staged in the summer. The marina also operates a sailing club and you will see Optimists and Lasers heading out for training and racing in the summer months.

It is easy to be seduced into just staying put in the marina, but I suggest you get out and wander into the village for an evening or two. It's a pleasant walk around the waterfront, and the warren of alleys and the hustle and bustle of shops and restaurants around the old harbour are an entertaining contrast to the ordered calm of the marina.

Note The marina has recently changed hands and the new owner, an Azeri oil billionaire, has plans to turn it into something of a superyacht marina. There are plans to completely re-develop the shoreside and to modify the pontoon layout so the layout may not be exactly as shown, though it is thought it will not be too radically different.

① 0252 311 0611
www.palmarinayalikavak.com.tr

GÜMÜSLÜK

Pilotage

Approach As you come down or up through the islands it pays to keep a check on what is where. The islands are easily identified and Çavus Adası off Gümüslük is readily identified. From the north the village at Gümüslük will be seen across the low-lying isthmus in the approaches and from the south you will see some of the village once you are up to Karabakla Burnu. A military observation tower (often not manned) on the promontory above the entrance is conspicuous.

Once up to the entrance care is needed of the submerged ancient breakwater running out from the western side of the entrance. The extremity is sometimes marked by a small buoy, but do not rely on this. It generally shows up well in good light, but in any case proceed through the entrance closer to Tavşan Adası than to the end of the submerged breakwater. With the *meltemi* there are strong gusts down into the approaches and inside the inlet as well, so it is best to have all sail off.

Mooring Anchor and take a long line ashore to the western side where shown or anchor off in the middle. Depths are considerable except at the northern end. Yachts may also be able to find a berth on the T-jetty off the village. Just north of the jetty there are a number of laid moorings that can be used by visitors. It's best to pick up the mooring and then take a long line ashore as space is restricted. The bottom is mud and weed, good holding once the anchor has cut through the weed, though this can take some doing in places. Good shelter from the *meltemi* although there are strong gusts into the bay. Some boats are left on permanent moorings at the head of the bay so all-round shelter is good.

Facilities

Services Water on the T-pier by arrangement.

Provisions Minimarkets and bakers in the village.

Eating out Restaurants and cafés all around the water's edge. I habitually go to the Myndos which has good seafood (especially fresh *barbunya*, red mullet) and tables by the water's edge looking out over Tavşan Adası and the entrance to Gümüşlük, but there are other good restaurants nearby. There is a good café/restaurant by the T-pier with sofas and tables by the water.

Other Dolmuş and taxi to Bodrum. Internet café.

General

The charm of Gümüşlük is that the protected site of ancient Myndos on the hump-backed peninsula guarding the anchorage keeps out the rampant development that has scarred the coast around Gümüşlük. The village retains a cohesive shape and although the number of restaurants and trinket shops has mushroomed, it is still recognisable from several decades ago. This is a place to linger in and many of us return as often as possible to the genial charms of the place.

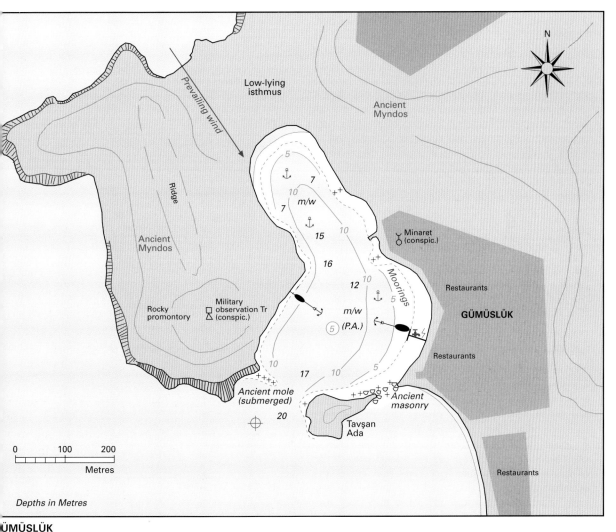

ÜMÜSLÜK
37°02´·96N 27°13´·72E WGS84

Gümüslük looking over the isthmus on which part of ancient Myndos was built

Gümüslük to Gökova Körfezi

The coast between Gümüslük and Paşa Rock, before you turn the corner to enter Gökova Körfezi, is fringed by above and below-water rocks, with a number of islands lying a short distance off. The channel between the coast and the islands is easily negotiated, with good depths in the fairway. The islands off the coast are all easily identified. Hüseyin Burnu, where you turn the corner to go up into Gökova Körfezi, has a white lighthouse and dwelling on it. Paşa Rock, on the reef running out from the corner, has a beacon on it. It is all too easy when turning the corner here to cut across Paşa Rock too finely, so keep an eye on what is going on as you close the cape.

When the *meltemi* is blowing, you either whoosh down this channel or have a struggle to get up it. When heading north it is sometimes prudent to anchor at Akyar or Aspat and wait for the *meltemi* to die down so that you can motor up the channel in the morning.

Çatalada

The island lying in the western approaches to Turgutreis Marina. It is easily recognised because it is very nearly divided into two with just a narrow sandy isthmus joining the two halves (actually more like one-third and two-thirds, but it looks like half from seawards). In settled weather you can anchor off the south side of the isthmus and get quite good shelter from the *meltemi*, although it does tend to gust through the gap. The bottom is sand and weed over rock and poor holding. There is a wooden pier off the

Ancient Myndos

Ancient Myndos occupied not only the peninsula on the western side of the harbour, but also an area twice this size in a square roughly east of the peninsula, with the southern wall running down through one of the carparks to a point about where the Myndos restaurant is. Off the restaurant you can see the remains of a causeway which ran across to the island. Myndos was not a Lelagian city although there was a city of this name closer to Bodrum. Myndos here was established by Mausolus as a fortified outpost of Bodrum in the 4th century BC. Much of the wall of the fortified city can be traced, though parts of it on the peninsula have deteriorated somewhat and some of the land wall has been carted off for construction elsewhere.

Myndos was never a powerful city and Diogenes, that Cynic wit of the 4th century BC, when looking at the large ornamental gates of the city and the small population housed inside, quipped that 'they had better keep the gates closed or the city would be running away'. Later, when Alexander asked him if he desired anything Diogenes is reputed to have said, 'Yes, that you stand out of my sun a little'. To add to their woes the Myndians produced what must have been some truly awful wine. In *Turkey Beyond the Meander* George Bean relates that

'It was one of those which were mixed with sea-water, a not uncommon monstrosity in ancient times; it is described as relaxing the stomach, causing flatulence, and leaving a hangover'. This unattractive beverage led to the Myndians being dubbed "brine-drinkers".'

I can think of a few Turkish wines I've drunk that were a bit like that.

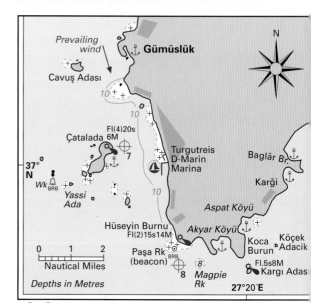

GÜMÜSLÜK TO ASPAT

⊕7 0·5M E of Çatalada light
      37°00'·72N 27°13'·96E WGS84
⊕8 0·5M S of Hüseyin Burnu light
      36°57'·33N 27°15'·85E WGS84

beach, but this is used by tripper *gulets* operating out of Turgutreis.

The anchorage is the one used by the boat hired by INA when they were diving on the various wrecks off the end to excavate the site. Some of the artefacts and a history of the excavation will be found in the Underwater Archaeology Museum in Bodrum.

D-MARIN TURGUTREIS MARINA

A marina built near the old fishing harbour at Turgutreis. What was a small fishing village has just grown, like Topsy, to become a huge resort spreading over the nearby slopes. You can't miss it.

Pilotage

Approach The marina lies immediately SE of the fishing harbour at Karatoprak (Turgutreis). Çatalada can be identified easily in the approaches from the north or south. The twin minarets behind the fishing harbour also show up well. Closer in the outer breakwater can be seen and the light structures are easily identified, although the entrance is not obvious until quite close to.

Mooring In the approaches call up the marina on VHF Ch 72 (Callsign *D-Marin*) and wait for instructions. Marina staff will come out to the entrance in a RIB to guide you to a berth and help you tie up. There are finger pontoons and laid moorings tailed to the quay for yachts over 14m. Excellent all-round shelter and boats are kept here all year around. Charge band 5.

Facilities

Services Water and electricity at all berths. Telephone and TV connections. Wi-Fi. Showers and toilets. Laundry. Chandlers and all yacht

Turgutreis Marina *D-Marin*

Yassi Ada: The ship trap

In ancient times, before there were adequate charts of the region, this maze of islands and reefs was a lethal trap for trading ships coasting to and from Halicarnassus and other ancient ports along the coast. Numerous wrecks litter the islands, and local fishermen are constantly hauling up old amphorae in their nets. Peter Throckmorton, who did much of the early work locating wrecks around the nearby coast, astutely sums up the trap these islands presented to ancient seafarers:

'From the big island's peak I could see Yassi Ada, where our wrecks lay. Watching the boil of waves on the west reef, I came to a clearer understanding of why shipwrecks lay there. Yassi Ada was the westernmost of the group. One hundred yards to the west of it was the reef, its top just below the surface. A prudent seaman would want to clear the whole Chattal group, thinking,

'"Why pick your way among those rocks if you don't have to?" He would be running, at this time of year, before the *meltemi*, if he were headed from the north toward Rhodes, seventy miles away, or Halicarnassus, fifteen miles away from Yassi Ada. He would want to stay away from the lee shore of Pserimos or Kós, six miles downwind. So he would stay close to Yassi Ada, then sail on a broad reach: twelve miles to go with a lee shore under him all the way until he was free of the easternmost point of Kós and ready to stand away for Rhodes or Knidos or Kós harbour. Not wanting to go too close to the outermost island, and knowing that almost all Aegean islands are steep-to, he would stand a cable length off and running before the strong *meltemi* in fairly heavy seas, would be on the reef before he could do a thing about it. Yassi Ada was, and is, a very subtle ship trap.'

Peter Throckmorton *The Lost Ships*

services. 100-ton travel-hoist and yard. Port of entry with customs and immigration.

Provisions Supermarket in the marina and others a short distance away. Big market day on Saturday in the town.

Eating out Restaurants and bars in the marina. The Yacht Club in the marina is a plush place where you can get a drink and snacks. The Seaman's cafeteria near the boatyard does cheap self-service food at lunch-time. In the town there are numerous restaurants including some good *pide* restaurants and *lokantas* in the back streets. The Gazientep Kebab in the garden behind the marina and The Family Tree near the market are good and modestly priced.

Other Banks and ATMs. PO. Internet cafés. Doctors and dentists nearby. Hire cars and motorbikes. Bus and *dolmuş* to Bodrum. Ferry to Kós.

Local boats

On the outskirts of Bodrum, along the coast road to the southeast, are the principal boatyards building the traditional Turkish boats that line the town quay. The boats are still built using traditional methods, though modern materials have imposed some new techniques on the builders. Some are built using plans, but many are built by eye using forming pieces to get the shape of the hull right. The keel is laid first and then the ribs are attached to give the skeleton of the boat. It is then planked up, the cabin built and the deck laid, before the interior is completed. The hull is then caulked and painted and varnished. Many of the metal fittings are made up locally and, in a country where yacht fittings are few and far between, ingenuity is the keyword. Though the finished article tied up to the quay looks impressive, the timber used is often of poor quality and the wood-working skills that put the boat together are not always what they should be. Most of the boats are built of local pine that has not been properly seasoned and is full of knots. This is reflected in the life expectancy of these boats, which is reckoned at best to be 30 years and for many not much more than 20 years. (A properly constructed yacht built of quality hardwood has a life expectancy three times this.)

There are numerous myths about the boats, the *gulets* and *tirhandils*, now built and being built for chartering. In the 1980s there was virtually no local boat-building except for a few boats for private owners and a few new fishing and sponge boats. The most popular type of boat, the *gulet*, with a clipper bow and a wide counter over the stern, is an extension of a traditional Italian design known as the *varkalas* in Greece and related to the Arab *baggala*. The name comes from the French *goelette* meaning a schooner, though many of the Turkish *gulets* built today are not schooners. They have been used for trading in the Aegean for several centuries, though the hull has evolved considerably in that time. In earlier designs the counter was not as large nor did it overhang the stern as much as it now does. The reasons for making it larger on modern *gulets* was simply to get more room on deck and to accommodate a permanent table for that all important 'al fresco' life. The beam of the boats increased considerably as well, again an expedient measure to fit more spacious accommodation into the traditional hull shape. The rig has changed too, not that it matters today as few *gulets* rely on sails for motive power when there is a big diesel below. Originally a low aspect lateen rig and later a gaff rig was used. With high aspect bermudan rigs fitted, the *gulet* is top-heavy and later versions have a ballast keel bolted on the bottom to counteract this tendency.

The *tirhandil* is closer to the traditional boats of the area. This double-ended sweet hull form is found throughout the Aegean and the Turkish name is almost identical to the Greek name for it, the *trehandiri*. It is a more seaworthy boat than the *gulet* and properly rigged it is a better sailing boat. It is not as popular as the *gulet* for charter simply because it is difficult to distort the hull lines too much to get more deck space and volume down below. You will find few of the *gulets* or *tirhandils* actually sail. They are motor-

Wooden *gulet* on charter

sailers and rely principally on a big engine to get around, the few scraps of sail that are hoisted are to steady the boat or to save a few litres of diesel.

Recently boat-building techniques have improved and with more care and attention to detail and better quality wood, some wonderful new boats have been built. A good number of boats are now built using epoxy with strip planking or cold moulded techniques. The design is not only ideal for a charter boat, with lots of space above and below deck, but is also aesthetically pleasing to the eye. Many of the charter skippers are great characters and the crew look after your every need, including preparing meals. For those who enjoy 'gin and tonic' cruising it is hard to beat a charter on one of these local boats.

Part of the impetus for this move has been the Bodrum Wooden Cup started in 1989 to encourage local charter *gulets* to put some sail up and, well, sail. There was a proviso that boats could motor and log their engine hours whereupon time would be deducted, but after accusations and near fisticuffs this proviso was dropped and boats had to stop motoring after the 5-minute gun and sail the whole course. Paying guests are taken on most of the *gulets* and can actively participate or sit back and watch the crew race. The race is over four days in mid-October.

Over the years the Bodrum Cup, has attracted more *gulets* and, true to the initial aim, better sailing performances. New *gulets* were built with sailing

Caulking the decks on a *gulet* in Bodrum

performance in mind and older *gulets* have ordered proper sails, attended to standing rigging to cut down on mast losses, and educated the crews into the black art of sail performance rather than engine performance. Prizes are awarded for all categories, but the coveted trophy is the Bodrum Cup, awarded to the overall winner in the traditional category.

The race is every bit as good as a tall ships regatta for the spectacle and excitement of 90-odd boats, most of them *gulets* upwards of 18m, under full sail and not always strictly in control. The parties afterwards are dangerous affairs, with calculated *raki* poisoning directed at winning skippers to handicap them the next day. The competition on the water is fierce but don't expect normal racing rules to be obeyed even if they are known: a 20m *gulet* is a difficult beast to tack. The organisation is first class, with referees on the water, a medical team following the race, and a quite spectacular prize-giving at the end complete with certificates, plaques, cups, and of course, *raki*.

General

Turgutreis Marina is an upmarket development with attentive staff and enough chic boutiques to tire even the most ardent shopaholic. Yet it gets its hands dirty as well: next to the marina is a boatyard and service agencies to effect the care and repair of yachts. On the slopes around what has become a small town, but was once a fishing village, are the white blobs of holiday villages spreading like a canker over the barren rocky slopes of the peninsula. From the distance the serried ranks of houses could be mistaken for the barracks of a vast army. In fact, most of these villas are retirement or holiday homes for the middle classes from Istanbul, Ankara and Izmir. Some of the houses are leased out to tour operators for package holidays and there are a number of largeish hotels along the foreshore and elsewhere, which swells the numbers in Turgutreis to five or 10 times the winter population.

The town is named after Admiral Turgut Reis who is said to have been born here in the early 16th century. He succeeded those other better known Ottoman admirals, the Barbarossas, in 1544, and commanded the Ottoman navy until his death in 1595 in the Great Siege of Malta against the Knights of St John. Piri Reis, the notable Turkish Admiral and cartographer, was a nephew of Turgut Reis.

☏ 0252 382 9200
www.dogusmarina.com.tr

Turgutreis Marina

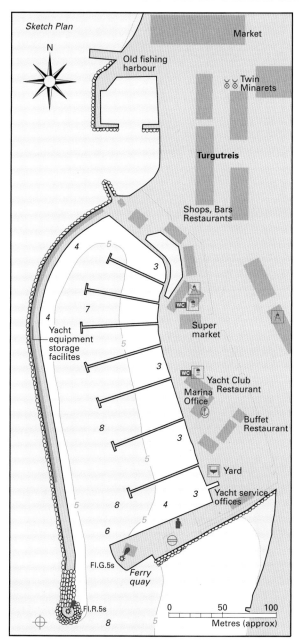

Sketch Plan

N

Market

Old fishing harbour

Twin Minarets

Turgutreis

Shops, Bars Restaurants

WC

Super market

WC

Yacht Club Restaurant

Marina Office

Buffet Restaurant

Yacht equipment storage facilites

Yard

Yacht service offices

Fl.G.5s

Ferry quay

Fl.R.5s

0   50   100
Metres (approx)

D-MARIN TURGUTREIS MARINA
⊕36°59'·89N 27°15'·30E WGS84

GÖKOVA KÖRFEZI (THE GULF OF GÖKOVA, ANCIENT GULF OF KERAMOS)

Gökova Körfezi (the Gulf of Gökova) bites deep into the mountains of the hinterland and forms an enclosed cruising area, a contrapuntal equivalent of an island's cruising area where the coast of the island is unravelled and stretched around the body of water. The Turkish name means something like 'The plains of blue heaven'. The gulf is the ancient Gulf of Keramos which once hummed with activity and had a number of important ancient cities around it. In common with all of the Turkish coast covered in this book, it is a mountainous region cut by deep gorges and ravines and until recent years an area as remote as any in the Mediterranean.

Bodrum is the undisputed tourist hotspot of the coast, an all-singing-and-dancing tourist resort in startling contrast to the simpler pleasures of the small villages and bays in the gulf. The only way to explore the gulf properly is by boat. It is quite simply impossible to easily visit many of the places by road, though adventurous souls can get to some of them on newly constructed gravel roads carved through the hills to coastal villages. But to get the feel of the region there is nothing to touch the approach from seawards where you creep into rocky inlets camouflaged in pine down to the water's edge and take a long line ashore to pull the boat in close to the shore. A word of warning: if you come here looking for long sandy beaches you will be disappointed. There are few beaches in the gulf, though that matters little if you are on a boat as there is nothing to beat diving off the back of a boat and swimming around under pine-clad rocks.

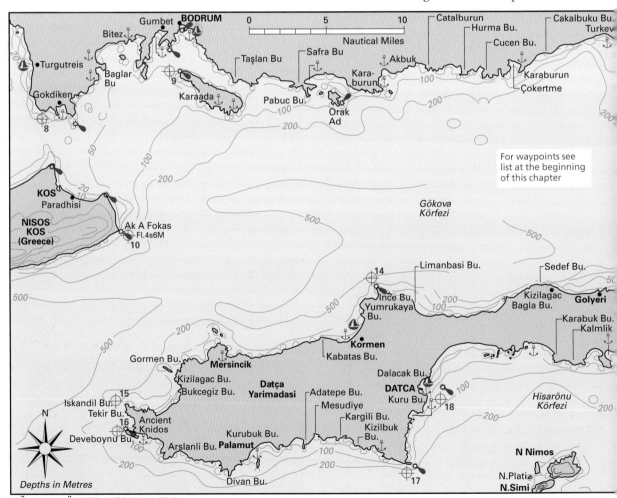

GÖKOVA KÖRFEZI WESTERN END

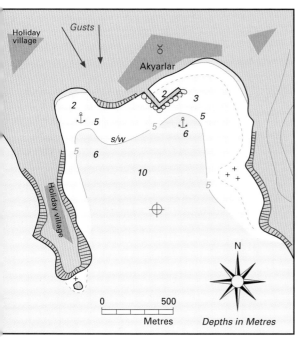

Akyarlar looking into the bay with the small harbour off the village

AKYARLAR

As you turn the corner to go east towards Bodrum, the white houses of Akyarlar can be seen tucked into a little bay. The small harbour is usually crowded with *gulets* and local boats, but you may find a berth inside. Alternatively anchor off in the bay in 3–5m on sand and weed. Good shelter from the *meltemi*, although there are gusts.

Before 1923 this was a summer resort for the Greeks and several Greek houses and a church can be seen in the village. There are several small restaurants with wonderful views over the water to Kós.

ASPAT KÖYÜ

⊕36°58′·3N 27°18′·4E

A double-headed bay sitting under a steep crag by the water with a fort on the very top. On the south side of the crag are the twin bays of Aspat and Karaincir, popular stops for the trip-boats and charter *gulets* in the high season. Anchor in either bay off the shore. Good shelter from the *meltemi*, although there are gusts into the anchorage. A holiday village and restaurants ashore.

Aspat Kalesi (Castle of Aspat) is on the top of the conical hill facing Aspat Cove in Akyarlar. It is a steep climb up to the summit and most are deterred from the ascent in the summer heat. Little is known about the so-called castle although it is said to be ancient Aspartos, a place not mentioned in any references I have seen. Inland from here was ancient Termera, a Lelagian settlement, though not of any importance.

KARĞI BÜKÜ

⊕36°59′·7N 27°20′·1E

A small bay just north of Aspat. With the *meltemi* there are gusts off the land, but the holding in here is good. In settled weather this is not a bad spot to spend the night. Holiday villages have now been built around the shore and inland around the lower slopes. Still, there is a good beach and some restaurants and crystal clear water.

BAĞLAR KÖYÜ

⊕37°00′·5N 27°20′·2E

The large bay on the north side of Bağlar Burun. In calm weather or light northerlies you can anchor off the beach here. Ashore there are restaurants on the beach. Tripper boats use the bay, but usually depart after lunch.

ORTAKENT

A new small harbour at the N end of Bağlar Köyü in the coastal development known as Yali. The basin lies on the west side of a canalised river.

Call ahead on VHF Ch 77. Go stern-to where directed by the harbourmaster. Laid moorings tailed to the quay. There are sufficient depths in the outer harbour, shallowing towards the inner berths. Mooring blocks reduce depths in places. Good shelter from the prevailing wind. Showers and toilets. Water and electricity. Charge band 4/5.

There are a number of restaurants and cafés along the waterfront. For minimarkets head

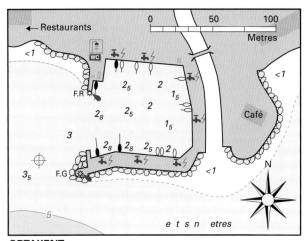

ORTAKENT
⊕37°01'·2N 27°20'·8E

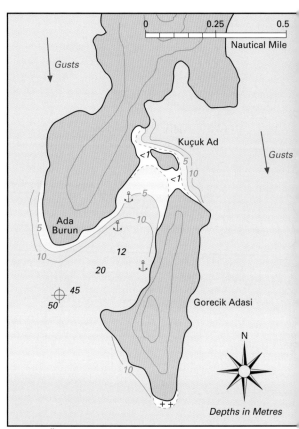

ADA BOĞAZI (The Aquarium)
⊕36°59'·8N 27°22'·7E

towards the minaret. Better shopping will be found in Ortakent. Take a mini-bus, which can also take you to Bodrum.

Yali is a popular resort in summer, owing to its sandy beach running around the bay – one of only a few in this area.

BITEZ

A more sedate beach resort compared with the noisy neighbours to the east, though it is not a quiet place at night. Anchor in the eastern half of the bay clear of the watersports area and the buoyed-off swimming area off the beach. The bottom is sand and thick weed and you may have to anchor a couple of times before you get the anchor to hold. Shelter from the *meltemi* is good, although it gusts off the high land. On the far eastern side there is a concrete quay and a

jetty, but as the prevailing wind blows straight onto here it is not really a good place to be unless you have a good laid mooring like the local boats. In strong southerlies you should head for Bodrum.

The bay has a number of hotels and numerous restaurants around the shore. I suggest you just dinghy in and use your nose to find somewhere you like. In recent years there has been an expansion of trinket shops and tourist tat, but wander around the outskirts and it is still a likeable enough place.

Dinghy sailing and board-sailing holidays are run from here and you can usually negotiate the hire of a sail-board for the day. Behind the hotels and restaurants on the waterfront are the few remaining citrus orchards that the bay was once famous for. A friend of mine, Zeke, grew up here and I have watched the family fortunes change over the years from citrus orchard to a small hotel to a much bigger hotel and apartments. Needless to say, the family doesn't have much in the way of orchards left.

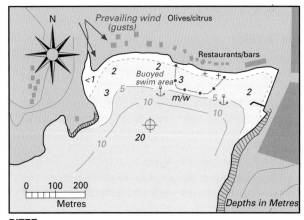

BITEZ
⊕37°01'·56N 27°22'·66E WGS84

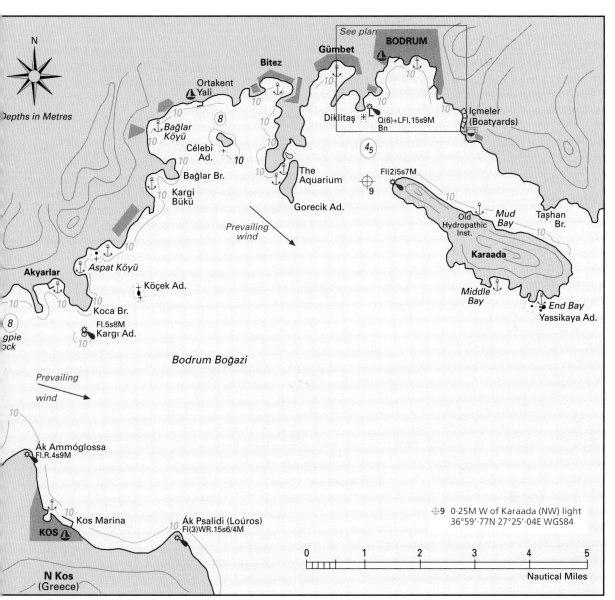

RUM BOĞAZI

ADA BOĞAZI

The headland dividing Gümbet from Bitez has a series of coves between the tip and a small island, an area known as the 'Aquarium' or less imaginatively as 'Paradise Bay'. The clear turquoise water is a favourite stop for tripper boats from Bodrum, but yachts should not attempt to follow small *gulets* in through the shallow winding channel at the north end of Gorecik Adası. Instead enter from the west side and anchor off the headland with a long line ashore. Depths come up quickly from 8–9m to the shore so care is needed once inside. Good shelter from the *meltemi* and quite peaceful at night once the tripper boats leave.

GÜMBET

Just to the west of Bodrum and virtually a suburb of it is Gümbet. You can anchor off here, taking care to avoid local moorings and the waterski boats and water-bikes. Shelter from the *meltemi* is good although there are gusts off the land.

Gümbet is the local dialect for the domed water cisterns that dot the peninsula and used to provide water through the summer for this rocky peninsula in pre-tourist days. It is popular, (some would say too popular) as the nearest beach to Bodrum, and consequently hotels, restaurants and bars line the foreshore to accommodate and refresh the summer invasion of tourists. It is a bit of 'Little England' and the decibel level is acute even in the anchorage. If you are looking for things Turkish then it is best to give Gümbet a miss. On the other hand, if you are looking for pubs, bars and clubs, Gümbet is the place to be.

MILTA BODRUM MARINA

Bodrum is the hub of this area and the place to stock up on provisions and get most things done. The marina is packed to the gills in the summer, but the staff will usually manage to squeeze you in somewhere.

Pilotage

Approach The cluster of white buildings around the slopes of Bodrum are fairly easy to identify, but it is difficult to determine just where the harbour is until you are closer in. Care needs to be taken of Dikilitas Reef, although once you have identified the beacon it is a useful pointer to

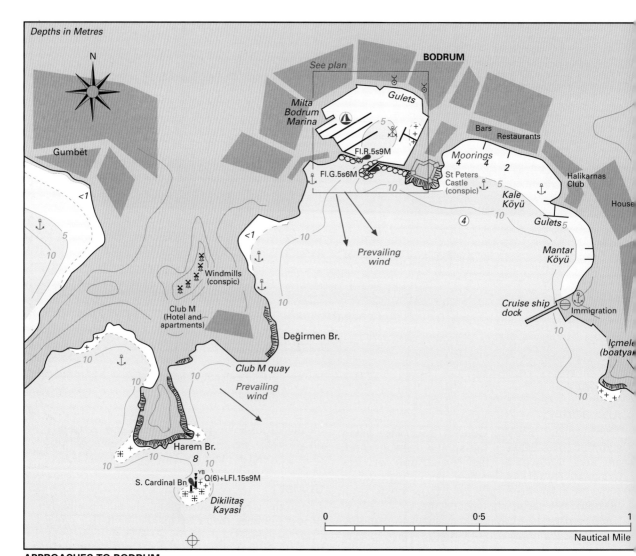

APPROACHES TO BODRUM
⊕ 0·5M S of Dikilitaş Beacon 37°00´·61N 27°24´·82E WGS84

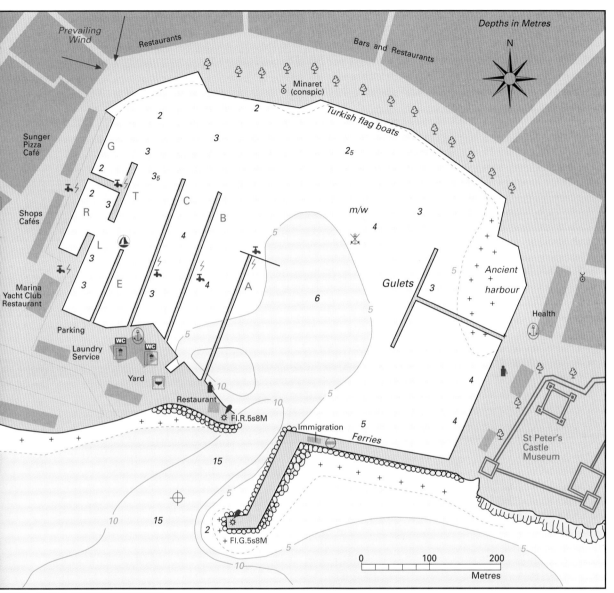

Depths in Metres

N

Prevailing Wind

Restaurants

Bars and Restaurants

Minaret (conspic)

Turkish flag boats

2

2

3

2₅

Sunger Pizza Café

G

3

3

3₅

Shops Cafés

2

2

3

T

C

B

R

4

m/w

3

5

4

L

E

3

3

4

A

6

5

Gulets

3

Ancient harbour

Health

Marina Yacht Club Restaurant

Parking

Laundry Service

WC

WC

Yard

Restaurant

10

FI.R.5s8M

15

Immigration

Ferries

5

5

4

4

St Peter's Castle Museum

10

10

5

10

15

2

FI.G.5s8M

5

5

0   100   200
Metres

DRUM - MILTA BODRUM MARINA
7°01´·88N 27°25´·44E WGS84

Castle of St Peter in the approaches to Bodrum

where you are. There will often be a cruise ship or two on their dock outside the harbour and this also helps to sort things out. Closer in St Peter's Castle will be seen and the entrance can be identified. Care is needed of craft zooming in and out of the entrance and *gulets* in particular tend to enter and exit at speed.

Mooring All yachts must go into the marina. The berths around the town quay are for local *gulets*.

Call up Milta Bodrum Marina on VHF Ch 73 or 16 (callsign Milta Bodrum Marina), preferably an hour or so before you are due to arrive. Large yachts over 15m or so should phone in advance to make a booking. Marina staff will come out in a RIB to guide you to a berth and help you tie up. It can be tight in some of the inside berths but the staff will use the RIB to nudge you into place. There are laid moorings tailed to the quay. Shelter inside is excellent. Charge band 5.

Facilities

Services Water and electricity at all berths. Telephone and TV connections. Wi-Fi. Shower and toilet blocks that would not disgrace a five-star hotel. Fuel quay at the entrance to the harbour. Laundry. Chandlers. Yacht clearance can be arranged. Customs and Immigration are at present on the cruise ship dock although new offices are under construction in the harbour on the south breakwater.

Provisions Small supermarket at the marina and others nearby. Or take a taxi to the massive Migros supermarket on the Bodrum-Gümbet road. Market on Thursday and Friday.

Eating out At night Bodrum throbs to the sound of amplified music and the babble of conversations from bars and restaurants. There are any number of good restaurants. (In general I operate on the principle that a good restaurant does not need to tout for customers.) The usual yachtie haunt is the Sunger just behind the marina. In the marina

Milta Bodrum Marina *Milta Bodrum Marina*

the Yacht Club has live music and is good value for money. Bars are littered all the way around the waterfront from the marina to the Halicarnassus night club at the far end of the eastern bay.

Other Banks and ATMs. PO. Internet cafés. Hospital. Dentists. Hire cars and motorbikes. Buses and *dolmuş* to most places. Internal and European flights from Bodrum Airport around 40 minutes away. Ferry to Körmen for Datça. Ferry for Kós.

General

Whether you enter Bodrum by land or by sea, two things immediately impress themselves on your senses. The first is the Castle of St Peter, a giant medieval silhouette that dominates the town. From the sea it appears as a grey blob amongst the houses and as you close it, crenellated towers, battlements and defensive walls gradually take form. In the harbour you are under the shadow of its high walls. The other thing is the hustle and bustle and sheer energy of the town. There are yachts and *gulets* crammed into every available space. Cars and motorbikes hurtle around the waterfront narrowly missing pedestrians. Bodrum has been called the 'St Tropez of Turkey' and if the panegyric is not quite accurate, it is a reflection of the feeling you get of a lot of people busily enjoying themselves. If you have come from some tranquil anchorage around the coast you will initially feel quite lost in the noise and confusion of the town. Once used to it the cosmopolitan feel of Bodrum comes as a welcome diversion to the simpler pleasures of other places around the coast and for entertainment and a few nights out there is little to rival it nearby.

All of this is quite recent. Thirty or so years ago Bodrum was a remote fishing village that was easier to get to by sea than by land. Until the new road to Milas was built it used to take four hours to get there on the old road via Mumcular: a trip that now takes half an hour. In the 1950s Lord Kinross described what it was like trying to get something to eat in Bodrum: '... no restaurant was open. They closed, I learnt, at 6.30 p.m. I dined off a biscuit and a bowl of yoghurt in a milk shop'. Earlier on Bodrum was considered such a remote place that dissident writers and artists were exiled here. The most famous of them all was Cevat Sakir Kabaağac, exiled here for his criticism of the Turkish Republic after its formation in 1923. He soon earned the title 'the Fisherman of Halicarnassus', a fisher of stories,

and his tales of Bodrum and its local characters became famous in Turkey, though sadly few have been translated into English. Others followed the 'fisherman' here and the village soon had a reputation for being a bit bohemian, though evidently this was not enough to keep the restaurants open, as Lord Kinross found out.

In the 1970s the rich and those in the know from Istanbul and Izmir followed the writers and artists here and the village developed into a small resort that in recent years has grown and grown and looks like keeping on growing. It now spreads over the nearby hillsides and although a council restriction on the height of buildings (limiting them to three storeys) has stopped the development of huge apartment blocks, the sheer scale of development has changed its character from that of a large village to that of a large town.

It does still retain the character of a market town. On Friday, (traditionally market day because it is the Muslim equivalent of the Christian Sunday and the faithful could combine a trip to the mosque with their buying and selling) farmers and traders block the roads into Bodrum as they bring their produce and goods into town. The market is now held in the sports ground near the old village and the new industrial area. Here fresh fruit of every kind: oranges and tangerines, lemons, grapefruit, peaches, nectarines, water melons, honey and rock melons, plums, apples and cherries can be found heaped up in huge piles according to the season. Tomatoes and more tomatoes, green peppers, hot peppers, aubergines, potatoes, carrots, green and red cabbages, cauliflower, lettuces, onions and spring onions, fresh garlic and coarse Mediterranean parsley can be found in over-abundance. Not for nothing is Turkey called the market garden of Europe. As well white village cheeses, green and black olives, nuts and dried fruit, herbs and spices, live chickens and ducks, sheep and cattle and the occasional camel, pots and pans, cloth and carpets are all displayed under cotton awnings in a scene straight out of a bazaar in the *Arabian Nights*. If you are in Bodrum for a few days only, contrive to be there on a Friday for market day.

A few nights on the town will soon revive memories of the quieter places down the coast where your eardrums and your liver can recover from the after-effects of too much Bodrum nightlife.

☎ 0252 316 1860

www.miltabodrummarina.com

Excursions from Bodrum

EPHESUS

Of all the sites this is the most well known, and deservedly so. The city was of Greek origin, founded in the 11th century BC, but it had been a place of worship to the 'Earth Mother' long before this. Though it was an important Greek city, it was the Romans who really made it what we see today. They chose the city to be the Roman capital of their Asian provinces and for 200 years it enjoyed great prosperity and power. Most of the grand buildings and monuments we see today date from this period and the scale and ornateness are a reflection of the importance of the city. There is much to see here: the theatre with seats for 25,000; the much-embellished facade of the Celsus Library; and the marble street with ruts from the chariots, and the buildings (including rich merchants' houses and a bordello) lining it. You are not finished yet, as there is the Temple of Hadrian; the city walls and gates from where you can view the silted harbour that ultimately led to the demise of Ephesus; and scattered up the hillside the ongoing excavations that reveal more and more of the extent of the city. The impact of Ephesus is in its completeness and its size. From Bodrum it is best to take an organised coach tour as it is over 200km to Ephesus; or you can take a bus to Seljuk and a *dolmuş* from there.

APHRODISIAS

Less well known than Ephesus, but in many ways more impressive, a visit to the site of this ancient city is best combined with an overnight trip to Pamukkale. Though there is still a great deal of reconstruction to be done, the site has been much excavated in recent years and there is more than enough to see here. There is a wonderful 30,000-seat theatre with a colonnaded area beyond it; an *odeon* with a chess-board *cavia* and a small sunken pool in the centre; a huge temple to Aphrodite; and just beyond the city a vast stadium virtually intact.

MILAS

Milas stands on the site of ancient Mylasa, one-time capital of Caria until Mausolus moved it to Halicarnassus. Little remains of the ancient city except for a Roman mausoleum and an ornamental gateway. What Milas does offer are a number of fine Ottoman mosques dating from the 14th century: the Orhan Bey Camii, the Ulu Camii, and the Firuz Bey Camii with a pink marble facade. There are also numerous old Ottoman houses with typical wooden balconies, mostly dating from the 19th century. Just outside Milas on a steep hill are the remains of a fortified castle, Pecinkale, a stronghold of the Mentese Turks who ruled this area just prior to the Ottomans. Milas is also known for its carpets, more so than Mumcular. In particular it is famed for some of the browns and greens it gets from vegetable dyes, and for patterns particular to the area. From Bodrum regular buses run to Milas, about a 30-minute trip.

Library of Celsus (Caesar) at Ephesus

Anchorage in
Kale Köyü off
Bodrum town

Anchorages around Bodrum

1. *Kale Köyü* This is the best anchorage for shelter, but it suffers from high decibel levels from the night clubs scattered around the bay. Anchor in 7–12m keeping clear of the laid moorings in the bay. The moorings with orange buoys are for visitors (Charge band 2). The bottom is sand and weed, good holding once you get through the weed. Good shelter from the *meltemi* but open south. Make sure you have an anchor light on as *gulets* return at all hours to moorings here.

   In the east side of the bay is a jetty used by *gulets* and a few yachts, but there is rarely a free space here and in any case the *meltemi* tends to blow straight down onto it, making it very uncomfortable.
2. *Under Değirmen Burnu* You can anchor off to the north of Değirmen Burnu and even in the bight under the harbour breakwater if there is room. Good shelter from the *meltemi* here, although it tends to gust off the high land making it a wet dinghy ride into Bodrum. Anchor in 6–10m on mud, sand and weed. It can be a bit rolly in here from the wash of passing craft coming and going from Bodrum.
3. *İçmeler* In calm weather it is possible to anchor off İçmeler. When the *meltemi* gets up it blows straight into the anchorage making it very uncomfortable, though it usually dies down at night. *Gulets* anchor off the yards here even when the *meltemi* is blowing, but I don't recommend it for yachts.

Note There are plans to put a wavebreaker pontoon in the bay at İçmeler to provide berths for yachts here. At the time of writing the exact position of the wavebreaker pontoon and the layout inside is not known.

KARAADA

Karaada (Black Island) is the large hump-backed island lying across the approaches to Bodrum. There are a number of places you can anchor off around the island.

Mud Bay In calm weather you can anchor off the few dilapidated buildings on the north side where a hot spring bubbles up into a sea cave in the rocks. The water is said to have therapeutic qualities and the fine grey mud in the immediate vicinity is reputed to be used by Elizabeth Arden for those very expensive facial mudpacks – get yours here for free!

Middle Bay Lies approximately two-thirds of the way down the south side of Karaada. You need to get a long line ashore and although there are strong gusts into the anchorage, it is reasonably safe with the *meltemi* blowing.

End Bay Lies at the southeast end of Karaada. Anchor and get a long line ashore as at Middle Bay. There tend to be fewer gusts here and it is an attractive spot with pine down to the water's edge. Both of these bays are visited by tripper boats in the summer, but they usually depart after lunch. In calm weather you could spend the night here but often you will get an early morning easterly blowing out of the gulf and this can make these anchorages uncomfortable.

Halicarnassus

For somewhere that was the capital of Caria and the site of one of the Seven Wonders of the World, precious little remains in present-day Bodrum to remind you of it. The town itself is a collage of ancient bric-a-brac. You will find a section of column used as a base for a potted plant, blocks of ancient marble built into houses and the castle, part of a frieze used as a doorstep, a capital serving as a garden table, reliefs and pediments built into the walls of houses: everything that could be used has been. All of the ancient marble and stone has been recycled in some way or another and while this may offend the classical sensibility, it pleases the senses. The city is a palinpsest in which bits of old history poke through into the modern world.

Halicarnassus was established as a Dorian city by colonists from the Peloponessus around the beginning of the tenth century BC. In 484BC Herodotus, 'the father of written history', was born here and much of what we know about the origins of Halicarnassus and Asia Minor in the fifth century we owe to him. Herodotus stands apart as an early writer because of his ability to arrange his material systematically and to look critically at his sources. He was surprisingly free of racial prejudice and his appreciation of the personalities he wrote about and his awareness of the foibles of human nature elevate his writings way above most earlier and many later writers. After travelling throughout the known world he returned to Halicarnassus, but he was not to stay long. He left after disagreements with the Dynasts and spent the last years of his life in Thuria in Italy.

It was the Dynasts who were to put Halicarnassus squarely on the map of the ancient world. In the fourth century BC the region was in Persian hands and ruled by local satraps. In 377BC Mausolus took over and set about making Halicarnassus the capital of Caria. He

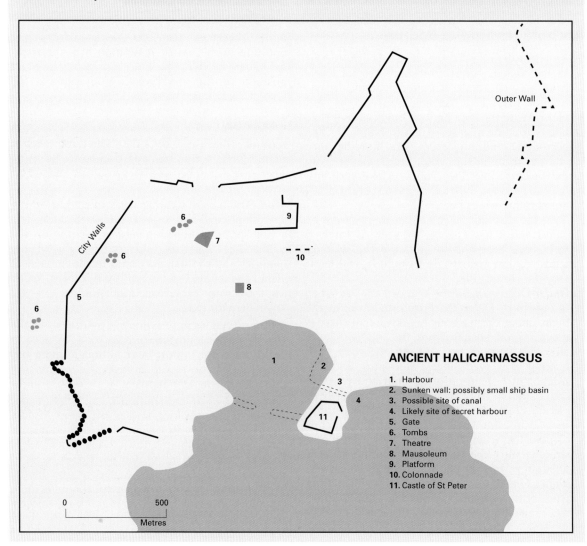

ANCIENT HALICARNASSUS

1. Harbour
2. Sunken wall: possibly small ship basin
3. Possible site of canal
4. Likely site of secret harbour
5. Gate
6. Tombs
7. Theatre
8. Mausoleum
9. Platform
10. Colonnade
11. Castle of St Peter

cannot be accused of mean ideas: he constructed three and a half miles of fortified city walls, the remains of which can still be traced on the western side of the town. He enclosed the harbour we see today and had a canal dug across the isthmus that now connects the castle to the mainland. He built temples and the theatre that remains today on the hillside above the main road to Gümbet. And for himself he built a large palace of sun-dried bricks decorated with marble from the Sea of Marmara, though the site of this edifice is not known with any certainty.

When Mausolus died he was succeeded by Artemisia, his sister and wife, it being common practice for a king to marry his sister as the Pharaohs did in Egypt. In his memory she constructed the magnificent tomb which became one of the Seven Wonders of the World. It also gave us the word 'mausoleum'. Today little remains apart from a hole in the ground where it stood, a few foundations and odd bits of marble. The small museum on the site at least has a reconstruction of what this huge tomb-monument looked like, but the site itself is disappointing. The mausoleum was

Reconstruction of the Mausoleum in the British Museum

reported to be still standing in the 12th century, but when the Knights of St John arrived in 1402 it was in ruins, presumably destroyed by an earthquake. The knights found the large quantity of marble a useful source of building materials for the castle and you can see bits and pieces of marble in the walls.

Although she ruled for just three short years, Artemisia proved to be a formidable successor to her brother and husband. When the Rhodians learnt that a woman now ruled Halicarnassus, they decided the city would be easy meat for their forces to take. When the Rhodian navy entered the harbour Artemisia led her fleet out of a secret canal on the eastern side and counter-attacked from the rear, routing the Rhodians and capturing their ships. Not content with simply defeating the Rhodians she sailed the ships back to Rhodes and those left behind, believing their triumphant fleet was returning, put up no resistance. She captured the city and the Rhodians, overawed as well as overwhelmed by this Amazon-like Queen, erected a statue in her honour.

Halicarnassus got its come-uppance in 334BC when Alexander arrived on the scene. The Halicarnassians declined to surrender so Alexander in his methodical way invested the city and after a long and fierce siege the defenders fired the city and retreated to two strongholds on the east and west of the harbour. Alexander sacked the city and left a detachment of troops to blockade the defenders, who surrendered a short time after. Between the fire and Alexander's troops sacking the town, much of it was destroyed and it never really recovered. Thereafter its fortunes followed the ups and downs of other more important cities along the coast until its decline in Byzantine times.

Gökova Protected Area (SEPA)

A local yachtsman, Sadun Boro, has successfully campaigned to have the area from Ören to Knidos established as a nature reserve. Sadun, a celebrity in Turkey since he became the first Turkish national to sail around the world (see separate section under Değirmen Bükü), hopes to restrict hotel development in order to keep this remote area in its present natural state, a sentiment I cannot help but share, having spent many pleasant days pottering in and out of the bays and coves along this coast. Unfortunately, the government decided to site a low-grade coal-burning power station near Ören, and this caused much anger in Bodrum over the ecological damage it will do. The

anger of the locals even caused the government to delay the start-up date for the power station.

The area from Ören to Knidos is now designated a Special Environment Protection Area (SEPA) under the Turkish Government's EPASA (Environmental Protection Agency for Special Areas) programme to promote Integrated Coastal and Marine Management (ICMM). Hopefully this project will do more than develop complex acronyms and make a real difference to protecting the coastal environment. For more information see www.smap.eu or www.sadafag.org

The Castle of the Knights

While most of ancient Halicarnassus has disappeared, the castle the Knights of St John built has remained virtually intact since its construction in the early 15th century. The Order of St John of Jerusalem was born in the 12th century in the dust of Jerusalem and the blood of the Holy War. Originally the order was purely a nursing brotherhood providing hospitals for the sick and wounded. Later its duties were extended to the defence of pilgrims visiting Jerusalem and it is from here that its military side appeared. In 1291 the knights were compelled to leave Palestine with the collapse of the last Christian stronghold and they went first to Cyprus and then to Rhodes. In Rhodes they developed new

military skills and became sailors. In their swift galleys these Christian corsairs became a respected and feared fighting force along the coast of Asia Minor. After Rhodes the knights established a string of castles on the islands of the Dodecanese and then turned their attention to Asia Minor. The site at Bodrum, where an earlier Seljuk castle had stood, was perfect, and construction began in 1402.

The layout of the castle roughly followed the divisions of the order into eight Langues or tongues, the eight European nationalities from whom the knights were recruited. These were Auvergne, Provence, France, Aragon, Castile, England, Germany, and Italy. In the

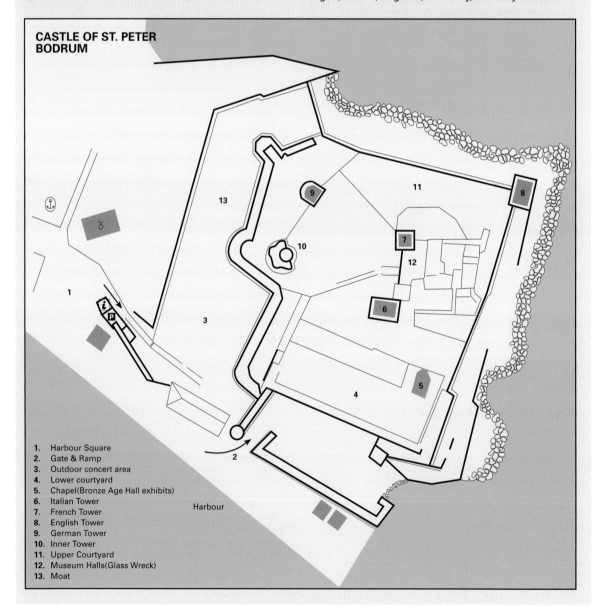

CASTLE OF ST. PETER BODRUM

1. Harbour Square
2. Gate & Ramp
3. Outdoor concert area
4. Lower courtyard
5. Chapel(Bronze Age Hall exhibits)
6. Italian Tower
7. French Tower
8. English Tower
9. German Tower
10. Inner Tower
11. Upper Courtyard
12. Museum Halls(Glass Wreck)
13. Moat

Harbour

Castle of St Peter there are four towers: the Italian, French (incorporating Auvergne and Provence), German, and English towers. I presume Aragon and Castille were accommodated in one of the towers or were not represented in the castle at Bodrum.

The knights of the order were all men of noble birth from the great houses of Europe. To be recruited the noble blood had to be traced through four generations and any possibility of illegitimacy or common blood in the line barred a man from joining. Once accepted, the novice knight served on the military side for a year, usually in the sleek galleys. One year of duty in the galleys was called a 'Caravan' and after three 'Caravans' the knight had to reside for a further two years in the order, in somewhere like the Castle of St Peter, before he

St Peter's Castle in Bodrum from Kale Köy anchorage

was a fully fledged Knight of St John. After this many would return to their estates in Europe, but on being summoned by the Grand Master in times of crisis, it was their duty to return. There were lower orders with no restrictions on birth, the Chaplains and Brothers, who served in the hospitals and with the soldiers on the military side, all of them along with the knights bound by those medieval dictates of chastity and obedience. At their best these knights probably came as close as any to the ideal knight imagined by romantics, what Chaucer called the 'verray parfit gentil knight', but they were also a skilled fighting machine as brutal and cruel in battle as any foe they fought against.

The knights occupied the Castle of St Peter until the fall of Rhodes to Suleiman the Magnificent in 1523. Suleiman allowed the Knights of Rhodes to leave, he considered them gallant adversaries whose lives should not be wasted and is reputed to have said of the Grand Master '… it is not without some regret that I oblige this old Christian to leave his home'.

The Castle of St Peter is a wonderful example of medieval military architecture, now partially restored to house a Museum of Underwater Archaeology. In the museum finds from the numerous wrecks excavated along the coast are imaginatively displayed. Peter Throckmorton got the museum off the ground in the early 1960s and the work has been continued by Dr George Bass and the Institute of Nautical Archaeology. Finds ranging from the contents of a Bronze Age ship that sunk off Cape Gelidonya around 1200BC, 6th and 7th century AD wrecks from Yassiada, an island at the tip of the Bodrum peninsula, and an 11th century Levantine trading ship loaded with exquisite glassware that foundered in Serçe Limanı, are all exhibited along with models and drawings showing how the delicate and dangerous job of underwater archaeology is carried out. The finds are arranged in different rooms and halls so that you get to wander around the gardens and towers and along the galleries of the castle to see the different exhibits, and a visit is as much a promenade through the castle as a tour of the museum.

Exhibit in the underwater archaeology museum in St Peter's Castle showing how amphorae were carried in a ship's hold

Statue of Herodotus, 'the father of history', outside St Peter's castle in Bodrum

GÖKOVA KÖRFEZI

The Gulf of Gökova extends in a great jagged gash for over 40 miles from Bodrum to the small village of Gökova at the eastern end. On the northern side of the gulf high mountains rise abruptly from the sea and until relatively recent times no roads connected the villages along this shore to the towns and villages in the interior – the only communication with the outside world was by boat or by donkey over rough paths through the mountains. The south side of the gulf is lower, but just as remote and wild as the north side.

The gulf takes its name from the hamlet of Gökova on a marshy plain at the head, but in times past it had a number of other titles. On the British Admiralty charts surveyed in the late 19th century by Commander Graves in HMS *Beacon* it is called the Gulf of Kós after the Greek island that sits in the open mouth of the gulf. In the Graeco-Roman period it was known as Sinus Ceramicus or the Gulf of Keramos, after the important port and city of Keramos on its northern side near the present-day village of Ören (Ören means ruins).

Today the gulf is popular with yachts and *gulets* based in Bodrum, offering an enclosed area ideal for a one- or two-week cruise. For some time there has been an attempt to declare the gulf a national park and forbid the construction of hotels or any buildings that would detract from the natural beauty of the area. Unfortunately little

WINDS

In the summer the *meltemi* curves around into the gulf to blow into it from the west. The high mountains have a significant effect on the winds by either compressing them into acceleration zones down valleys or in narrow channels or by lifting the wind so you suddenly run into a light spot, though the swell still rolls on. On the northern side of the gulf the wind gusts down with some ferocity off the high land and care is needed not to shred sails. On the southern side the wind either lifts, leaving light airs and confused seas, or accelerates across low land to blow off the other side of the Datça peninsula. There are several areas where the wind will accelerate and care is needed as the gusts can be significantly higher than the wind in areas out to sea.

Kós to Knidos The wind is accelerated around the eastern end of Kós and blows off the SE corner with violence. At Knidos the wind may be lifted or it can blow with violence around and across the cape.

Pabuç to Çökertme Gusts blow down off the high land, although the sea is relatively flat.

Akbük to Gökova The wind gusts down into Akbük and is accelerated to the eastern end of the gulf by the high mountains on either side. At night a katabatic wind can blow down off the mountains from the northeast. At times it will blow at Force 7–8 for 3–4 hours and then die down. Care is needed in Akbük, Gelibolu and Sehir Adalari where you will have normally anchored for the *meltemi* blowing from the northwest to west, only to have a katabatic NE wind blast into the anchorages late in the evening.

Teke Burun to Küçük Çati The wind is funnelled across the Datça peninsula, especially around Yedi Adalari.

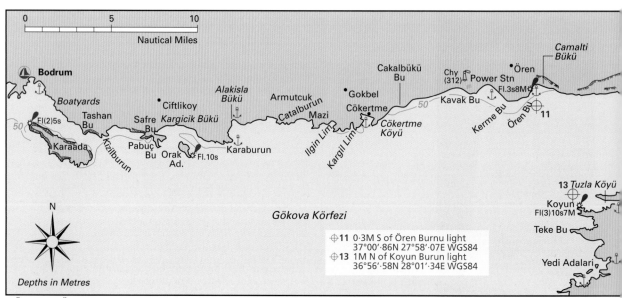

⊕11 0·3M S of Ören Burnu light
37°00'·86N 27°58'·07E WGS84
⊕13 1M N of Koyun Burun light
36°56'·58N 28°01'·34E WGS84

GÖKOVA KÖRFEZI

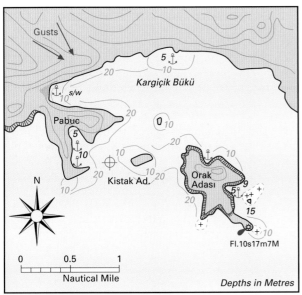

PABUÇ, KARGIÇIK AND ORAK ADASI
⊕36°58'·68N 27°34'·37E WGS84

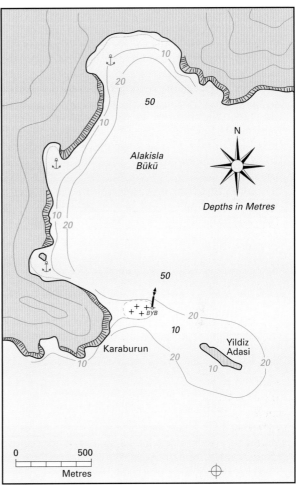

ALAKISLA BÜKÜ
⊕36°58'·19N 27°39'·37E WGS84
(0.5M S of Yildiz Adasi)

has yet happened and some parts of the area have hotels planned or built, though nothing really detrimental yet. Worse than hotels is the construction of a coal-fired power station behind Ören where there is a coal mine to supply the fuel for it. Hopefully something will be done in the future to save the area from development or at least to put a stop to the sort of environmentally unsympathetic buildings that blight some Mediterranean coastlines. Waterborne visitors should be aware of the fire risk to the pine forests in the summer and take every care with barbecues and cigarette ends.

PABUÇ AND KARGIÇIK

(Kargiçik = 'Little Spear') Two bays immediately northwest of Orak Adası. Both bays make ideal lunch stops although there is no reason why you cannot stay overnight. The holding in Pabuç and Kargiçik is poor on a sand and rock bottom. Most yachts take a long line to the shore as the *meltemi* gusts off the land with some strength. At lunchtime you will find lots of tripper boats here, but by mid-afternoon most of them have left and you pretty much have the place to yourself – at least on the water. Ashore there are several large hotels and of course the attendant restaurants and bars and (inevitably) the thumping bass of dance music.

ORAK ADASI

A stark rocky island lying a short distance off the coast. There is a cove on the north side (36°58'·72N 27°35'·59E WGS84) suitable for a lunch stop when the *meltemi* is not blowing and a more sheltered cove on the eastern side. The attraction of this little island is its seclusion and the remarkably clear water around its shores: ideal for snorkelling. If you have a long line ashore care is needed as there have been reports of big and very bold rats on the island.

ALAKISLA BÜKÜ

A large bay three miles NE of Orak Adası. An islet, Yıldız Adası lies in the entrance and a reef is situated in the entrance between Yıldız and the southeastern entrance point to the bay. A rusty buoy with ♦ topmarks marks the reef although it is easily spotted. While the local *gulets* pass inside the reef, the prudent course is to go around the outside between the reef and the islet to get into the bay. Anchor with a long line ashore in either of the two coves on the west side or at the head of the bay. The bottom is hard sand and weed, reasonable holding once the anchor is in, though it is best to take a long line ashore. Good shelter from the *meltemi* although there are strong gusts into the bay.

The setting here is wonderful and the water a wonderful turquoise and blue, especially over the reef. Restaurant/café on the beach in the summer.

ÇÖKERTME

Pilotage

Approach Çökertme is a popular first-night stop for yachts bound into the gulf. After a night of revelry in one of the restaurants ashore it is often a last-night stop as well. From Bodrum the entrance to the bay is difficult to make out until you are nearly upon it. The huge power-station chimney at Ören will be seen further to the east of the bay and closer in three communication towers on the eastern entrance point will be seen.

Mooring Yachts can anchor in one of the coves on the western side of the bay with a long line ashore or go stern-to one of the jetties off the restaurants

on the coastal flat the hamlet is built upon. In the western anchorage a long line ashore is essential as the *meltemi* gusts down into the bay with some ferocity. The bottom is mud, sand and weed, poor holding in places. There are laid moorings off the restaurant jetties so that you don't have to use your own anchor. The restaurant owners will row out or stand on the wooden jetties with the mooring lines entreating you to berth there. Take your time and make up your own mind where you are going. When the *meltemi* is gusting down it will tend to be on the beam as you head into the catwalks that can make it a tad difficult at times. Good shelter in the bays on the west side as long as you are securely tied to the shore. On the restaurant jetties you will hopefully be tied to something solid so the gusts should be of little consequence.

Facilities

In the west bays a boat from one of the restaurants will come out to visit you to enquire if you are going ashore to Captain Ibrahim's, Rose Mary or the Çökertme Restaurant and whether you will want a lift ashore and back again. You can take up the offer or potter over in the dinghy. Apart from the restaurants there is a small minimarket and if you are on one of the restaurant piers there is water and electricity and the possibility of showers.

General

The setting is spectacular with the mountains rising from the shore in layered folds and tucks enclosing steep gorges and gullies. The gentler slopes around the bay are planted in olives and a few crops while the higher slopes are covered in pine – a landscape that will be repeated many times down the coast. The only flat land is the sandy patch by the water's edge where the houses of the hamlet are built.

The raffish Captain Ibrahim, looking not unlike a latter-day corsair from the Barbary coast, is a well known character in the gulf. The evening's entertainment starts after dinner with Ibrahim bringing out his *nargile* and offering everyone a puff: a sort of Çökertme peace-pipe. The tobacco is placed in a bowl on the top with a live coal to keep it burning, and the smoke is sucked through the water to the coiled pipe and mouthpiece. The smoke is cooled as it bubbles through the water and has none of the harshness of cigarette or cigar smoke. Then the music starts and the dancing follows soon after. The evening runs on *raki*. The Rose Mary is a family-run affair

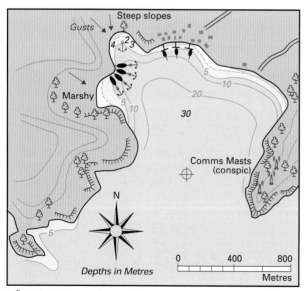

ÇÖKERTME
⊕36°59'·96N 27°47'·52E WGS84

Çökertme looking W along the N coast of Gökova Körfezi
Kadir Kir

Restaurant pier in Çökertme complete with laid moorings and assistance

with friendly service and a show of sorts to rival Captain Ibrahim's. The Çökertme Restaurant is the quietest and more convivial of the three. If you are anchored out it is best to leave your dinghy behind and get a lift back on the restaurant's runabout as the *raki* will more than likely have stacked the odds against you finding your own way back.

In the morning, in a more sober light, you can see carpets being woven on hand looms in the village. The carpets from Çökertme and the surrounding region as far as Mumcular are distinctive and pleasing pieces, and here is as good a place as any to get one if you happen to find one you like.

Around Çökertme

To the west of Çökertme are a number of coves that make ideal lunch stops and, depending on the weather, can be used as overnight stops. These should be explored with caution as there are numerous rocks and reefs off the coast. One of my favourite places is below the village of Mazi where a fish restaurant sits on a rocky bluff by the shore, with steps cut into the rock to get up to it. There is a jetty here now that you can go stern-to on or you can anchor immediately west of the restaurant off the beach, although it can be a bit rolly from the swell that curves around the headland. There are strong gusts with the *meltemi* but tied up to the jetty you should have few problems in settled weather. In unsettled weather this is not a good place to be.

From the restaurant you have an uncluttered view out over the bay and the gulf to the Dorian Promontory ten miles away on the other side.

ÖREN

⊕37°01'·55N 27°58'·52E WGS84

From Çökertme the coast is fairly straight, with the mountains rising abruptly from the sea to 600m (2,090 ft) and more. Ören sits on the only flat bit of land along the coast, a narrow strip of land under Kiran Daği, a sheer curtain of rock between Ören and Akbük. Really the most prominent feature here is the huge coal-fired power station that burns low-grade coal from a mine just inland. There has been a lot of local anger over the siting of this power station in this wonderfully savage landscape and for a while the government agreed to delay operation of the power station. It is now up and running though its long term future is in doubt.

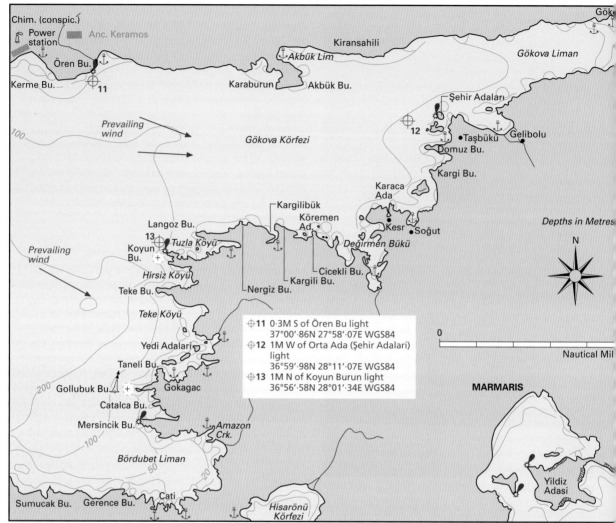

GÖKOVA KÖRFEZI EASTERN END

The following labels appear on the map:

Chim. (conspic.)
Power station
Anc. Keramos
Kiransahili
Gök
Akbük Lim
Gökova Liman
Ören Bu.
Kerme Bu.
11
Karaburun
Akbük Bu.
Şehir Adaları
12
Taşbükü
Gelibolu
Prevailing wind
Gökova Körfezi
Domuz Bu.
Kargi Bu.
Karaca Ada
Kargilibük
Köremen Ad.
Langoz Bu.
Kesr
Soğut
Depths in Metres
13
Koyun Bu.
Tuzla Köyü
Değirmen Bükü
N
Prevailing wind
Hirsiz Köyü
Cicekli Bu.
Teke Bu.
Kargili Bu.
Nergiz Bu.
Teke Köyü
Yedi Adalari
Taneli Bu.
Gollubuk Bu.
Gokagac
MARMARIS
Catalca Bu.
Mersincik Bu.
Amazon Crk.
Bördubet Liman
Yildiz Adasi
Sumucak Bu.
Gerence Bu.
Cati
Hisarönü Körfezi

⊕**11** 0·3M S of Ören Bu light
37°00'·86N 27°58'·07E WGS84
⊕**12** 1M W of Orta Ada (Şehir Adalari) light
36°59'·98N 28°11'·07E WGS84
⊕**13** 1M N of Koyun Burun light
36°56'·58N 28°01'·34E WGS84

0

Nautical Mil

The steel light structure on Ören Burnu is conspicuous. Once around here and into Camalti Bükü the short mole off the village, with a white pillar and statue, will be seen. Further around the beach to the east is a fishing boat mole and coastguard post.

In calm weather a boat can anchor in 6–12m off the beach. With the *meltemi* blowing it would be uncomfortable and perhaps untenable here. There is a pier off the power station, but this is not available to yachts.

Note There are plans to build a marina at Ören, as part of a major tourism development of the area. At the time of writing no plans are available showing the layout, although it is likely that construction work will start in the near future.

The small harbour at Ören with the tall chimney of the power station in the background

Ancient Keramos

The very forces that formed the coastal plain Ören is built on are the same forces that spelled the end of the ancient city of Keramos. A river cuts its way down through the mountains behind Ören and although it only runs above the ground in the winter (in the summer the smaller volume of water runs in underground channels), it brings down sufficient silt to build up an alluvial plain. Keramos originally stood by the sea and was an important port in antiquity, but today the ruins are a mile from the sea and the city walls are partially buried in the silt brought down over time.

As for the city that the gulf was named after, remarkably little is known about it. The walls and remaining masonry indicate a Carian city that was Hellenised and was evidently of some size and importance. The name is identical to the Greek word for 'pottery' or 'tile', from which we get the word 'ceramic', and although George Bean states that this is only a coincidence, is it also a coincidence that a small trading boat carrying pottery was excavated by George Bass and his team from Bodrum Museum a short distance along the coast from ancient Keramos. This and other finds in the area have led to the conclusion that there was a pottery workshop somewhere in the gulf, and what better place than the city called Keramos. The city survived into the early Roman period but declined soon after that, probably because the port silted.

AKBÜK

From Çökertme to Gökova at the head of the gulf there are no real indentations in the coastline except for a headland which shelters the bay of Akbük (White Bay). From the distance the low line of the headland stands out prominently against the

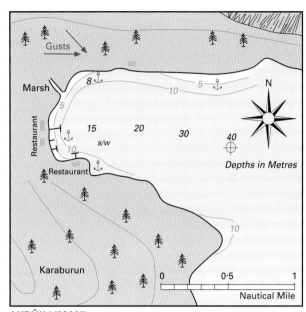

AKBÜK LIMANI
⊕37°01´·61N 28°06´·87E WGS84

Akbük Limani (right) looking NW over the two headlands Karaburun (left) and Akbuk Burnu (bottom) Kadir Kir

rock face of Kiran Daği behind. Once around the headland you enter a wide bay that slopes gently up to the foot of the mountains, much of it covered in pine. Anchor in the southwest corner off the restaurant prominent on the shore and take a line ashore. The restaurants in here have jetties and laid moorings. If you go on the jetty then you should eat at the restaurant there. Alternatively anchor off the restaurants or anchor off in the cove immediately east of the restaurants under a small rocky bluff. If the *meltemi* is blowing its useful to take a line ashore. The *meltemi* can gust into here so some care is needed. At times a katabatic wind may blow down off the mountains at night from the east to northeast. If this happens you need to get out of the western corner and either get some sea room until it blows over (normally 2–4 hours) or try to anchor off on the north side of the bay where shown.

Ashore there are several restaurants and that is about it. The bay is quite simply spectacular, with steep slopes covered in pine rising almost vertically from the sea on the headland and the sheer rocky cliffs of Kiran Daği along the coast.

GÖKOVA ISKELESI

The small village at the head of the gulf. The small harbour here is shallow (it dries in parts) so is of little use to most yachts. Anchor off on the

Gökova Iskelesı

IDYMA

Idyma was an important city of the Rhodian Peraea but little remains of it. The fertile alluvial plain at the head of the gulf would have been cultivated by the inhabitants of Idyma though the acropolis was built high up, in a better defensive position, on the hill above Gökova. Little remains apart from some of the defensive walls and a necropolis by the road where there are several rock tombs, a fairly rare example in the Gulf of Gökova. The tombs are thought to be from the 4th century BC and are probably Carian, though in an Ionian style.

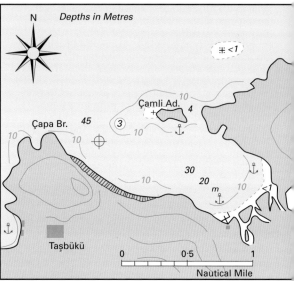

GELIBOLU BÜKÜ
⊕37°00´·0N 28°13´·7E

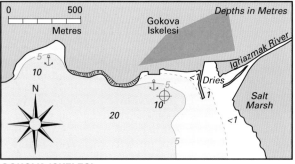

GOKOVA ISKELESI
⊕37°02´·9N 28°19´·3E

outside of the mole or in the bight a short distance west. Neither of these two anchorages is secure when the *meltemi* is really blowing, but in calm weather makes an interesting lunch stop. There is a fish restaurant near the village and a few provisions can be obtained.

At the head of the gulf the Igriazmak River (ancient Idyma) wends its way down through the alluvial plain and spreads out over the salt marsh that borders the sea. There is a mole off the river mouth that local boats use, but the approaches and most of the space inside the harbour is shoal. Even shallow-draught yachts should not attempt to get in here.

GELIBOLU (GALLIPOLI)

Going west from Gökova the first anchorage you come to on the south side is Gelibolu. Care is needed of the isolated reef northeast of the entrance. Anchor at the head of the bay or under the islet, Camlı Adası, on the eastern side of the entrance. It is often best to anchor under the islet in case a katabatic wind gets up and blows in from the northeast in the night. In the southwest corner of the bay there is a T-pier with an extension which is used by tripper boats and a few local boats. Most of the pier is shallow and in any case there is little room to berth. Simple restaurant near the harbour.

At the head of the bay there is a flat marshy area and on the high ground to the north and to the south are a few ancient ruins. Gelibolu is probably a corruption of Callipolis, an ancient

Antony and Cleopatra

In 44BC when Julius Caesar was stabbed to death by an aristocratic clique including Cassius and Brutus, the Roman Empire was left without an obvious successor. Two figures emerged as likely candidates: Octavius, Caesar's nephew, and Mark Antony, Caesar's best general. The two came to terms with one another and quickly quelled the aristocrats and any other candidates they thought might pose a threat. The Empire was divided between Octavius and Antony, with Antony taking the east, including Asia Minor. The difference between the two could not have been more marked. Octavius was a sickly youth, a methodical and careful ruler who was planning for the future of the Roman Empire and his succession. Antony was more in the mould of Caesar, a devil-may-care General, albeit a brilliant one, who led his men into battle and was popular with them. He drank heavily and was notorious for his womanising. When Caesar had tamed Egypt he took Cleopatra as mistress and Antony followed him in this. Cleopatra's fatal beauty did not appear to have dimmed over time and she exercised a hold over Antony that ultimately led to his death.

In the period Antony ruled over the eastern Roman provinces he spent a good deal of his time with Cleopatra, enjoying himself in the cities around the coast of Asia Minor. The partying was on a scale seldom seen before or since. Plutarch described one such event in Samos like this: 'While nearly the whole world was filled with groans and lamentations this one island for many days resounded with the music of flutes and harps. The theatres were filled, and choruses competed against one another. Every city sent an ox for sacrifice and kings vied with one another in entertainments and gifts. Everywhere men began to ask how on earth the conquerors would celebrate their victory when their festivities at the opening of the war were so expensive.' As Antony spent more time with Cleopatra his popularity with the legions declined. His popularity in

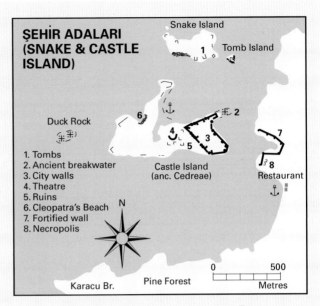

ŞEHİR ADALARI (SNAKE & CASTLE ISLAND)

1. Tombs
2. Ancient breakwater
3. City walls
4. Theatre
5. Ruins
6. Cleopatra's Beach
7. Fortified wall
8. Necropolis

Snake Island
Tomb Island
Duck Rock
Castle Island (anc. Cedreae)
Restaurant
Karacu Br.
Pine Forest
0   500
Metres
N

Part of the ancient wall around Cedreae on Castle Island

Rome also declined and it was all but inevitable that a showdown with Octavius was in the offing.

Octavius had to take action against Antony when he declared Cleopatra joint ruler of Egypt and her offspring, including her illegitimate son by Caesar, the heirs of the Eastern Roman Empire. Octavius gathered his forces against Antony and the two rivals met at Actium in western Greece. The outcome was decided almost before the battle began. Antony's legions and generals deserted to Octavius and when the fleets came out to do battle, Octavius's superior forces quickly routed Antony's fleet. The story of Cleopatra fleeing the battle in her purple-sailed galley and Antony deserting his men to follow, is well known, and a sad finale to his brilliant life. Shakespeare catches the shame and despair of it all in this passage from *Antony and Cleopatra*:

> She once being loofed
> The noble ruin of her magic, Antony,
> Claps on his sea wing, and like a doting mallard,
> Leaving the fight in height, flies after her.
> I never saw such an action of such shame.
> Experience, manhood, honour, ne'er before
> Did violate so itself.

The conclusion to it we all know. Antony committed suicide as did Cleopatra soon after her capture. The illegitimate son of Caesar was quietly disposed of.

Inevitably the liaison of Antony and Cleopatra and their pursuit of pleasure along the coast of Asia Minor has spawned a whole host of apocryphal tales about what went on where. Many of the ancient Graeco-Roman ruins have had a tale and a name tacked onto them: Cleopatra's Island, Cleopatra's Beach, Cleopatra's Bay, Cleopatra's Baths, and so on. Poor old Antony hardly gets a mention. There may be some truth in some of the tales, and even if there is not, there should be.

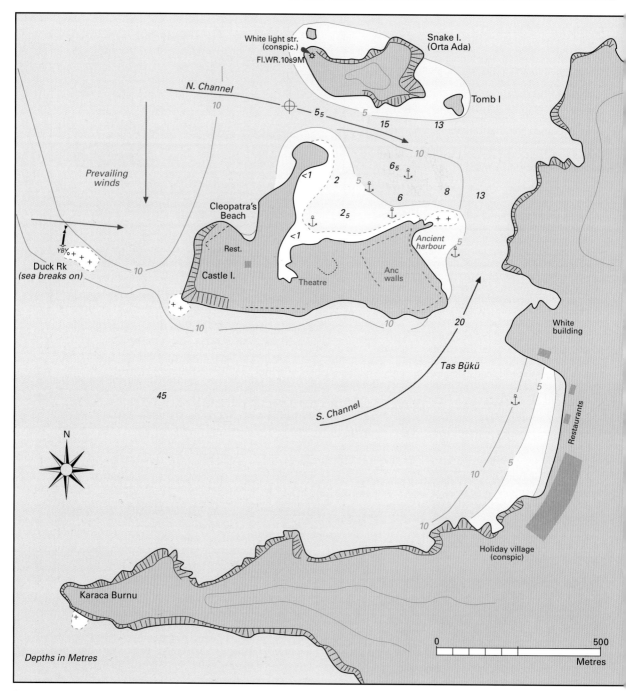

ŞEHIR ADALARI (SNAKE AND CASTLE ISLANDS)
⊕36°59′·81N 28°12′·21E WGS84

city situated six miles inland to the east. The site on the coast was probably the port for the city proper and somehow retained the name when the inland site declined in the early Middle Ages.

ŞEHIR ADALARI

Pilotage

Approach The islands tucked close into the land in the southwest corner of the gulf are difficult to make out from the distance, although the white buildings in Tas Bükü will be seen. Care is needed of Duck Rock off the western side of the islands. It is marked by a west cardinal beacon. The approach can be made by either the North or South Channel, though care is needed of depths and rocks lying close to the islands.

Mooring Yachts normally anchor in the bay on the northeast side of Castle Island although it can get very crowded in the summer. Trip boats run from Tas Bükü ferrying holidaymakers across to Cleopatra's Beach, and they take up a fair amount of room in the inner part of the bay. Alternatively anchor off the eastern side of Castle Island or in Tas Bükü. Shelter is good from the *meltemi*, although in the night a north or northeast katabatic wind may blow, making it uncomfortable here.

Facilities

Virtually none. A restaurant/café opens in the summer and also in Tas Bükü. *Dolmuş* run to Marmaris from Tas Bükü. If you are in the main anchorage there is a warden who will collect a fee to pay for rubbish disposal and caretaker duties.

There have been reports that the restaurant has closed and visitors are denied permission to land. Play it by ear and see what is what when you get here.

General

It has numerous names. In Turkish it is called Şehir Adalari, Şehirlioglu and Sedir Adası, meaning variously the Island city and the Island of cedars. In ancient times it was known as Cedreae (as in the cedar tree), though none are to be seen today. On Admiralty chart 1533 the islands are

The anchorage on Castle Island with Snake Island top of photo   *Kadir Kir*

rather theatrically called the Snake and Castle Islands: the 'castle' is easily derived from the ancient ruins of Cedreae and the snake comes from a symbol found on a tomb on the smaller island. More recently it has been dubbed Cleopatra's Island and the tale behind the name is fascinating. When the Roman Empire was divided up between Antony and Octavius, Antony and his mistress Cleopatra spent a great deal of their time in the Roman provinces of Asia Minor. Evidently Cleopatra spent some time in Cedreae, but was distressed by the lack of a sandy beach to cavort upon. In an age when anything seemed possible and frequently was, she ordered sand to be brought by ship from the Sahara and had the perfect little beach constructed on the west side of the island. Is it just an apocryphal tale? The sand has been examined by a geologist, Professor Tom Goedike, and pronounced to be untypical of the region and to conform to the type of sand found in the Sahara.

The approach to the islands and the anchorage on the north side of Castle Island is a beguiling one. Tombs litter the slopes of Snake Island. In the passage between the islands the water shallows to a sandy turquoise that is so clear you can see the bottom 5m (16ft) below as if you were standing on it. From the anchorage little can be seen of ancient Cedreae apart from a section of the city wall and a few piles of masonry. The city proper was situated on the eastern half of the island and to get to the theatre, the temple, and the city walls you will have to pick your way through the olive trees and thick undergrowth. The small theatre is romantically sited in a dense thicket and is well preserved, though much overgrown. Once it would have had a view out over the anchorage, but today the dense thicket shuts out the sky and the sea. Other buildings are scattered around the undergrowth and as you come across a building here or there it is a bit like being let loose in an archaeological toyshop, discovering one new treat after another.

On the northeast tip of the island the remains of an ancient breakwater (now partially submerged) can be seen. Galleys and trading ships would have used either the anchorage on the north now used by yachts and *gulets*, where they could beach the vessels at the head, or this small harbour tucked under the city walls. Further to the east of the ancient harbour, the walls of the city, some of it in good condition, can be traced for much of their length.

On the mainland opposite a necropolis and parts of an ancient wall can be seen. To the south of the necropolis is the bay of Tas Bükü with a few houses and a restaurant and a recently built holiday village at the southern end. In recent years numbers of land-based visitors have been attracted to Tas Bükü and from here small boats run them across to Castle Island. The inevitable despoiling of the islands from rubbish thoughtlessly discarded by visitors has recently had a stop put to it with the appointment of a warden and the provision of containers for litter. Waterborne visitors should know better than to dump non-biodegradable rubbish, especially plastic, in the sea; but even biodegradable litter such as orange peel or vegetable matter should not be thrown overboard in a bay like this where the prevailing wind will blow it onshore. Cleopatra must be turning in her grave.

DUCK ROCK

Care needs to be taken of this razor-back reef just to the west of Castle Island. Now it is marked by a beacon with a west cardinal mark on it there should be little excuse for not spotting it, though in the past it has claimed several yachts. One can only wonder if a slight phonetic mistake was made by the midshipman surveying it for the Admiralty, but one that couldn't be printed on a chart.

SÖĞÜT (Karacasöğüt)

Pilotage

Approach From Şehir Adalari it is a short passage around Karaca Burnu and Karaca Island to Söğüt (pronounced 'So-oot'). The entrance can be difficult to see from the distance, but closer in the houses and yachts are readily identified. It's well worth pottering around the inside of Karaca Adası just for the wonderful views between island and shore.

Mooring There are several places a yacht can berth.
1. *Söğüt jetty* In the southwest corner there is a long catwalk jetty with some laid moorings. Go stern or bows-to where convenient or directed. Charge band 3.
2. *Karacasöğüt Jetty* The long T-pier off the village where you can go stern or bows-to where directed. Laid moorings to pick up. VHF Ch 73. Charge band 3.

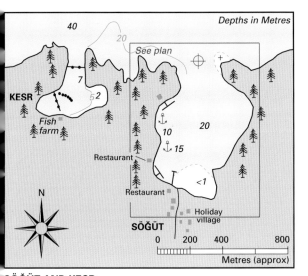

SÖĞÜT AND KESR
⊕36°56´·92N 28°11´·39E WGS84

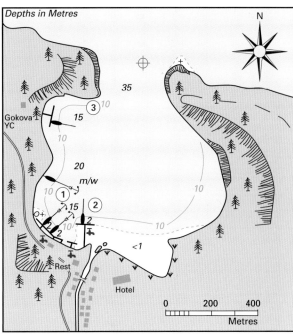

SÖĞÜT
⊕36°56´·92N 28°11´·39E WGS84

3. *Gökova Yacht Club* A T-pier in the northwest corner of the bay. At weekends several charter companies do turn-arounds here so space is limited. Laid moorings to pick up. VHF Ch 72. Charge band 3/4.

4. There are still a few places left to anchor off and take a long line ashore on the west side of the bay. It is very deep for anchoring so you will need plenty of chain out.

There is excellent shelter in here and you would hardly know the *meltemi* was blowing further out in the gulf.

Söğüt looking into the anchorage. On the left of picture is Karacasöğüt jetty, then the Söğüt jetty around the shore and on the right the Gökova Yacht Club   *Kadir Kir*

Karacasöğüt pier

Facilities

Services Water, electricity, showers and toilets at Karacasöğüt Pier and Gökova Yacht Club. Water and electricity on Söğüt jetty.

Provisions Small minimarkets. Good local honey. Ice.

Eating out I'd suggest you eat in whichever restaurant is nearest the boat or has the best view. At the root of Karacasöğüt jetty there is a good restaurant and there are several others though some have been closed down because they were built without planning permission. Gökova YC has an up-market restaurant with superb views that mostly caters for the charter boats based here.

Other Dolmuş into Marmaris.

General

The approach to Söğüt from behind Karaca Island is a gently pleasing one with the slate-coloured cliffs of the island in contrast to the wooded foreshore. In calm weather you can anchor in the cove on the shore for a swim and lunch; but be prepared to move out when the wind gets up.

Söğüt is an enclosed bay surrounded by thick pine forest. A small holiday village has been built on the flat land at the head of the bay but doesn't intrude overly on the bay. A spring favours this spot with water renowned for its purity, so much so that the place has been dubbed 'Honey Water Bay' by some.

KEŞR (Canak Limanı)

⊕36°57'·11N 28°10'·33E WGS84

This narrow fjord-like inlet immediately west of Söğüt is little frequented, partly because mooring space is restricted with the fish farm in here and partly because it is a dark, almost ominous spot, that the sun hardly seems to reach. The creek is now buoyed off at the entrance blocking ingress inside.

DEĞIRMEN BÜKÜ

A large, deeply indented bay with a number of coves and inlets dotted around the edge.

Pilotage

Approach Like Söğüt, the entrance to the large bay is difficult to identify until closer to. Care is needed of the isolated reef under Karaada off the eastern entrance. If you keep to the west of Karaada and Zeytinli Ada there are no dangers in the approaches.

Mooring There are a number of places a yacht can anchor around the large indented bay.

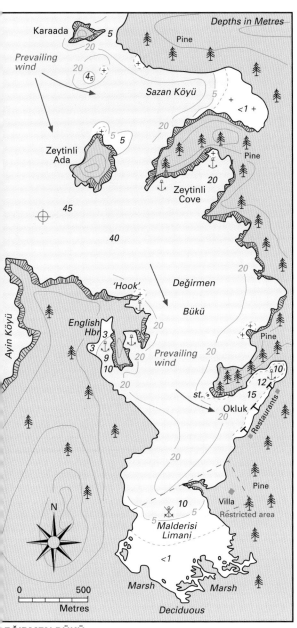

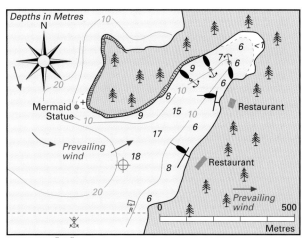

OKLUK KÖYÜ
⊕36°55′·05N 28°10′·1E

Restaurant jetty in Okluk Köyü

EĞIRMEN BÜKÜ
⊕36°56′·18N 28°08′·79E WGS84

1. **Okluk Köyü** The inlet on the eastern side (see plan) with several restaurants on the southern side. Off the entrance there is a statue of a mermaid erected by Sadun Boro. The two restaurants here have T-piers where you can go stern or bows-to. There are some laid moorings, but usually you will have to use your own anchor. If you are using one of these piers then it is only politic to eat in that restaurant. Alternatively anchor and take a long line ashore on either side at the head of the inlet. Be careful opposite the jetties where anchors can cross in the middle of the inlet. Care is needed at the very end where the depths come up quickly to a shelf with less than a metre over it. Good shelter in the inlet, although the prevailing wind tends to blow down into Değirmen Bükü and then perversely curl around and blow into the inlet. More uncomfortable than dangerous until the wind dies down in the evening.

Sadun Boro

I first met Sadun Boro when I sailed into Değirmen Bükü over 30 years ago. His Atkins ketch was anchored in Okluk and after we had looked in there we decided to anchor for the night in English Harbour. In the morning there was a loud 'halloo' from the shore and there was Sadun. He had walked all the way around the shore and over a cuppa in the cockpit invited us for dinner on *Kismet* the next day. On subsequent visits we have dined and wined and renewed our friendship with this wonderful man, the first Turk to sail around the world in a small sailing yacht.

Sadun was born in 1928 in Istanbul and started sailing on the Sea of Marmara while still a teenager. While studying textile engineering in Manchester he signed up for a transatlantic crossing on a 36-foot yacht and fell in love with the whole idea of cruising the seas. Back in Turkey he was assigned to run a textile factory in Iskenderun and resolved to build a boat and go cruising. In 1963 he had *Kismet*, a 36-foot Atkins ketch, built and began equipping her for long passages. He had to make up much of the equipment like the deck hardware and fixings and fittings himself as they were not readily available in Turkey. In 1965 he set off with his German-born wife Oda and spent three years circumnavigating the world on the Trade Wind route. This was the era of the Hiscocks, of Humphrey Barton, of the Smeetons and John Guzzwell, of Dr Peter Pye, many of whom the Boros met on their travels. You can find a photo of the young Sadun and Oda in Eric Hiscock's *Voyaging Under Sail*.

Sadun on his circumnavigation catching breakfast

Sadun Boro on *Kismet* getting ready to head down into the gulf

The whole enterprise was sponsored and made public by the Turkish daily *Hürriyet* and its editor, Necati Zincirkıran, a sailor himself. When the Boros arrived back in Turkey they were feted by the press and overnight Sadun became a national hero. A stamp was issued in *Kismet*'s honour and his account of the voyage, *Pupa Yelken* ('Running Downwind', literally 'Wind under the Stern'), became a bestseller. I still have the copy of his book he gave me all those years ago. Up until recently Sadun was still sailing his beloved *Kismet* around the Aegean, but in 2010 it was donated to the Rahmi M. Koç Maritime Museum in Istanbul and he now sails a modern catamaran called *Son Bahar* ('Fall' or 'Autumn', literally 'The last Spring').

And he still spends most of his time in Gökova Körfezi, a place he calls 'the most beautiful place to sail in the world'. When you sail into Okluk Bükü you will see the statue of a mermaid Sadun had made perched on the rocks off the entrance, and inside the cove don't be surprised to find a still sprightly Sadun anchored under the pines at the end.

2. **Malderesi Köyü** Yachts are now prohibited to anchor here. On the western side there is the holiday home of a prominent Turkish politician and when he is in residence or there are guests a patrol boat is usually in evidence, keeping yachts out of this part of the bay.

3. **English Harbour** The bay opposite Okluk. Anchor where convenient and take a line ashore to the eastern side. The bottom here is sticky mud and good holding. Good all-round shelter. There is a cove immediately east that also affords good shelter. In English Harbour and several of the other coves tripper boats will anchor briefly for lunch or a swim, but they are all gone by mid-afternoon.

4. **Hook cove** Just up around from English Harbour there is a short headland right on the corner where you can anchor and take a long line ashore. In settled weather there is a surprisingly good lee from the *meltemi* here.

5. **Ayin Köyü** The large bay on the western side of Değirmen Bükü. In settled weather when the

Okluk Köyü in Değirmen Bükü. Note the shoal at the head of the bay *Kadir Kir*

meltemi is not blowing too hard you can anchor on the west side and take a long line ashore. Some swell rolls around into here and it is not as sheltered as some of the other anchorages.

6. **Sazan Köyü** The large bay between Karaada and Zeytinli on the eastern side of Değirmen Bükü. The prevailing wind blows into here, but in calm weather it is an attractive spot to stop for a swim.

7. **Zeytinli Cove** Opposite Zeytinli Ada there is a bay where you can anchor and take a long line ashore to the north side. It's a bit uncomfortable until the *meltemi* dies down, but usually quite tenable. You will be dropping your anchor in deep water here so make sure you have plenty of it. Zeytin means 'olive' and is presumably a reference to olives growing on the islet.

Facilities

In the eastern cove you will find the only facilities here at the restaurants. The restaurants often have good fresh fish and a hose from a nearby spring supplies water nearly as good as that from Söğüt. There is also a minimarket with limited provisions.

General

On the eastern side of the bay the slopes are covered with thick pine forest and the eastern cove is a little gem with pine on the slopes and a few deciduous trees near the shore. The slopes around English Harbour have recently been replanted with pine after a fire sadly destroyed the mature forest: a salutary reminder to us all of the fire risk from a cigarette carelessly discarded or a barbecue fire. At the head of Değirmen Bükü there is a stand of fragrant amber trees (*Liquidamber orientalis*) which are tapped for their resin. Gashes are cut in the trunks and a tin nailed to the tree collects the resin in much the same way that natural latex is collected from rubber trees. The resin from the fragrant amber is used in soaps and perfumes for its antiseptic properties and its fragrance, though in days gone by it had all sorts of properties attributed to it. The Chinese believe it is a cure-all for a wide range of ills: ulcers (in particular stomach ulcers), haemorrhage, toothache, swellings, some cancers, and that it improves circulation and healing of wounds and cuts. Certainly in the west in medieval times it was reckoned to cure, if not all

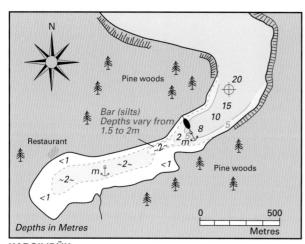

KARGILIBÜK
⊕36°56'·1N 28°05'·8E

these ills, then a goodly number of them. The Turks call it *gunluk* (fragrant) or *sigla* (gum) and use it for its antiseptic properties, and in soaps and perfumes for its fragrant smell. In autumn when the leaves are turning, the surroundings are reminiscent of parts of northern Europe.

English Harbour, the inlet on the western side of the bay, is so named from the Second World War when English torpedo boats are reputed to have holed up here during daylight hours before venturing out at night. The name and the tale are difficult to relate to the Turkish situation in the war, which was to take a neutral stance with non-aggression treaties towards both the Axis and the Allied powers. Turkey did not declare war on Germany until February 1945 by which time it was evident that Germany's fate was sealed and surrender was not far off. A friend of mine, Johnny Guard, has written an interesting account of this period of the war when the Special Forces conducted a maritime guerrilla war in the Aegean using any craft, including sailing boats, to harry the Germans. If you have an interest in this period of war history I recommend his book *Improvise and Dare: War in the Aegean 1943–1945*.

KÖREMEN ADALARI

⊕0.25M N of Köremen Ad 36°56'·57N 28°07'·46E WGS84
A group of small islets lying 1½ miles west of Değirmen Bükü. Under the islets is a headland and on the eastern side there is a cove with good shelter from the *meltemi*. Anchor where convenient with a long line ashore tucked in as far as possible under the headland.

KARGILIBÜK (Longoz Köyü)

A long narrow inlet a few miles west of Değirmen Bükü. The inlet is deep until you get to a narrow waist inside where the inner half shallows, although there are 2–3m depths in the middle up until halfway in. You can anchor around the edges in the outer part of the inlet with a long line ashore, although it is quite deep here and you will be anchoring in 20m plus. Tripper boats pop in in the morning and anchor here, but don't stay long.

If you venture past the bar into the inner part just be careful, and if you do go aground it is all soft mud and pretty easy to get off. Anchor in the inner half with a line ashore to the north side where there is all-round shelter.

The inlet is a wonderful place, almost a little spooky, and very hot in the summer as little wind penetrates. It is a hurricane hole if you get down into the inner half of the inlet as little wind and no sea get this far. Ashore a simple restaurant opens in the summer, though they seem to get little custom.

TUZLA KÖYÜ

Tuzla Köyü (Salty Gulf) is the long inlet running east from Koyun Burun. The light structure on Koyun Burun is easily spotted and you then just proceed around until you get to your chosen cove. If coming from the west care is needed of Karamuk Reef which used to be marked by a west cardinal buoy, though in recent years it has not been in place. Take the prudent course and keep well north of Koyun Burun.

Once inside there are several coves you can anchor in just inside the entrance where shown on the plan. There are a few rocks bordering the

Tuzla Köyü looking over the anchorages tucked under the entrance

coast, but these are easily seen by day. It is quite deep until close to the coast and you will frequently need to drop the anchor in 12–20m, so make sure you have a good length of cable and take a long line ashore to the south side. The shelter from the prevailing *meltemi* blowing outside from the west to northwest is better than it looks in here.

A few *gulets* use the anchorages, but in general this is a wonderfully peaceful place with a knobbly red rock landscape covered in pine and clear blue water.

You can also anchor further down or at the head of the bay, but shelter is not as good as in the coves near the entrance.

HIRSIZ KÖYÜ

⊕36°54′·5N 28°02′·4E

A few *gulets* squeeze up around into this small inlet where there is some shelter from the *meltemi*. I would suggest you look at it in calm weather though take some care over depths.

YEDI ADALAR

This corner of the gulf is a windy old place, renowned for the *meltemi* accelerating over the narrow neck of the Datça Peninsula and into Hisarönü Körfezi on the other side. When the *meltemi* is blowing it pushes a confused sea into this corner and if you add to that a number of above and below-water rocks littered all over the place to compound the pilotage, it all adds up to an area you need to exercise some care over. You should really make the approach through the northeast or southwest channel as shown on the plan. It is possible to thread your way through the islets off the coast, but the two channels at either end are more straightforward.

Once under the islets there are several places a yacht can anchor.

1. **North Cove** The small cove at the northern end of the chain of islets. Anchor in 10–14m and take a line ashore to the western side. Good shelter from the *meltemi*. Restaurant close by.
2. **East Creek** The long inlet on the eastern side. You can anchor just inside the entrance on the

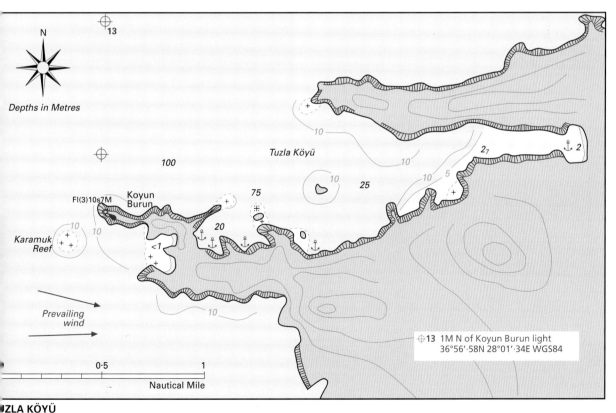

⊕13 1M N of Koyun Burun light
36°56′·58N 28°01′·34E WGS84

TUZLA KÖYÜ
36°55′·73N 28°01′·28E WGS84

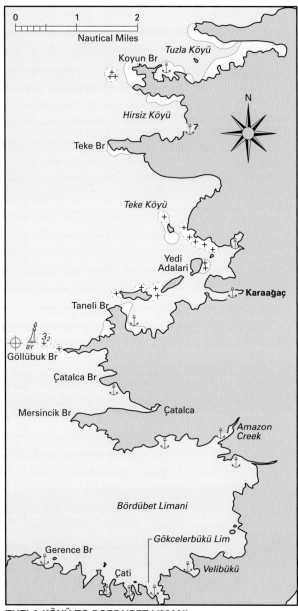

TUZLA KÖYÜ TO BORDUBET LIMANI
⊕0.25M W of Göllübuk Br.
36°51′·34N 27°59′·44E WGS84

Yedi Adalari looking down the straggling chain from North Cove to Gökağaç   *Kadir Kir*

south side with a long line ashore or proceed into the inner lagoon. Proceed slowly into the inner lagoon as there is a sandbank running out across it. The tip of the southern entrance in line with the extremity of the northern side leads you over the bank with just 1·8m under you. The bar has silted since my earlier surveys and if in doubt reconnoitre by dinghy to check

depths over it. Inside anchor and take a long line ashore, usually to the north side. Excellent all-round shelter inside.

3. *Karaağaç* A bight just under East Creek where you can anchor and take a line ashore to the western side.

4. *Gökağaç* An anchorage at the southwest end. Anchor and take a line ashore to the western side.

The name means the 'seven islands', but as there are only five easily recognised as such; whoever named the place must have counted a detached rock or two. The area has a wilder and more rugged aspect to it than the softer pine covered slopes further east. Here the trees are stunted and

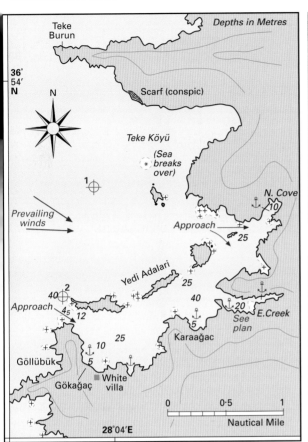

YEDI ADALARI ANCHORAGES
⊕1 0.45M W of islet, 36°53´.02N 28°01´.48E WGS84
⊕2 Close E of 4m shoal, 36°52´.00N 28°01´.06E WGS84

The anchorage in the east creek at Yedi Adalari

YEDI ADALARI EAST CREEK
⊕36°52´.12N 28°02´.74E WGS84

twisted by the prevailing westerlies that howl over the islands and adjacent coast in the summer months. The islands are lumpy rocky things bereft of any vegetation, and the waters around them are spiked with razor-back reefs and jagged pinnacles of rock. East Creek is used by a few fishermen and is a little oasis for water-birds (heron, cormorant, curlew and the electric blue kingfisher).

CATALCA

⊕36°50´.3N 28°01´.3E

A long skinny inlet under Catalca Burnu. The prevailing wind tends to blow straight into the inlet, but some *gulets* anchor in the bight under the cape where there is better shelter.

AMAZON CREEK

Normally I abhor the renaming of bays and islands along the lines of 'Dream Bay', 'Paradise Island', and others of the same mould, but in the case of Amazon Creek the name fits the surroundings. Proceed into the inlet with care as the bottom comes up quickly to less than a metre, though fortunately it is mud. Anchor clear of the end of the inlet and take a long line ashore to the north side or swing to an anchor in the middle. Alternative anchorages are under the southern entrance point and in some of the coves on the underbelly of Mersinçik Burnu. Inside the creek there is some shelter from the *meltemi* although there can be strong gusts into the inlet. The best

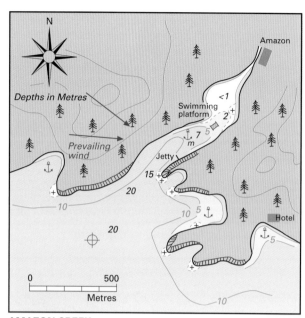

AMAZON CREEK
⊕36°49´·60N 28°02´·74E WGS84

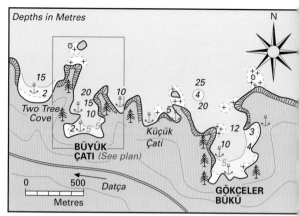

GÖKCELER BÜKÜ AND BÜYÜK ÇATI

policy is to anchor with a long line to the north side. In the other anchorages shelter is also good, though not all-round.

The Amazon restaurant is open from May–September. From the anchorage there is a sign-posted track of about 500m leading up the river. If you call *Amazon* on VHF Ch 77 they will come to the jetty to take you to the restaurant. The jetty is a bit rickety and care is needed of protruding nails. Alternatively you can anchor off the hotel in settled weather.

VELIBÜKÜ

⊕36°47´·9N 28°02´·4E

A bay in the southeast corner of Bordubet Limanı that can be used in light conditions. If the *meltemi* is really blowing this is not a good place to be, although the wind does tend to lift a bit here. If in doubt about the viability of the anchorage head for Gökceler Bükü or Çati.

GÖKCELER BÜKÜ (Balikasiran Köyü)

⊕36°47´·5N 28°01´·8E

An indented bay offering good shelter from the *meltemi*. The wind tends to lift a bit here and you should tuck yourself into the west side of the bay. Proceed with care into the bay taking care of the reef and shoal water. A few local boats are kept in the southwest corner and if you can get in here

there is good shelter. Anchor and take a long line ashore on the western side or near the head of the bay. The bottom is mud and good holding.

Here you are on the other side of Bençik, where the inhabitants of Knidos attempted to dig a defensive canal across the isthmus. The alternative Turkish name, Balikasiran, means the place where 'fish jump across' (the isthmus).

BÜYÜK ÇATI AND KÜÇÜK ÇATI

These two bays afford good shelter from the *meltemi*, especially in Büyük Çati where you can tuck right inside and get all-round shelter. In the approaches One Tree Island, an islet off the entrance to Büyük Çati, will be seen and closer in a stunted tree will be seen growing on it. Küçük Çati lies a short distance east. Off the coast there are numerous rocks and reefs, but the water is very clear here and in calm weather the dangers are easily spotted. There are a number of places yachts can anchor.

Büyük Çati anchorage

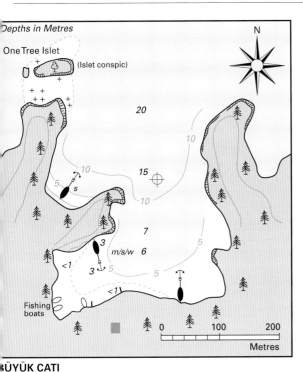

Depths in Metres

One Tree Islet

(Islet conspic)

20

10

10

15

10

5 s

10

3

m/s/w 6

5

<1

3

5

5

<1

Fishing boats

0   100   200

Metres

ÜYÜK ÇATI

⊕ 36°47´·60N 28°00´·92E WGS84

Büyük Çati and Küçük Çati looking east *Kadir Kir*

1. ***Büyük Çati*** Proceed into the bay and around the dogleg to the inner anchorage. Anchor and take a long line ashore to the north side. The bottom is mud and the shelter all-round.
2. ***Büyük Çati beach*** In calm weather you can anchor off the beach in the outer part of the bay. The *meltemi* will not always blow home here, but if it does just chug around into the inner anchorage.
3. ***One Tree Cove*** Immediately west of Büyük Çati there is a cove that can be used in calm weather. In earlier visits I called this Two Tree Island and Cove, but one of the trees has gone.
4. ***Küçük Çati*** The small bay just east of Büyük Çati. If the *meltemi* is blowing strongly this is not a good place to be and you should head around into Büyük Çati. Anchor and take a line ashore to the western side.

These anchorages are all in idyllic surroundings with clear turquoise water everywhere. Ashore there is rough red rock, with pine growing out over the water everywhere. A few *gulets* will put into Büyük Çati, but frequently you will have this place to yourself, especially at the beginning and end of the season. As yet there has been no construction around these wonderful bays, but the construction of a new road around the steep hills above Çati doesn't bode well for the place.

GERENCE BURNU

⊕36°47´·9N 27°59´·5E

There is a reasonable lee here from the *meltemi* tucked under the cape with a long line ashore to the western side.

GÖLYERI

⊕0·45M N of N cardinal off Kuzgun Bu
  36°49´·07N 27°55´·07E WGS84

An anchorage off the hamlet of Gölyeri tucked under Kurzgun Burnu. Care is needed in the eastern approaches of the detached reef off Kuzgun Burnu which is now marked with a north cardinal buoy (⚉ topmark). Care is also needed of rocks and reefs bordering the coast. Enter the bay with caution as the water shoals inside and anchor in 4–6m with a long line ashore to the western side. Reasonable shelter from the *meltemi* although some swell rolls around the cape into the anchorage.

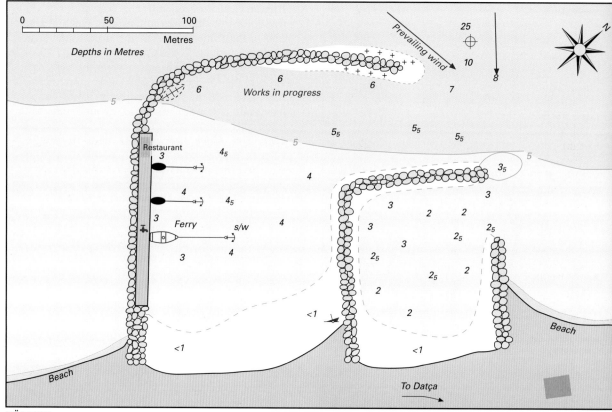

KÖRMEN
⊕36°46'·31N 27°37'·01E WGS84

KÖRMEN

Most of the Dorian Promontory is mountainous except for the coastal plain at Körmen. As you approach from offshore look for the valley gap between the mountainous slopes either side.

Pilotage

Approach Look for the coastal flat and then closer in you will see a few white houses and the rough stone breakwaters. With the *meltemi* a confused swell heaps up at the entrance so you need to keep a bit of speed on until inside the breakwater where it will be calm.

Mooring Proceed into the main basin and go stern or bows-to the quay leaving the ferry space clear. Good shelter in here although the *meltemi* tends to blow somewhat beam-on, so make sure your anchor is well in.

Note Work is in progress developing a new 270-berth marina. It is likely that parts of the harbour will be closed and berths restricted until work is completed. The project has a completion date of

Körmen looking NW over the old harbour

2013. Further details will be included in future supplements available on the Imray website.

Facilities

Services Water and electricity on the quay.

Provisions There is not a lot here. The best idea is to go into Datça which is around 6km away. A *dolmuş* runs at times, or try hitching. You can get a taxi back.

Eating out A restaurant ashore. Restaurants seem to come and go: at times there have been three and at others just the one.

General

Körmen is not a place many yachts head for; most find it a bit depressing. It seems somehow ordinary, the harbour a bit scruffy, after the other anchorages in the gulf. But the place grows on you and the surroundings, the steep northern slopes of the promontory and the fertile plain, are really quite grand.

In antiquity a harbour existed here, although virtually nothing remains of it. George Bean discovered a capital built into the village mosque that has been reused as a boundary stone and is inscribed, in letters of the fourth century 'Boundary of the Harbour'. He also traced the route of an ancient road (the modern road has been built along much of its course) to Triopium (Palamut) on the other side of the peninsula.

MERSINÇIK

Mersinçik is the most westerly bay suitable for an overnight stay on the south side of the gulf before you turn the corner to Knidos and Datça. The anchorage off the hamlet is rather exposed and most yachts and *gulets* make for a small cove north of the hamlet if the *meltemi* is blowing with any strength. Anchor and take a long line to the north side of the bay. It is quite deep in here,

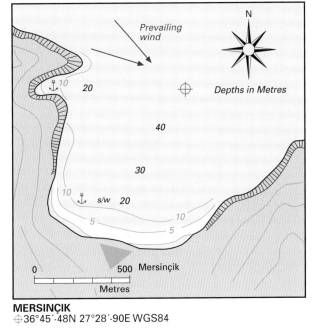

MERSINÇIK
⊕36°45'·48N 27°28'·90E WGS84

although you can pull yourself quite close in to the northern side. The bottom is hard sand, mud and weed with a few rocks thrown in for good measure which makes the holding uncertain in places, so make sure your anchor is well in. The

The cove on the west side at Mersinçik

Badem the Mediterranean Monk Seal

In December 2006 a badly dehydrated and abandoned monk seal pup was rescued from a beach near Didim and taken to the Monk Seal Rehabilitation Centre near Foca. After several months' care 'Badem', meaning 'almond' in Turkish, was deemed ready for re-release back into the wild in the Spring of 2007. A suitable site in the gulf of Gökova was selected, and Badem was transported down from Foca, her care and expenses paid for by a local businessman. As sometimes happens with seals following rehabilitation, Badem has found it difficult to disassociate from humans, and was seen in several places around the gulf playing on the beaches and around small boats, even climbing into the cockpits of charter boats, much to the amusement of tourists.

It was clear that Badem needed a few more lessons in how to be a wild Monk Seal, and so a further period of rehabilitation ensued. During this time the rescue centre also mounted a campaign of awareness for the local community and tourists, to inform them of the best way to discourage Badem's interaction with humans so that she might make a complete return to the wild. Look out for Badem next time you are sailing around the gulf, though she roams around, and enjoy the fact that you are watching one of the world's most endangered species frolicking around you. But please follow the advice of the experts, and do not encourage direct interaction with her. It may just make the difference between Badem, and others like her, surviving or being lost as a species forever. And besides, she bites!

For more information on Badem see www.sadafag.org or www.monachus-guardian.org

DATÇA YARIMADASI

cove is an idyllic little spot surrounded by steep pine-covered slopes except for the pebbly beach and flat land at its head.

There is little in the hamlet ashore, just a few fishermen and some small-holders.

THE DATÇA PENINSULA: KNIDOS TO DATÇA

KNIDOS

This is the old harbour of Knidos, the same harbour used by the ancients over 2,000 years ago, tucked under Cape Krio at the end of the Datça peninsula.

Pilotage

Approach The bold promontory of Cape Krio (properly Deveboynu Burnu, although most people still call it Cape Krio) is easily identified from seaward. From the north you will not see the entrance to the harbour on the south side until

⊕**14** 0·5M N of İnce Burun light
36°49'·19N 27°38'·45E WGS84
⊕**15** 0.5M W of İskandil Burnu (Knidos)
36°42'·75N 27°21'·17E WGS84
⊕**16** 0·75M W of Deveboynu Bükü (Knidos)
36°41'·45N 27°20'·90E WGS84
⊕**17** 0·75M S of İnce Burnu
36°38'·69N 27°40'·69E WGS84
⊕**18** 0·25M S of Uzunca Ada lt (Datça)
36°43'·28N 27°42'·83E WGS84

you are nearly upon it. From the east it can be seen from some distance off. When the *meltemi* is blowing there can be severe gusts in the approaches and in the harbour itself and, combined with the confused seas off the cape, calls for some care. Shorten sail before you get close to the cape or alternatively motorsail the last bit as there can be frustrating patches with no wind followed by strong gusts when off the high land near the cape. Care is needed of the submerged breakwater on the northeast side of the entrance which can be difficult to identify when the *meltemi* is whipping up whitecaps. The

Cape Krio on a good day

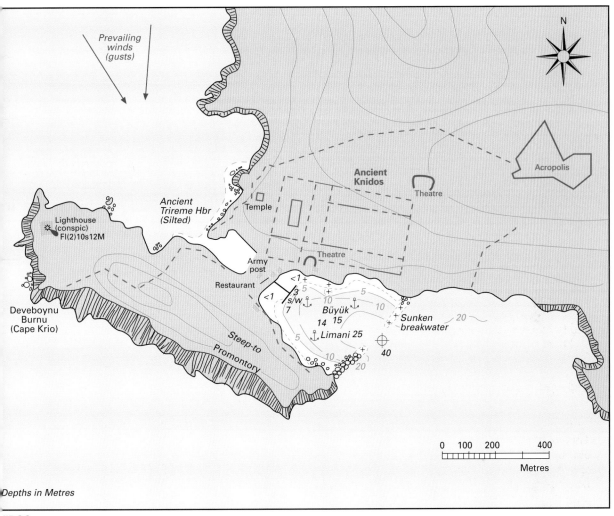

NIDOS
36°41´·01N 27°22´·65E WGS84

best policy is to stay around 20m off the end of the breakwater on the southwest side and have someone up front con you in if you are at all uncertain. I've seen several boats mangle keels and rudders on the underwater breakwater, and it's not pretty.

Mooring There is a long jetty off the restaurant where you can go stern or bows-to with care. Reconnoitre first as depths are variable off the jetty. Charge band 2/3. Alternatively anchor off where possible. The holding is uncertain in places so make sure your anchor is well in before leaving the boat to go ashore. Good shelter from the *meltemi* although there are severe gusts into the old harbour which can fray the nerves. In the event of strong southerlies it is best to leave and go to Körmen or Bodrum.

Facilities

A restaurant ashore which often has fish. Infrequent *dolmuş* to Datça. *Jandarma* (gendarme) post. The caretaker for the site makes a small charge for visitors and both the caretaker and the *jandarma* may want to check your bags to make sure you are not walking off with some ancient bric-a-brac.

General

Knidos is one of those places where you can easily transport yourself back in time. The old city has gently crumbled away into the rocky foundations

Knidos

When the energetic Charles Newton, British Consul to Turkey in the mid-nineteenth century, discovered a massive stone lion, all eleven tons of it, at Knidos, he wrote afterwards that 'the lion seemed made for the scenery, the scenery for the lion'. The scenery on the rocky promontory is just like this. Indeed, the scenery has altered little since the city was deserted sometime in the Middle Ages and, apart from the modern lighthouse on the cape, not at all since Newton visited it and shipped off tons of antiquities, including the lion, to the British Museum. The view from seaward is that which small trading ships would have seen 2,000 years ago as they approached the harbour.

Knidos at the extremity of the Dorian Promontory sits on tiered rocky slopes dominated by the slab-sided Cape Krio. It was the second city to bear the name Knidos. The original site was near Datça, but the inhabitants soon realised the strategic advantages of a city on the end of the promontory and subsequently established new Knidos there. Maritime commerce was on the increase in the 4th century BC and the inhabitants of old-Knidos, halfway along the Dorian Promontory, must have watched enviously as trading ships sailed by and around Cape Krio heading for Halicarnassus and points

further north. All through the summer the *meltemi* blows from the north and often the traders would have to anchor in the lee of Cape Krio to wait for the wind to die down before they rounded the cape. In the summer you can wait some time for the northerlies to drop (as any yachtsman in the area knows) and the Knidians were onto a good thing when they moved to the end of the promontory.

The move from the old site near Datça to the new site occurred sometime in 360BC. The craggy Cape Krio was then an island, so the Knidians laid a causeway to it and constructed harbours on either side. The island was largely used for private residences while the public buildings were laid out on a generous scale on the flatter mainland opposite. From the skeleton that remains the size and scale of the city is easily visualised, mostly because no modern buildings obscure it and little grows on the dry rocky ground to conceal the ancient streets and buildings. The city walls, the small theatre by the harbour, several temples including the temple of Aphrodite, patron deity of the city, the *agora*, the streets, the large theatre, and the acropolis on a bluff above the city are all easily identified. It is the isolation and size of the site which is impressive, not its

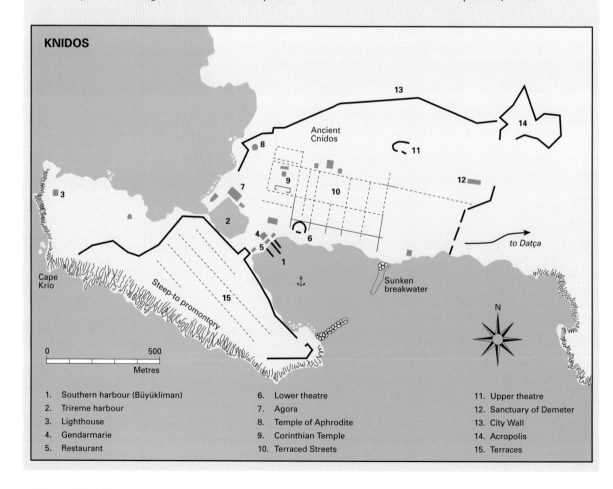

KNIDOS

Ancient Cnidos

to Datça

Cape Krio

Steep-to promontory

Sunken breakwater

0   500
Metres

N

1. Southern harbour (Büyükliman)	6. Lower theatre	11. Upper theatre
2. Trireme harbour	7. Agora	12. Sanctuary of Demeter
3. Lighthouse	8. Temple of Aphrodite	13. City Wall
4. Gendarmarie	9. Corinthian Temple	14. Acropolis
5. Restaurant	10. Terraced Streets	15. Terraces

completeness. If you sit for a while in the upper part of the city you can mentally reconstruct it from the jumbled pile of stones and get a fair idea of what it must have looked like. A few signs around describing the buildings on the site also help.

If Knidos captured wind-bound ships in its harbour, Praxiteles captured the hearts of the Greeks with what was apparently the most beautiful statue of the era. Men literally fell in love with his statue of Aphrodite and they came from far and wide to look at it. In this Knidos had some of the earliest tourist trade, long before the English deserted their own damp climate for the Côte d'Azur, or more recently jetted around the skies looking for sun, sea, and sand. The statue was a source of some contention. It was modelled on Phryne, the most famous and beautiful *hetaera* of the age, and it was sculpted nude, a revolution in an age where only men had been sculpted nude. Praxiteles first offered the statue to the citizens of Kós, who had also recently moved their city from a site inland to the site of present-day Kós. These prudish citizens are said to have refused the nude Aphrodite and ordered another with cloth chipped into the marble for modesty. So the Knidians got the nude Aphrodite, which they mounted on a circular platform in a temple on the northern slopes. The temple base is still there, but sadly Aphrodite is not.

Many stories are told of the beautiful statue. Lucian relates that the shrine had a back, as well as a front door so that the posterior of Aphrodite, said to be as lovely as the front, could be seen. With the old woman who held the key to the vital back panel, Lucian viewed Aphrodite from the rear and pronounced that she was indeed as lovely behind as she was in front. During his tour of inspection he noticed a dark mark on the inner thigh and asked the old woman whether it was a flaw in the marble. She replied that it was not. A lovesick admirer, unable to control his desire for her, contrived to hide inside the shrine and so have her to himself for the night. In the morning the statue was discovered to have a dark stain on the inner thigh, the mark of the young man's passion, that proved impossible to remove from the marble. Another tale relates how the King of Bithynia offered to pay off all of the city's debts (a not inconsiderable amount) if he could have the statue in exchange. The good citizens of Knidos quite rightly preferred the beauty of Aphrodite to a clean slate in the city's financial affairs.

What happened to the statue is uncertain. One source says it was taken to Constantinople and later destroyed there in a fire. Iris Love, who excavated here under the American School, believes she found the head in the cellars of the British Museum, shipped back in 1859 by the enthusiastic Newton. The museum denies that the head came from Knidos and the fate of the statue is still very much clouded in mystery.

The paradox of Knidos is why it went downhill. It is easy to understand why ancient cities such as Ephesus and Caunos expired as the rivers their harbours were built near silted up: the traders just couldn't get their ships in, despite dredging. Since trade was almost exclusively by sea this spelt death to a city; up until twenty years ago most trade between the small villages and towns along

Looking NW from the ruins of ancient Knidos over the ancient trireme harbour to the lighthouse on the cape

this coast was still carried out by sea. But the harbour at Knidos did not silt. It's still there and is now called Büyük Limanı, 'Big Harbour'. Yachts and *gulets* use it as a convenient stopover when going north or south or, as in the days of old, as a refuge from the northerlies. The ancient breakwaters are still in place, though the eastern arm is now just under the water and a danger to craft unaware it is there. The western arm is virtually intact, its extremity in water some thirty metres deep. Around the inside of the harbour large sections of the ancient quay are still in place, though the sides have crumbled making it unsafe to go alongside. The smaller northern harbour is the one Strabo called the 'Trireme Harbour' and it held around 20 of these warships. It is open to the north and has consequently silted from the sand deposited in the entrance by the waves pushed down onto it by the northerlies, but otherwise it is essentially intact. So why did Knidos decline? By Roman times it was no longer a major city and in the Byzantine era it is barely mentioned. There is no evidence of a great calamity like a fire or an earthquake destroying it. There is no good answer to the question; it just gradually went downhill until it was no more than a provincial town, finally abandoned in the Middle Ages.

Knidos looking across the ancient harbour to the ruins of ancient Knidos

it was built on and has not been trammelled under reinforced concrete. The city just wound down and never regained its former importance and glory. Today there is a small fish restaurant, a modest *pension* built by one of the locals, and a small gendarmarie post, but these are recent additions to the landscape. The gendarmes guard the ruins and will sometimes take the opportunity to request cigarettes and whisky. The restaurant often has good fresh fish, sometimes lobster, and drinkable local wine. Perhaps the wine is similar to Knidian wine of two millennia ago that was described as 'nourishing, enriching the blood and promoting easy movement of the bowels, but relaxing the stomach if drunk in excess' (Bean). Come to think of it, that describes today's wine pretty well.

ECHO BAY

⊕36°39'·6N 27°29'·5E

A steep-sided bay just south of Palamut. It offers a bit of a lee from the *meltemi*, but some swell tends to work its way around the corner making it uncomfortable. I'd guess the steep vertical sides of the bay lend it the name Echo Bay.

PALAMUT

Pilotage

Approach The low island in the approaches, Palamut Adası (Baba Adası), will be seen and the harbour lies northwest of it. It is difficult to make out initially, but closer in all becomes clear. Getting into the small harbour is a hair-raising business as you must head straight for the beach

before making a sharp turn to port through the narrow entrance. The exceptionally clear water makes the approach look far worse than it is, though care is needed of rubble on either side. The harbour is prone to silting, especially at the entrance, so care is needed over depths. The entrance and harbour are dredged periodically. Depths are usually somewhere around 2–2·5m and more if it has just been dredged.

Mooring Go stern or bows-to the quay on the northeast side or opposite on the southwest side where there is a stub quay. If all these spaces are taken go bows-to the rough quay outside the stub quay, though care is needed of underwater ballasting. The *meltemi* blows at an angle to the beam and you need to make sure your anchor is well in. The holding on mud with a bit of rubble is good. Good shelter inside and only strong southerlies cause a surge in the harbour. Charge band 2.

Facilities

Services Water and electricity on the quay. Showers in some of the restaurants.

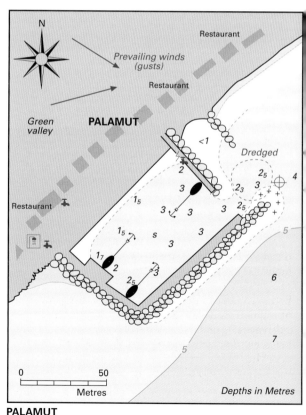

PALAMUT
⊕ 36°40'·17N 27°30'·37E WGS84

Palamut *Kadir Kir*

Provisions A couple of minimarkets. Wonderful local fruit and almonds available in season.

Eating out Restaurants on the waterfront. I suggest you make your choice on locality and what is offered. Up the main road running inland is a wonderful *pide* (Turkish pizza) place though no alcohol is served.

General

The southern side of the Dorian Promontory is for the most part bare rock where little grows except stunted and thorny bushes and pungent thyme. Palamut is one of the few spots where the green of trees and crops relieves the dull grey limestone, though from seaward you can easily miss the hamlet tucked into the corner of the bay with the island of Palamut Adası shielding the view. The island was called Baba Adası, which somehow sounds more interesting to me than plain Palamut Adası. Palamut means 'tuna' (bonito) and a lot of tuna is caught around the Datça peninsula – it might be worth trying that lure again, although the word can also mean acorn, so then again maybe not.

Palamut is one of a group of villages known as Betçe, the 'five villages'. The others, little huddles of white houses and trees and patches of cultivated land, are scattered over the hill-side between Palamut and Datça. It is a little-visited area that relies on agriculture and fishing to keep the village economies ticking over.

Ancient Triopium

The little hamlet of Palamut is the most likely site of ancient Triopium, a city that was once the equal of Knidos. Thucydides mentions how a Spartan fleet sheltered in the harbour at Triopium between new Knidos and old Knidos at Datça. In 1984, while investigating the harbour at Palamut , I very nearly came to grief on what I first assumed to be a short reef running out from the coast on the west side of the bay. Later on when I snorkelled over it, it turned out to be the remnants of an ancient breakwater which probably enclosed a small harbour slightly larger than the present-day one. George Bean has theorised that breakwaters extended from the end of the island across to the shore to enclose a large harbour. While there are no reasons why a harbour of this size could not have been constructed with the technology of the age, it is unlikely a harbour on so grand a scale would have been needed and it would surely have been much commented on as a maritime wonder of the world. It was not, and Thucydides mentions it as one of several harbours along this stretch of coast.

Triopium was a place of some importance early on. It was a meeting place for the Dorian states and the festival of Triopian Apollo, a sort of early Olympics with athletics and running races, we are told. Probably the stadium and the temple of Apollo stood on the level ground around Palamut, but today there is no trace of them. Up above Palamut are the remains of a sizeable town and an acropolis and this is the likely site of the city. The walk up to the site is a pleasant one, but don't go expecting to find anything like the ruins at Knidos. For the more indolent traveller it is far better to sit in the simple restaurant on the beach and contemplate over a glass or two what the harbour of Triopium may have looked like.

KÜRÜBÜKÜ

⊕36°40'·50N 27°32'·20E

Kürübükü (Dry Bay) is a bay under Kürübükü Burnu at the other end of the long Palamut Bükü. You can anchor off the beach in a light *meltemi*, but if it blows strongly a swell tends to creep right along the coast and into the bay, making it uncomfortable.

MESUDIYE BÜKÜ

(Also called Kalaboshi, Hayit Bükü and Ova Bükü)

A small cove lying close east of Adatepe Burnu (Kalaboshi Point). The craggy hump of Adatepe Burnu is easily identified and has an old military watchtower on the summit. The small bay is somewhat hidden away and you will not see the buildings in the hamlet until up to the entrance. Once into the bay care is needed of the reef running out from the north side of the shore.

Yachts usually berth stern-to on the jetty in Mesudiye

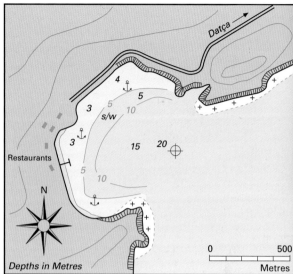

KARĞI KÖYÜ
⊕36°42´·1N 27°41´·1E

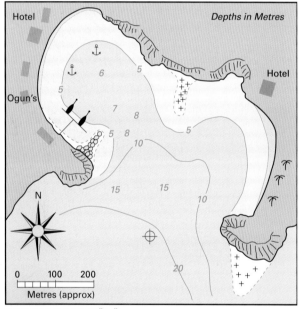

MESUDIYE (OVA BÜKÜ)
⊕36°40´·86N 27°34´·58E WGS84

A jetty runs out from the western side and you can go stern or bows-to to the end where there are 2·5m depths. Depths shallow up further along the jetty. Alternatively anchor off in the bay. Another alternative in settled weather is to anchor just east of the small rock breakwater and take a long line to it. Good shelter from the *meltemi* on the jetty where you are out of the bit of residual swell that curves into the bay. At anchor you will roll around a bit. Charge band 2 on the jetty.

Ashore there is the redoubtable Ogun's restaurant which has excellent home-cooked food. Also toilets and showers and (sometimes) internet access. There are several other restaurants around the bay. The little bay is popular with flotillas so can be crowded at times.

PARMAK

⊕36°40´·3N 27°38´·2E
This bay (Parmak means 'finger') lies around two miles WNW of Ince Burun, the long low finger of a cape that runs out just where you turn the corner to go up to Datça. A delightful cove with pine forest down to the water's edge and reasonable shelter from the *meltemi*. There are some laid moorings but their condition is suspect. Ashore there is a small hotel and restaurant.

KARĞI

The large bay (Karği means 'spear') just around the corner from Ince Burun before you get to Datça. There is some shelter from the *meltemi* here although there are gusts and some swell penetrates into the bay. There are several restaurants ashore and it is a popular place for the locals to come and swim and unwind.

DATÇA

Datça sits up under the belly of the Datça peninsula just before you get to Hisarönü Körfezi.

Looking north over Datça bay and harbour

Pilotage

Approach Coasting from the west you won't see the town until a fair way up into Datça Limanı. From the east the town is easily identified. Once up into Datça Limanı, Uzunca Ada, the islet off the town, will be seen and the approach to the harbour is straightforward. Once up into the bay head for the harbour on the west side of the headland. The *meltemi* screams across this cut in the peninsula right across to Sími. The gusts can be ferocious and you should reef right down before turning up towards Datça.

Mooring Go stern or bows-to the north quay on the south side. Care is needed of the ballasting off

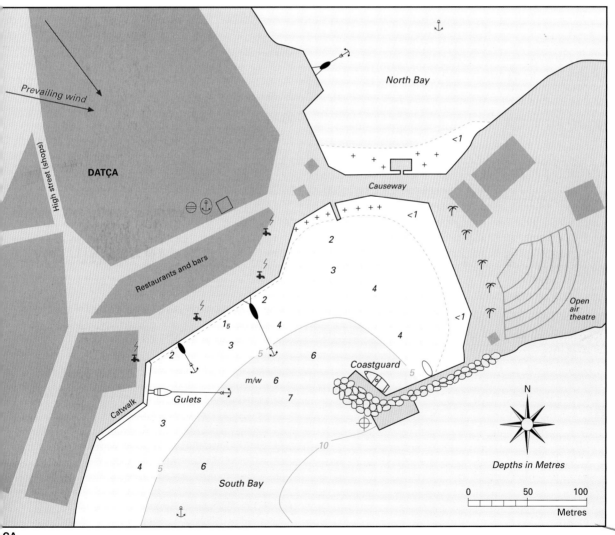

Datça harbour

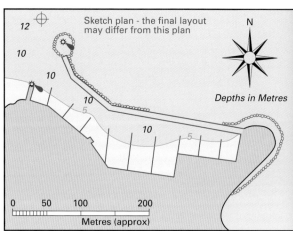

DATCA MARINA - PLANNED FUTURE DEVELOPMENT
⊕36°43'·1N 27°41'·5E

the quay so when stern-to be careful the rudder is not damaged. The local harbourmaster is helpful and will guide you in. Care is also needed not to lay your anchor too far out so it fouls on *gulet* anchors running out from the catwalk. Alternatively anchor out in the bay. The bottom is mud, patchy holding in places. Good shelter from the *meltemi*. Southerlies send in a swell. In southerly gales this is no place to be and you should head off east into Hisarönü Körfezi to find better shelter in somewhere like Keçi Bükü. Charge band 3.

Note There are plans to develop a new marina in the bay to the south of the town. The proposed layout is shown in the plan, but no further details are available, and is probably undergoing planning permission.

Facilities

Services Water and electricity on the quay. Showers and WC. Fuel can be delivered by mini-tanker.

Provisions Good shopping in the town for all provisions. Wander up the high street and you will find minimarkets and towards the top a supermarket. There is sometimes a small market in town.

Eating out A wide choice of restaurants and bars on or near the waterfront. Up the main street there are some less flashy restaurants, including a couple of good *pide* restaurants. The Titanic and Kucuk Ev ('Little House') overlooking the harbour are good if a bit pricey. In town there are more homely *lokantas*.

Other Banks and ATMs. PO. Internet cafés. Hire cars and motorbikes. Bus and *dolmuş* to Marmaris. Ferry to Bodrum from Körmen. Port of entry with Customs and Immigration.

General

Datça (or, to give its proper name, Datça Iskele, *iskele* meaning a landing place for an inland village) is a fishing village which in recent years has developed into a goodly sized tourist resort. It lies around the water's edge on either side of a small isthmus and straggles in a higgledy-piggledy way inland. The village, and especially the new buildings, cannot be described as attractive, but somehow it works as a pleasing and happy place

Perili anchorage looking west over Yolluca Adası   *Kadir Kir*

that I have grown attached to over the years. The small harbour is invariably packed with yachts and *gulets* and if a yacht arrives late in the afternoon it may have to anchor off outside the harbour. Just above the harbour on a low rocky outcrop are several restaurants with views out over the bay to the Greek island of Sími seven or so miles across the water. In one or other of these restaurants you can watch yachts and *gulets* beating up against the *meltemi* towards Datça and competing for space in the harbour – entertaining if you have already arrived and found a space.

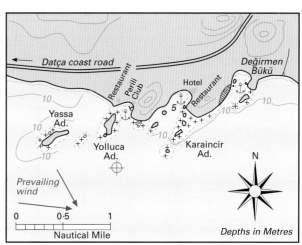

YASSA ADASI TO DEĞIRMEN BÜKÜ
⊕36°45′·0N 27°46′·8E

'Old' Knidos

Datça Iskele is on the southeastern side of the only good fertile land on the otherwise barren and rocky Dorian Promontory. This precious fertile plain, remarked upon by Spratt in the 19th century as having 'fine groves of olive and valonia (Mediterranean oak), and of almonds and other fruit trees', was more than likely the reason for siting old Knidos here. The city was founded by Dorians sometime in the 11th or 12th century BC, though the site is mentioned earlier than this date. From the 7th century the city rose to some prominence and embarked on some colonisation of its own. A band of colonists from old Knidos settled on Sicily, but problems with the locals forced them to move to the Lipari Islands off the northeast coast of Sicily. One of this group of islands is Stromboli, the active volcano dubbed the 'lighthouse of the Mediterranean' as the dull red glow from its continual burping of lava and ash can be seen from many miles away at night. Finds from these early colonists have been discovered on Stromboli and the other Lipari islands. Trade with Egypt was also an important ingredient of old Knidos's wealth and the city helped to establish Naucratis, a Greek-Egyptian trading colony on the Nile delta.

Today little remains of old Knidos and, compared with new Knidos on the end of the promontory, it hardly warrants looking for the old bits of rubble left behind. Near the harbour there is a large platform with terrace walls and this was probably a sanctuary. The acropolis lies to the north of the present village and from the extent of the city walls, some of it submerged in the sea either because the land has sunk or the sea level risen, it has been calculated that there was an enclosed area of over two square miles. The move to new Knidos occurred sometime around 360BC, but the old site was not abandoned. Probably it continued as a small client town producing the crops that could not be grown on the barren ground at the end of the promontory. According to George Bean the name was later recorded by Pliny as Stadia and this name survives in the modern Turkish name of Datça, though I can't see the connection between the two.

Yassa Adası to Değirmen Bükü

From Datça the shoreline runs in a shallow curve until you get to a group of jagged rocks and islets at the eastern end of the bay. Behind and between these islets there are a number of anchorages that afford some protection from the *meltemi*. All the anchorages are open south.

Perili The bay lying under Yolluca Adası. Care is needed of the reef around the islet. Anchor as close to the shore as possible. In the corner there is a T-pier used by a beach club using the small hotel ashore. With a strong *meltemi* some swell is pushed into the bay, but it is generally tenable if a little uncomfortable at times. On the beach there is an interesting restaurant with a neo-Ottoman architectural style.

Karaincir Adalari Immediately east of Perili is another bay with a hotel and restaurant ashore. Care is needed of the islets and reefs in the approaches. Shelter as for Perili.

Değirmen Bükü A little further east is Değirmen Bükü that can be used in calm weather or a light *meltemi*.

Hisarönü Körfezi

The small gulf at the southeastern end of the Dorian Promontory is as wild and beautiful as its larger counterpart on the northern side. Many of the places around its shores are easiest reached by boat: the road around the south side winds interminably through the rocky landscape and under the hot sun you are better off on the sea

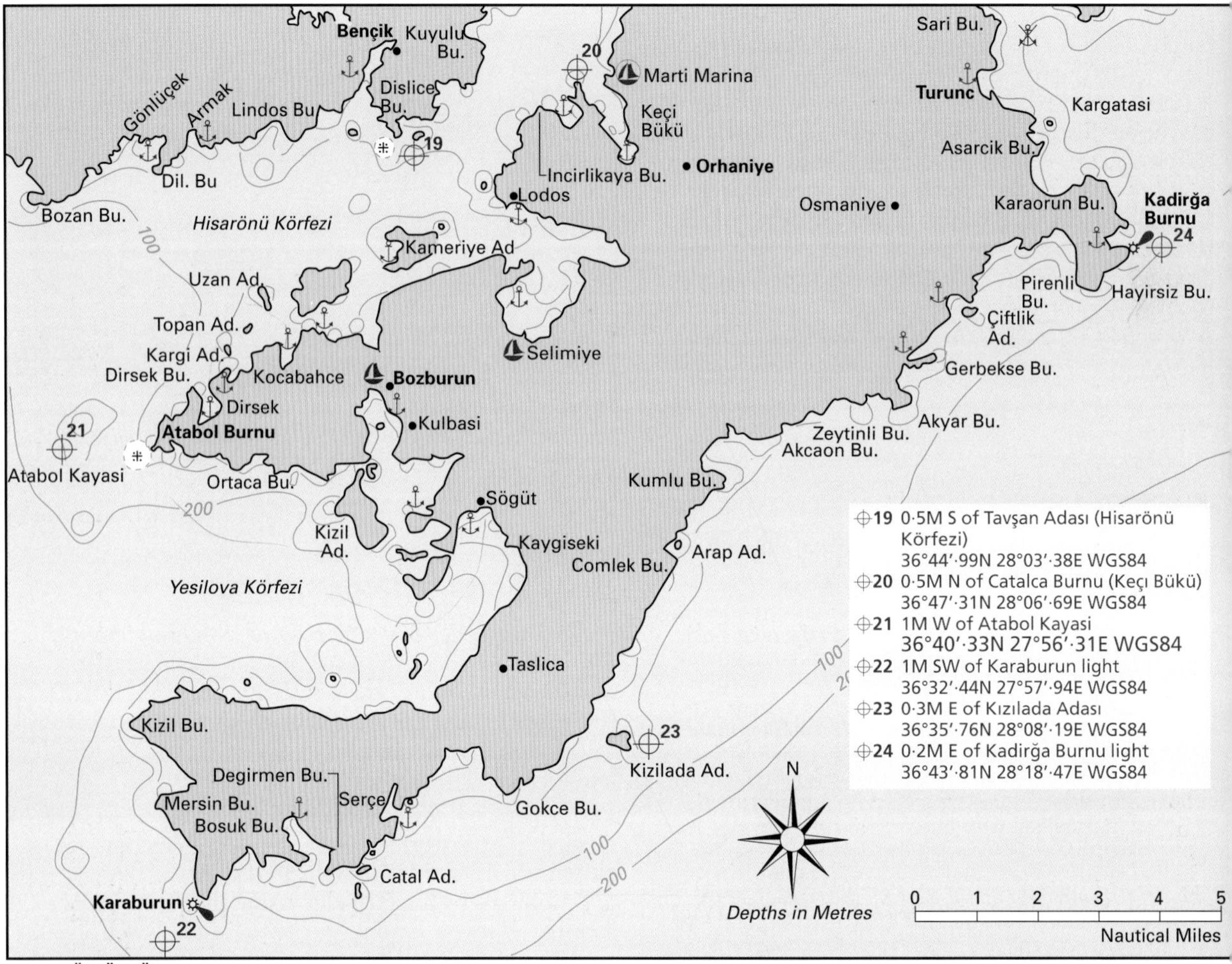
Bençik
Kuyulu Bu.
Dislice Bu.
Gönlüçek
Armak
Lindos Bu.
Dil. Bu
Bozan Bu.
Hisarönü Körfezi
Marti Marina
Keçi Bükü
Incirlikaya Bu.
Orhaniye
Lodos
Kameriye Ad
Uzan Ad.
Topan Ad.
Kargi Ad.
Dirsek Bu.
Kocabahce
Bozburun
Selimiye
Dirsek
Atabol Burnu
Kulbasi
Atabol Kayasi
Ortaca Bu.
Sögüt
Kizil Ad.
Kaygiseki
Comlek Bu.
Yesilova Körfezi
Taslica
Kizil Bu.
Degirmen Bu.
Mersin Bu.
Bosuk Bu.
Serçe
Gokce Bu.
Catal Ad.
Karaburun
Kizilada Ad.
Kumlu Bu.
Arap Ad.
Zeytinli Bu.
Akcaon Bu.
Akyar Bu.
Gerbekse Bu.
Çiftlik Ad.
Pirenli Bu.
Hayirsiz Bu.
Kadirğa Burnu
Karaorun Bu.
Osmaniye
Asarcik Bu.
Turunc
Kargatasi
Sari Bu.
19
20
21
22
23
24
100
200
⊕19 0·5M S of Tavşan Adası (Hisarönü Körfezi) 36°44'·99N 28°03'·38E WGS84
⊕20 0·5M N of Catalca Burnu (Keçı Bükü) 36°47'·31N 28°06'·69E WGS84
⊕21 1M W of Atabol Kayasi 36°40'·33N 27°56'·31E WGS84
⊕22 1M SW of Karaburun light 36°32'·44N 27°57'·94E WGS84
⊕23 0·3M E of Kızılada Adası 36°35'·76N 28°08'·19E WGS84
⊕24 0·2M E of Kadirğa Burnu light 36°43'·81N 28°18'·47E WGS84
N
Depths in Metres
0 1 2 3 4 5
Nautical Miles

HISARÖNÜ KÖRFEZI TO KADIRGA BURNU

where the breeze cools things down. Like the shores of the Gulf of Gökova, its shores are extensively covered in pine forest and there are a number of ancient sites, though none of them measure up to Cnidos or Cedreae.

ÇIFTLIK LIMANI

A large bay easily recognised by the large holiday village at the head. The rocky landscape now changes to thick pine forest again, corresponding to the pine forests on the Gökova side. The approaches are free from danger except for a reef off the east side of the bay and another along the headland between Çiftlik and Kuruca Bükü. Anchor off the holiday village where there is good shelter from the *meltemi,* although there are gusts into the anchorage. Restaurants ashore.

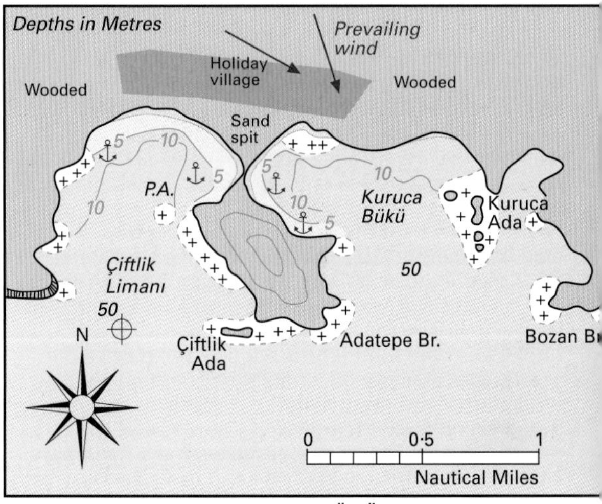
Depths in Metres
Prevailing wind
Holiday village
Wooded
Wooded
Sand spit
P.A.
Kuruca Bükü
Kuruca Ada
Çiftlik Limanı
50
Çiftlik Ada
Adatepe Br.
Bozan B
N
0 0·5 1
Nautical Miles

ÇIFTLIK LIMANI AND KURUCA BÜKÜ
⊕36°44´·6N 27°52´·8E

Kuruca Bükü

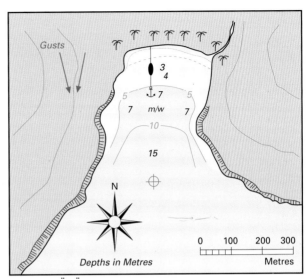

ARMAK BÜKÜ
⊕36°45'·45N 27°58'·6E

Depths in Metres

KURUCA BÜKÜ

On the east side of the headland shaping Çiftlik is the large bay of Kuruca Bükü (Dry Bay). Anchor in the northwest corner off the sandy isthmus dividing the two bays. Shelter here is a bit better than in Çiftlik, although there are still gusts.

The holiday village is said to be popular with the elderly and an amusing anecdote is told to account for this. Just before construction of the holiday village began in the early 1970s, seven old and useless donkeys were turned out to pasture in Kuruca. Two years later when the construction team turned up to begin work, they found a healthy family of 28 donkeys grazing peacefully around the shores. What Kuruca can do for the virility of a donkey, it can do …

GÖNLÜÇEK BÜKÜ

⊕36°45'·6N 27°58'·1E

The large bay to the east of Kuruca Bükü. Anchor where convenient around the bay taking care of the reef running out from the middle of the bay. In places it is worth taking a long line ashore. Reasonable shelter from the *meltemi*, although by now it has been funnelled to blow from the west into Hisarönü Körfezi, so a bit of swell may be pushed into the bay.

ARMAK BÜKÜ

A smaller bay on the east side of Dil Burnu. Anchor at the head of the bay with a long line ashore or anchor free in the bay. The bottom is mud and weed, reasonable holding once the anchor is in. Reasonable shelter from the *meltemi*, although there are gusts into the bay and some swell seems to creep around into here. Around the beach at the head of the bay are palm trees, looking a little incongruous with the pine behind.

BENÇIK

Pilotage

Approach The large hotel on the eastern entrance point is easily seen and the knobbly red outline of Dislice Adası can be seen when closer to, although it can be difficult to pick out against the land behind it. Care is needed of Sunk Rock off the eastern entrance point although it is usually marked by a south cardinal buoy.

Mooring Anchor near the head of Bençik or around the edges. The inlet is mostly fairly deep so it is a good idea to take a long line ashore where possible. There is a quay on the eastern side that can normally be used although yachts have been asked to leave in the past. You can also anchor in the cove on the east side of the eastern entrance point where the hotel has a jetty. If there is room on the jetty you may be able to go stern or bows-to. Good shelter in the inlet from the *meltemi* although there are gusts.

Facilities

Water on the quay in Bençik, though it is not always turned on at the main. Water on the hotel jetty and a restaurant and bar in the hotel.

General

Bençik is situated at the narrowest part of the

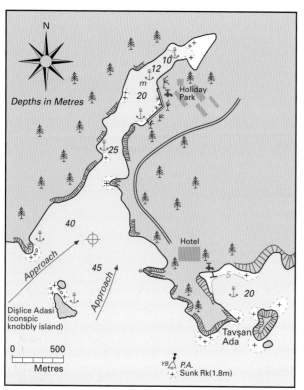

BENÇIK
⊕36°46'·0N 28°02'·25E

Looking NNW into Bençik *Kadir Kir*

Dorian Promontory so that only a short neck of land, about half a mile wide, joins the promontory to the mainland. The local Turkish name for it is 'Balikasiran' which means 'the place where fish jump across' and neatly sums up the size of the neck. The bay on the opposite side in Gökova Körfezi is also sometimes called Balikasiran. This narrow neck of land figured prominently in the history of old Knidos. In the 6th century BC the Persians were rapidly mopping up the Greek cities in their conquest of Asia Minor. The Knidians realised they were threatened and hit upon the idea of turning the promontory into an island by digging a canal from Bençik to the other side. Work proceeded slowly and the rock tended to shatter and splinter a lot, injuring the workmen. If you enter Bençik from seawards one of its outstanding features is the knobbly red rock that makes it look not unlike a mini-Grand Canyon. It certainly looks dangerous stuff to work with though I have not tried to imitate the Knidian workmen and see if it does splinter when hit. The difficult nature of the job gave the city elders cause to consult the oracle at Delphi and the reply was unequivocal:

'Dig not nor fence your isthmus: Zeus himself
Had made your land an island, had he so wished.'

The Knidians stopped work and the Persians encountered no resistance when they arrived, which just goes to show you can't trust an oracle all of the time. When Spratt explored the area in 1838 he believed he found evidence of work on the canal, but nobody since has.

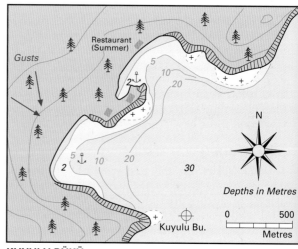

KUYULU BÜKÜ
⊕36°47'·06N 28°05'·13E WGS84

Kuyulu Bükü looking SW over the bay

KUYULU BÜKÜ

Two coves near the end of Hisarönü Körfezi. Anchor in either cove with a long line ashore. With the *meltemi* there are strong gusts off the land into the bays, but the bottom is mud and good holding so you can generally hang on until the wind drops in the night. In the northeast inlet there is an idyllic cove under the southern entrance point. Anchor and take a long line ashore to the southern side of the cove. Although the *meltemi* gusts straight onto it, it is normally tenable.

These two bays are idyllic places with steep slopes clothed in pine all around. Ashore there are fine walks amongst the pine and the marshy ground around some of the bays. A summer restaurant opens in the northerly cove.

MARTI MARINA

A marina situated on the east side of the entrance to Keçi Bükü.

Pilotage

Approach The marina will not be seen until you are up to the entrance of Keçi Bükü. Once in the entrance the hotel on the slopes behind the marina and the masts of the yachts in the marina will be seen. The approaches are clear of dangers with deep water up to the entrance (in fact the entrance has some 25m depth). VHF Ch 73 and 16 for the marina. Callsign *Marti Marina*.

Mooring Marina staff will direct you to a berth. Laid moorings tailed to the quay. Good shelter inside and yachts are left here through the winter. Charge band 4.

Facilities

Services Water and electricity at all berths. Showers and toilets. Wi-Fi. Laundry. Fuel quay.

Provisions Minimarket in the marina. Other minimarkets nearby in Keçi Bükü. Minibus to Marmaris where there is excellent shopping.

Eating out The Mistral restaurant and bar at the marina has good food in an enviable setting. The Wheelhouse café/restaurant in the marina has good honest food including a set menu lunch. Other restaurants around the bay in Keçi Bükü.

Marti Marina looking south

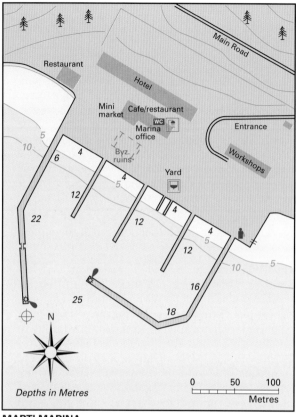

MARTI MARINA
⊕36°46´·20N 28°07´·50E WGS84

Other Customs and immigration can be arranged to clear you in. Exchange facilities. Minibus to Marmaris.

General

The marina is one of the most sympathetic in Turkey. It sits under pine-clad slopes at the entrance to Keçi Bükü with views out across the end of Hisarönü Körfezi and down into Keçi Bükü itself. In the marina some ruins, probably Byzantine, have been left intact amongst the yachts hauled out on the hard. While the charms of Keçi Bükü and a berth at one of the jetties further into the bay beckon, it's still worth spending a night here for the facilities and, yes, for the ambience.

KEÇI BÜKÜ

Pilotage

Approach Keçi Bükü lies at the southeast corner of Hisarönü Körfezi. The approach is straightforward to the entrance although once into the bay some care is needed. If you fork to starboard between the islet with a fort on top and the western side of the bay, care is needed of the reefs and shoal water at the northern end extending out from either side with a 3m bar

Keçi Bükü looking over the sandbar out towards the entrance to the bay to right of photo *Kadir Kir*

Oracles

Time and time again, as with the Cnidians asking whether or not they should continue to dig their canal across the Dorian Promontory in the face of the Persian invasion, the matter of oracles comes up. Whether it was going off to start a war, whether or not to build a new city in a chosen spot, whether to fight an invader or submit, or on a more mundane level whether it was going to be a boy or a girl or whether to pursue a romance, one of the oracles was consulted. The oracle at Delphi was pre-eminent and known all over the civilised world, but other oracles of lesser fame existed. The oracle at Didyma in the gulf above Halicarnassus was one such. Others were situated in Crete, at Paphos in Cyprus, at Mycenae and Epidavros, at Colchis at the eastern end of the Black Sea, at Ammon in Libya, in Athens, and for a short time even in unbelieving Rome.

An oracle was the answer of a god or demi-god to an inquiry about the future. Apollo was the preferred god for prophecy and the sanctuary at Delphi, dedicated to him, the preferred oracle. The oracle was delivered by a priestess, the Pythia, who was said to sit astride a chasm from which intoxicating vapours issued. Alternative accounts state that laurel leaves were burnt and the fumes from these caused the priestess to fall into a trance. The answers the priestess gave were always interpreted: in some cases the answers were apparently unintelligible gibberish, but the interpreters at the temple always managed to get something down, usually in hexameter verse, and it must be supposed the real power of the oracle lay with these poet-interpreters. The oracle was frequently ambiguous and some of the ambiguities had tragic consequences. When Phillip of Macedon was about to set off against the Persians he asked the Delphic oracle what the outcome would be and received this answer:

'The ready victim crowned for death
Before the altar stands.'

Assuming the victim to be the King of Persia, Phillip went ahead with his campaign. Unfortunately for him, he was the victim. The ambiguity of the responses meant the oracle had, de facto, an excellent success rate. When the Greeks asked if they would succeed against the Persians, this cryptic answer was given:

'Seed-time and harvest, weeping sires shall tell
How thousands fought at Salamis and fell.'

Whether it was to be the Greeks or the Persians who fell in their thousands it did not say.

The oracle was not above being partisan, or even being bribed. When the Cnidians asked the oracle whether or not to continue digging the canal, the Delphic oracle was in a pro-Persian period despite being under Greek control. Possibly the priests thought the temple would be under Persian management in the near future when they looked at the success rate of the Persian army against the Greeks. Yet despite the often partisan nature of the oracle, despite bribery and wars over who controlled Delphi and so controlled the prestigious oracle, it continued to be the most revered of all the sacred places. Delphi itself was considered to be the 'navel of the earth' and for those who have been to the precipitous mountain site on which the temple stands, it is not too difficult to understand why. The site is on one side of a great crack in the Parnassus mountain range, a crack that opens up to the plain of Itea and the sea a long way below. Delphi was more to the Greeks than just a fortune-telling enterprise, it was a focus for Greek civilisation and a secure centre for a world constantly on the move and threatened by enemies without and ideas within. On the walls of the temple a number of precepts were inscribed, among them one that has survived in various forms down through the ages: 'Know thyself'. The Delphic oracle was a focus for Greek civilisation to know itself.

One of the last oracles delivered from Delphi before its destruction by the Goths in AD396 captures something of the desolation and mystery of Delphi. It was to be an epitaph for the Roman world as well as the Greek, since Christianity and monotheism was ascendant in the world:

'Go, tell the king – the carven hall is felled,
Apollo has no cell, prophetic bay
Nor talking spring, the cadenced well is stilled.'

---

between them. Further down into the bay care is needed of the sand bar dividing the end of the bay almost into two. The sand bar is relatively easy to spot and as long as you stick to the western side of the bay there is no problem.

Mooring Go stern or bows-to one of the catwalk jetties off your restaurant of choice. Most of them have laid moorings with a long line tailed to the jetty and inevitably someone from one or other of the restaurants will come out and signal for you to come in there. Just take your time and choose where you want to go. Alternatively anchor around the islet taking care of the reef or further down into the bay. In places it is useful to take a long line ashore. The bottom is mud and good holding once the anchor is in. Although the *meltemi* curves around to blow into the bay, it does not do so with any strength and shelter is all-round in here.

Note Several incidents of theft have been reported from yachts at anchor near the islet. Lock up securely before going ashore.

Facilities

Services Water and electricity on the wooden jetties off the restaurants. The restaurants all have toilets and showers.

Provisions Several minimarkets.

Eating out If you are berthed off one of the restaurants you should, out of politeness, eat there at least a couple of times. If you don't eat

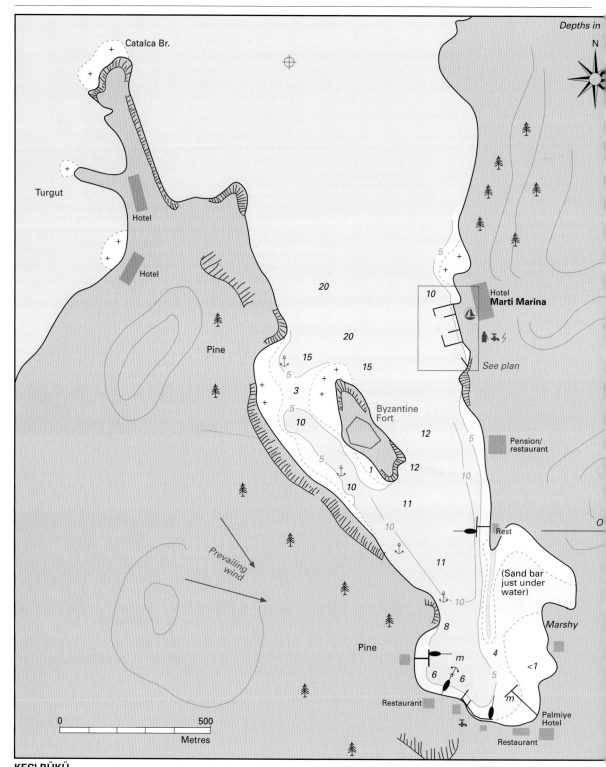

Depths in

N

Catalca Br.

Turgut

Hotel

Hotel

Pine

20

20

15

15

5

3

5

10

Byzantine
Fort

12

5

Pension/
restaurant

5

1

12

10

10

11

Prevailing
wind

10

10

Rest

(Sand bar
just under
water)

11

Marshy

8

Pine

4

m

<1

6

6

5

m

Restaurant

Palmiye
Hotel

Restaurant

0

500

Metres

Hotel
Marti Marina

See plan

0

KEÇI BÜKÜ
⊕36°46´·70N 28°06´·98E WGS84

Anchorage under the islet in Keçi Bükü

Hisarönü Limanı and Bybassus

At the end of the gulf on the flat plain deposited by silt brought down by the river which enters the sea here, stands the small village of Hisarönü. In calm weather you can anchor off in the bay at the end, but normally the *meltemi* sends a swell right onto the beach. Up the river there are some good restaurants: with care you can take the dinghy up the river.

On the flat plain at the head of the gulf lies the village of Hisarönü, from which the gulf takes its name. In antiquity it was called Bybassus and on a rocky outcrop nearby the remains of the acropolis can be seen, but little else remains. Like the other cities in this area, Bybassus was part of the Rhodian Peraea and was important for its association with a temple complex to the south (and to the east of Keçi Bükü). It is likely that Keçi Bükü was the ancient harbour for Bybassus and a landing place for those making a pilgrimage to the temple.

The temple was dedicated to Hemithea, literally the 'demi-goddess', who was revered for her healing powers, particularly for women in childbirth. The method used is described by George Bean as incubation, a method in which the goddess stood over the sick woman and cured her in her sleep. It is speculation on my part, but it occurs to me that all these references to incubation and curing people in their sleep – the method was also practised at Epidavros and by Hippocrates in Kós – refer to hypnosis. It is common knowledge that hypnosis can act as an analgesic and that pain can be almost entirely eliminated under a hypnotic suggestion, or at least that consciousness of pain can be eliminated. I have no concrete references, but I have seen statements to the effect that major open-body surgery has been conducted with the patient under hypnotic suggestion. Certainly hypnosis would make childbirth relatively pain-free and it may be for this that Hemithea was famous.

However cures were effected, the temple was popular for some 200 years from the 4th to the 2nd centuries BC. A festival, the Castabeia, was held here at intervals, and so crowded did it get that an inscription on the site records how accommodation could not be found for the numbers attending and there were worries that revenue was being lost. The historian Diodrus relates that the temple was honoured throughout the Rhodian Peraea and even further afield. Votive gifts were showered on the site from pilgrims who came from far and wide. To get to it today, (it is called *Pazarlik*, 'the market place', in Turkish) entails a fair hike and then a stiff climb some 270m (900ft) to a ridge on Eren Daği. Little remains apart from the platform of the temple and a small theatre in poor condition; and the curious tale relating the strange healing powers of Hemithea.

at the restaurant a small charge will usually be made. Most of them have fairly standard fare and all have wonderful views out over the bay and the yachts moored there.

Other Dolmuş to Marmaris and Bozburun.

General

Keçi Bükü is one of the loveliest places in the gulf. From seawards you enter the inlet with thick pine cover on one side and banks of tall reeds on the other. Halfway down the inlet a steep-sided islet blocks one side of the channel and on the top is perched a fortified structure. The surroundings are nothing short of spectacular and a good-sized handful of the adjectives commonly found in tourist brochures would not do Keçi Bükü justice.

Above the anchorage the small village of Orhaniye is shut in by vertical walls of rock. The gorge behind the village channels a stream down to the sea and this bubbles through the village and surrounding farms. On my first visit here in 1983 a wedding was scheduled for the next day and I was invited to attend. It took place at the farm of the bride's parents and a more beautiful setting is hard to imagine. A brook bubbled through a yard hemmed in by the farmhouse and outbuildings and conveniently supplied crystal-clear water for the farm. It was springtime and the yard was covered in peach and almond blossom. Dogs, chickens, goats, and a donkey puzzled by all the commotion wandered about the tables set up for the occasion.

The wedding party was segregated into a reception party for the males and another for the females, each party with their own separate band of musicians, this being the correct way to stage the wedding, I was told. Only the groom, the father of the bride, and a few village elders were allowed to attend the reception for the bride and the women; a local 'sheriff' with a stout staff kept the local lads from creeping up to watch the women dancing. As a foreigner I was an honoured guest and one of the few males allowed to watch the women. The formal part of the ceremony and the signing of the register were brief, and most of the afternoon was taken up with drinking *raki*, eating, dancing, and drinking more *raki* while the musicians, principally the clarinet player, wailed for all they were worth. My memory of the latter part of the reception is clouded by a *raki*-induced fog, but I remember making my way back to the boat with the help of several men from the village, the clarinet player tootling away in the lead, and none of us very co-ordinated.

Around Keçi Bükü itself there are a few ancient ruins on the eastern side of the inlet, and the fortified structure on the islet. The latter may have had ancient foundations, but is more than likely of medieval origin. Of more recent origin are the restaurants here serving simple but delicious fare. Water from a nearby spring has been analysed in Izmir and found to be just about as uncontaminated as you can get, so yachts and *gulets* often fill their tanks here. The village of Orhaniye is about 2km away, a pleasant walk around the bay and through farmsteads to the foothills of Eren Daği.

TURGUT

⊕ 36°46'·1N 28°07'·4E

The large bay immediately west of Keçi Bükü. With the prevailing wind blowing down into the gulf a swell is pushed into here. In the southwest corner of the bay where shelter is better there are several jetties which *gulets* use. There is little room for yachts, but you can anchor off here. In calm weather it is worth stopping for lunch, but chug around into Keçi Bükü for the night. The coast is slowly being developed, with several hotels built around the slopes and a couple of restaurants.

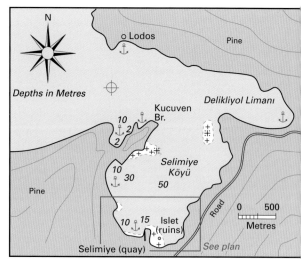

DELIKLIYOL AND SELIMIYE
⊕36°44'·08N 28°05'·36E WGS84

SELIMIYE AND DELIKLIYOL

Immediately south of Keçi Bükü a large bay loops back on itself and fans out into two arms. The first of these is Delikliyol Limanı and the southern arm is Selimiye.

Pilotage

Approach The approaches to Delikliyol Limanı are deep and free of dangers. At the entrance to Selimiye there are reefs on either side. On the western side a reef extends out from the shore with less than 2m depths over it. Because of the size of the bay it is easy to underestimate how far the reef comes out (around 200m) so head for the centre of the entrance. On the eastern side there is a large detached reef (shown as an islet on most charts). Both reefs are easily identified in calm weather. With any wind ruffling the surface the reefs are more difficult to pick out. Apart from these reefs Selimiye Köyü is deep and free of dangers except for the shallows and the islet surrounded by shoal water and reefs at the far southern end (see plan).

Mooring There are a number of places a yacht can bring up.
1. *Selimiye* The village sits at the far southern end of Selimiye Köyü around a stubby headland. The houses of the village are easily seen. A pontoon runs out on the western side of the headland with the village. Berth stern or bows-to either side of the pontoon or on the boardwalk running north to south off the

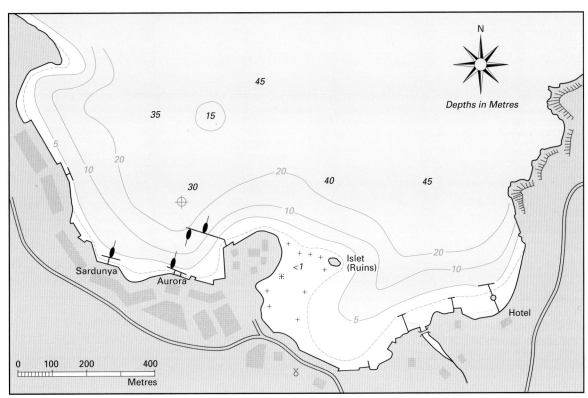

SELIMIYE
⊕36°42′·51N 28°05′·57E WGS84

Selimiye looking W from above the village

village. Care is needed of depths towards the southern end of the boardwalk where there is still some underwater ballasting projecting. Laid moorings tailed to the pontoon and boardwalk. Some of the longer stay boats here will sometimes use more than one mooring so you may need to use your own anchor at times. Remember it is deep off the pontoon, 20m in places, so you will need to have plenty of chain ready to let go. Charge band 2/3.

2. Around the bay from Selimiye village are a number of restaurant jetties and quays. Going westwards from the village.
Aurora T-jetty off the restaurant. 2·5–4m. Laid moorings. Water and electricity.
Sardunya T-jetty off the fairly up-market restaurant. 4m. Laid moorings. Water and electricity.
SW corner Quayed area off several restaurants at the far western end. 2–5m. Laid moorings. Water and electricity.

    A charge is made, usually Charge band 2, though it is often waived if you eat at the restaurant.

    In any of these places there is good protection from the *meltemi* which tends to swirl around at the southern end of the bay. You can also anchor off the village though depths drop off quite steeply. The bottom is mud and weed, poor holding in places.

3. **Delikliyol Limanı** In calm weather you can anchor off the beach here in 3–7m. With the *meltemi* some swell is pushed into here and it is best used in calm weather only. Restaurant ashore opens in the summer.

4. *Lodos* On the northeast side of the entrance to Delikliyol there is a restaurant/bar built on the rocky headland. Here there is a rough quay where you can anchor and take a long line ashore. Off one part of the quay you can actually go stern-to. There is reasonable protection from the *meltemi* blowing down the gulf outside although a bit of slop disturbs the bight. At one time the place was much used by flotillas and charter yachts, but in recent years a 'No entrance: Private' sign has been up and the enterprise appears to have been abandoned. It may open again.

5. *Kucuven Burnu* Under this headland on the southern entrance to Delikliyol there is a bay which can be used in calm weather or light westerlies. It is mostly quite deep so anchor and take a long line ashore to the western side.

Facilities

Services Water and electricity on the pontoon and restaurant jetties. Fuel by mini-tanker.
Provisions Mini-markets in the village and baker and butcher. Market on Wednesdays.
Eating out In Selimiye there are several restaurants on the front including 'Golden Teeth' who turns out to be none other than Osman who was at Serçe many years ago and now here. He doubles as informal 'dockhand' tying boats up and the restaurant is not half bad. And he does have a mouthful of gold teeth. If you are on one of the restaurant jetties such as the Aurora or Sardunya then you will probably be eating there.
Other ATM. Internet cafés. *Dolmuş* to Marmaris and Bozburun.

General

The bay is a remote place, though less so than a few years ago when Selimiye had little more than a simple village restaurant and café. The bay is a magnificent place with wooded slopes all around and steep rocky cliffs cutting down to the sea in places. In antiquity a small city flourished here, either near present-day Selimiye where there are a number of ancient ruins, or on the northern side of the bay where there is an ancient acropolis with a fort from the Middle Ages built on top of it. The bay was called Sinus Schoenus (the Bay of Reeds), in antiquity and the city, most likely near Selimiye, was called Hyda or Hyla.

Selimiye to Bozburun

From Selimiye the steep coast is a wild and rugged landscape with little sign of habitation. A chain of islands, two of them quite large and three smaller ones, lie just off the coast. Once around the corner into Sombeki Körfezi the landscape changes dramatically to barren rocky hillside and a rubble-strewn coastline, a harsh glaring landscape hard on the eyes after the green pine of Hisarönü.

    In calm weather there are a number of anchorages off the islands that can be used for lunch stops.
Kameriye Ada On the west side of the island there is a cove that can be used before the westerlies blowing into the gulf get up. On the south side of the island there is an old Greek church or small monastery, long ago abandoned in the population transfers at the beginning of the 20th century.
Koca Ada On the southeast corner there is a bight affording some shelter from the westerlies and with suitable depths to anchor in. In settled weather it is a possible overnight stop depending on the strength of the westerlies blowing down.
Kocabahçe 36°42'·29N 28°00'·64E WGS84 A bay on the mainland opposite Kargí Adasí. In the southwest corner there is the Sailors Paradise restaurant with a jetty. Go stern or bows-to the jetty where there are laid moorings tailed to the

Old Greek monastery on Kameriye Ada

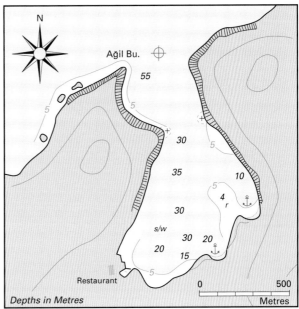

DIRSEK
⊕36°41´·65N 27°58´·78E WGS84

Sailor's Paradise Restaurant in Kocabahçe

jetty. Alternatively there are a few laid moorings with buoys near the jetty. Good shelter from the *meltemi*, but open north. The restaurant is a convivial place with simple fare including good fresh fish.

DIRSEK

On the east side of Agil Burnu just before you turn the corner to head into Yeşilova Körfezi. The approach and entrance are free of dangers until you get down into the bottom of the inlet. There are a number of places to anchor.

1. In the southwest corner at the very end of the inlet there is a stone jetty and pontoon off a simple restaurant. Go stern or bows-to the pontoon. There are mostly 2m depths. Good shelter from the *meltemi*.

2. Anchor off the south side near the restaurant with a long line ashore. Good shelter from the *meltemi* and wonderfully clear water for swimming.

3. In the southeast corner of the inlet a rocky reef with 4m least depth runs out from the coast. Anchor on either side of the shoal patch with a long line ashore. Reasonable shelter from the *meltemi*, although some swell is pushed into the inlet with the *meltemi*.

   The restaurant at the end of the inlet serves simple fare in idyllic surroundings.

The restaurant jetty in Dirsek is popular with charter sailors

Yeşilova Körfezi

The end of the Loryma Peninsula divides into two ragged headlands which look like the jaws of a snake on a chart. The inside of the jaws is Sombeki Körfezi, the ancient Gulf of Symi after the Greek island a short distance offshore. Bozburun sits in a cavity where the upper jaw should be. The approach between a number of islands and the rubble-strewn hills of the peninsula is quite different from the landscape further north – the land around is baked hard by the sun and the few strips of cultivated land do little to relieve the starkness of the vista. The coast and waters are littered with rocks and reefs. Atabol Kayası claimed a number of victims before the beacon (red bands and a ⁑ topmark) was erected on it. It is particularly dangerous because it comes up suddenly from considerable depths and a number of yachts, blown down by the *meltemi*, simply sliced off the bottom of the boat before sliding over and sinking in deep water on the other side.

BOZBURUN

The harbour of Bozburun ('Grey Cape') lies at the head of the bay at the northern end of the gulf. There are a number of islands in the approaches and two passages into the bay. The safe approach is around the southern end of Kızıl Adası. In calm weather and with due care it is possible to use the passage around the north end of Kızıl Adası.

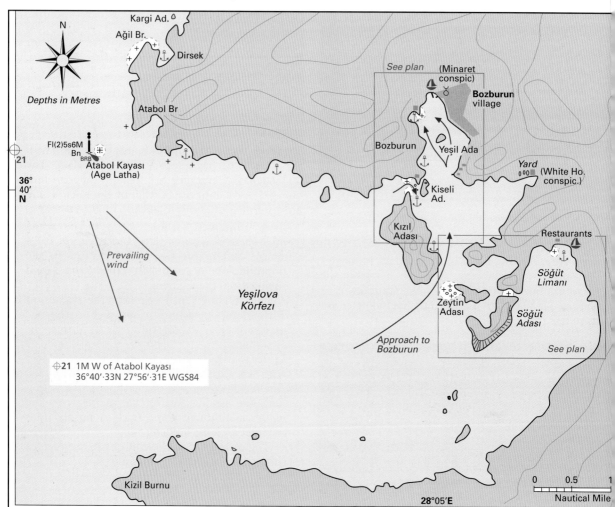

YEŞILOVA KÖRFEZI

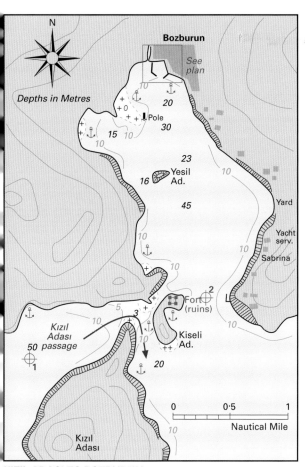

KIZIL ADASI TO BOZBURUN
⊕1 36°40´.14N 28°01´.70E WGS84
⊕2 36°40´.39N 28°02´.67E WGS84

Bozburun town with the conspic silver-domed mosque

Pilotage

Approach The approach around the southern end of Kızıl Adası is straightforward as long as you stay clear of the reef and rocks off the western end of Zeytin Adası. You then proceed up the bay towards Yesil Ada which can be passed on either side. Once past the islet the buildings of Bozburun will be seen. Care is needed of the reef running out from the west side of the bay in the final approaches to the harbour. The end of the reef is marked by a pole with a flag, though it should not be relied on.

The passage around the north end of Kızıl Adası has least depths of 3–3·5m though it looks a lot less. For a first-time transit it should only be attempted in calm weather and with someone upfront conning you through. There is a reef and shoal water on the north and east side of the passage and you should proceed through here slowly. Keep closer to the north end of Kızıl Adası than to the north and east sides, though not too close. Do not attempt to pass between Kiseli Adası and the coast as the passage is shallow and obstructed by a reef. Care is also needed of a reef off the south end of Kiseli Adası.

Mooring Berth stern or bows-to wherever there is space in the harbour. There are a few shallow spaces on the eastern side of the quay but generally there are sufficient depths. You can also anchor and take a long line ashore outside the harbour on the eastern side of Bozburun where shown. Alternatively swing to an anchor on the west side of the harbour. In the summer the wind tends to blow in from the west to northwest and shelter in the harbour is good. In southerly blows it is not a good place to be.

Facilities

Services Water on the quay, although it can be brackish. Drinking water can be delivered by tanker. Electricity connections. Toilets and showers. Bozburun is known as a place where you will be fined heavily for pumping out the holding tank, so don't even think about it. Fuel quay.

Provisions Most provisions can be found around town. Market on Tuesdays.

Eating out Numerous restaurants on the waterfront. The Liman Restaurant has been recommended but have a wander around and then make a choice.

Other PO. Bank. ATM. Internet café and Wi-Fi. *Dolmuş* to Marmaris.

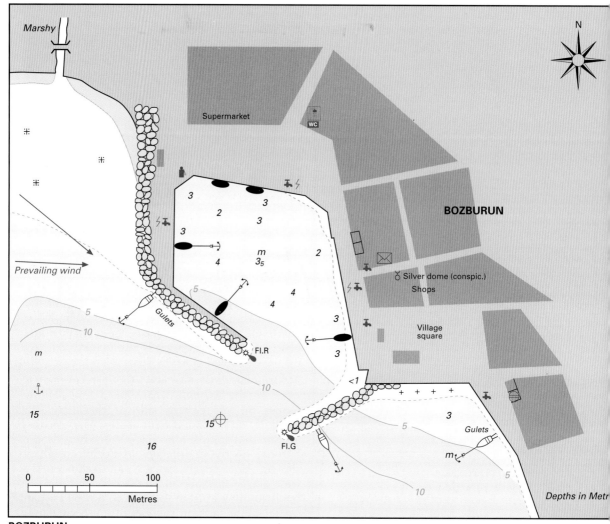

BOZBURUN
⊕36°41´·43N 28°02´·52E WGS84

General

Bozburun has always been a place where the inhabitants made their living from the sea: one look at the landscape tells you that there is little livelihood to be gained from the land. So it is no wonder that the inhabitants of Bozburun, like the inhabitants of the equally parched and rocky island of Sími just across the water, turned to the sea for their livelihood. Bozburun has long been a sponge-fishing village, although as elsewhere, fewer of the young men contract to carry on the arduous and often dangerous work when the pickings of a bar or restaurant job is so much easier.

In Bozburun you are unlikely to see any of the sponge-fishing boats in the harbour during the summer, but you might see them around the coast. Bozburun has developed into a small resort in the last few years, relying on charter boats for much of the custom. The road around the peninsula mostly travels inland after Keçi Bükü and it is still more pleasant to arrive here by boat than by land. The village council has improved the harbour and the locals have been quick to build a few restaurants around the quay to cater for waterborne visitors. After the harsh and glaring landscape encountered in the approaches to

Kızıl Adası looking into the north passage and anchorage

Bozburun, the cool shade of the awnings and a cold beer are a bit like paradise.

On the outskirts of the village and in a bay to the east the local boatbuilders have found a new trade building *gulets* for charter boats. A few years ago the boatyards were struggling to make ends meet building and repairing the sponge-fishing boats, but now the yards are populated with the half-finished hulls of *gulets* for the charter market and some large wood-epoxy motorboats.

Anchorages around Bozburun

Bozburun Bay Yachts often anchor immediately west of the harbour or in the cove under the reef on the western side. Care is needed at the northern end of the bay where it shallows up some distance from the shore. In the cove anchor in 5–10m on mud and weed. Both of these anchorages provide good shelter from the *meltemi*.

Kiseli Adası north passage Yachts often anchor in the northern passage around the northern end of Kızıl Adası. Most yachts anchor with a long line ashore to Kiseli Adası on the eastern side or to the northern end of Kızıl Adası on the west side.

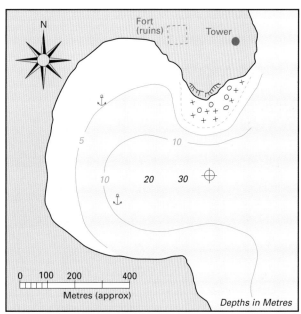

KISELI ADASI ANCHORAGE
⊕36°40′·27N 28°02′·50EWGS84

Good shelter from the *meltemi* here in enchanting surroundings. The water is a startling turquoise over a sandy bottom and on Kiseli there is a sprinkling of Byzantine ruins to add to the fairy-tale appeal of the place. It is used by *gulets* for a lunch time stop, though by dusk most have left and you can stay here overnight in solitude and safety. Do put the anchor light on as a few *gulets* and fishing boats use the passage at night.

Kiseli Adası east side On the east side of Kiseli Adası there is a cove that can be used in settled weather. Anchor in 5–12m and take a long line ashore if necessary. The bottom is mud and weed, good holding once you are in. Reasonable shelter from the *meltemi* and usually not as crowded as the northern passage anchorage.

Yacht Service and Sabrina's Haus On the east side of Bozburun Limanı, just before the boatyard, are a number of moorings tailed to buoys. Sabrina's Haus has a restaurant as does Yacht Service. At the latter there is a catwalk with 3m off it and advertising water, electricity and showers. Both of these places are exposed to a bit of chop kicked up by the *meltemi*, but as long as the moorings are beefy enough, you should be alright.

SÖĞÜT LIMANI

Söğüt Limanı is the large bay on the SW end of Yeşilova Körfezi. Leave Söğüt Adası to port and don't attempt to pass between Söğüt Adası and the mainland as it is shoal here even though some charts show a clear passage through here.

Head up into the northern end of the bay where you will find a dog-leg jetty on the NE side. Go stern or bows-to the outside of the jetty. The inside

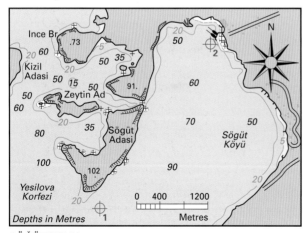

SÖĞÜT KOYU
⊕1 36°39'·0N 28°03'·6E
⊕2 36°39'·5N 28°04'·95E

KARABURUN TO MARMARIS

⊕22 1M SW of Karaburun light
    36°32'·44N 27°57'·94E WGS84
⊕23 0·3M E of Kızılada Adası
    36°35'·76N 28°08'·19E WGS84
⊕24 0·2M E of Kadirğa Burnu light
    36°43'·81N 28°18'·47E WGS84
⊕25 S entrance to Sark Boğazı (Marmarıs Limanı)
    36°47'·83N 28°15'·84E WGS84

of the dog-leg jetty is shallow. Mooring can be a bit difficult if the *meltemi* is blowing as it tends to blow beam-on. Laid moorings tailed to the jetty.

Water and electricity on the jetty. Limited provisions. Several restaurants ashore, of which the Octopus is popular.

Along the eastern side of the bay there are other restaurants and a number of T-jetties where you can go stern or bows-to. An alternative is to anchor off where convenient. There are a couple of coves NW of the dog-leg jetty in the north that afford good shelter from the *meltemi*.

On the rocky headland are the remains of the acropolis to ancient Amnistus, an important *deme* of the Rhodian Peraea. Some of the wall and a gate are in good condition and at the water's edge there is a section of ancient quay, but unless you have the stamina of a Hercules for exploring under the hot summer sun, you are better off cooling off in the clear waters of the bay and looking for any sponges that might have been overlooked in the rocky shallows.

BOZUK BÜKÜ

The large bay ('Broken' or 'Broken-down Bay') lying just two miles up from Karaburun. This low finger of a cape is easily recognised with the light structure on the end prominent. Usually the *meltemi* heaves down onto the cape and then gusts off the high land of the Loryma Peninsula from the west. Care is needed of these gusts blowing off the land and of the confused seas kicked up by the wind against the southwest-going current following the coast in an anticlockwise direction. As you close the bay the citadel atop the entrance mostly shows up well, although in some light it can be more difficult to see as the ancient stone blends into the rocky landscape.

Inside the bay there are a number of places a yacht can moor.

1. Just inside the entrance under the citadel there is a bight with a jetty off the restaurant on the shore. Anchor and go stern-to the jetty which mostly has 2–4m depths off it. Someone from

the restaurant will usually come down to help. Good shelter from the *meltemi*. The restaurant ashore has basic food in idyllic surroundings under the citadel and looking out over the clear turquoise water.

2. On the west side of the bay there is a restaurant in a bight with a catwalk off it. Go stern-to the catwalk. Someone from the restaurant will usually direct you to a berth and help you tie up. Good shelter from the *meltemi*, although there are gusts down into the head of the bay. Simple fare ashore.

3. To the north of this restaurant is another restaurant in a bight with moorings off it.

The Rhodian Peraea

The Dorians moved down from northern Greece into the Greek islands and Asia Minor between 2200 and 1000BC. They brought with them the iron slashing sword and quickly overcame any resistance from tribes equipped with mere bronze weapons. In the southeast corner of the Aegean the Dorians took the island of Rhodes for their principal settlement and in 408BC founded the city of Rhodes on the site it still occupies today. With the foundation of this new site the Dorians set about managing the cities in Asia Minor which had hitherto only been loosely under Rhodian dominion. Not surprisingly, the Loryma Peninsula, a short eight miles away, formed the power base of Rhodian territories in Asia Minor, an area known as the Rhodian Peraea.

Though the Loryma Peninsula as far as present-day Hisarönü and Marmaris formed the heart of Rhodian territory, at times it included a much larger region. The area at the end of the Gulf of Gökova, including Idyma, Callipolis, and Cedreae, was part of the Peraea and control extended as far north as Stratoniceia for a while, an area near the ugly open-cast coal mine at present-day Yatagan. In 190BC Caunos was bought from the Egyptians and added to the territory. A year later the whole of Lycia was given to the Rhodians by the Romans, though this was a nominal gift only since no real Roman control was exercised over much of Lycia.

The cities in the Peraea were governed by officials from Rhodes, though the majority of the citizens were native Carians. It is strange to think of this now isolated and wild Loryma Peninsula as a bustling landscape with towns dotted around it. Important *demes* such as Physcus at Marmaris near the sea can be comprehended, but it is difficult to think of Söğüt or Syrna or Thyssanus, now isolated ruins in a rocky wilderness and little-known outside academic libraries, as important and busy places at the centre of life in this region. The Rhodian Peraea declined in the second century AD and the cities dotted around the peninsula were never revived.

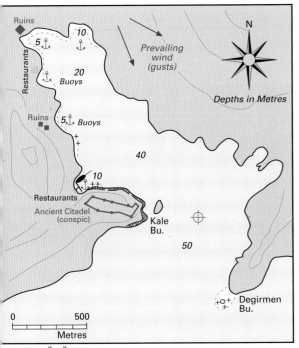

BOZUK BÜKÜ (APLOTHEKA)
⊕ 36°33′·94N 28°01′·28E WGS84

Bozuk Bükü looking into the cove under the ancient citadel on the western entrance

4. At the very head of the bay there is a restaurant with a jetty and laid moorings where yachts can moor. Someone from the restaurant will usually come out in a dinghy to lend a hand.

Note All these restaurants serve simple fare, mostly adequately cooked, but they are not necessarily cheap – still I guess most everything

Ancient Loryma

Bozuk Bükü was formerly called Loryma and the measure of its importance was that the peninsula was named after it. It was primarily a harbour of refuge and not a trading harbour, the acropolis for the city being situated at the head of the bay. It was used at various times to assemble naval fleets, most notably in 395BC by Demetrius Polioketes before his attack on Rhodes. Polioketes is remembered for the gargantuan siege machine he had constructed for the assault on Rhodes, a huge catapult estimated to be nine storeys high and weighing around 125 tons. The bits and pieces of this contraption would have sat in Bozuk Bükü on transports before the short voyage across to the island. The attack failed, but Polioketes, ever magnanimous in defeat, sold his siege machine and donated the money to the Rhodians to build a statue to commemorate the battle. The result was the huge bronze statue of Hellos, the sun god, that stood astride the harbour at Rhodes and was one of the seven wonders of the ancient world.

Later in Byzantine times the bay was called Aplotheka from the Greek hoplotheke meaning an arsenal, after the ancient fort standing at the entrance. On older British charts it was still called by this name. It is well worth the short climb up to the fort for a brief inspection; some of the stone blocks are over 5m (17ft) long and more than a metre (3ft) square, all of them fitting perfectly together without mortar. There is also a fine view across to Rhodes.

has to be brought in by boat. Although gusts blow down into the head of the bay you are secure enough on the laid moorings.

Getting around Kızıl Burun and Karaburun to the underside of the Loryma Peninsula can be a rough and windy business when the *meltemi* is blowing, and the anchorage at Bozuk Bükü, like that of Cnidos on the end of the Dorian Peninsula, has been used since antiquity by boats waiting for the wind to drop before heading north. So it is not surprising that the first thing you see on approaching the bay is a well preserved fortification composed of gigantic ashlar masonry blocks on the headland enclosing it.

ÇATAL ADALARI

⊕ Fairway between the two islets
36°33'·61N 28°02'·13E WGS84

Two islets just east of the entrance to Bozuk Bükü. Yachts can use the passage between the two islets with the deepest part of the passage (10–12m) about one-third of the way off the northernmost islet. Do not attempt to pass between the northernmost islet and the mainland coast.

A short distance north of the islets there is a very small inlet (36°34'·10N 28°02'·45E) on the mainland coast that has room for about one yacht to anchor and take a long line ashore. An islet lies off the southern side of the entrance. It is in effect your own little mini-fjord with wonderful turquoise water and with adequate protection from the prevailing wind.

SERÇE LIMANI

Before you can see the entrance to Serçe it looks as if you are headed for sheer cliffs with no obvious gap in them. Then, just when you think the chart must be wrong or the skipper has made a glaring mistake in his navigation, the entrance to Serçe opens up between the cliffs and you sail into a completely landlocked natural harbour. The narrow entrance opens up into a large bay with two arms running north and west; you may feel a bit like Alice disappearing down the rabbit-hole and discovering a whole new world on entering Serçe.

In the southern arm anchor with a long line ashore or swing to anchor if there is room. The bay is fairly deep further out and you will be anchoring in 20m plus.

In the northern arm pick up one of the restaurant moorings and take a long line ashore to the west side of the arm. The *meltemi* tends to

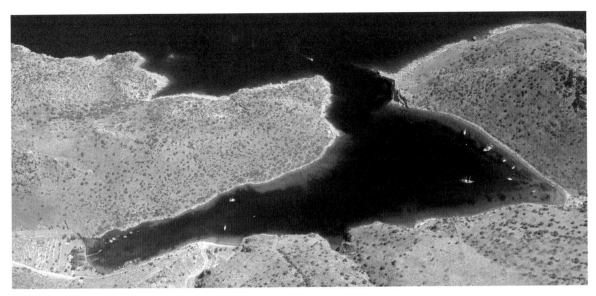

Serçe looking SE towards the entrance   *Kadir Kir*

Serçe Limanı looking over the southern
arm of the anchorage

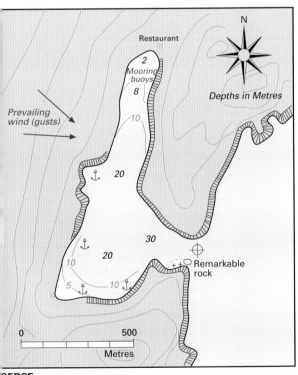

SERÇE
⊕36°34'·64N 28°03'·10E WGS84

blow from the west or NW so you are being
blown off on the western side of he arm.

The bottom is hard sand, rock and weed and
not the best holding everywhere, so make sure the
anchor is well in. Shelter in the bay is good in

The Glass Wreck

Serçe has no ancient remains and the reason for this is that while it appears a good natural harbour to us in our modern watertight boats, for the ancients it was not. The bay has a very narrow entrance which would have made it difficult for the unhandy craft to sail into. Nor does it have a good sandy beach where craft could be hauled ashore. However, it was known as a port of refuge. In several of the rooms in the castle museum in Bodrum there are extensive exhibits of Islamic glass, exquisite pieces with delicate designs and hues. One outstanding exhibit is a very thin glass beaker with a fine design of lions chasing each other. The glass beaker and many other artefacts were excavated from the wreck of a small 11th-century trading ship which sank in the entrance to Serçe. The wreck was excavated by Dr George Bass and his underwater archaeological team in 1977 and from the remains of the wreck and the artefacts found a reasonable picture of what happened can be built up.

It would appear that the ship, a wooden trader of about 15m (50ft) overall length, was voyaging along the coast from a Fatimite port somewhere in the east. Curiously enough, it appears to have been a Byzantine ship carrying a cargo of Islamic glass and not an Islamic ship. (Among the artefacts fish and pork bones were found, the remains of the crew's last meal. The strict Islamic orthodoxy of the time meant no Muslim, however lax, would touch pork.) In addition Byzantine coins, official seals, and lead weights were found, adding to the evidence for the wreck being a Byzantine ship. Most likely the ship was heading for Loryma, but was encountering difficulties with the *meltemi* which blows up this stretch of coast, and so decided to put into Serçe to wait for more favourable winds. While attempting to sail through the entrance the ship hit a rock and sank instantly in 32m of water near the north side of the entrance.

By one of those strange coincidences, I discovered the difficulties the Byzantine ship would have encountered. The engine on my yacht refused to start as I approached Serçe in 1984 and so I decided to sail in. In the entrance the wind constantly changes direction so that one minute it is behind, the next in front, and for a minute or two I thought my yacht might join the Byzantine ship on the bottom. Compared to the Serçe ship, my modern yacht and rig gave me far more manoeuvrability than it had and yet I experienced some difficulty negotiating the entrance under sail. The difficulties of the Byzantine ship with its tubby hull and clumsy rig would have been immense. Herein lies the clue as to why Serçe was not developed as a harbour by the ancients: the entrance is too narrow and the shifting wind in the entrance makes it too difficult for a sailing ship to enter or leave. Better that an ancient harbour should have a wide entrance like Bozuk Bükü with fairly constant winds blowing down on it.

From the personal belongings and valuables found it appears the skipper and crew had no time to rescue their personal effects and had to immediately jump overboard and swim ashore, fortunately not far away in this instance. One interesting fact about the ship is that it is the oldest known example of a ship built in a 'modern' way. The ancient method of building a ship was to build up the planks of the hull and then fit strengthening ribs and floors inside. The 'modern' method is to build a skeleton of ribs and then plank over it. Despite its 'modern' method of construction, externally the ship looked not unlike merchant ships of 1,500 years earlier.

settled weather, although the *meltemi* tends to gust down and swirl around in the steep-sided bay. In strong southerlies a considerable surge builds up in the bay and you should leave.

In the north arm there is a restaurant, Captain Nemo's Farm, which has basic fare and good village bread.

GERBEKSE

Gerbekse Burun sticks out from the coast, connected to it by a low isthmus on the west. Tucked into the north side of Gerbekse Burun is a small cove with room for a few boats to get into it. Anchor off or anchor and take a long line ashore to the south side of the cove. Good shelter from the *meltemi*, but completely open to the north. By day a number of *gulets* will usually be found in the cove, but most of these disappear by dusk. It is possible to stay overnight here in settled weather, but you should be ready to leave if the wind goes anywhere into the north.

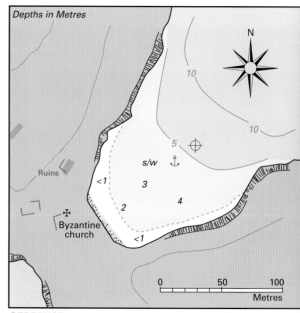

GERBEKSE
⊕36°42´·0N 28°13´·6E

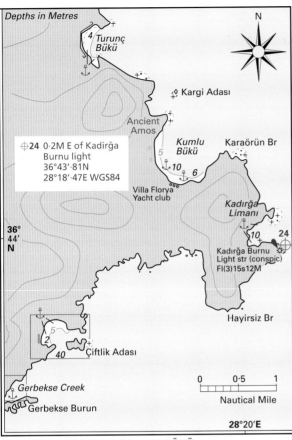

GERBEKSE BURUN TO TURUNÇ BÜKÜ

The cove is often called Byzantine Creek after the ruins of a Byzantine trading station ashore. Around the shore and overgrown by bushes and trees are the ruins of several Byzantine churches and other buildings belonging to what was a sizeable settlement. Quite possibly the 'glass-ship' that foundered at Serçe had visited here before its disastrous voyage south.

ÇIFTLIK

Behind Çiftlik Adası there is an anchorage out of the prevailing winds. Enter on either side of the islet in the entrance and anchor off or go stern or bows-to one of the catwalks on the western side.

The options, running northwards from the southwest corner are:

1. *Alarga Sail* Go stern or bows-to where directed. Laid moorings. This is probably the most upmarket place in Çiftlik. Restaurant and café. Water and electricity. Wi-Fi. Hotel.

2. *Mehmets Place* Stern or bows-to or alongside where directed. Laid moorings. Water and electricity. Restaurant.

3. *Deniz* Stern or bows-to or alongside where directed. Laid moorings. Water and electricity. Restaurant. Popular with the cruising community.

4. *Rafet Baba* Stern or bows-to where directed. Laid moorings. Water and electricity. Wi-Fi. Restaurant. Popular with cruisers and charter boats.

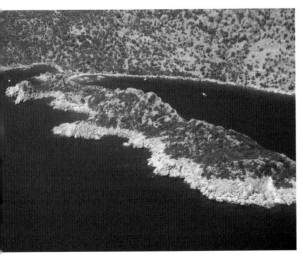

Gerbekse looking over the headland into the anchorage off the old Byzantine settlement

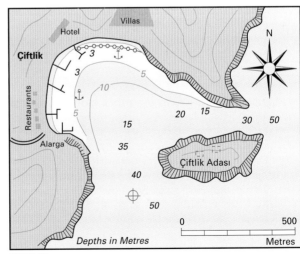

ÇIFTLIK
⊕36°42′·78N 28°14′·49E WGS84

Çiftlik looking into the bay sheltered by the island

5. *Green Platan Hotel pier* Not often used by yachts though there are sufficient depths off the end.

Good shelter from the *meltemi* although a strong *meltemi* can send a bit of swell in here, a little uncomfortable rather than dangerous. Southerlies send in a swell and this is no place to be in strong southerlies.

Tripper boats from Marmaris often use Çiftlik and berths on the catwalks may be reserved for them and their cargo of potential restaurant customers. By late afternoon the tripper boats will have departed and there is plenty of room on the catwalks.

Around the slopes the barren terrain at the bottom of the Loryma Peninsula here gives way to pine and maquis, making this a greener place, softer on the eyes, and yet still possessing the wild beauty of the anchorages further down the coast.

KADIRĞA LIMANI

('Galley Harbour') On the north side of Kadirğa Burun there is a large bay surrounded by low cliffs that is used by charter *gulets* as a lunch stop. Anchor and take a long line ashore at the head of the bay. It is quite deep for anchoring here and the holding is not everywhere the best. Good shelter from the *meltemi* although you tend to get the wash from passing craft turning the corner en route to or from Marmaris.

Ancient Amos

On the north side of Kumlu Bükü, atop the headland, are the ruins of ancient Amos, a member of Rhodian Peraea. Parts of the acropolis walls and towers and a gate remain, as well as the platform of a small temple and a small theatre. The site has either subsided or, as the locals allege, it was damaged by an earthquake, though whether this was long ago or more recently is difficult to know. Eliciting information on ancient ruins from the locals can sometimes be an amusing experience. After struggling in my bad Turkish to get some information on Amos from a local, he was eventually able to assure me that the ruins were very old, they had been there at least since his grandfather's time. Amos yielded some interesting information when George Bean visited it in 1948. He discovered a number of tablets inscribed with the terms of land leases from around 200BC, and it is surprising just how explicit and detailed these leases were:

'(The leases had) … precise instructions for the payment of rent, provision of guarantors, and development of the property; the tenant must build a minimum number of sheds, plant a minimum number of vines and figs, with a minimum space for corn between, and dig a drainage trench. Penalties are fixed for failure to observe these conditions, and also for cutting wood on the property, burying a corpse in it, or encroaching on the public roads.'

George Bean *Turkey Beyond the Maeander* (1980)

Kadirğa Limanı just where you turn the corner to head towards Marmaris   *Kadir Kir*

KUMLU BÜKÜ

⊕ 36°45'·0N 28°16'·4E

A mile above Kadirğa lies the bay of Kumlu Bükü ('Sandy Bay'). The development spreading around the coast from Marmaris has touched this area and there are a number of new villas and small hotels built or being built. In the southwest corner there is the Villa Florya Yacht Club, a restaurant with a jetty off it where you can go stern or bows-to. Laid moorings for the jetty and also laid moorings in the bay with a bumboat service to the shore. Charge band 2. Alternatively anchor off in the bay, although the holding here is bad and you must ensure your anchor is well dug in. Reasonable shelter from the *meltemi* which tends to blow down into Marmaris Bay or up the coast of the Loryma Peninsula, leaving something of a wind hole here.

Restaurants and hotels around the bay and a *dolmuş* runs into Marmaris. Small tripper boats also run regular routes between here and Marmaris.

TURUNÇ BÜKÜ

A bay just before the island passage into the huge Bay of Marmaris. Yachts anchor around the edge of the bay. The cove on the south side is cordoned off as a swimming area and so is not accessible to yachts. On the western side of the cove there is the Turunç Bükü Yacht Club (see entry below). Anchor off around the bay where possible. Good shelter from the *meltemi*, although it can gust with some force into the bay off the high land.

Turunç Bükü Yacht Club The 'club' maintains a number of moorings in the southwest corner of the bay. The moorings are a bit shabby and you may want to check them carefully before mooring. You can also go stern or bows-to the T-pier here, but depths are variable and care is needed close in. Laid moorings. Water and electricity. Charge band 2. Yacht Club restaurant ashore.

Ashore there are villas and hotels and a fair number of restaurants and bars line the shore, a visual reminder that you are close to the tourist hub of this section of the coast. It is a very busy place with watersports boats of all types carving up the waters of the bay, so not a quiet spot for a swim or a snooze in the cockpit.

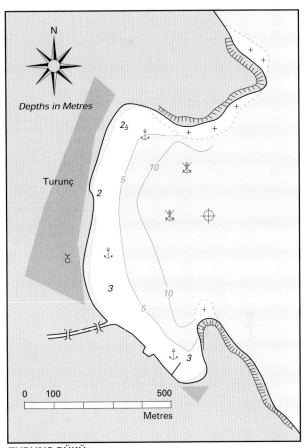

TURUNÇ BÜKÜ
⊕ 36°46'·5N 28°15'·2E

George Bean

Scattered around this section on the Turkish coast there are references to George Bean and his books on the Graeco-Roman sites in Turkey. At many of the sites I have come across locals who remember him with great affection and in one out-of-the-way spot I had no choice other than to donate a copy of one of his books to a local who had known him. George Bean became something of a legend as he criss-crossed the Turkish coast looking for little known sites and identifying and translating the inscriptions he often found on ancient material transplanted from its original site to a Turkish village. In the 1950s and 1960s when he collected most of his material, travel was not as easy as it is now and most of the sites could only be reached after a long and arduous hike on foot. George Bean was a big man (he stood at least 6'6" tall and was broad of shoulder) and as Professor Cook has related in a memoir to the man, this made for a problem or two in a country where most things were designed for smaller men:

'George put up with a good deal of hardship; in a Turkish bus the luggage rack at the back was often the only place he could be fitted into, and in hotels he never found a bed that didn't contort him. As he said, things were not made for a full-grown man.'

Professor Cook goes on to tell of George Bean's method of finding out from the locals where old bits of rock might be lying around. He spoke perfect Turkish and on arriving in a village would sit down over coffee and talk to the locals about the crops, the weather, events in the outside world, eventually getting round to the matter of ancient sites in the area. Professor Cook, who accompanied him on some of his travels, admits that he used to get annoyed with this apparent time-wasting, until he realised that unless the villagers accepted them, they were not going to get anywhere. While other archaeologists whizzing around in jeeps found little that was new, George Bean confirmed and named many sites and discovered a number of new ones.

George Bean spent over 25 years travelling the coast of Asia Minor from the Sea of Marmara in the north to Mersin and Iskenderun near Turkey's border with Syria. He published numerous scholarly papers and in 1964 started on the series of archaeological guides to the Graeco-Roman sites that he is best known for: *Aegean Turkey*; *Turkey Beyond the Maeander*; *Lycian Turkey*; and *Turkey's Southern Shore*. These are the best of any guides to the sites and as a bonus you get Bean's pithy asides and witty comments on all sorts of aspects of life in ancient times. He is still known in some of the villages as Bin Bey – a larger-than-life character in the mould of those 19th-century adventurers like Spratt and Newton.

MARMARIS NETSEL MARINA

Marmaris sits at the northeastern end of Marmaris Limanı, the large enclosed body of water entered either side of Keçi Adası at the southwest corner. Apart from Marmaris Marina there are several other places which will be detailed later where a yacht can bring up around the large bay.

Pilotage

Approach Yachts can enter Marmaris Limanı on either side of Keçi Adası, though the passage on the east side, Sark Boğazi, is more commonly used. Some care is needed of *gulets* and ferries hurtling through the passage from either direction. Once into Marmaris Limanı the cluster of buildings of Marmaris town are easily recognised and closer in the marina will be seen. The floating boom that was deployed off the entrance to protect the cruise boat dock in previous years is now only used when military vessels berth here. If the boom is deployed it is easily spotted by day and will be lit at night. VHF Ch 06, 16. Callsign *Port Marmaris*.

Mooring Once up to the marina a member of staff in a RIB will come out to show you to a berth and help you tie up. Laid moorings tailed to the pontoons. Space is tight between the pontoons for manoeuvring and yachts will sometimes go astern from the centre of the marina down between the pontoons. He will also give you a form to fill out and deliver to the marina office. Excellent all-round shelter inside. Charge band 5.

Note The pontoon layout on the southern side may be changed slightly in the future.

Sark Bogazi, the entrance channel into the Bay of Marmaris looking southeast. Nimara Adası is top left of photo *Kadir Kir*

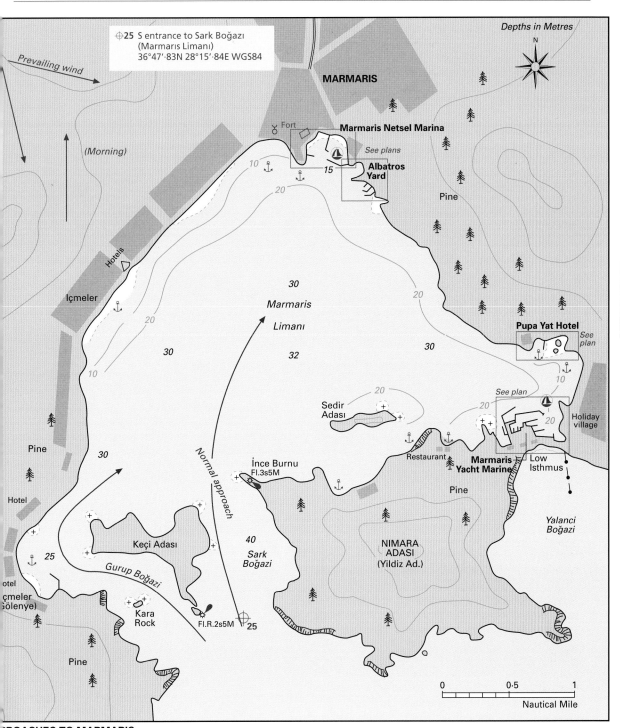

APPROACHES TO MARMARIS

Marmaris Netsel Marina looking southwest over towards Marmaris old town   *Kadir Kir*

Facilities

Services Water and electricity at every berth. Showers and toilets. Wi-Fi. Laundry service. Fuel quay.

Provisions Supermarket in the marina. Minimarkets nearby in Marmaris town and a large Migros on the outskirts of town. Market on Friday at the west end of town.

Eating out Several restaurants in the marina and a wide choice in and outside Marmaris town. In the marina, tucked into the back of the marina near the car park is a small local restaurant, the Rota, that serves good Turkish food including *pide* at good prices. On the front is Pineapple and My Marina that has a more international cuisine and good views over the marina. Nearby in Marmaris town are numerous restaurants along the waterfront serving Turkish and 'international' cuisine. There are also Indian and Chinese restaurants near the front. Its worth a walk around the backstreets where there are some good local eateries without the touts and the noise. Bar street in Marmaris has bars of all types and persuasions, mostly loud and naff, and most yachties tend to frequent one or other of the bars along the waterfront just after the footbridge.

Other PO. Banks. ATMs. Internet cafés. Hire cars and motorbikes. Bus connections to everywhere and flights from Dalaman Airport about one hour away. Ferries to Rhodes.

General

When Nelson was pursuing Napoleon and the French Fleet around the Mediterranean in 1798, he put in at Marmaris to make some repairs and give his long-suffering sailors a short respite from the hectic business of keeping up with Napoleon. Nelson thought Marmaris the best fleet anchorage in the eastern Mediterranean and thereafter the Admiralty recommended it as '... suited to the various purposes of airing stores, stretching rigging, repairing boats, erecting tents for carpenters, armourers and coopers, and for unloading and carrying transports and prizes.' (The Admiralty's prose never did stretch to much more than the utilitarian.) It is not difficult to see why Nelson and the Admiralty thought Marmaris an excellent fleet anchorage. From seaward you pass through a narrow passage between two islands and enter a huge landlocked bay. Pine

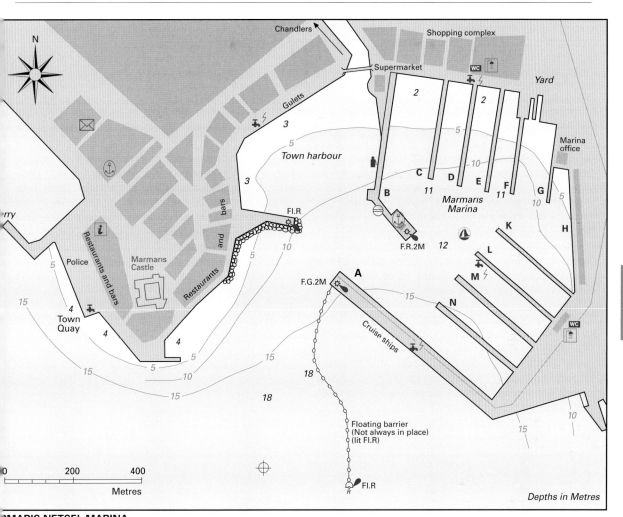

RMARIS NETSEL MARINA
6°50′·91N 28°16′·58E WGS84

forest (useful to the carpenters and coopers) carpet the slopes of the hills and islands enclosing the bay. In the northeast corner the white houses and red roofs of Marmaris town can be seen. Today it is not the lofty masts of ships-of-the-line that will be seen, but a thicket of yacht masts advertising that Marmaris is the hub of yacht charter along this section of the coast.

What was the small village of Marmaris sits in one corner of the bay. Around it large hotels line the foreshore, reflecting the new found prosperity of the place. Marmaris village was largely destroyed by an earthquake in 1958 and though much of the rebuilding does not have the rustic charm of the older buildings, it all works as a reasonably sympathetic place. The same cannot be said for the development spreading to the west

of Marmaris, which is a tourist ghetto of the worst type. Awful pour-and-fill hotels and self-catering apartments spread like a canker around the foreshore and behind so that you would hardly believe you were in Turkey. Touts from the restaurants will harangue you in slang in a dozen different languages and it should take no more than a few signs advertising 'cheap chicken and chips and a big beer' or cocktails like 'sex on a Turkish beach' to persuade you that this is tourist hell.

On a low rocky spur by the shore, a partially ruined castle will be seen, with some of the older houses built into and against the walls. The castle was built by Suleiman the Magnificent in 1522 as a base for his assault on Rhodes against the Knights of St John.

The quay and esplanade is the centre of life in Marmaris and whether you are dining out, having a quiet drink or just strolling around the waterfront, this is the place to be. Here there are all the restaurants and bars you could desire. The attraction is the boats berthed stern-to the quay and there seems to be an eternal fascination with watching people messing about in boats. The boats themselves vary from battered but loved cruising boats to the giant gin-palaces of millionaires. And of course there are rows of the traditional wooden *gulets* waiting to whisk charterers off around the coast. Around the marina is a mini-nautical village with all facilities including restaurants and bars of all types.

Behind the town quay lies the old quarter of the town with shops selling everything and anything that visitors to Marmaris might want: fashionable leather goods, carpets, kilims, brass and copperware, beachwear, lace, ceramics, not to mention more mundane things like sunblock and freshly made fruit juice to quench your thirst. Recently the local town council banned vehicles from many of the narrow streets and the road around the quay, which makes walking around much more pleasant than it used to be when one had to dodge cars and motorbikes trying to force a way through hordes of pedestrians.

Marmaris is the site of ancient Physicus, a deme of the Rhodian Peraea, but virtually nothing remains of this ancient city. The acropolis was sited on a hill to the north of the present town, but there is little to see and an excursion is not worthwhile for the ruins, but it is worthwhile for the delightful walk up a rocky gorge hemmed in by pine and kept cool by a stream. It is strange that so little should remain of ancient Physicus when it was considered to be the most important of all the cities in the Peraea, the only one to be named separately, according to George Bean, and a city that enjoyed a special relationship (presumably commercial) with Lindos on Rhodes. In all likelihood the city was carried away piecemeal by ships for building projects elsewhere, or perhaps just as ballast, the accessibility of the site and the safe anchorage denying it the longevity of the other less accessible sites on the Loryma Peninsula.

☎ 0252 412 2708
www.netselmarina.com

Marmaris Netsel Marina looking out from one of the restaurants

Other harbours and anchorages around Marmaris

ALBATROS MARINA

A yard and associated mooring lying about half a mile southeast of Marmaris Marina. It is not really a place for visiting yachts to head for, more a yard with moorings and some quay space for resident boats. Shelter on the laid moorings or on the south side of the quay is adequate from the prevailing wind, though there is often a bit of swell here making it uncomfortable. Enquire in advance if you want to berth here.

Water and electricity on the quay and toilets and showers in the yard.

Note There are plans to develop a marina here along the lines shown on the plan. At the time of writing work has not started.

PUPA YAT HOTEL

In the southeast corner of Marmaris Bay is Pupa Yat Hotel tucked under a stubby headland. You can anchor off here or go on the pontoon. Some care is needed of the shallows spreading out from the marshy land on the east side of the pontoon and yachts should also leave the swimming area off the hotel beach clear. There is better shelter

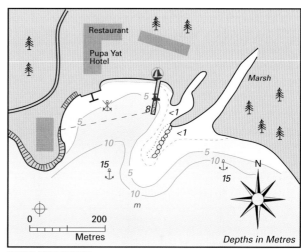

PUPA YAT HOTEL
⊕36°49′·61N 28°18′·55E WGS84

ATROS MARINA
°50′·72N 28°17′·07E WGS84

Albatros Marina looking northeast over the basin and south quay

Pupa Yat Hotel pier

from the prevailing northwesterlies in this bight than a glance at the chart might indicate.

The small hotel is an intimate sort of place in a green corner of the bay and it's well worth a wander ashore for a drink in the bar and a meal in the restaurant. Water and electricity on the pontoon and showers and toilets ashore for pontoon users.

MARMARIS YACHT MARINE

A large marina (incorporating the old Marmarin Marina) and yard.

Pilotage

Approach The marina sits in the far southeast corner of the bay off the narrow isthmus of Yalanci Boğazi connecting the mainland to Nimara Adası. Care is needed of the shoals and reefs to the west off Nimara Adası. VHF Ch 72. Charge band 2.

Mooring Berth where directed. Marina staff will come out to you in a RIB and show you to your berth and help you tie up. There are laid moorings tailed to the quay or pontoons. Good shelter in the enclosed basin and on the pontoons, although there can be a bit of a surge in the outer part of the harbour when the wind blows briskly from the north.

Facilities

Services Water and electricity. Showers and toilets. Wi-Fi. Laundry service.

Provisions A well-stocked minimarket in the marina. You can also catch the *dolmuş* or small ferry into Marmaris town and shop there.

Eating out An up-market restaurant and bar in the marina. Alternatively take the dinghy across to Pupa Yat restaurant or catch the *dolmuş* into Marmaris town.

General

Marmaris Yacht Marine has built up a good reputation for providing economical berthing with an upmarket ambience ashore. The yard can handle very large yachts, so not surprisingly, some

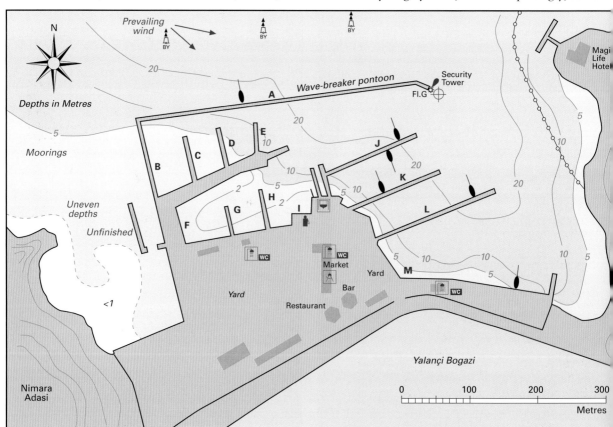

MARMARIS YACHT MARINE
⊕36°49'·14N 28°18'·48E WGS84

Marmaris Yacht Marine looking west over the marina and yard towards Nimara Adası   *Kadir Kir*

super-yachts haul here for a refit. The architecture ashore is quite spectacular, with a lot of monumental marble adorning the buildings and atriums. If there is a downside to the marina it is that is in the middle of nowhere and to get into Marmaris requires a 15-minute *dolmuş* ride or a trip on the small ferry that runs back and forth from the marina to Marmaris. That said, there are good (if limited) facilities ashore and by all accounts most people enjoy their stay here.

☎ 0252 422 022

www.yachtmarin.com

Anchorages around Marmaris Bay

Marmaris town Anchor off to the west of the old town and castle where possible. The area is used by *gulets* snd other boats so pick a spot with an eye on other anchored yachts and keeping clear of the approaches to the town quay. You should be able to find a spot in 8–15m though sometimes you have to anchor in deeper water. The bottom is mud and weed and generally good holding once the anchor is dug in. The *meltemi* tends to blow off the land though there can be southerlies in the morning. Obviously not a place to be in strong southerlies.

Northwest side Yachts often anchor around the northwest side of the bay. The depths mostly come up to depths suitable for anchoring. The bottom is mud and weed and not always the best holding until the anchor is well dug in. Off a number of the large hotels around the shore are T-jetties where you may be able to find a berth although most are taken up by tripper boats.

Içmeler The bay on the west side behind Keçi Adası is lined by beachside hotels. A long jetty on the south side of the bay is usually full with trip boats and mega-yachts. Anchor off outside the swimming area. The bay throbs with jet-skis, para-scending boats, and the background beat from bars and clubs. A peaceful retreat it is not.

Nimara Adası There are a number of places you can anchor off on the north side of Nimara Adası although it is mostly quite deep (15–20m) and exposed to the *meltemi* when it gets up.

Adakoy On the headland close west of Marmaris Yacht Marine is a stylish small hotel with a private quay, where yachts can go stern-to. Further west opposite Sedir Adası is the Pruva Marina boatyard, though there are no actual berths here, only a slip and yard ashore.

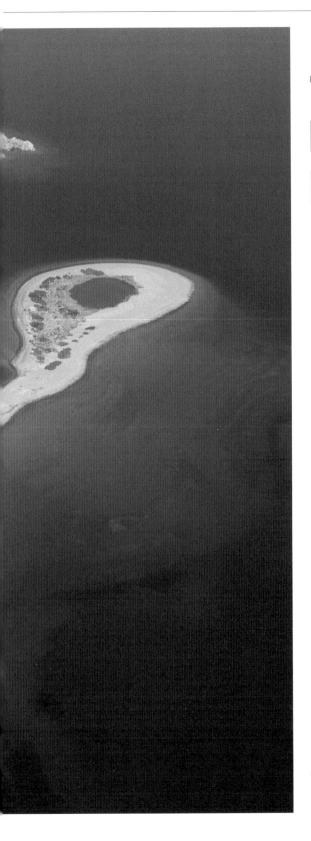

4
Marmaris to Kekova

Yassica Adası north end *Kadir Kir*

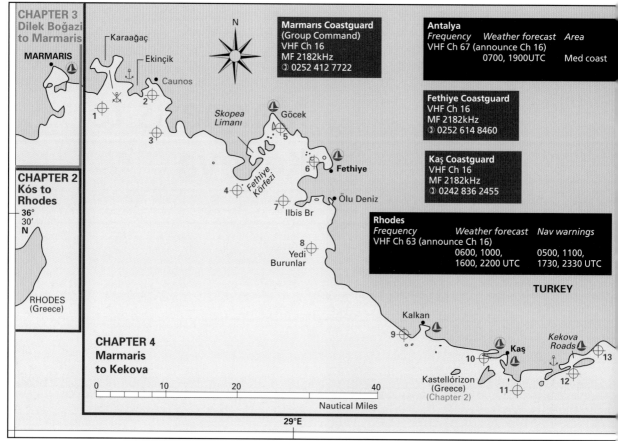

MARMARIS TO KEKOVA

USEFUL WAYPOINTS

⊕**1** 0·5M S of Yilancik Adası light
36°45'·75N 28°26'·31E WGS84

⊕**2** Entrance to Köyceğiz Limanı
36°46'·96N 28°33'·76E WGS84

⊕**3** 1·25M SW of Disibilmez Burnu
36°41'·18N 28°36'·31E WGS84

⊕**4** Mid-channel between Peksimet Adası and
Kurtoğlu Burnu
36°34'·76N 28°49'·89E WGS84

⊕**5** 0·18M E of light on Göcek Adası
36°43'·54N 28°57'·28E WGS84

⊕**6** 0·3M N of Batikkaya Beacon
(approaches to Fethiye)
36°39'·06N 29°05'·18E WGS84

⊕**7** 0·5M W of Iblis (Dökükbaşı) Burnu light
36°32'·71N 28°59'·88E WGS84

⊕**8** 1M W of Kötü Burnu light
36°23'·31N 29°04'·70E WGS84

⊕**9** Mid-channel between Yilan Adası and Yali
Burnu
36°13'·49N 29°20'·98E WGS84

⊕**10** 0·5M S of Ada Burnu (approaches to Kaş)
36°10'·52N 29°35'·38E WGS84

⊕**11** 0·5M S of Ulü Burun
36°07'·43N 29°40'·97E WGS84

⊕**12** Kekova Roads W entrance
36°10'·04N 29°49'·81E WGS84

⊕**13** Kekova Roads E entrance
36°12'·26N 29°54'·89E WGS84

Quick reference guide

	Shelter	Mooring	Fuel	Water	Provisions	Eating out	Plan
Karaağaç	Prohibited to yachts						•
Ekinçik	B	AC	O	A	C	C	•
Delikada	O	C	O	O	O	O	•
Baba Adası	C	C	O	O	O	C	•
Kızılkuyruk Köyü	B	C	O	O	O	O	•
Küçük Kuyruk	B	C	O	O	O	O	•
Ragged Bay	C	C	O	O	O	O	
Skopea Limanı							
Kapi Creek	A	A	O	O	O	C	•
Twenty-two Fathom Cove	B	AC	O	O	O	C	•
Seagull Bay	B	AC	O	O	O	C	•
Ruin Bay	B	AC	O	O	O	C	•
Wall Bay	B	AC	O	O	O	C	•
Sarsala Iskelesi	C	C	O	O	O	C	•
Deep Bay	B	C	O	O	O	C	•
Tomb Bay	B	C	O	O	O	C	•
Domuz Adası	C	C	O	O	O	O	
Tersane	A	C	O	O	O	C	•
Yassica Adalari	C	C	O	O	O	O	•
Boynüz Bükü	B	C	O	O	O	C	•
Ortisim Bükü	B	C	O	O	O	O	
Göcek							
Municipal Marina	B	A	A	A	A	A	•
Skopea Marina	B	A	B	A	A	A	•
Marinturk Village Marina	B	A	B	A	A	A	•
Club Marina	A	A	A	A	A	A	•
D-Marin Göcek Marina	A	A	B	A	A	A	•
MarinTurk Exclusive Marina	B	A	B	A	C	C	•

	Shelter	Mooring	Fuel	Water	Provisions	Eating out	Plan
Fethiye Körfezi							
Innice Iskelesi	C	C	O	O	O	C	
Küçük Kargi Köyü	C	C	O	O	O	C	
Kargi Bükü	C	C	O	O	O	C	
Kızıl Ada	C	C	O	O	O	O	
Fethiye Adası	B	C	O	O	O	C	•
Ece Fethiye Marina	A	A	A	A	A	A	•
Fethiye anchorages	A	C	O	O	C	B	•
Letoonia Marina	B	A	B	A	C	C	•
Paçariz Bükü	C	C	O	O	O	C	•
Battikaya Bükü	C	C	O	O	O	O	•
Coast to Kekova							
Gemiler Anchorages	B	C	O	O	O	C	•
Ölü Deniz	C	C	O	O	C	B	•
Yeşilköy Limanı	C	C	O	O	O	O	
Kalkan	B	A	B	A	B	A	•
Kaş Marina	A	A	A	A	A	A	•
Büçak Deniz	B	AC	B	B	B	C	•
Kaş	B	A	B	A	A	A	•
Bayindir Limanı	B	C	O	O	O	C	•
Asar	O	C	O	O	O	O	
Woodhouse Bay	B	C	O	O	O	O	•
Pölemos Bükü	A	C	O	O	O	C	•
Tersane	B	C	O	O	O	O	•
Kale Köy	C	BC	O	A	C	B	•
Üçağiz	A	AC	O	A	C	B	•
Karaloz	B	C	O	O	O	O	•
Gökkaya Limanı	A	C	O	O	O	C	•
Andraki	B	C	O	A	C	C	

PREVAILING WINDS

This coast curves in great semicircle from the NW to SE before turning to the NE towards Antalya. It has two distinct weather patterns on either side, with the dividing line more or less around Kekova.

In the summer on the W-facing coast from Marmaris to Kekova the prevailing wind is the *meltemi* blowing NW to W down the coast. It is strongest in July to September when it can blow up to Force 6–7 and sets up considerable seas, especially onto the stretch of coast between Fethiye and Kekova. In the early and late summer the *meltemi* blows less strongly and less frequently although there can still be blustery days. In places, especially in the Gulf of Fethiye, the *meltemi* will often die late at night and not get up until the morning. At other times it will blow day and night for a week or more. In places like Skopea Limanı the wind tends to curve right round and blow into the gulf from the SW–S.

The wind tends to gust down off high land and these gusts can be significantly stronger than the wind over the open sea. It will also be channelled and funnelled through any islands and channels, where again it will be significantly stronger. At the SE end of this stretch of coast the *meltemi* effectively blows past the end of the bulge and out to sea. Generally it runs out of steam 20 or so miles off the coast and you will be left with a confused sea and no wind when this happens.

In the sea area between Kekova and Finike there is a transition area between the *meltemi* on the W and the land and sea breezes on the E. At times one or other prevailing wind may blow along this stretch of coast, but often there is just a flat calm.

In the spring and autumn winds are more evenly distributed between N and S, although there are still more northerlies than southerlies. Gale-force winds can be from N or S, although again strong northerlies seem to predominate.

Along this coast the prevailing NW–W winds mean that going SE down the coast is straightforward but coming NW back up the coast is a slog to windward. In the pocket of coast between Marmaris and Fethiye winds tend to be lighter and more variable, with a definite calm in the morning before the wind fills in. On the passage back up this makes Ekinçik a popular staging area from where it is easy to motor to Marmaris in the morning or get a good sail later in the day. Yachts coming N from Kekova usually do so in stages, with the most difficult leg being that past the Seven Capes from Kalkan to the Fethiye area. Yachts will often leave very early in the morning (often at 0400–0500) and motor as far N as possible until the *meltemi* fills in.

Marmaris to Kekova

From Marmaris the coast turns south towards the huge rocky hump sticking out of Anatolia into the sea, a region known in ancient times as Lycia and a region as inhospitable as any in Asia Minor. Close to Marmaris is ancient Caunos, sited on the delta of the Dalyan River, a sort of halfway house between ancient Caria and ancient Lycia. In common with the coast described in the previous chapter, much of it was inaccessible by road until recently and some of it is still inaccessible except by sea.

The Lycian coast seems to be one vast necropolis, with tombs and sarcophagi scattered all around the landscape

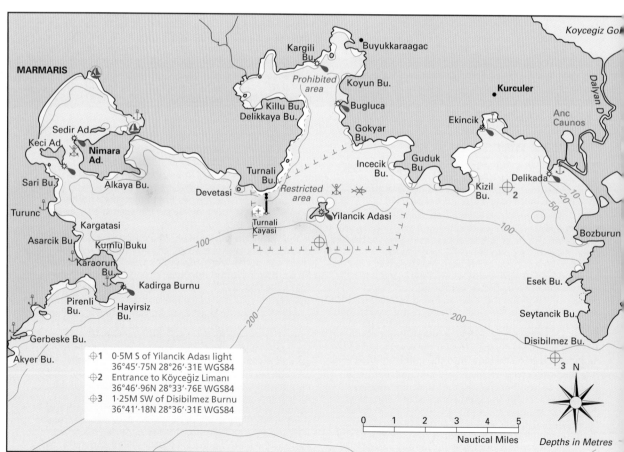

⊕1 0·5M S of Yilancik Adası light
36°45'·75N 28°26'·31E WGS84
⊕2 Entrance to Köyceğiz Limanı
36°46'·96N 28°33'·76E WGS84
⊕3 1·25M SW of Disibilmez Burnu
36°41'·18N 28°36'·31E WGS84

MARMARIS TO DISIBILMEZ BURNU

THE LYCIANS

Ancient Lycia encompassed the sea-girt bulge that runs from Ekinçik and ancient Caunos around as far as Antalya, a semicircle of some of the most mountainous and wild landscape to be encountered anywhere in Turkey. During the Ottoman period it was called 'Uch', the 'Frontier', a name that conjures up the nature of the landscape. It is a region hemmed in by mountains. On the west and east two high mountain ridges, the tallest peaks standing well over 3,000m (10,000ft) high, cut off Lycia from neighbouring Caria to the west and Pamphylia to the east. In the north a lower but no less rugged range and a great plateau cut Lycia off from central Anatolia. Around the coast a series of mountain ranges drop precipitously into the sea and though the peaks are not as high as those in the interior, the aspect from seaward is of an inhospitable coast. Right into early summer the highest peaks in Lycia, Akdağ in the west and Bey Daği (ancient Mt Solymnus) in the east, are covered in snow on the highest slopes.

As the landscape is wild, so were the men who lived here. The Lycians enjoyed a reputation for independence and fought for it tooth and nail, often to the last man. This last statement is not just a cliché, as on at least two occasions we know it to be fact. In 546BC the Persians defeated Croesus (the same 'rich as Croesus'), the last Lydian king, and advanced upon Lycia. On the Plain of Xanthos the Lycians met the much superior forces of the Persians, to no avail. Herodotus tells us of the tragic finale to the battle:

'When Harpagus advanced into the plain of Xanthos, they met him in battle, though greatly outnumbered, and fought with much gallantry; at length, however, they were defeated and forced to retire within their walls, whereupon they collected their women, children, slaves, and other property and shut them up in the citadel, set fire to it and burnt it to the ground. Then having sworn to do or die, they marched out to meet the enemy and were killed to a man.' Five hundred years later in 42BC it all happened again when Brutus besieged Xanthos. Against a superior force the Lycians fought to the finish, and when they saw there was no hope of victory, they once again slew their women and children and burnt the city down. Plutarch recorded Brutus's feelings on this second mass suicide:

'… it was so tragical a sight that Brutus could not bear to see it, but wept at the very mention of the scene. Thus the Xanthians, after a long space of years, repeated by their desperate deed the calamity of their forefathers, who after the very same manner in the Persian Wars had fired their city and destroyed themselves.'

Such was the feeling of the Lycians towards independence that they were the last region to be incorporated into the Roman provinces in Asia Minor.

Who were these Lycians and where did they come from? They are mentioned in Homer's *Iliad*, where they fought on the side of the Trojans in defence of Troy, as a gallant force from 'distant Lycia and the eddying Xanthus'. Herodotus fills us in on the details. The Lycians, he says, came from Crete after 'Sarpedon and Minos, fought for the throne, and the victorious Minos expelled Sarpedon and his party'. They were then called the Termilae, and only adopted the name Lycian when the noble Lycus, son of King Pandion, was expelled from Athens and came to join Sarpedon. From Lycus they adopted the name Lycian. It's all a bit tortuous, and not as interesting as the light Hittite and Egyptian references throw on the

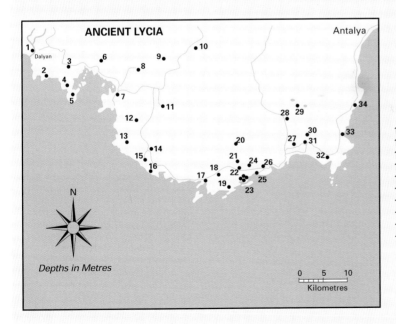

1.	Caunos	20.	Arneas
2.	Prepia	21.	Corba
3.	Calynda	22.	Cyanae
4.	Lissa	23.	Simena,
5.	Lydae		Teimiussa,
6.	Daedala		Istlada,
7.	Telmessus		Tyberissus
8.	Cadyanda	24.	Trysa
9.	Araxa	25.	Sura
10.	Oenoanda	26.	Myralstlada
11.	Tlos	27.	Limyra
12.	Pinara	28.	Arycanda
13.	Sidyma	29.	Acalissus
14.	Xanthus	30.	Rhodiapolis
15.	Letoum	31.	Corydalla
16.	Patara	32.	Gagae
17.	Antiphellus	33.	Olympos
18.	Isinda	34.	Phaselis
19.	Aperlae		

Typical Lycian
rock tomb
(Myra)

origins of the Lycians. The Hittites record that a maritime people called the Lukka lived here sometime in the 14th century BC. Egyptian records mention a people called the Lukki living here, a people feared as sea-raiders. This latter reference makes a good deal of sense on later evidence.

The Lycian coast has often been referred to as the 'pirate coast', and with its many strategically sited coves and islands where these sea-raiders could lie in wait for plump merchant ships tramping up and down the coast, it deserves the epithet. Numerous campaigns were mounted to clean up the coast from as early as 1194BC right up until the 19th century. A relief at Medinet Habu in the Nile delta records how Rameses III put together a great fleet to take on the Lukki and decisively defeated them, leaving the coast free of piracy for a while. When Xerxes assembled his huge force for the invasion of Greece in 480BC the Lycians contributed fifty ships, and Herodotus gives us this tantalising description of the piratical bunch that manned them:

'They wore greaves and corslets; they carried bows of cornel wood, cane arrows without feathers, and javelins. They had goatskin slung round their shoulders, and hats stuck round with feathers. They also carried daggers and rip-hooks.'

Piracy is again mentioned in the 5th century BC, but it is not until the Roman occupation of Asia Minor that attempts were again made to bring it under control. In 78BC a campaign was mounted by Servilius Vatia, governor of Cilicia, and though he had moderate success, it did little to check it. In 67BC Pompey, an able and intelligent admiral, was given wide-ranging powers and almost unlimited resources to tackle the piracy problem, which he did with total success. However, Pompey was reluctant to give up his power and his ships and became something of a thorn in the Senate's side. After the fall of Rome the Lycian coast once again became a haven for pirate fleets and not until the 18th

and 19th centuries and the presence of the British Navy was the piracy problem again tackled and the Lycian coast cleaned up.

In this remote region the sites of over forty cities have been found and much remains to identify the culture of the Lycians. The most obvious features of the Lycian landscape are the tombs and sarcophagi left behind. They are everywhere, and it is difficult not to think of the region as a vast necropolis peopled with the shadowy figures of Lycian nobles and warriors. Ancestor-worship was evidently important to the Lycians and the tombs are extravagant affairs, the more grandiose decorated with a frieze and inscriptions placing a curse on anyone tampering with the tomb. Five distinct types of tomb can be distinguished: pillar-tombs, temple-tombs, house-tombs, pigeon-hole tombs, and the ubiquitous sarcophagi.

Pillar-tombs are specific to Lycia and consist of a long tapering pillar set on a stone base with the grave chamber at the top. These were for important dynasts and the best examples are at Xanthos. Temple-tombs are, to my mind, the most impressive of the Lycian tombs and consist of a temple facade with a grave chamber behind it. Those at Caunos are the most romantically-sited while those at Fethiye the most accessible. House-tombs were modelled on the wooden houses of the Lycians and so give us some idea of what everyday accommodation was like several thousand years ago. They are smaller than the temple-tombs, though often several storeys high, and the stone has been hewn to imitate wooden roof beams and the doorway and portico. The house-tombs were sometimes decorated with reliefs and painted, as at Myra, where fragments of a painted relief have miraculously survived. Pigeon-hole tombs were the downmarket version of temple and house-tombs, small unadorned chambers cut into a cliff-face. The best examples are at Pinara where the cliffs are pockmarked by these tombs. Sarcophagi are found everywhere: scattered over hill-sides, on the summits of hills, by the shore, and in the sea where the land has subsided. The older sarcophagi are the largest, with massive stone bases, grave chambers, and heavy lids often with a peaked 'gothic' look to them. In Roman times the sarcophagi became smaller and less ornate, perhaps as the importance of ancestor-worship declined.

With the decline of the Roman Empire, so too Lycian fortunes declined. In Byzantine times there were small settlements around the coast (a number of Byzantine churches will be seen in isolated spots) but the interior was not heavily populated as in Lycian times. In the late Middle Ages this region was viewed as a wilderness, the region of 'Uch', the 'Frontier' of the Ottomans, and the coast was the haunt of pirates who had semi-permanent settlements ashore. The Lycians and Lycian culture faded into vague folk-memories of a proud and independent people who had built great stone cities and buried their dead in magnificent tombs. Not until those intrepid travellers of the 19th century – Francis Beaufort, Charles Newton, Thomas Spratt and Edward Forbes – was the existence and extent of Lycian culture to be brought to the notice of the West.

KARAAĞAÇ

Karaağaç Limanı is a large indented bay lying close east of Marmaris. The bay is a military area and prohibited to yachts. It is prohibited to enter the bay and outside the bay there is a restricted area shown on the plan. In practice yachts transit through the restricted area without hindrance, though it is possible that during exercises you would be prohibited from doing so. Monitor VHF Ch 16 when in this area. Care is needed of Turnalı Kayası, a reef lying on the western side of the restricted zone. It is now marked by an isolated danger buoy (❖ topmark).

Some *gulets* anchor just inside the entrance to the bay inside the prohibited area, but it is not advised. The area is patrolled from time to time and you may find yourself on the receiving end of an irate patrol, or worse.

EKINÇIK

A well-protected bay tucked into the northeast corner of the coast before it curves south.

Pilotage

Approach From Marmaris you follow the coast around until it curves south. Ekinçik is tucked right in the northeast corner of this stretch of coast and once up to the bay you will see a cluster of houses and, most probably, quite a few yachts and *gulets*. Ekinçik (or 'eggs-n-chips' to charter skippers) is a popular first-night stopover for boats heading out of Marmaris and consequently it is crowded in the summer.

Mooring There are several places a yacht can go.

1. **My Marina** A catwalk in the southeast corner of the bay with a T-pier. Berth stern-to where directed. Call up *My Marina* VHF Ch 16 or wait until the RIB comes out to show you to your space and help you berth. Laid moorings tailed to the catwalk. The prevailing wind blows lightly into here from the west during the day until it drops in the evening. Good protection tucked into this corner (although see the *caution* below).

   Water and electricity on the catwalk. Showers and toilets. Charge band 3, although this will often be waived if you eat at the My Marina restaurant.

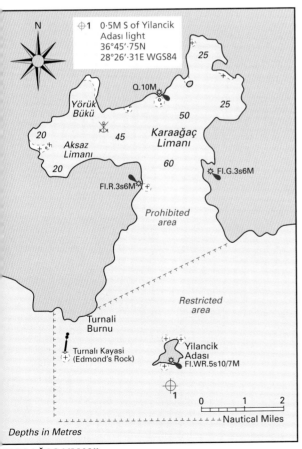

⊕1 0·5M S of Yilancik Adası light
36°45'·75N
28°26'·31E WGS84

Q.10M
Yörük Bükü
20
Aksaz Limanı
20
45
Karaağaç Limanı
25
25
50
60
Fl.G.3s6M
Fl.R.3s6M
Prohibited area
Restricted area
Turnalı Burnu
Turnalı Kayasi (Edmond's Rock)
Yilancik Adası
Fl.WR.5s10/7M
0   1   2
Nautical Miles
Depths in Metres

KARAAĞAÇ LIMANI

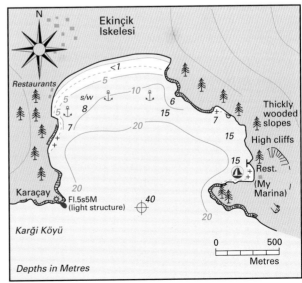

N
Ekinçik Iskelesi
Restaurants
<1
5
5   s/w
5   8
7
10
20
6
15
7
15
15
15
Rest.
Thickly wooded slopes
High cliffs
(My Marina)
Karaçay
20
Fl.5s5M (light structure)
40
Karği Köyü
20
0   500
Metres
Depths in Metres

EKINÇIK
⊕36°49'·12N 28°33'·27E WGS84

Karği Köyu anchorage in the bay on the western side before you enter Ekinçik proper

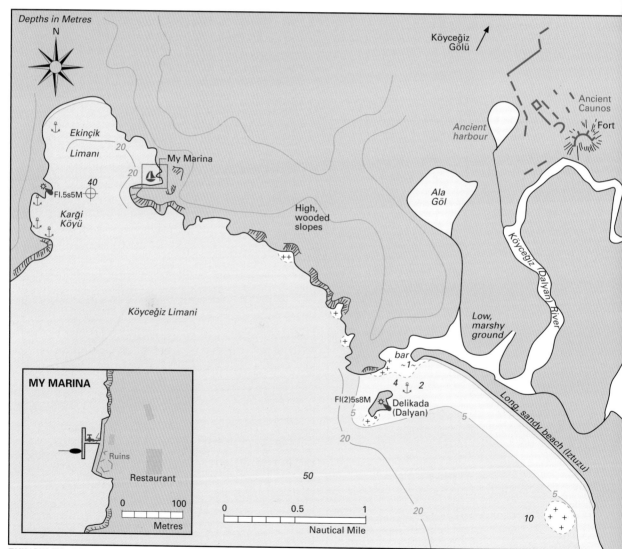

Depths in Metres
N

Köyceğiz Gölü

Ancient Caunos

Fort

Ancient harbour

Ekinçik Limani

20

My Marina

20

Fl.5s5M

40

Karği Köyü

Ala Göl

High, wooded slopes

Köyceğiz Limani

Low, marshy ground

Köyceğiz (Dalyan) River

bar
~1~

4   2

Fl(2)5s8M

Delikada (Dalyan)

5

5

Long sandy beach (Iztuzu)

20

50

20

10

5

5

MY MARINA

Ruins

Restaurant

0   100

Metres

0   0.5   1

Nautical Mile

EKINÇIK TO DELIKADA
36°49´.12N 28°33´.27E WGS84

My Marina in the southeast corner of Ekinçik
Marc Labaume

Ekinçik   *Kadir Kir*

2. **Tripper boat pier** A quay on the western side of the bay, though it is usually occupied by the boats doing trips up the Dalyan River.
3. Anchor in the bay. The bottom is mud and weed and for some reason not the best holding everywhere.
4. **Karği Köyü** The bay on the west side before you enter Ekinçik proper. Anchor and take a long line ashore to the north or south side. It is fairly deep in here so you will be dropping your anchor in considerable depths. Reasonable shelter from the prevailing wind and an utterly lovely place away from the hurley burley of Ekinçik central.

Caution At times a katabatic wind blows off the hills from the N–NE with some strength. The bad holding in the bay means that boats often drag anchor. With southerlies a considerable surge enters Ekinçik and the only really safe place is tucked into the southeast corner at My Marina.

Facilities

Water and electricity at My Marina. Meagre provisions and several restaurants, including the My Marina restaurant above the southeast corner with stupendous views and good (if somewhat expensive) food.

General

The bay itself is hemmed in by pine-clad slopes with a spectacular flat-topped red rock outcrop on the eastern side. At the head of the bay there is a pebbly beach and a short walk away the small village of Ekinçik. There are several restaurants, the one on the eastern side of the bay being justifiably popular for the view over the anchorage and its good food. A flotilla of small boats is permanently stationed in the bay for excursions up the Dalyan River to ancient Caunos – though excursion rates have escalated in recent years (in 2010 rates were €50 per head or €200 per boat). Rates can be haggled over and it really depends on demand and how well the season has gone what sort of price you will get. The trip is well worth the effort, both for the magnificent surroundings and the visit to Caunos. See the section below on Caunos.

KÖYCEĞIZ AND THE LAKE

The village of Köyceğiz sits at the northern end of Lake Köyceğiz (Köyceğiz Gölu), the lake that feeds the Dalyan River. Köyceğiz itself is a pleasant little place, unpretentious to a fault, with a most helpful tourist information office. From Köyceğiz you can hire a boat to go to Caunos and/or to the Sultaniye hot springs in the southwest corner of the lake, though this is a much longer trip than from Dalyan.

The Sultaniye hot springs were described to me as a thermal establishment with rooms for hire and luxuriantly appointed baths. They are nothing like this. The buildings and baths are dilapidated and in the spring the visitors mostly appear to be the shepherds and their goats. The springs are said to be the most radioactive in Turkey and the second most radioactive springs in the world, but post-Fukushima I'm not sure whether this is really the best way to advertise

Delikada and the Dalyan River

Off the entrance to the Dalyan River (properly the Köyceğiz River, but everyone calls it the Dalyan) is the small islet of Delikada. Yachts can anchor with a long line ashore to the islet in the shallows off the river mouth. Some swell penetrates into here, but it is usually tenable though at times it may be best to leave someone on board. From here you can hire a tripper boat to go up the river or you can take your own dinghy, though you may face some approbation from the tripper boat skippers. They will tell you it is prohibited for you to do so: the fish trap barriers will not open, and so on, none of which is true. It is really up to the individual skipper to decide whether he wants the hassle of taking his own dingy or a relaxed ride in one of the local boats.

Dalyan village sits on the east bank of the river and its name literally means a 'fish-trap'. Mullet and bass (*kefal* and *levrek* in Turkish) swim up the river to Lake Köyceğiz to spawn and on their return are caught in a trap stretched across the river. The barrier fish-trap used to be situated at the village of Dalyan, but now it is sited a kilometre downstream. Basically it is a great mesh barrier across the river with enclosures in it from which the trapped fish can be taken. Excursion boats are locked through one side of the barrier to ensure that as few fish as possible escape. In Dalyan village there are several restaurants by the river which specialise in mullet and bass dishes and either fish is excellent eating.

It is likely that the ancient Caunians also employed a fish-trap across the river to catch mullet and bass (in ancient Greek *kephalos* and *labrax*). George Bean has identified an inscription regulating catches of fish in the river and we know that Caunos produced salted fish for export. In an age where salting fish was just about the only way of preserving them, salted fish was a valuable commodity. Even today you can get salted cod throughout the Mediterranean, where it is known as *baccala* or a variation on that name. Today the *baccala* mostly comes from Scandinavia and one of its advantages over frozen fish is that it weighs less, as little as one-fifth the weight of frozen cod, and so costs much less to transport. One of the other things the Caunians would have made was *garum*, an essence of fish much valued by Roman epicures, but which sounds revolting. It was made by filling a barrel with fish entrails and salt and drawing off the liquid which formed from this evil mixture. The *pissalat* still used in Provence is probably a direct descendent of the Romans' *garum* and in the Sea of Marmara an essence made from mackerel livers soaked in brine is also probably descended from ancient *garum*.

Looking over Delikada Islet on the right and the Dalyan River delta on the left   *Kadir Kir*

CAUNOS

Caunos is usually remembered as much for the experience of getting to it as for the site itself. The boat-trip from Ekinçik takes you along a rocky coast with small inlets and craggy headlands covered in pine to the mouth of the Dalyan River. The small islet of Delikada protects the mouth of the river and a sand bar across the mouth prevents all but shallow-draught boats from proceeding up it. Once into the river tall reeds shut out the scenery and divide it up into countless different channels. You could be on the Norfolk Broads or some other northern European river delta until you turn a corner and see several imposing rock-tombs carved out of the cliff-face. If you have come by road to Dalyan village you take a boat from there to the site and the approach from upriver is much the same sort of river-scape as from downriver. After chugging through the reedy channels you come to a landing stage on the western side of the river and the track that leads to the site of ancient Caunos.

The track winds through low land with a steep rocky hill prominent from afar. This is the acropolis hill, about 150m (500 ft) high, but appearing to be more when looking up at the sheer cliffs from below. At the base of the acropolis hill are a theatre in good condition, a large Roman bathhouse with the heating cavities intact and a smaller building thought to be a library. A Byzantine church also stands nearby. Down towards the ancient harbour a temple and agora have been uncovered in the excavations. Close to the harbour a quite fascinating structure has been excavated and restored, fascinating because its precise function is still somewhat mysterious and the likely function makes it unique. Two concentric pools are ringed by low walls and columns with a circular platform in the middle pool. Notches in the columns were probably there for an attached screen around the pool. Leading away from the pools is an enclosed garden that was also partly screened off from full public view. The pools may have been purely ornamental with a fountain in the middle, but if so why are there steps down into the pool and why was it all screened off? The Turkish excavators have suggested that it was used as a shallow swimming pool and the flat platform in the middle was for sitting on. The existence of an outdoor bathing pool as luxuriantly appointed as this, an enclosed arbour leading off it, and a prominent site close to the harbour and the centre of the city, leads to pleasant sybaritic musings on the lifestyle enjoyed by the inhabitants of Caunos. The idea of young Caunian maidens in diaphanous silk cavorting in the shallow pool by the harbour brings to mind those wonderfully naive drawings in children's books of everyday life in ancient Greece and Rome, where nothing as nasty as disease or ugliness touched the inhabitants of the drawings.

Disease is something we know the Caunians suffered dreadfully from: the Greek and Roman writers and commentators tell us so. Stratonicus (4th century BC), renowned for his scathing tongue, visited Caunos and commented on the greenish complexion of the inhabitants by saying he now knew what Homer had meant when he said: 'As are the generations of leaves, so are the generations of men'. The Caunians thought it unkind of him to call their city unhealthy to which Stratonicus replied he had meant no such thing, after all 'how could I dare to call a city unhealthy where even dead men walk the streets'. Strabo (63BC–AD21) remarked that although the city and its territory were rich, the city was notoriously unhealthy because of the heat and the abundance of fruit. Over-indulgence in fruit was generally supposed to cause disease, a theory still prevalent throughout Europe until the 17th century. Dio Chrysostom (AD40–115), the wandering philosopher, was especially caustic about the Caunians: 'Their misfortunes are due to their extreme folly and rascality, and if they were all but wiped out by fever, it is no more than they deserve'. From Stratonicus and his reference to the green complexion of the Caunians to Dio Chrysostom's desire that they all succumb to fever, it is not too difficult after looking at the marshy hinterland around Caunos to conclude that malaria was the scourge of the city. The area is ideal for the mosquito to breed in and no doubt in antiquity Caunos throbbed to the irritating whine of the malarial *Anopheles*. In fact, it was not until 1948 that the area around Caunos was sprayed and malaria brought under control. There are still mosquitoes in the Dalyan area, though thankfully not of the species that transmits malaria.

Continued on next page

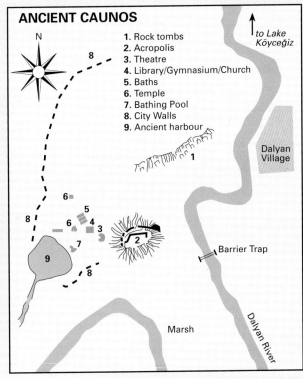

ANCIENT CAUNOS

N

1. Rock tombs
2. Acropolis
3. Theatre
4. Library/Gymnasium/Church
5. Baths
6. Temple
7. Bathing Pool
8. City Walls
9. Ancient harbour

to Lake Köyceğiz

Dalyan Village

Barrier Trap

Marsh

Dalyan River

CAUNOS *continued*

Caunos. Rock tombs above the Dalyan River

culture evidently owed much to the Lycians. Herodotus tells us it was neither Carian nor Lycian and it is interesting that though inscriptions have been found in Carian script, there are sufficient different and unique characters for us to assume there was a Caunian language. While the language was largely Carian, the rock tombs in the cliffside are typically Lycian.

The exterior of the tomb is hewn to look like the entrance to a temple with columns, friezes, and a pediment. Despite the grand exterior, inside there is only a small chamber with benches on which the dead were laid. The largest of these temple-tombs is incomplete and we can see how they were constructed. The roof, pediment, and frieze are complete, but the columns have only been roughly shaped and work on the chamber had not started. With the arrival of Alexander the Great Caunos adopted Hellenic practices and by the 1st century BC Greek institutions and culture had entirely taken over. Though it was a prosperous city (Pliny mentions Caunian salted fish and slaves as its principal exports) it was not well known outside Asia Minor. No great artists or writers were claimed by Caunos and it seems the only thing the city was renowned for was its unhealthy site. Rather than support artists and philosophers as other cities did, the profits from the city coffers were spent on a sybaritic lifestyle, if the bathing pool by the harbour is anything to go by.

The climb up to the acropolis is not recommended for anyone short of breath. Although not very far, it is very steep, an ideal spot for an acropolis. Most of the walls and the tower are of medieval origin, but on the summit the ruined fort is of ancient masonry. The climb up to the summit is worth it, as much for the view out over the river to the sea nearly two miles away as for the ancient bits of rock. In antiquity it is likely that the sea came right up to the acropolis hill. The ancient harbour, now a small lake known as Suluklu Gölu, was either right on the sea or connected to it by a channel and it suffered the same fate as other harbours such as Ephesus and Patara situated at the mouth of a river. It silted. From the acropolis hill you can see the vast swampy area, knitted together by reeds, that now cover what was once sea. George Bean has surmised that an inscription found by the harbour detailing tax exemptions in the 1st century AD may have been an effort to encourage ships to use the harbour at Caunos, and that these exemptions were necessary because the approaches to the harbour had already begun to silt up and consequently ships were avoiding it. Certainly the fortunes of the city had begun to decline by the 2nd century AD.

Caunos sits on the border between ancient Caria and ancient Lycia. It is mentioned as a Carian city, but its

Looking out on to what was the harbour at Caunos before it silted

Iztuzu and the turtles

Though the title may sound like something out of a Zen tale, Iztuzu is a beach and the turtles in question are the beleaguered loggerhead turtles who lay their eggs on that beach. To the east of Delikada and the mouth of the Dalyan River, a long fine sandy beach known as Iztuzu runs around the shore, the sort of place photographers for travel brochures drool over. Apart from a few shacks and the locals, little else intrudes on the peace and quiet of this beach, certainly not sun-starved northerners frying their bodies in the heat of summer. There is, however, another visitor to the beach and that is the loggerhead turtle, *Caretta caretta*, which comes ashore to lay its eggs here. There are few places left in the Mediterranean where the right conditions, a south-facing beach, fine uncompacted sand, and the absence of noise and bright artificial lights, remain for the loggerhead to breed. One of these is Iztuzu.

At one time it appeared that Iztuzu might be threatened by tourism. It was planned to build accommodation providing 3,000 beds on the beach, a hotel and holiday village complex. Tourists *en masse* compact the sand, making it difficult for the female to excavate a pit in which to lay her eggs. Noise will drive her away from the beach. And if, somehow, baby turtles are born, the bright lights of the hotel will disorientate them and cause them to head inland instead of towards the sea and relative safety. If a newly born turtle doesn't make it to the sea in time, and is not picked off by predators, it fries in the sun – an irony that may have escaped the hotel developers.

In the eastern Mediterranean there are known to be two principal breeding spots for the loggerhead: on Zante in the Ionian Sea, and at Iztuzu. Hotel development has already occurred along Laguna Beach on Zante and has significantly affected the breeding population of loggerheads using the beach. Now, with hindsight, the Greeks have restricted further development and the beach is patrolled during the breeding season to minimise disruption to the turtles, though in fact the amount of beach left for the turtles is little more than a joke. At Iztuzu the development of a hotel and holiday village complex has been halted for now and a programme set up to police the beach during the breeding season. This at least gives the turtles a fighting chance and the authorities are to be commended for their foresight.

DISIBILMEZ BÜKÜ

⊕ 36°43'·29N 28°38'·94E WGS84

The anchorage under Delikada islet off the mouth of the Dalyan River

them. The tourist office handout goes on to say that the hot springs are beneficial for rheumatism, neuralgia, neuritis, gall-bladder disorders, mental disorders, liver complaints, and women's diseases. Since I was suffering from none of these I declined to try the baths, a reluctance encouraged by the absence of people in the vicinity who perhaps knew more about the effects of radioactivity than I did. Apparently the establishment has now been tidied up and is not the tumbledown place it used to be.

Further on towards Dalyan there is another thermal pool amongst the trees. Despite the presence of strange algae-like growth in the pool, which earned it the title of 'the slime pool' from a companion, I have bathed here. The mud here is said to be good for you and the idea is you coat it all over yourself, more it seems for photos to send home than for its therapeutic properties. In these pools, or any hot pool for that matter, never put your head under the water. There are sufficient cases of meningitis contracted from immersing the head and all its orifices in a hot pool to make it an unnecessary risk to take.

The large bay between Disibilmez Burnu and Kara Burun. In the northwest corner of the bay there is a cove that can be used in calm weather. Anchor in 10–15m with a long line to the shore near the restaurant. Reasonable shelter here although the *meltemi* pushes some swell up into the bay. A restaurant opens in the summer.

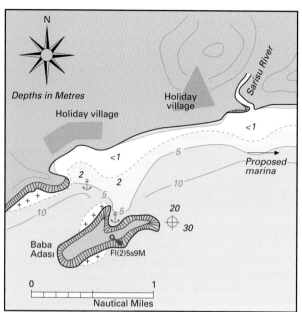

BABA ADASI ANCHORAGE
⊕36°41'·6N 28°42'·05E

Looking NW over Baba Adası into Disibilmez Buku   *Kadir Kü*

BABA ADASI

From Ekinçik and Dalyan there are several rocky capes before the slab-sided island of Baba Adası ('Papa' or 'Daddy Island') can be seen close off a long sandy beach. You can pass behind the islet from either end, taking care of the shallows off the coast and the bar going across to the islet. Anchor off the holiday village or behind the islet. Neither anchorage is completely protected from the *meltemi,* which pushes a swell in here making it uncomfortable. There are a number of large holiday villages around the shore and restaurants around the beach.

On the summit of the island there is a remarkable pyramidal structure built in brick, the purpose of which has been disputed. It has been variously described as a mausoleum, a monument and a lighthouse, the general consensus being that the latter was the most likely purpose. Although the holiday villages are sited next to the beach and the sea, they are also directly under the flightpath of planes landing and taking off from Dalaman Airport – perhaps they didn't mention that in the brochures.

From Baba Adası you can visit the ruins of a sizeable town near the shore. Most of the ruins to be seen are of a medieval town, probably of Prepia, a place in this vicinity mentioned in medieval Sailing Directions (the 'Portolans').

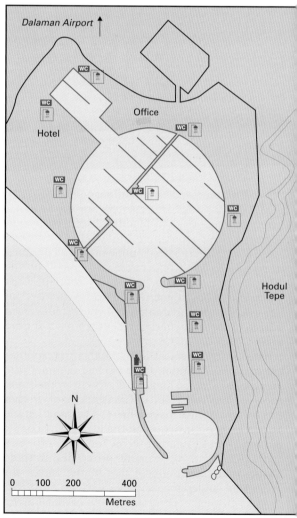

D-MARIN DALAMAN MARINA (PROPOSED LAYOUT)
⊕36°40'·5N 28°47'·4E

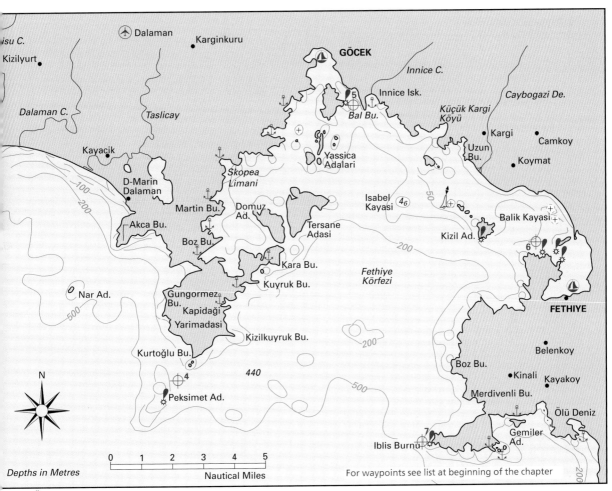

ԶIYE KÖRFEZI (GULF OF FETHIYE)

Evidence of a more ancient settlement, probably the town of Pisilis, are also scattered around the site and incorporated into the medieval buildings. It may be that a harbour was situated on the Dalaman River that flows into the sea near here, that in antiquity and the Middle Ages the river's course was different to what it is today and formerly it flowed close to Pisilis/Prepia, so that the harbour silted as at Caunos. The fact that Prepia was mentioned in the Portalans does not mean it necessarily had a harbour, but the existence of the lighthouse, if that is what it was, indicates it had an importance over and above simply being there.

D-MARIN DALAMAN MARINA

There are plans by the Dogus group to build a marina at the eastern end of the bay close S of the end of the runway at Dalaman airport. A holiday village is conspicuous on the hill. Work is planned to start in 2012 with projected completion due in 2014.

Data 650 berths. Max LOA 60m.

www.dogusmarina.com.tr

Fethiye-Göcek SEPA
(Special Environmental Protection Area)

The Fethiye–Gocek SEPA covers the area from the beach off Dalaman airport, all of Fethiye Körfezi around to and including Olu Deniz. More about the SEPA general regulations can be found in the introduction.

SEPA Anchorages

Within the SEPA I have marked the restrictions on anchorages as defined by the current advice at the time of writing. I have left all the plans intact (except where they needed amending), as who knows what new interpretations there will be in the next few years and who knows what will happen in practice concerning anchoring and mooring around the gulf.

In all likelihood these restrictions will change or may be modified depending on how the interpretation of the SEPA goes and how it is policed. It should be noted that at present the coastguard (Sahil Güvenlik) and harbourmasters will be responsible for implementation and policing. Marina staff are not involved, although they are required to check the scheme, and some waste discharge points will be sited in marinas.

In 2011 there were just not enough buoys for the numbers of yachts here and many yachts were anchoring and taking a long line ashore or swinging free. Many of the buoys are sited some way off the coast so yachts were swinging free. Most of the restaurant catwalks are operating although a few have been removed. I suggest you play things by ear and see what the situation is when you get into the gulf. As ever local practice is usually different to official edicts.

Below is an abridged translation of the latest regulations concerning yachts within the SEPA of Fethiye-Gocek. Further restrictions for trip boats, cargo vessels and diving also apply. This is our interpretation of the regulations, and is as accurate as possible, but it does not replace the original Turkish document as the definitive reference:

**MINISTRY OF ENVIRONMENT AND FORESTS
4.05.10 NUMBER 2540 PUBLICATION
PRINCIPLES TO PROTECT THE GULF OF GÖCEK AND
THE COVES IN THE GÖCEK/DALAMAN REGION**
Section 5

These regulations apply to the entire area except where specified.

5a.   The objective is to protect the biodiversity and the environmental values and to avoid pollution in the Fethiye-Göcek Special Environmental Protection Area.

5b.   Polluters are liable for costs to stop and reverse the effects of any pollution. Costs of fines to be determined.

5c.   Yachts without black water holding tanks are not permitted to stay overnight in the areas of restricted use.

Note Foreign yachts will not be inspected, but must be able to show their Blue Card when asked, and if yachts remain here for several days without using pump-out facilities they will be liable to a fine.

5c₁. No anchoring in restricted areas – vessels must only use moorings in the areas as detailed in Section 8.

5d.   Noise pollution prohibited.

5e.   No barbecues on deck or on shore.

5f.   No discharge of waste water or solid waste – this must be passed to collection vessels.

Note Waste water is defined as black water, bilge water, and grey water.

5g.   All documents and digital card to control waste must be carried on board.

Note Blue cards are available from most nearby marinas at a one-off cost of 70YTL

6.   Area prohibited for diving: area enclosing Kapidağ Yarimadasi and most of Skopea Limani.

7.   Area prohibited to all vessels: Hammam Köyü (Ruin Bay)

8.   Restricted Areas

8b   No Anchoring N of a line E–W across the N end of Göcek Adası

Note There are two ship anchorages within the area.

8c   Protection of *Posidonia* sea grass beds

Vessels are prohibited from anchoring, but may secure to mooring buoys and bollards or eye-pads on shore, in the following areas:

a. Göcek Adası NW corner and bay on NE side of Göcek Ad. light

b. Tersane Creek

c. Corner between 22 Fathom Cove and Seagull Bay

d. Inner Sarsaya Koyu including Pilloried Cove

e. Deep Bay (Siralibük Koyu)

8d   Overnight stays

f. Anchoring is prohibited in Yassica Adaları including Zeytinli Adası. All vessels must only use moorings and bollards.
The area around Dil Burnu is out of bounds to all but trip boats during the hours of 1000–2000. Yachts may stay overnight here, but must only use moorings and bollards.

9.   General Rules within the entire area:

9a.   Vessel numbers limited to numbers of moorings

9b.   No lines may be taken to trees

9c.   Solid waste container locations

9d.   Maximum permitted stay is limited to three days in one place, and max 11 days total in the area

9e.   Max speed 6kns in roadsteads, bays and coves

9f.   Watersports permitted – excluding jet skis

10.   Further restrictions

10a. Fuel can only be transferred at fuel quays

10b. Restriction of vessel types

0c. Exceptional permission (short term) may be obtained by the harbour office.

My thanks to Yusuf Civelokoglu for the translation and making sense, as much as we can, of the official document.

In Practice

As of November 2011 the practice on the ground as experienced by us on *Skylax* was as follows. What will happen in 2012 and later is guesswork. We have talked to marina managers, charter operators, those in the marine trade, officials and harbourmasters. The only conclusion that can be drawn from all this is that no one knows exactly what will happen in practice, how the regulations will affect private boats or what the final ramifications will be for charter boats. Nearly all are agreed that the SEPA regulations are skewed to unduly penalising yachts on pollution issues compared to land-based pollution. See the section on pollution in the Mediterranean in the introduction.

In November 2011 in the Mugla area

1. All boats are required to have a blue card. This can be obtained from all marinas in the area and most will issue the card free of charge. At this time no readers were available for the cards so any inspections (and I know of none) were just to see if you had the card. It is planned to introduce card readers in 2012.

2. Monitoring of the blue card will be carried out by the harbourmaster and the coastguard.

3. In the Fethiye/Göcek area yachts were required to present evidence of a pump-out to obtain a new transit log. This only really impinged on charter yachts where a new transit log is issued for every charter. Because the readers for the new blue cards were not working a paper receipt was issued as evidence, referred to as a 'poo paper' by the charter companies.

4. There are pump-out stations in the marinas and these work efficiently. A conical rubber collar means all deck fitting sizes for pump-out can be accomodated. In practice this works well without messing up the deck or topsides. As one marina manager said, "... in over 3,000 pump-outs we have yet to cover a yacht in sh**." A charge is made for pump-out, usually 15–20TL.

5. Grey water is still included in the SEPA regulations. Charter companies are employing a wait-and-see policy and if required will plumb grey water into the black water holding tank. It should be evident that any yachts away from a pump-out station for even a few days will have filled the holding tank. Here you can draw your own conclusions to what happens in practice.

Coda

It is important to know that the SEPA regulations are intended to be implemented around all Turkish coasts. The Mugla region is the pilot for the scheme and originally it was planned that all of the Turkish coast would be under SEPA regulations by 2013–2014. Given the problems encountered implementing the scheme in Fethiye Körfezi this roll-out date is now unlikely.

FETHIYE KÖRFEZI (GULF OF FETHIYE)

From Baba Adası the bold silhouette of Kapi Daği, the headland at the western entrance to the Gulf of Fethiye, can be seen. The gulf is a jagged bite out of the mountains of Lycia with a number of small islands scattered around the perimeter. The locals call it the Gulf of Twelve Islands, though that is counting some fairly small ones to get to that number. It takes its better known name, Fethiye Körfezi, from the town of Fethiye tucked into its eastern corner. In ancient times it was called Sinus Glaucus, Glaucus being one of the Lycian generals mentioned by Homer in the *Iliad*.

To get to most places in the gulf, particularly to the islands and coast on the western side, there are few alternatives but to go by boat, though a rough road around the western side now brings some land-based tourists. These islands and the much indented coast on the western side, called Skopea Limanı, are a popular cruising ground for yachts and *gulets* offering sheltered waters behind the islands and attractive coves and bays within short distances around the coast. Formerly the shores were virtually deserted, but in recent years with the increasing numbers of yachts and *gulets* about, small restaurants have sprung up in the more popular bays.

It is common practice in many of the bays to anchor and take a long line ashore. As well as allowing more craft to moor in a limited space, it is a sensible way to moor your boat in relatively deep water. Trees are a tempting anchoring point, but since many have been badly damaged by this practice, they should never be used. The authorities have cemeted bollards to the foreshore in many bays, and it is to these, in preference to trees or rocks, that you should take your long line to.

KIZILKUYRUK KÖYÜ

Within marine reserve but outside restricted area.

A bay ('Redstart' or 'Whitecap' Bay) just inside the western entrance to the gulf that can be easily recognised by the prominent red cliffs around it. Anchor in the western or northern coves with a long line ashore. It is quite deep for anchoring so have plenty of anchor chain and line ready. Good shelter, although after the *meltemi* has been blowing for a bit some residual swell is pushed around into the bay – more uncomfortable than worrying.

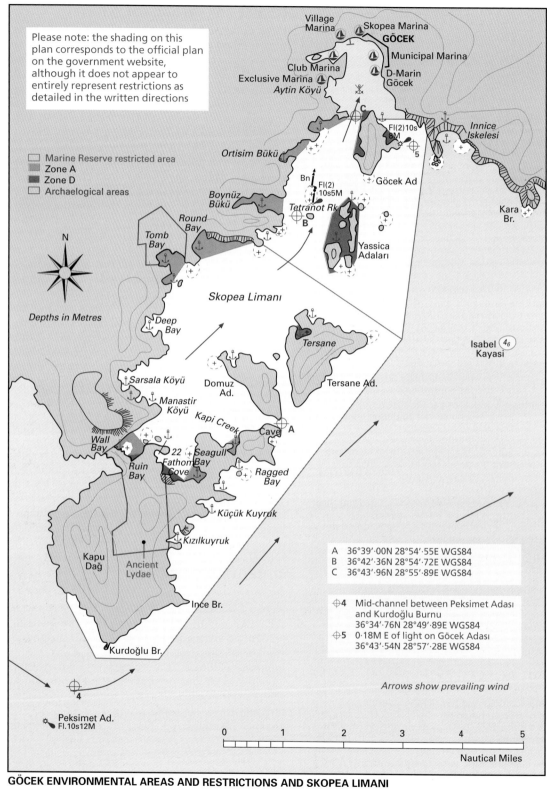

Please note: the shading on this plan corresponds to the official plan on the government website, although it does not appear to entirely represent restrictions as detailed in the written directions

☐ Marine Reserve restricted area
◼ Zone A
◼ Zone D
☐ Archaelogical areas

N

Depths in Metres

Village Marina
Skopea Marina
GÖCEK
Municipal Marina
Club Marina
Exclusive Marina
D-Marin Göcek
Aytin Köyü

C

Fl(2)10s 8M
5
Innice Iskelesi

Ortisim Bükü

Bn
Fl(2) 10s5M
Göcek Ad

Boynüz Bükü
Tetranot Rk
B
Kara Br.

Round Bay
Tomb Bay

Yassica Adaları

Skopea Limanı

Deep Bay

Tersane

Isabel Kayasi 4₆

Sarsala Köyü

Domuz Ad.

Tersane Ad.

Manastir Köyü
Kapi Creek

Cave A

Wall Bay
Ruin Bay
22
Fathom Cove
Seagull Bay
Ragged Bay

Küçük Kuyruk

Kızılkuyruk

Kapu Dağ
Ancient Lydae

A   36°39′·00N 28°54′·55E WGS84
B   36°42′·36N 28°54′·72E WGS84
C   36°43′·96N 28°55′·89E WGS84

⊕4 Mid-channel between Peksimet Adası and Kurdoğlu Burnu
      36°34′·76N 28°49′·89E WGS84
⊕5 0·18M E of light on Göcek Adası
      36°43′·54N 28°57′·28E WGS84

Ince Br.

Arrows show prevailing wind

Kurdoğlu Br.

4

Peksimet Ad.
Fl.10s12M

0   1   2   3   4   5

Nautical Miles

GÖCEK ENVIRONMENTAL AREAS AND RESTRICTIONS AND SKOPEA LIMANI

Kızılkuyruk

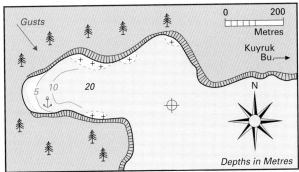

KÜÇÜK KUYRUK
⊕36°37'·74N 28°53'·01E WGS84

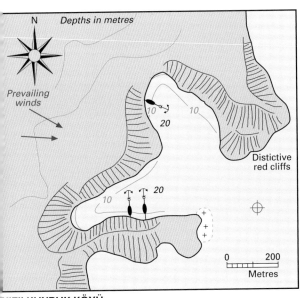

KIZILKUYRUK KÖYÜ
⊕36°37'·04N 28°52'·40E WGS84

The anchorage is a delightful one in peaceful surroundings and it was probably known and used by the ancients.

KÜÇÜK KUYRUK

Within marine reserve but outside restricted area.

A spectacular anchorage less than a mile north of Kizilkuyruk. The entrance can be difficult to see from the south although once up to the entrance things become obvious. Anchor on the south side with a long line ashore. Like Kizilkuyruk a bit of residual swell is pushed into here until the *meltemi* dies in the evening. The surroundings are stupendous with pine growing at odd angles out of the steep slopes and cliffs around the anchorage.

When seeking translations of some of these names you can get some unexpected results. Küçük means 'little'. Kuyruk means a 'tail' or 'rear end', presumably because it looks a bit like one. However, the colloquial use of *kuyruk* is 'prick'. Work it out for yourself.

RAGGED BAY

Within marine reserve but outside restricted area.

Just north of Küçük Kuyruk is a large bay with an islet in the middle. Around the rocky coast there are several places where a yacht can anchor with a long line ashore. Generally the southwest corner and a cove behind the islet are favoured. It is

Ancient Lydae and Arymaxa

From Kizilkuyrak a path leads to ancient Lydae, about an hour's easy walk to the west, with parts of an ancient path evident along the way. The site is set in splendid isolation and there are the remains of the *agora*, several indeterminate buildings, part of a colossal statue, and the remains of other buildings scattered about; but the most striking feature of the site is two large mausoleums in reasonable condition. The ruins are of Roman and Byzantine origin and little is known about the city at this time and virtually nothing of its existence in pre-Roman times bar a brief mention in the *Stadiasmus* and later by Ptolemy in his *Geography*.

To the north of Lydae, near the narrow neck joining the headland of Kapi Daği to the mainland, are a few ruins and a fort belonging to Arymaxa, a *deme* of Lydae. A wall runs right across this neck of land from the cove on the east side to the sea on the other. Whether the wall is of recent origin or has older antecedents is uncertain, but it would have made an effective defensive wall, cutting the whole headland off from a land attack.

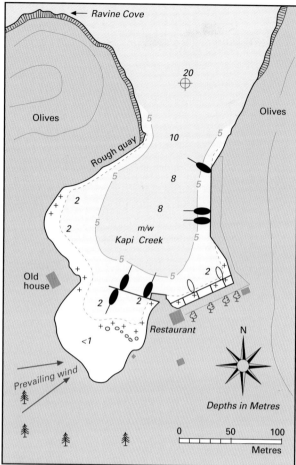

KAPI CREEK
⊕36°38'·87N 28°53'·67E WGS84

Kapi Creek and Ravine Cove

mostly fairly deep here so have plenty of chain ready to let go. Shelter is good with a light *meltemi*, but once it blows up a swell is pushed around into the bay and it is probably best to leave and go around into Skopea Limanı proper.

KAPI CREEK (Göbün Köyü)

Within marine reserve and anchoring restrictions apply here. The quay and pontoon have laid moorings.

('Gateway' or 'Door Creek') Between Domuz Adası and the northern tip of Kapi Daği there is a narrow channel leading into Skopea Limanı. Just around from the channel an inlet, barely visible until you are at the entrance, runs in. Go stern or bows-to one of the rough quays taking care of underwater rubble. You will usually be waved into a berth on the catwalk on the south or east side by a waiter from the restaurant here. Laid moorings tailed to the catwalk. Good shelter from the *meltemi*, although there can be strong gusts off the western side which make manoeuvring difficult.

There are a few old houses around the shore and the restaurant (there used to be several), but otherwise there are just olive groves and pine on the higher slopes. It is an idyllic spot and not surprisingly it is popular with yachts. The restaurant serves simple but good fare and will often supply 'village bread', the huge round leaves of unleavened bread cooked in an outdoor oven.

On the west side of the bay there is a triple-vaulted house – at least I have been assured it is simply a house – of unusual design and with no obvious explanation for its complex construction. There are others of similar design around Skopea Liman, presumably a local architectural feature. A short walk over the ridge behind the inlet you come to the sea again and here there is a delightful rocky cove, shaded by pine, just right for a secluded dip.

Large yachts that can't get into the creek will often use Ravine Cove immediately west of the creek. Cliffs on either side implode into a ravine dropping steeply to the sea. Just impressive and savagely beautiful.

Looking from Ragged Bay over into Skopea Liman with Kapi Creek on the right and Seagull Bay and Wall Bay on the left   *Kadir Kir*

TWENTY-TWO-FATHOM COVE

Within marine reserve. Use moorings if available and take the long line to a shore bollard or swing free. Long lines go to bollards only and not to trees or rocks. Anchoring permitted 2011.

⊕ 36°38'·42N 28°51'·93E WGS84

A small cove just across from Kapi Creek. Go bows-to the rough quay at the head or pick up a mooring and take a long line ashore on the southwest side. On the southwest side you will be anchoring in 35–40m (22 fathoms!). Take a long line ashore to a bollard. Good shelter from the *meltemi* although some chop is kicked up across the bay – more uncomfortable than anything else, although you need to ensure your anchor is well in.

Restaurants seem to come and go in the cove. At the moment there is a 'boat' restaurant moored in the NE corner. It has limited but excellent fare; you get *mezes* and a choice of *guvec*, the traditional Turkish casserole. They also cook village bread in the morning.

Looking into Seagull Bay with Küçük Kuyruk bottom left
Kadir Kir

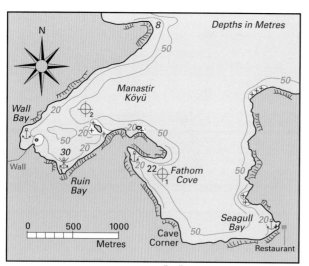

SEAGULL BAY TO MANASTIR KÖYÜ
⊕1 36°38'·42N 28°51'·93E WGS84
⊕2 36°38'·79N 28°51'·44E WGS84

head of the bay. A peaceful place not crowded with *gulets*. Seagull Bay restaurant was demolished by the authorities, though it is rumoured it may open again. Best advice is not to rely on finding a restaurant here for the time being.

CAVE CORNER

According to the regulations this is a prohibited area, but since moorings have been laid it suggests this is currently a permitted area, but that anchoring may be prohibited.

Between Seagull Bay and 22 Fathom Cove are a couple of indents in the coast where yachts can pick up a mooring and either take a long line to a bollard or swing free.

Manastir Köyü

Directly west of Twenty-two-fathom cove lies Manastir Köyü, a large bay with two stunningly beautiful anchorages in it.

The cove takes its name from Admiralty chart 1986 (surveyed by Commander T Graves back in 1840) which has a 22-fathom sounding shown at the entrance of the cove. On the eastern arm of the cove the rock has weathered into jagged and weird columns to create a curious landscape.

SEAGULL BAY

⊕ 36°38'·19N 28°52'·76E WGS84

Opposite Twenty-two-fathom Cove in the E corner of the bay, Seagull Bay is easily identified by the large white seagull painting on the shore. Yachts berth stern or bows-to on a T-pier at the

Wall Bay at the west end of Manastir Köyü with the stone wall it takes its name from in the background

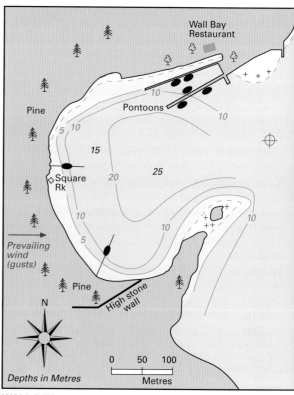

WALL BAY
⊕36°38'·67N 28°51'·12E WGS84

Ancient Crya and the 'fish'

On the north side of Ruin Bay there are several temple-tombs and pigeon-hole tombs and steps cut into the rock leading up to a miniature acropolis. The site has been identified by George Bean as Crya, which Pliny called by the evocative name 'Crya of the fugitives'. There is no explanation for this strange appellation and little is known about this small city other than the fact that it controlled two islands, Carysis and Alina, presumably the two largest islands, now called Domuz and Tersane. To the east of the tombs there is a painting of a fish on a boulder apparently executed by an Istanbuli artist, Bedri Rahmi Eyupoglu in 1974. It probably gets touched up from time to time, judging by its pristine appearance.

RUIN BAY (Hamman Köyü)

Yachts are prohibited from entering Ruin Bay but often anchor with a long line ashore just outside.

Local knowledge claims these as Cleopatra's Baths, but it is unlikely they were built until after Cleopatra was long gone, despite the locals claims. If everywhere called Cleopatra's bay/beach/palace in the eastern Mediterranean was actually visited by Cleopatra she would have needed a Lear Jet to get around in. Whatever story has become attached to the place, it is enchanting with clear turquoise water and pine overhanging the shore.

WALL BAY

Within marine reserve and anchoring restrictions apply here. Use moorings if available and take the long line to a shore bollard. Long lines go to bollards only and not to trees or rocks. Alternatively use the catwalk off the restaurant. Anchoring permitted 2011.

At the far western end of Manastir Köyü there is a cove with several places to moor around its perimeter. A remarkable square rock sits in the water near the head of the cove. Pick up a mooring and take a long line ashore to a bollard or anchor and take a line ashore to a bollard. Alternatively go alongside one of the pontoons off the restaurant on the north side. Good shelter from the *meltemi* although it tends to gust down into the bay until it dies in the evening.

Thick pine forest overhangs the water except on the northern side which is planted in olives. At the southern end of Wall Bay, a solid stone wall crossing the isthmus can be seen, from which the bay takes its name. This is the same wall mentioned in connection with ancient Arymaxa, the *deme* of Lydae.

The area ashore is now part of a protected archaeological site (see map). The restaurant on the north side serves good food and if you are using the catwalk it is only politic to eat here.

SARSALA KÖYÜ

Within marine reserve and anchoring restrictions apply here. Use moorings if available and take the long line to a shore bollard. Long lines go to bollards only and not to trees or rocks. Alternatively use the catwalk off the restaurant in the middle cove.

Note *Although not marked on the official plan, Sarsala Köyü is listed under 8c of the notes as a place where anchoring is prohibited to protect Posidonia.*

A large bay on the coast north of Manastir Köyü. It is one of the few places on this side of the gulf you can reach by road. The best anchorages here are not off the small settlement on the north side

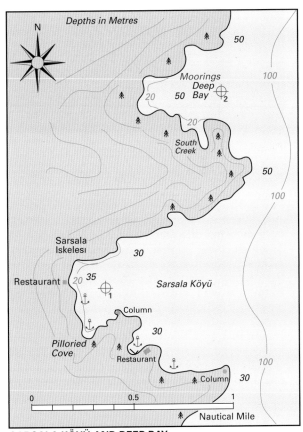

SARSALA KÖYÜ AND DEEP BAY
⊕1 36°39'·67N 28°51'·29E WGS84
⊕2 36°40'·64N 28°51'·84E WGS84

Pilloried Cove in Sarsala Köyü

Looking S from Deep Bay, past Sarsala Koyu towards Seagull Bay   *Kadir Kir*

but in the coves and bights along the southern side. There are a number of places you can pick up a mooring or anchor with a long line ashore. Most of these afford good shelter from the *meltemi* and most are relatively free of gusts. In the 'middle' inlet on the south side there is a restaurant with a catwalk you can go stern or bows-to. Laid moorings tailed to the catwalk.

My favourite is Pilloried Cove in the southwest corner. Pick up a mooring if one is free and take a line ashore if possible. Alternatively you will find a shallower patch as you enter the bay and you can drop your anchor nearby and take a line to the western side. Good shelter in a wonderful situation.

At the entrance a marble column used to poke out of the vegetation, beautifully evocative of a past age, but on a recent visit here I couldn't locate it, perhaps it has been removed or perhaps it has just been overgrown. Around the bay the heavily forested slopes plummet dramatically down to the sea and you can easily hole up in here, wonderfully cut off from the world, and just do those simple things like swimming, reading and contemplating the gourmet delights you will cook for dinner.

DEEP BAY (properly **Siralibük Limanı**)

Within marine reserve and anchoring restrictions apply. Yachts may only use moorings in Deep Bay. Long lines go to bollards only and not to trees or rocks. Anchoring permitted 2011.

A deeply indented bay immediately north of Sarsala Iskelesi. Yachts are theoretically prohibited from anchoring in the bay and may only use the laid moorings with a long line ashore to a bollard or swing free. Despite the ban on anchoring yachts were anchoring here in 2011. Good shelter from the prevailing wind although it gusts down off the slopes in places.

Pine covers the slopes and it is a peaceful spot. As its name suggests it is quite deep, although the creek on the south side provides an enclosed anchorage.

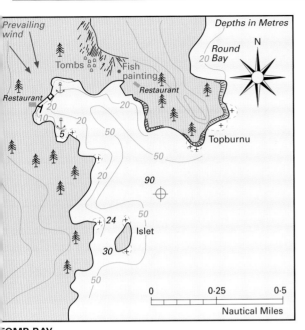

TOMB BAY
⊕36°41'·47N 28°52'·39E WGS84

TOMB BAY (properly Tasyaka Bükü)

Within marine reserve and anchoring restrictions apply. Yachts may only use moorings in Tomb Bay. Long lines go to bollards only and not to trees or rocks. Anchoring permitted 2011.

Note *Shown on official plan, but restrictions listed in the official notes.*

This bay lies to the northwest of Domuz Adası and Tersane Adası, under the prominent headland of Topburnu. There are least depths of 24m in the

Tomb Bay looking E with Round Bay top left of picture
Kadir Kir

channel between the islet and the coast in the southern approaches. There are numerous anchorages around the bay.

In 2011 there were no laid moorings, although this may change in future. The regulations prohibit anchoring here but in practice yachts do anchor with a long line ashore to a bollard. The restaurant in the NW corner of the bay has a catwalk with laid moorings. Someone will usually help you to tie up. Good shelter from the prevailing wind although there are gusts with the *meltemi.*

The bay is popular by day, but is less populated at night when tripper boats and others return home. The restaurant serves good local fare and in the early evening you can take the dinghy across to the tombs and contemplate the sun going down with the ancient souls of Crya. If you go on the restaurant jetties then it is only politic to eat at the restaurant.

ROUND BAY (Killeiskelesi Köyü)

Within marine reserve and anchoring restrictions apply. Yachts may only use moorings if they are available here. Long lines go to bollards only and not to trees or rocks. Anchoring permitted 2011.

Note
Shown as restricted on the official plan, but no specific restrictions listed in the official notes.

⊕ 36°41'·90N 28°52'·78E WGS84

The bay just north of Tomb Bay. It is quite deep until close in where it shallows quickly to the beach. Pick up a mooring if available. Reasonable shelter although the prevailing wind will sometimes blow up and around the corner into the bay. The flat flood plain at the head is a popular spot and an unofficial camp site for weekending locals. Otherwise there are some old olive and almond trees and some curious goats.

DOMUZ ADASI

(Boar or Pig Island) This is the southernmost of the chain of islands strung through Skopea Limanı and one of the largest along with Tersane Adası. Part of the island is privately owned, apparently by the owners of *Hurriyet* ('Freedom'), one of the largest Turkish daily newspapers. A large residence and ancillary buildings have been built on the northeastern side of the island with a quayed area nearby, but it should come as no surprise that yachts and *gulets* cannot use it and landing on the island is not permitted.

Tersane Creek   *Kadir Kir*

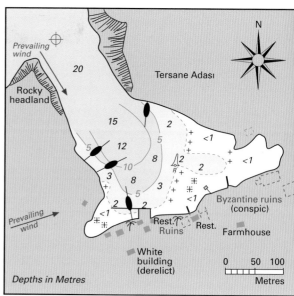

TERSANE CREEK
⊕36°40′·71N 28°54′·70E WGS84

At the northwest end of the island there is a bay sheltered from the prevailing wind, although it is very deep to anchor in here.

TERSANE ADASI

Within marine reserve and anchoring restrictions apply. Yachts may only use moorings in the area of Tersane Adası. Long lines go to bollards only and not to trees or rocks. Anchoring permitted 2011.

The largest island in the gulf, lying immediately east of Domuz Adası and separated from it by a narrow channel. There are good depths in the fairway of the channel. On the northwest side of the island a narrow inlet opens up into a T-shaped cove, an almost totally enclosed anchorage providing good shelter. The approach to the anchorage is free of dangers, but the head of the bay is encumbered by rocks and shoal water so some care is needed.

Yachts can pick up a mooring and take a long line ashore. Yachts also anchor and take a long line ashore although theoretically it is prohibited to anchor here. Alternatively go on the restaurant catwalk if it is in place. Laid moorings tailed to the catwalk and someone will usually help you tie up here. Good shelter, although there are strong gusts into the anchorage with the prevailing wind and in the afternoon is will sometimes blow straight through the entrance. Numerous tripper boats stop here so it can get very crowded at times. The restaurant is reputed to serve the best lamb in the area.

Tall palms around the shore give the place the feel of a tropical anchorage. Ashore there are numerous buildings, now deserted and partially ruined, of what was evidently a sizeable community. A number are older Byzantine buildings with more recent additions, but most date from after this period.

Apparently there was a prosperous Greek village here until the exchange of populations between Greece and Turkey after the First World War. Now there is a solitary family who farms the surrounding land, and a restaurant which opens in the summer. Tersane means 'boatyard' and it is likely that before the village was abandoned the inhabitants were engaged in building and repairing boats. There is a poignant atmosphere about this deserted village and it is a pleasant irony that once again boats visit Tersane, though for a pleasure-seeking purpose rather than the utilitarian purposes of days gone by.

YASSICA ADALARI

*Within marine reserve and anchoring restrictions apply. Yachts may only use moorings on the west side of Yassica Adaları and **only at night**. Tripper boats can use the moorings by day. Long lines go to bollards only and not to trees or rocks. In 2011 yachts anchored around the islands by day and night. It is likely that in the future the restrictions will apply, but play it by ear and see what is happening here.*

Yassica Adası north end *Kadir Kir*

A group of islets to the north of Tersane Adası with a number of dangerous offlying rocks and reefs. Despite the official edict in 2011 yachts used mooring buoys here by day and anchored as well. Like other places here you need to play it by ear. If a mooring is free pick it up and take a line ashore to a bollard or swing free. Lines must not be taken to rocks or trees. Care is needed of the reef and shoal water between the islands at the northern and southern ends. Care is also needed of above and below-water rocks fringing the coast.

Old Admiralty charts had a fairly serious error (which was duplicated onto the Turkish metric charts) showing 43 fathoms (79m on the Turkish chart) between the two southernmost islets, when in fact there is a reef with less than a metre over it joining them. Some boats didn't put the brakes on hard enough once the reef was spotted and for a while a fair amount of damage was done here.

BOYNÜZ BÜKÜ

Within marine reserve and anchoring restrictions apply. Yachts may only use moorings in Boynüz Bükü or go on the restaurant jetty. Long lines go to bollards only and not to trees or rocks. Anchoring permitted 2011.

Note *Shown as a restricted area on the official plan, but no specific restrictions listed in the official notes.*

A large bay on the coast directly opposite Yassica Adalari. The entrance is difficult to spot until you are up to it. Care is needed of a reef running out from the second point in on the north side. Pick up a mooring and take a long line ashore to a bollard. Yachts anchored here in 2011 and it is again a matter of playing it by ear. Off the restaurant at the head of the bay there is a T-pier

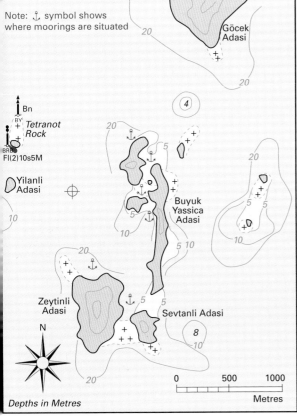

YASSICA ADALARI
⊕36°42′·4N 28°55′·45E

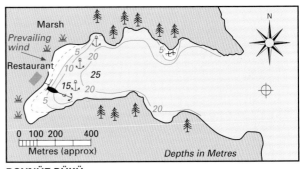

BOYNÜZ BÜKÜ
⊕36°42′·58N 28°54′·59E WGS84

Boynüz Bükü restaurant jetty

and yachts can go stern or bows-to on here. Laid moorings tailed to the jetty. The bay affords good shelter and has become something of a summering spot for those who make it as far as Skopea Limanı and decide to go no further.

A river flows into it at the head, ensuring it is well watered through the summer and consequently a green and shady place. A stand of deciduous trees and oleander grow around the river mouth with pine on the rocky slopes around. Reeds grow in the choked mouth of the river, giving it the appearance of a mini-Dalyan. The restaurant here is popular in the summer and serves good food in wonderful surroundings.

ORTISIM BÜKÜ

⊕ 36°43'·43N 28°54'·97E WGS84

Within marine reserve and anchoring restrictions apply. Yachts may only use moorings in Ortism Bükü. No anchoring is allowed. Long lines go to bollards only and not to trees or rocks.

Note
Shown as restricted on official plan, but no specific restrictions listed.

A bay north of Boynüz Bükü which also affords good shelter. It is deep until close to the head of the bay so you will often be anchoring in fairly deep water. Anchor and take a line ashore at the head or around the south side of the bay.

GÖCEK

Within marine reserve and anchoring restrictions apply. Yachts may berth in any of the six marinas around the bay. Anchoring permitted 2011.

The large bay and yachting centre for this part of the coast at the northern end of Skopea Limanı.

Pilotage

Approach Closing on the bay you will see the buildings of Göcek around the bay and inevitably a lot of yachts and *gulets* coming and going. There

Göcek   *Kadir Kir*

are no dangers in the approaches, although when closing on Port Göcek there are a number of large navigation buoys.

Mooring There are basically six yacht harbours which are detailed separately below.

Anchorage Yachts can also anchor in the bay at the time of writing, though things may well change in the future. There has long been talk about prohibiting anchoring in Göcek Bay. The bottom comes up quickly from 12–15m to under 5m so potter into the shore carefully. Further out in the bay depths are considerably more. If you are pottering around in 3m or so be careful of the fringing shoal water which extends some distance off the shore. The holding here is mediocre and you should ensure the anchor is well in. You must also exhibit an anchor light as there is a lot of traffic even after dark.

Facilities

In Göcek town you can find most things that you need.

Provisions Several supermarkets in or near town and mini-markets, bakers and butchers in town. Market in the town car park on Fridays.

Eating out There is a good selection of eateries in Göcek. On the waterfront near Skopea Liman are the Limon and the Can (John) provide a wide variety of excellent Turkish fare. Off the town square just in from the Municipal Marina is an excellent and very reasonable *pide*

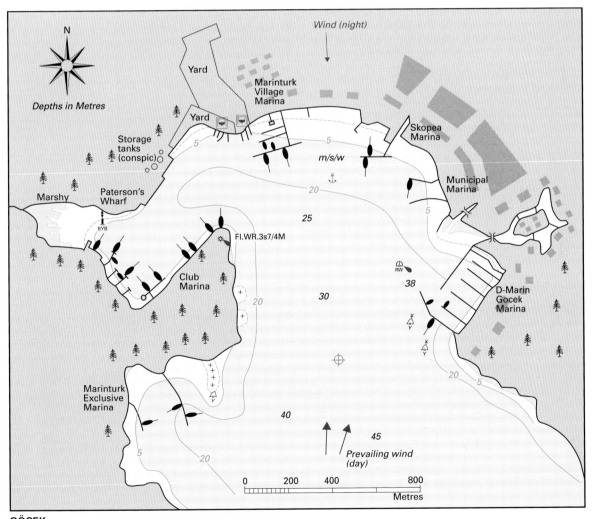

GÖCEK
⊕36°44′·92N 28°56′·31E WGS84

restaurant the Göcek Pide Salonu. In town the Mercan on the high street is an excellent local for lunch and at some time you have to try the Kebab Hospital just for the name.

Other PO. Banks. ATM. Internet cafés. Hire cars and motorbikes. Buses and *dolmuş* to Fethiye, Dalaman and points northwest. Flights from Dalaman which is about half an hour away.

General

At the very northern end of the gulf there is a large bay with the small town of Göcek strung around the shore. On the western side there is a wharf and storage tanks that rather mar the otherwise beautiful bay. The wharf is marked on early charts as 'Patersons Wharf' and the modern name, the 'Turkish Chrome Company Wharf', doesn't convey quite the same tone as the old name. Turkey has extensive workable deposits of chrome ore and exports much of Europe's requirements of the stuff, essential for making hardened steel.

The town of Göcek, formerly a small agricultural centre, has blossomed in recent years with the increased numbers of charter yachts around. It possesses the important advantage of being a mere 20 minutes from Dalaman Airport, so charterers can be off the plane and on the boat in half an hour. As a consequence it has become an important charter boat base for the area.

To supply the needs of visiting yachts and *gulets* a number of marinas have been built around the bay. Overall the effect is more pleasant than it sounds and Göcek remains a pleasant little town that has grown sympathetically to satisfy the needs of the boats based here.

GÖCEK MUNICIPAL MARINA

The two piers of the marina are located at the southeast end of the village. Here you are basically right in the heart of the village so all the facilities described above are on your doorstep.

Mooring Berth where directed. Most berths have laid moorings tailed to the jetties or the quay. Care is needed if you are going on the quay directly northwest of the piers as the dredging has left some shallow patches. Care is also needed of the shallow patch from halfway along the town quay to Skopea Limanı which often catches yachts out as they manoeuvre before berthing. Shelter here is generally good although the prevailing breeze does send an annoying chop onto the piers and jetties, which can make them uncomfortable. VHF Ch 13.

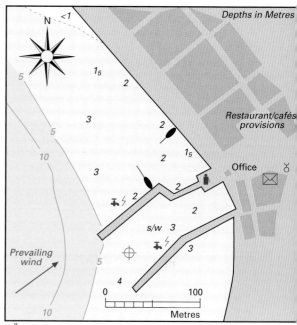

GÖCEK (Municipal Marina) ⊕36°45'·19N 28°56'·4E

Services Water and electricity. Showers and toilets. Laundry service. Fuel quay. Security. Charge band 3/4.

SKOPEA MARINA

A pier at the northwest end of town and the town quay. As at the municipal marina, you are right in the heart of town here.

Mooring Berth where directed. All berths have laid moorings tailed to the jetty. Shelter here is

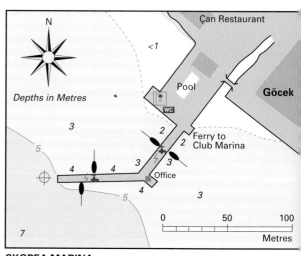

SKOPEA MARINA
⊕36°45'·26N 28°56'·24E WGS84

good, although like the municipal marina it gets an annoying chop from the prevailing wind blowing up the gulf.

VHF Ch 72, callsign *Skopea Marina*.

Services Water and electricity. Showers and toilets. Laundry service. Swimming pool. Security. Charge band 4/5.

☎ 0252 645 1794
www.skopeamarina.com.tr

VILLAGE MARINA

A new marina on the northern shore of Göcek. The masts of yachts in here and the pontoons and buoyed off areas are easily identified. The marina provides good shelter in the summer as the chop kicked up by the afternoon breeze is much attenuated by the time it gets this far into the bay. Winter southerlies send in a bit more swell and the marina is not as well protected in these winds.

Mooring As you approach the marina give them a call on VHF Ch 73. Most yachts will be heading for the buoyed channel on the southern side. Two large buoys mark the channel into the marina. A RIB will show you to a berth and help you tie up. Laid moorings tailed to the pontoons. When approaching the inside berths at the northern end of the marina you need to keep inside the dredged area conveniently marked by small yellow buoys with 'stop' on them. Inside the marina the pontoons are quite close together so some care is

needed in manoeuvring. Some yachts prefer to turn around and reverse between the pontoons to the berth.

VHF Ch 73 callsign *Marinturk Village Marina*.

Services Water and electricity. Showers and toilets. Wi-Fi. Laundry services. Waste pump-out. 24 hour security. Charge band 5.

Provisions Supermarket in the marina. It is a pleasant 10 minute walk around the waterfront to Göcek town.

Eating Out Restaurant and café in the marina. Otherwise wander around to Göcek town.

Other Boatyard with comprehensive service facilities. 75-/200-ton travel-hoists.

☎ 0252 645 2229
www.marinturk.com.tr

CLUB MARINA

When you enter Göcek Limanı you will not at first see Club Marina which is tucked into the inlet in the southeast corner of the bay. It sits nestled under the pines on the slopes around it, in a peaceful cul-de-sac out of the hustle and bustle of downtown Göcek. It also has a startling façade that can only be described as neo-Lycian.

Mooring Berth where directed. A RIB will direct you to your berth and help you tie up. Laid moorings at all berths. Many of the berths here are permanently taken so it is a good idea to enquire in advance to see if you can get a space. Excellent all-round shelter here in convivial surroundings.

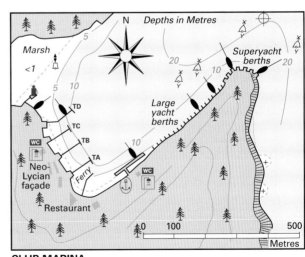

VILLAGE MARINA
⊕36°45'·20N 28°55'·89E WGS84

CLUB MARINA
⊕36°45'·11N 28°55'·87E WGS84

Club Marina in the southwest corner of Göcek Bay
Kadir Kir

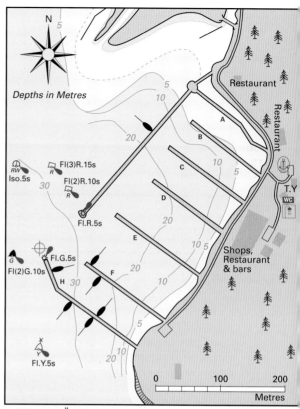

D-MARIN GÖCEK
⊕36°44'·92N 28°56'·43E WGS84

VHF Ch 72, callsign *Club Marina.*

Services Water and electricity. Showers and toilets. Wi-Fi. Laundry service. Fuel barge where you can go alongside to fill up. Waste pump-out. Charge band 5.

Provisions Minimarket. Really it is best to go to Göcek for shopping.

Eating out The restaurant here serves good and interesting food in a wonderful location. Otherwise head for Göcek town.

Other A small passenger ferry runs regularly to and from Skopea Marina from 0800 to midnight in the summer.

☎ 0252 645 1800
www.clubmarina.com.tr

D-MARIN GÖCEK MARINA

D-Marin Göcek is very much an upmarket place, with the architecture blending into the rock and pine on the slopes around it and some very chic shops and restaurants.

Approach The harbour is enclosed by wave-breaker pontoons and there are a number of navigation buoys around it. Off the south side there are two yellow isolated danger (× topmark) buoys. On the west side there is a fairway buoy and two sets of channel buoys. There is deep water everywhere in the approaches.

Mooring Berth where directed. A marina attendant will come out in a RIB to guide you to your berth and help you tie up. Laid moorings tailed to the pontoons. Shelter inside is good although strong southerlies can make some outer berths uncomfortable.

D-Marin Port Göcek looking SW   *Kadir Kir*

VHF Ch 73, callsign *D-Marin Göcek.*

Services Water and electricity. Telephone and television connections possible. Wi-Fi. Showers and toilets of a standard that surpasses many five-star hotels, with green and ochre marble everywhere. Laundry service. Waste pump-out. Charge band 5.

Provisions Minimarket. Alternatively walk around the waterfront to Göcek village.

Eating out The Sailor's pub is wonderful for sundowners with a view over the bay and marina. The Şeherazat Bistro and Restaurant is upmarket, with Turkish and international fare, prices to match, and a superb view out over the marina and bay.

Other Hire cars. ATM. For other facilities it is about a 10-minute walk into Göcek around the waterfront.

MARINTURK GÖCEK EXCLUSIVE MARINA

A new marina for the larger yacht situated in Poruklu Bay which lies on the western side of the approaches to Göcek Bay. The two curved pontoons of the marina are easily identified when approaching Göcek. Some care is needed of the reef running out from the shore on the north side of the marina (marked by a small conical yellow buoy).

Mooring Berth where directed. A RIB will come out to guide you to your berth and assist with mooring. Tucked into the bay here there is a bit of a lee from the prevailing wind blowing up into Göcek Bay, but a bit of slop is still sent in, especially to outer berths on the northern pontoon. If your boat is of a certain size I guess that will hardly matter. Open to the east and southeast when things could get more agitated.

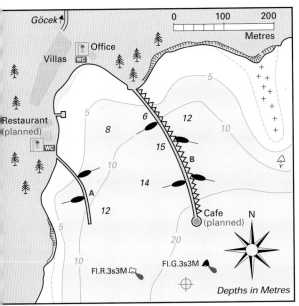

MARINTURK GOCEK EXCLUSIVE MARINA
⊕36°44'·52N 28°55'·63E WGS84

VHF Ch 73 callsign *Marinturk Exclusive Marina*.

Services Water and electricity. Showers and toilets. Wi-Fi. Laundry services. 24 hour security.

Provisions A provisioning service, otherwise in Göcek town.

Eating out Restaurant and café planned in the marina. Otherwise in Göcek.

Other Taxi and RIB ferry service to Göcek.

GÖCEK ADASI

On the east side of Göcek Adası in the eastern channel into Göcek there is a cove on the coast (36°43'·7N 28°56'·7E) with a restaurant that opens in the summer. It is fairly shallow close to the shore but yachts can go on the T-pier here with care. Most of the time the pier is used by tripper boats that stop here and you will probably have to anchor and take a long line ashore to the northern side. It is very deep for anchoring and although there are some mooring buoys laid in summer, the cove is best treated as a lunch stop.

INNICE ISKELESI

⊕ 36°43'·6N 28°58'·2E

On the mainland coast opposite Göcek Adası there is a deep inlet with precipitous slopes all around it. In calm weather or light winds anchor near the head of the bay or on the west side with a long line ashore. Once the prevailing wind has got up to any strength it pushes a swell in here, so it is really a lunch-cum-swim stop rather than an overnight anchorage.

Iskelesi means 'landing place' and presumably along this savage coast it was used before roads were cut through the steep mountains.

KÜÇÜK KARĞI KÖYÜ

⊕ 36°42'·6N 29°00'·7E

('Little Spear' Gulf) A large bay lying north of Katrancik Ada. It is very deep in here but local *gulets* use it. With the *meltemi* a swell is pushed into the bay.

KIZIL ADA

⊕ 0·2M S of light on Kızıl Ada
36°38'·92N 29°02'·64E WGS84

On the north side of Kızıl Ada (Red Island) are two bights where you can anchor with reasonable protection from the *meltemi* blowing up into the

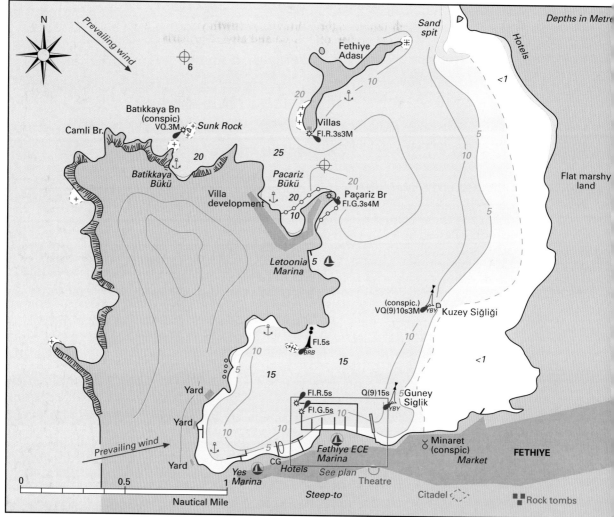

APPROACHES TO FETHIYE
⊕36°38'·66N 29°05'·88E WGS84

gulf. There are gusts but with a long line ashore you would be secure enough here in settled weather, assuming no breeze blows down off the land at night.

On the south side of Kızıl Adası there is a bay tucked around the corner under the lighthouse. On the western side of the bay is a rough quay where yachts can go stern or bows-to. Tripper boats from Fethiye stop here so at times the quay can be crowded. By evening the tripper boats will have departed. Good shelter from the prevailing wind blowing up into the gulf but open south. Ashore up near the lighthouse there is a restaurant.

FETHIYE ADASI

Fethiye Adası lies like a long breakwater across the entrance to Fethiye Limanı. The normal entrance into Fethiye itself is around the southwestern end of the island. Being so close to the mainland it has relatively easy access and there are a surprising number of houses on it. Many of them are holiday villas for rich Turks and there are a number of restaurants around the shores.

Yachts can anchor off the southern side of the island in suitable depths, mostly under 10m, where there is good shelter from the prevailing northwesterlies.

FETHIYE

Fethiye Limanı is a large bay which curves right round to the southwest. There are a number of anchorages and jetties, and a marina in the bay.

Pilotage

Approach You won't see the town and bay of Fethiye until you are right up to the entrance to the bay. Battikaya beacon will be seen on the way in and then the Hotel Letoonia around Paçariz Bükü. Once into the bay the buildings of the town will be seen and the masts of yachts in Fethiye Marina are easily identified.

Mooring There is one marina and several jetties which are detailed separately below. Yachts can also anchor in the bay. Yachts tend to anchor west of the municipal harbour or further down into the bay. In fact, you can anchor almost anywhere as there are suitable depths all around the bay. Good shelter from the prevailing winds and nearly all-round shelter in most places. The bottom is sticky mud, excellent holding, though messy when you are hauling anchor.

The City of Light

In ancient times Fethiye was Telmessus, the 'City of Light', a name that evocatively captures the varied and subtle pastel shades of the setting sun on the mountains around Fethiye. Of ancient Telmessus virtually nothing remains except a number of rock tombs and sarcophagi and the theatre. The rock tombs cut into the cliffs that rise up behind the town stand out clearly from seaward. To get to them you must climb up a lot of steps clearly signposted from the town.

The largest of the temple-tombs is that of Amyntas, an unknown citizen who must have been rich or famous, or both, to deserve such a grand tomb. It is a temple-tomb in the Ionic order built in the 4th century BC and embellished with a frieze and imitation iron studs on the door to the main chamber. Inside is a chamber with three benches for the dead; as always the interior is a bit of a let-down after the imposing exterior. To the left of this tomb are two other temple-tombs and below them some house-tombs and pigeon-hole tombs.

To the west of the tombs is a medieval castle, thought to have been built by the Knights of St John, and possibly modified later. Around the town are numerous sarcophagi, with a superb example in front of the town hall. It stands on a heavy stone base and has been carved to represent a two-storey Lycian house with a curved 'Gothic' lid adorned with a relief of rows of warriors. It says much for the Lycian artisans that when the 1957 earthquake flattened most of Fethiye, the lid on the sarcophagus moved slightly, but otherwise it was unaffected. Apparently the sarcophagus used to sit in the sea so the sea level must

Facilities

In Fethiye town you can find most things that you need and after Marmaris this is really the place to stock up on provisions or find basic gear.

Provisions There are a large number of minimarkets and a market on Mondays and Wednesdays on the eastern side of the shopping area. The produce from the surrounding area is excellent and varied. Small supermarket in Ece Marina.

Eating out There are numerous restaurants around town and along the waterfront. In town there are some good *pide* places and good local *lokantas* around the market area on the east side of town – wander around and take your time choosing one you like rather than one touts try to get you into. Try the Mozaik Bahce and the Megri Lokantsi in town for good Turkish food. The roof hotel restaurants, usually with 'yacht' in the name, are expensive and the food is not the greatest.

Other PO. Banks. ATMs. Internet cafés. Hire cars and motorbikes. Buses and *dolmuş* to Dalaman

have risen since antiquity. There is literally nothing else to see of ancient Telmessus. Charles Newton in 1838, and Thomas Spratt a little later, mentioned a theatre in good order on the west side of the town, but little is left of it today except a depression and some of the seats which have been unearthed, and a bit of modern licence. Ancient Telmessus, along with Physicus at Marmaris, was no doubt carted away bit by bit by ship or used by the locals for building materials.

Telmessus seems to have been an independent city in Lycia for some of the time. In the 4th century BC the Lycians besieged it and brought it into the Lycian League. George Bean relates a curious tale of its recapture in the time of Alexander the Great when it had been taken over by a certain Antipatrides. Nearchus, appointed satrap of the region by Alexander and coincidentally an old friend of Antipatrides, asked a favour of him: '... Nearchus asked permission to leave in the city a number of captive women singers and boys that he had with him. When this was granted, he gave the women's musical instruments to the boys to carry, with daggers concealed in the flute-cases; when the party was inside the citadel, the prisoners' escort took out the weapons and so seized the acropolis. This is described by the historian as a stratagem; others might call it sharp practice.' (George Bean: *Lycian Turkey*). Telmessus has been described as a place where divination was practised and Telmessian seers were well known in ancient times. However, as George Bean points out, it is likely that these seers came from another city called Telmessus in Caria, above present-day Bodrum and not from the site at Fethiye. Further down the coast at Patara there was another oracle famous throughout the ancient world.

and points east. Flights from Dalaman, which is around an hour away.

General

As you come into Fethiye by road you pass along a long cobbled street lined with shops selling anything and everything to do with the land, and workshops for servicing and maintaining agricultural machinery. Tractors and trailers compete with cars and buses for space on the roads. Mopeds with baskets of produce on the back bounce over the cobbles towards the town centre. This is one face of Fethiye. As you approach Fethiye from seawards you pass between the headland of Belen Daği and Fethiye Island, between shores covered in villas, into the almost landlocked bay of Fethiye where a forest of masts at one end of the town identifies the other face of Fethiye. Somewhere between the tractors and trailers and the hotels and yachts is Fethiye.

Whether you arrive by land or sea, it is to a comparatively modern town. Like Marmaris, Fethiye was progressively flattened by a series of earthquakes in the 1950s, that of 1957 doing most of the damage. The rubble from the collapsed buildings was pushed down into the sea to provide flat land around the waterfront for rebuilding, and most of the buildings in Fethiye date from this time or later. You cannot call Fethiye an attractive town – there is just too much reinforced concrete everywhere – but it has a bustling workaday charm to it that grows on you. The market on the edge of town is as good as anywhere, with stall upon stall of fruit and vegetables brought in from the rich agricultural land around Fethiye. There is a covered fish market with more variety than elsewhere along the coast, perhaps because the fishing grounds here are not hemmed in by offshore islands as they are further north. And there are stalls selling all manner of agricultural implements from scythes (a tool probably seen here two thousand and more years ago) to rolls of clear polythene for covering greenhouses.

The town has not always been called Fethiye. It was given its present name from a famous Turkish aviator, Fethi Bey, who was killed in a crash in the early years of the republic. Prior to this it was known as Makri, 'the far-off land', and it didn't get very good write-ups from 19th-century travellers to it. Dr Clarke recorded in his *Travels in Europe, Asia, and Africa* (1817) that most of the crew on the ship he was travelling on succumbed to malaria at Makri and that he himself soon became a striking example of the powerful influence of such air, not only in the fever which then attacked him, but in the temporary privation of the use of his limbs, which continued until he put to sea again. (quoted in Lord Kinross: *Europa Minor*). In the 8th century the place was called Anastasiupolis after the Byzantine emperor Anastasius II, so it must have been of some importance in Byzantine times. As a safe natural harbour it was used to ship timber, valona oak and pine, from the interior, a trade that continued right up into the 20th century.

The Bay of Fethiye, once used to sheltering small coasters and fishing boats, now shelters large numbers of yachts and *gulets*. From Fethiye there are the islands and bays in Skopea Liman a short distance across the gulf, and to the south after the Seven Capes, there are Kalkan, Kaş, and Kekova. Land-based visitors can take day-trips from Fethiye to Skopea Liman.

For the waterborne visitor Fethiye is the place to organise trips inland to a number of sites otherwise inaccessible from other places along the coast. There are some organised coach tours, or local buses can be taken to some of the places. A number of sites, such as Tlos and Pinara, can only be reached by hire-car or jeep.

FETHIYE ECE MARINA

Pilotage

Approach The marina is easily identified once into the bay. VHF Ch 73 (Ece Marina) 24/7.

Mooring Berth where directed. Marina staff will usually come out to you in a RIB to direct you to a berth and help you tie up. Laid moorings tailed to the pontoons. Shelter here is OK but the

Fethiye Ece Marina with its conspicuous control tower

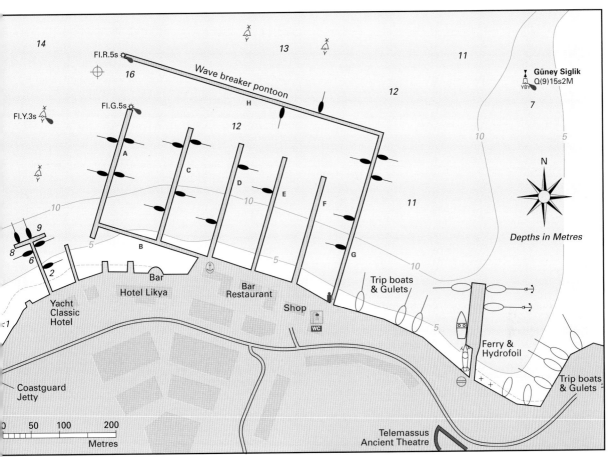

FETHIYE ECE MARINA
⊕36°37′·48N 29°05′·97E WGS84

prevailing wind does tend to cause a bit of surge in the marina, more uncomfortable than dangerous, though it goes flat when the wind dies at night. Charge band 4/5.

Facilities

Services Water and electricity. Telephone and TV connections. Wi-Fi. Toilets and showers. Facilities for disabled. Laundry service. Small supermarket. Café. 24-hour security. Waste pump-out.
For other services see the main entry for Fethiye.

① 0252 612 8829
www.ecesaray.net

YACHT CLASSIC HOTEL PIER

Tucked under the western side of Fethiye Ece Marina is a T-pier catwalk off a hotel.

Mooring Approach the marina where a marinero will direct you to a berth if one is available. Laid

Fethiye Ece Marina looking W over Yacht Classic pier towards the boatyards at Karagözler *Fethiye Ece Marina*

moorings tailed to the catwalk. It is a bit tight in places if there is any wind around. Good shelter in the summer and a number of boats are wintered afloat here.

Excursions from Fethiye

TLOS

Tlos lies high up on a rocky promontory in the Lycian hinterland. From Kemer the road is signposted to the site. The city is unexcavated, but there is much to see and the wild setting only enhances the site. From the acropolis hill with a more recent Turkish fort built on top of it you get a view right over the Xanthos valley and towards the mountains to the east. There are numerous rock-tombs cut into the cliff-face, including a magnificent temple-tomb with a relief of Bellerophon on his winged horse Pegasus. Bellerophon was the son of King Glaucus of Corinth who was wrongfully exiled, accused of murder and rape, to Lycia. (From Glaucus's blindness to his sons innocence we get the word 'glaucoma'.) In Lycia Bellerophon was set a number of Herculean tasks: to kill the Chimaera, and to do battle with the savage Solymi and the Amazons, which he successfully accomplished with the aid of his winged horse, Pegasus. Thus vindicated, he married the daughter of King Iobates of Lycia and ruled happily ever after. Tlos claimed descent from Bellerophon, hence the relief over the temple-tomb.

Around the flat area below, now cultivated, are the ruins of a stadium, gymnasium, a baths complex, and a theatre with carved actors masks on the stage building. It is a bit of a trek from Fethiye to Tlos, about an hour and a half, but well worth it to see this once grand city in a remote and wild landscape.

PINARA

Pinara lies off the main road south from Fethiye. The main attraction of the place is the site, a rocky promontory some 600m (2,000ft) high with nearly perpendicular cliffs which are honeycombed with rock-tombs. Of the city itself little remains except a well preserved theatre and the foundations of numerous buildings. The rock-tombs in the cliffs, nearly all of which are pigeon-hole tombs, are inaccessible and must have been constructed by workers dangling on ropes from above. A number of house-tombs lower down can be reached from the base of the cliff.

SIDYMA

Further along the main road through the Xanthos valley there is a turn-off to Sidyma. The Turkish village of Dodurga now stands in and on the site of ancient Sidyma and some of the ancient material has been used in the construction of the village. Virtually all the ruins here are of Roman origin: a baths complex, a small temple, a *stoa*, part of the theatre, and the inevitable necropolis with rock tombs and numerous sarcophagi. The city remained important into the Byzantine era, as evidenced by a substantial Byzantine fort on the acropolis hill.

XANTHOS

Of all the Lycian cities Xanthos was always pre-eminent, and indeed the term Xanthian was often synonymous with Lycian. It was the capital of Lycia, the richest and most powerful of the cities, and a city with a tragic history. It lies right on the main road through the Xanthos valley at the little agricultural village of Kinik. A gravel road leads up to the site where you can park opposite the *agora*. The custodian of the site will probably wander out to sell you a ticket to see the ruins and then retreat to the shade to snooze again.

The remarkable pillar tombs at Xanthos

Tlos rock tombs

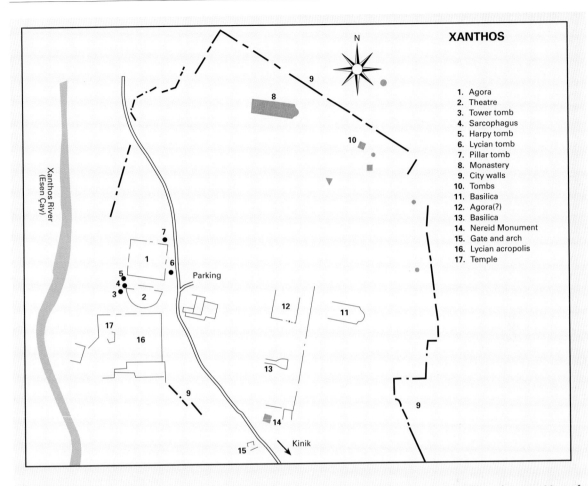

XANTHOS

1. Agora
2. Theatre
3. Tower tomb
4. Sarcophagus
5. Harpy tomb
6. Lycian tomb
7. Pillar tomb
8. Monastery
9. City walls
10. Tombs
11. Basilica
12. Agora(?)
13. Basilica
14. Nereid Monument
15. Gate and arch
16. Lycian acropolis
17. Temple

The site of the city on a low hillock is not as impressive as at Pinara or Tlos, but has the advantage of a view out over the flat land of the Xanthos valley on all sides. The Xanthos River, now the Esen Çay and the largest river in Lycia, flows close to the city on the west side, providing ample fresh water. Xanthos means 'yellow', and is the Greek name for the river and the city (in Lycian it was called Arnna, but was not generally called by this name). The city is mentioned by Homer in the *Iliad* and by Herodotus, and, later, Appian and Plutarch who relate the details of the two tragic mass suicides I have already described in the section on the Lycians. How any Xanthians remained after committing mass suicide twice in 400 years and burning the city to the ground is a mystery, but there were evidently a few survivors and no doubt an influx of new Lycian blood to rebuild and repopulate the city for it to again resume its role as capital of Lycia.

The site itself is much damaged, largely as a result of Sir Charles Fellows and the British Navy's wholesale export of some quite remarkable friezes and sculptures in 1842, much of which can now be seen in the Xanthian Room of the British Museum. No doubt the locals also helped themselves to the building materials so conveniently left behind by the Lycians. Despite the damage done by

Fellows and the navy, there is still much to see. Most of the buildings are of Roman origin, but dotted all around the site, as if carefully preserved by the Romans, are Lycian monuments. Opposite the car park are the theatre and the *agora*. Just above the theatre are two Lycian tombs.

The one on the north is called the Harpy tomb, from a relief on it showing bird-women carrying off children in their arms, interpreted by Fellows as the screaming Harpies described by Homer. This interpretation is now thought to be incorrect and the figures probably represent those other bird-women, the Sirens, carrying off the souls of the dead in the form of children. The original friezes were carried off by Fellows, but plaster casts have been made by the Turkish authorities and it is these that can be seen today. The other tomb is a sarcophagus standing on a stunted pillar, the pillar itself being hollow and a tomb. On the other side of the *agora* there is a tall obelisk, covered in Lycian script and the longest Lycian inscription known, though exactly what it says is not known as the Lycian language has not yet been properly deciphered. The obelisk is yet another tomb, though again of a novel type, underlining the importance of this city.

Further up the hill the remains of a Byzantine monastery built over a large Roman temple can be seen. Close to the car park another Byzantine basilica, with extensive mosaics, was built over what was the residential area. Scattered over the hillside are numerous rock-tombs and sarcophagi, enough to keep your average tomb enthusiast happy for days.

On the road down to the village from the car park are the remains of the southern gate to the city and a Roman arch. Just above here sat the Nereid Monument, the one that now graces the British Museum courtesy of Fellows and the British navy, though it is likely, as with the Elgin Marbles, that the British Museum and the British government have not heard the last of it yet. Xanthos is easily reached from Fethiye and there are organised excursions to the site. Alternatively you can take a bus or *dolmuş* to Kinik from Fethiye or Kaş. The rather ramshackle village doesn't offer a lot, though there are places to eat and a very good local market on Fridays.

LETOUM

Just before you get to Kinik and Xanthos on the main road from Fethiye, there is a turn-off signposted to Letoum (Letoon). A short drive along a good road you come to a small village with plastic-covered greenhouses covering every square metre of ground. After zigzagging through the greenhouses you come to one of the most delightful sites in Lycia. Letoum was a sanctuary precinct and not a city as such, though it did have a settlement around it. This was the spiritual heart of Xanthos and of Lycia, the federal sanctuary to the Lycian League and the place where national festivals were held. The sanctuary was dedicated to Leto, the national deity of Lycia, and several tales tell of how and why she came to this place. Leto was loved by Zeus, one of the many who put a firecracker up his skirt, and one of many hated by Zeus' wife Hera for doing so. Leto was driven out by Hera and exiled. She wandered far and wide, including Asia Minor, and finally arrived on Delos where she gave birth to Apollo and Artemis. During her travels in Lycia, she went to quench her thirst at a fountain, but before she could drink local herdsmen came and drove her away. After the birth of Apollo and Artemis it is said she returned and turned the churlish herdsmen into frogs, and certainly there are a lot of frogs in the sunken ruins of Letoum. Another tale tells of how she was guided by wolves to the Xanthos River to assuage her thirst. From the Greek lykos (wolf) the name 'Lycia' may have evolved.

There is no doubt that Letoum was a major sanctuary. There are no less than three temples side by side. The site was not excavated until the 1950s and most

LETOUM

1. Temple of Leto
2. Old temple
3. Temple of Apollon
4. Church
5. Nymphaeum
6. Exedra
7. Portico

0   50
Metres

N

of the foundations are now partially underwater, lending a watery tranquillity to the site. Frogs happily croak away, terrapins sun themselves on the steps of the portico, and a family of ducks paddle around the submerged northern *stoa*. Of the three temples, only the foundations remain, while to the south there is a large *nymphaeum*, partially underwater, and to the north a *stoa*, also underwater. Over the back is a theatre in good

The watery ruins of Letoum

condition. In the centre of the Temple of Apollo, one of the three temples, there is an unusual Lycian mosaic of a lyre, the sun, and a bow and arrow – the only known surviving Lycian mosaic. If, as is normally the case, the custodian seeks you out when you arrive, he will show you where to find the mosaic. Ask him to show you the masks at the theatre as well.

KAYA KÖY

This ruined town is an entirely different beast from the Lycian ruins as it dates not from thousands of years ago, but from mere hundreds. The ruined town built over the sides of a valley away from the sea was populated by Greeks until the 1923 exchange of populations between Greece and Turkey which left Kaya deserted. It is a poignant reminder of those troubled times, all the more so for being deserted now when it was so obviously once a prosperous large town with a population of 7,000 or so. Today a few crops are grown around the town and the decaying buildings have been preserved as a national monument. There are two large churches, though the murals are, sadly, defaced. It is interesting that the town is entirely hidden from the sea, a legacy of the piracy that afflicted this coast even in the 19th century.

You can reach Kaya by taking the road to Ölü Deniz, a road signposted but not easily spotted on the road out of Fethiye, and then continuing for a short distance until a turn-off signposted to Kaya. The road runs through the forest until the valley of Kaya is seen below. Coach excursions run from Fethiye. A more precarious but passable road continues on from Kaya to Gemiler. You

The abandoned Greek village of Kaya

can also get there from Gemiler – a long walk up and over into the hidden valley.

Kaya is the setting for Louis de Bernière's remarkable novel *Birds Without Wings* which describes events leading up to the population exchanges and the birth pangs of modern Turkey under Ataturk. If you haven't read it then get a copy now.

Charge band 4 or Charge band 2 if you eat in the hotel restaurant ashore.

Facilities

Services Water and electricity. Shower and toilets. Wi-Fi. Restaurant (mediocre) and bar ashore.

YES MARINA

A T-jetty lying further into the bay west of Fethiye Ece Marina.

Data c.35 yachts. Visitors' berths. Max LOA c.20m. Depths 2–4m.

Mooring As you approach the catwalk a marinero will direct you to a berth. Laid moorings tailed to the catwalk. Good shelter in the summer with the prevailing wind though a bit of chop is kicked up by the afternoon breeze. Yachts are wintered afloat here. Charge band 2/3.

Facilities

Services Water and electricity. Showers and toilets. Restaurant and café ashore. It is a bit of a walk into Fethiye town or there are mini-buses running around the coast road.

KARAGOZLER PARK MARINA HOTEL JETTY

Off the boatyards at the head of the bay there is a dog-leg catwalk. Yachts may find a berth here though most are taken up by 'permanent' berth holders. Good shelter from the prevailing wind, but open east. Water and electricity.

Note The boatyards at this end of the gulf may soon be moved out of Fethiye Bay to a location on the northern side of the Gulf of Fethiye at Karaot, close S of Kargi Köyü.

LETOONIA MARINA

Under Paçariz Burnu a concrete quay with a pier has been built around part of the bay. Yachts can berth here if space is available although most berths are private. Good shelter from the prevailing wind. You are a bit out of it here, although there are several restaurants and bars nearby. Water and electricity. Charge band 3.

Around Fethiye

CALIS BEACH

This is on the east side of Fethiye Bay, a wide sandy beach stretches for 4km around the shore. This is the 'resort' part of the town where Turks on holiday would come before tourists from overseas arrived. There are numerous hotels and *pensions* around the beach, but you can still find a patch of sand all to yourself.

PAÇARIZ AND BATIKKAYA BÜKÜ

On the headland forming the west side of Fethiye Bay there are several attractive bays. Paçariz is the bay on the northeast tip. Batikkaya is a little further around, tucked under a rocky headland with a small islet in the entrance. A floating boom now obstructs part of the E side of Paçariz Bükü. Batikkaya Bükü is entrancing, with a good beach and a wooded foreshore. Judging by the ranks of sun-loungers it can get pretty hectic here in the season, but probably quietens down in the evening.

Fethiye to Kalkan

From Fethiye the coast curves around in a mountainous bulge to Antalya. It is a rugged region that, like the rest of the coastline described in this book, is difficult to access by road for much of its length. Conversely the waterborne visitor must take to the roads to visit some of the ancient sites in the Xanthos valley and to see what the interior, cut off from the sea by rugged mountains, is like.

This region was the heartland of ancient Lycia and some of the ruins here are quite simply spectacular. Some of them, such as Patara, have not been excavated and the sight of a once great city half-buried by sand dunes is an evocative one. Some like Tlos are in a wild and savage setting in the mountains. All of them are worth a visit, as much for the landscape along the way as for the sites themselves.

Gemiler and nearby anchorages

On the south side of the great craggy lump that forms the eastern side of the Gulf of Fethiye lie the island and anchorages of Gemiler. This reef-strewn place could only be reached by boat until the new road was cut around the sides of Karadağ from Kaya, and given the state of the

road, the trip by boat is still much the easiest way to get here.

The attractions of Gemiler are two fold. It is an isolated wild place with a number of small coves just right for swimming and relaxing in. Several restaurants have opened around the shores, but these detract little from the place, whereas plans for more large-scale development may not be so benign. There are a number of anchorages around the coast and behind the island.

Note In recent years more and more tripper boats operating out of Ölü Deniz have been competing for space around Gemiler. Some are quite polite, but others can be aggressive and try to barge into small spaces between yachts.

Karacaören A cove tucked in behind the jagged rocks extending out towards Karaca Adalari. Don't attempt to cut across the reef but enter from the south with someone up forward conning the way in. Even through the passage between the islet and the reef where there are 10m least depths, the water is so clear it looks a lot shallower. Anchor in Karacaören Bükü on the west or south side of the bay with a long line ashore.

You will be anchoring in 10–15m here and you also need to avoid the improvised buoys off the swimming area at the head of the bay. Alternatively go stern or bows-to the restaurant jetty where there are some laid moorings.

Good shelter from the *meltemi* although a bit of swell can creep around into the bay. Restaurant ashore.

Karacaören means 'roe deer', though I haven't seen any here or anywhere nearby.

Northwest bay A bay tucked into the northwest corner of the bay in which Gemiler Adası sits. Anchor with a long line ashore to the west side taking care of the reefs off here. With the *meltemi* some swell creeps around and rolls into the anchorage.

Gemiler Adası Anchor off the north side at the western end with a long line ashore. It is quite deep here so you will dropping anchor in 15–20m. There can also be some W-going current which causes you to lie at an angle. Good shelter from the *meltemi*. At night care is needed of katabatic winds blowing from the northeast off the high mainland mountains.

The anchorage under the island is really the best place to be, given the number of *gulets* and tripper boats around here.

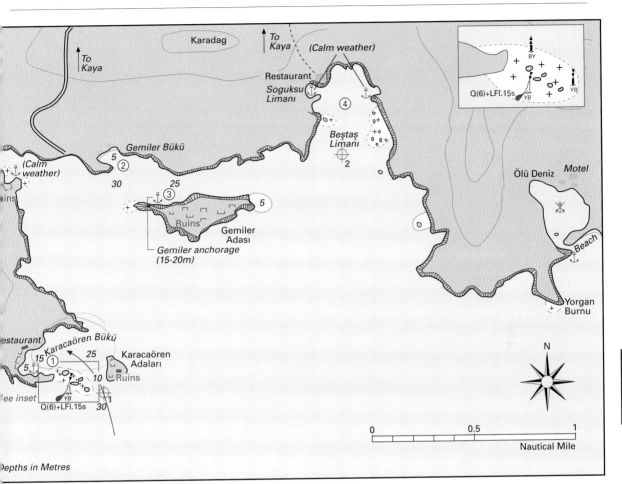

MILER ADASI AND NEARBY ANCHORAGES
36°32'·39N 29°03'·50E WGS84
36°33'·47N 29°05'·06E WGS84

The anchorage on the inside of Gemiler Adası

Gemiler Bükü A small nearly oval bay on the mainland opposite the anchorage off the island. The bay is pretty much full of fishing boats, watersports boats and tripper boats. Usually you will be waved away, though you may find a space late in the evening. The best place to be is on the western side with a long line ashore where there is good shelter from the *meltemi*. A restaurant opens in the summer.

Beştaş Limanı The large bay on the northeast side of the large bay in which Gemiler Adası sits. Care is needed of the reef fringing the eastern side of the bay and of a reef on the western side. Anchor in either of the coves on the west or east side. The cove on the west side (Soğuksu Limanı) is the most popular and is easily identified by a conspicuous white domed water reservoir. Depths are considerable here and you will be dropping anchor in 15–20m plus. You can anchor off the

Tucked into the crack in the cliffs where the cold spring bubbles up into Cold Water Harbour

Around Gemiler tripper boats compete with space for yachts and at times they can be a bit aggressive

boats as the cold spring that wells up here is a bit of an attraction. Soğuksu Limanı means 'Cold Water Harbour'. It is reasonably comfortable in here but if a katabatic wind blows off the hills it can get tricky. The bay is popular with tripper boats though these depart in late afternoon. It is also popular with flotillas so it can get crowded in here. On the slopes above is Ali's restaurant serving good basic food. You can also walk to the ruins at Kaya from here, about an hour's walk. The bay takes its popular name from the fresh-water spring that feeds the bay, and water temperatures here are significantly less than the average sea temperature, in fact really quite cold.

General

The attraction of this spot is Gemiler Island lying a short distance off the coast. On it are the remains of a sizeable Byzantine settlement and though many of the buildings are in ruins, there is still sufficient to see, including some marvellous mosaic floors, to make a ramble ashore

small beach with a kedge anchor out the back or a long line ashore where there is room for perhaps half-a-dozen yachts (with fenders out). Alternatively there is room for a couple of yachts in a nook on the south side with long lines ashore. In the latter you may be hassled a bit by tripper

worthwhile. According to local folklore the island was a pirate stronghold at some time and given its location on this lonely bit of coast, where a look-out on the high hills above could signal the approach of ships going north or south, it would seem a likely location for the thinking pirate to base himself at Gemiler.

At one time the island was said to be ruled by a queen who had skin extremely sensitive to the sun (an albino, perhaps?) A covered road was built from her palace on the top of the island down to the sea so she could walk in the shade to the water's edge for a swim. Parts of an arched road still exist, so perhaps there is some truth in the story.

There is a caretaker on the site and a modest entry fee is made.

ÖLÜ DENIZ

Ölü Deniz is tucked into a bight at the western end of a long sandy beach and under spectacular cliffs that go straight up from behind the beach. Space is restricted here as tripper boats occupy much of it and certainly all the best spots. It's probably best to consider Ölü Deniz a lunch stop and then chug around to one of the anchorages around Gemiler. Yachts anchor with a long line ashore off the western side of the entrance to Ölü Deniz, anywhere around from the large sign prohibiting entrance to the lagoon. It is very deep for anchoring here and you will frequently be dropping anchor in 15–20m before taking a line ashore. Shelter is adequate from the *meltemi*, though uncomfortable at times. Some care is needed of katabatic winds blowing down off the mountains at night from a north to northeast direction. These mostly occur in the spring and autumn and can reach Force 7 or more.

Ölü Deniz

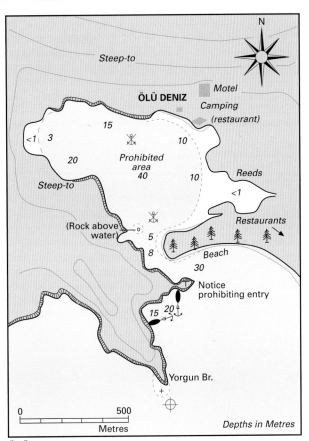

ÖLÜ DENIZ
⊕36°32'·55N 29°06'·64E WGS84

There are restaurants and bars around the beach and behind the lagoon.

Ölü Deniz means 'Dead Sea', not because it is dead like its namesake in Israel, but because it is so enclosed and protected from the sea that no swell penetrates inside. There may be a storm in the sea just outside while in Ölü Deniz it will be comparatively calm. The setting is spectacular, with mountains rising sheer from the sea to 1,000m (3,300 feet) and more. The cliffs are popular with base jumpers, who run off the top of the cliffs with specially designed parachutes. You have about 15 seconds from the top (at 3,300ft) to open the chute before you hit the ground at around 120mph. You can do trips here where you double up with a paraglider who simply runs off the cliff with the chute already open, which at least means you know it is working.

Underneath the cliffs is a narrow strip of blinding white sand that attracts lots of tourists in the summer. Thick pine grows wherever it can get a hold on the rocky slopes, often growing out at precarious angles. Fortunately a few trees also grow along the narrow coastal strip, providing welcome shade from the sun. A number of hotels and restaurants have been built around the shores, but someone somewhere with some pull has restricted development so it does not violate the magnificent surroundings, although the same cannot be said for the amplified muzak that pounds out over the bay at night.

Until 1984 yachts and *gulets* could anchor in Ölü Deniz, but since then entry has been prohibited and the only anchorage allowed is outside the entrance in a relatively unsheltered and sometimes dangerous bight on the rocky coast. This stern injunction on the use of Ölü Deniz was imposed by the Ministry of Culture and Tourism to stop the bay being polluted. Being a virtually land-locked bay connected to the cleansing sea by only a narrow and quite shallow channel, the cumulative effects of oil and sewage left by the yachts and *gulets* was badly polluting the water. It is to the credit of the Ministry that this prompt action was taken, though those on the water may think the action a little draconian.

BUTTERFLY VALLEY

Roughly 2·5M south of Ölü Deniz is a steep-sided bay that has been christened Butterfly Valley. The bay is open to the prevailing winds which blow onto the beach at the head of the bay. It is a bit of a bun fight with tripper boats from Ölü Deniz so is not exactly a peaceful spot, though they will all have departed by late afternoon. In calm weather anchor fore-and-aft or anchor and take a line ashore. If wind and sea conditions permit it can be used as an overnighter, otherwise think of it as a lunch stop.

The attraction of the place is the butterflies that always seem to frequent the place, hence the name.

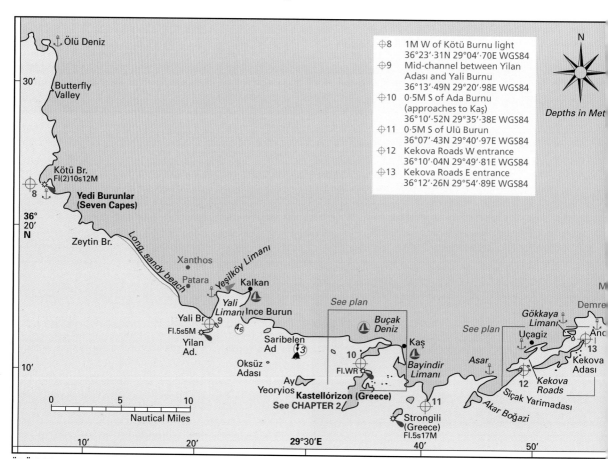

ÖLÜ DENIZ TO KEKOVA ROADS

YEDI BURUNLAR

The name means 'Seven Capes' and refers to the series of high bold capes that jut into the sea south of Ölü Deniz. The mountains here drop spectacularly into the sea, effectively cutting off the interior and the Xanthos valley that the main road passes through until it meets the sea again at Kalkan. These capes have a nasty reputation, a sort of Turkish 'Cape Horn' for this stretch of the coast, and yachts and *gulets* going north will often leave Kalkan early in the morning to get past them before the *meltemi* starts blowing around midday. After the seven capes there is a long sandy beach with sand dunes extending inland for some distance. At the southern end of the beach lies Patara near the mouth of the Esen Çay, the ancients' Xanthos River, with much of the site covered by the shifting sands.

YESILKÖY LIMANI

⊕ 36°15'·6N 29°22'·6E

A large bay on the west side of Yali Limanı in the approaches to Kalkan. Anchor and take a long line ashore to the west side as there are strong gusts in here with the *meltemi* and the holding on sand and weed is not the best. If you anchor free it may pay to lay a second anchor. Good shelter from the *meltemi* despite the gusts.

A new holiday village has been built around the shores and this doesn't do a lot for the landscape; otherwise there is just sun-baked rock and maquis.

KALKAN

The small harbour is situated in the northeastern corner of Yali Limanı under the steep slopes and houses of Kalkan.

Pilotage

Approach You won't see the harbour until well into the bay. Several large and despoiling holiday villages will be seen and closer in the village and harbour can be identified. The approach is straightforward once you are into Yali Limanı and although there are gusts and some chop, you don't have the large swell outside the bay.

Mooring Berth where directed or in a free spot on the breakwater quay. The harbour is quite narrow and fouled anchors from yachts and *gulets* berthed on the opposite side of the harbour are commonplace. *Gulets* especially, like to lay their anchors just under the quay opposite their berth. Good shelter from the *meltemi*. Charge band 3/4.

Kalkan looking W across the entrance

PATARA

The ruins at Patara are some of the most evocative in Lycia. Sand dunes cover most of the site, half-filling the theatre *cavea*, heaped up over massive stone blocks, and totally burying the harbour entrance and moles. What was the most important harbour in Lycia is now covered in sand and, more than Caunos or Ephesus, it illustrates the fate of a harbour built at the mouth of a river and thus prone to silting, and the inevitable demise of the city attached to the harbour.

Patara was Lycian in origin (its Lycian name of Patara has been found on inscriptions and coins) and was probably founded around the 6th century BC. Herodotus mentions it in connection with the Oracle of Apollo that practised here and which was said for a time to rival that at Delphi, at least in Asia Minor.

The origin of the oracle was attributed to Danaus, King of Argos, who was told by Apollo to search the world until he found a bull and a wolf fighting each other. He was to build a temple to whichever was the victor: a temple to Poseidon if the bull won or a temple to Apollo if the wolf won. The wolf was victorious and Danaus built a temple to Apollo at Patara. In truth, this and other eponymous founders were probably later inventions for a small harbour-city that grew as Xanthos prospered. Patara was in effect the port of the capital and its importance only overshadowed Xanthos and other inland cities when it was made the seat of the Roman provincial governor during the last years before the birth of Christ. Later it was at Patara that the Apostle Paul, that intrepid traveller and fervent evangelist, changed ships en route to Jerusalem at the end of his third missionary journey. In the 4th century AD Patara was honoured as the birthplace of Bishop Nicholas of Myra, the saint who metamorphosed into our Father Christmas.

From seawards little can be seen of the ruins as rolling sand dunes have formed between the sea and the site of the city. It can be visited from Kalkan by taxi or from Fethiye. The road to it is clearly signposted off the main road and you follow it, over a bridge across the present course of the Esen Çay, through a ravine-like pass until you get to a parking area by the theatre. Before this you pass an arch with an inscription to Mettius Modestus, governor of Lycia-Pamphylia around AD100. At the turn-off to the theatre the road leads on to a restaurant by the beach. From the theatre, half-filled with sand, you can look out over the site of the city which in its heyday covered a sizeable acreage. The harbour is now a marshy area cut off from the sea by at least half a kilometre of sand. On the top of a low knell by the theatre is an unusual round structure with steps cut around the inside and which was probably a cistern, though of unusual design. Nearby are the ruins of what may have been a lighthouse. Down from the theatre are parts of the city wall. After Brutus had witnessed the mass suicide of the Xanthians, he gave the inhabitants of Patara the chance to submit and not repeat the tragedy of Xanthos. After pleading with the Patarans for several days, Brutus eventually persuaded them to give in peacefully and true to his word, spared all the inhabitants. Despite his part in the murder of Julius Caesar, Brutus seems to have been an honourable man with no appetite for needless bloodletting. Around the east side of the harbour are two bath complexes and a small temple. On the other side of the harbour is the massive Granary of Hadrian, some 60m (200 ft) long and 24m (80 ft) wide, still virtually intact. Nearby are the remains of the *agora* and a tomb.

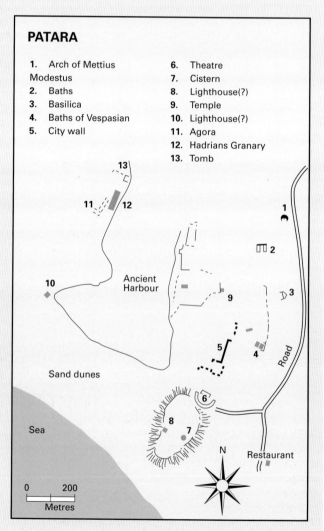

PATARA

1. Arch of Mettius Modestus
2. Baths
3. Basilica
4. Baths of Vespasian
5. City wall
6. Theatre
7. Cistern
8. Lighthouse(?)
9. Temple
10. Lighthouse(?)
11. Agora
12. Hadrians Granary
13. Tomb

Ancient Harbour

Sand dunes

Sea

Road

Restaurant

0   200
Metres

There can be no doubt that under the sands much remains of Patara. No trace of the Temple to Apollo, famous for its oracle, has been found. To date no systematic excavation of the site has been carried out. Sitting in the theatre and looking out across the sand dunes calls to mind those well known lines of Shelley's on the impermanence of man's constructions:

'My name is Ozymandias, King of Kings,
Look on my works, ye Mighty, and despair!
Nothing beside remains. Round the decay
Of that colossal wreck, boundless and bare
The lone and level sands stretch far away.'

Theatre at Patara

Facilities

Services Water and electricity. Showers and toilets (sort-of). Fuel by tanker.

Provisions Good shopping for provisions in town.

Eating out The bars and restaurants around the waterfront are popular, but the food often does not match the situation or the promises. On the corner of the road going up the hill from the northwest corner of the harbour is a good *pide* and kebab restaurant (part of a hotel) with outdoor seating. The Ozgur Café is a pleasant place to relax with good pancakes. Otherwise try the Palanin Yeri by the harbour with good food and lots of cats.

Other PO. Bank. ATM. Internet cafés. Hire cars and motorbikes. Bus to Antalya or Fethiye.

General

Kalkan was devastated by the same earthquake that flattened Fethiye and the government of the day decided not to repair the houses of the old village, but to build an entirely new village above it. In the 1980s a number of rich entrepreneurs bought up most of the old village and many of the old houses have been restored. With the addition of a small yacht harbour Kalkan has prospered and today it is a pleasant little resort village with a number of good hotels and pensions and some good restaurants.

The attractions of the place are simple. It is small enough to be comfortable but big enough to offer some variety for eating out. Amongst the old houses of the village are some good examples of

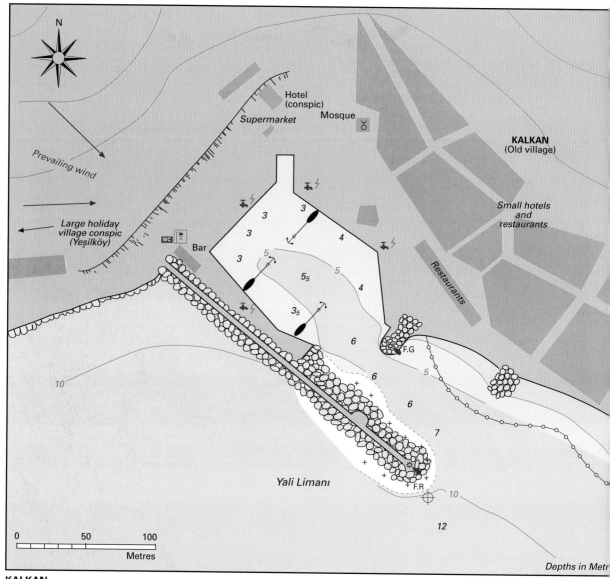

KALKAN
⊕36°15'·66N 29°24'·87E WGS84

traditional architecture with wooden balconies jutting out over the streets. Bougainvillaea and jasmine clothe the old plaster through the summer, making the village a green oasis amongst the otherwise rocky mountain slopes.

Kalkan means 'shield' or 'turbot' – take your pick of which applies. For waterborne visitors Kalkan is the nearest safe harbour after Fethiye and yachts and *gulets* going north will usually stop here before tackling the trip past the seven capes. For those with a few days to spare it is a pleasant spot to tarry in and a trip to Patara and Xanthos can be arranged from here if you feel like a bit of a wander around some ancient ruins.

BÜÇAK DENIZ

The long inlet on the north side of Çukurbağ Peninsula. Care is needed of the rock and reef just above water on the south side of the entrance, but otherwise it is deep and clear of dangers. In fact, it used to be called Port Vathi (meaning 'deep') when it was a Greek settlement.

Looking SW over the new Kaş Marina in Büçak Deniz

KAŞ MARINA

A new marina at the end of Büçak Deniz.

Pilotage

Approach Once into Büçak Deniz head towards the end of the bay when the marina and buildings ashore will be seen. Give the marina a call on VHF Ch 73 and a RIB will come out to show you to your berth and help you tie up.

Mooring Laid moorings tailed to the pontoons. Generally good shelter but with strong westerlies there is some surge on the end of the pontoons. There are plans in place to ameliorate this. Charge band 4.

Facilities

Services Water and electricity. Fuel quay. Showers and toilets. Telephone and TV connections. Wi-Fi. Laundry services. 24 hour security. Waste pump-out.

Provisions Small supermarket in the marina. Good shopping in Kaş nearby. If you walk up the hill to the crossroads in Kaş there are two supermarkets on opposite corners. Good market usually on Friday, just off the road to Kaş.

Eating out Restaurant planned for the marina. Otherwise in Kaş.

Other Yacht club, hotel and swimming pool. Boatyard with 100-ton travel-hoist. Chandlers planned. Yacht services. ATM. Hire cars. Taxi service.

General

The old harbour at Kaş is an enchanting spot, but in summer it is also impossibly crowded. Kaş marina will provide much needed berths, 450 of them, close to Kaş town. It's about 10 or 15 minutes' walk up the hill to the main crossroads and then wander down the hill to town and the old harbour. Around the marina itself the architecture has been sympathetically executed in local stone and tiles and it all blends in nicely with the shore rather than looking like a blot on the

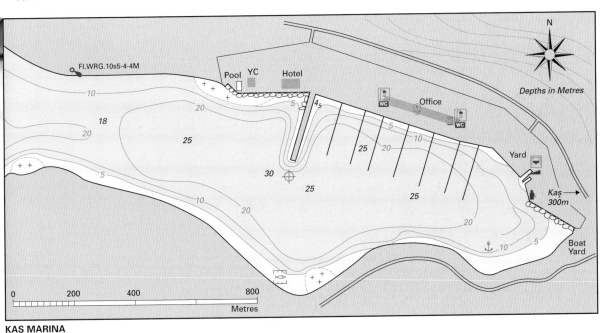

KAŞ MARINA
⊕36°12'·43N 29°37'·32E WGS84

landscape. And that's not something you can say for lots of the shoreside development in Turkey.

No doubt now the marina is open the land adjacent to it will be snapped up by developers and restaurants and cafés and local shops will no doubt open outside of the marina itself. Let's hope this development is sympathetically executed as well.

☎ 0242 836 3470
www.kasmarina.com.tr

⊕10 0·5M S of Ada Burnu (approaches to Kaş)
36°10'·52N 29°35'·38E WGS84

⊕A 0·75M N of Ada Burnu
36°11'·58N 29°35'·14E WGS84

KAŞ

Kaş lies tucked into the northeast corner of Kaş Limanı, the large bay hemmed in on the west by the Greek island of Kastellórizon. (See Chapter 2 for details on Kastellórizon.)

Pilotage

Approach It can be a windy old stretch of coast coming down towards Kaş and Kastellórizon from Kalkan and the Seven Capes, or up from Ulu Burun, so it comes as something of a relief to turn the corner into Kaş Limanı, though there are still severe gusts off the headland that shelters it. Coming from either direction, the approaches to Kaş are littered with rocks and reefs. Most are

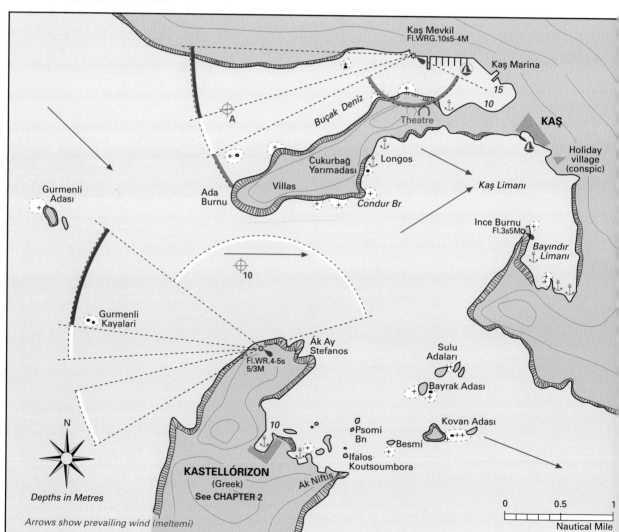

APPROACHES TO KAŞ AND KASTELLÓRIZON (See Chapter 2 for details on Kastellórizon)

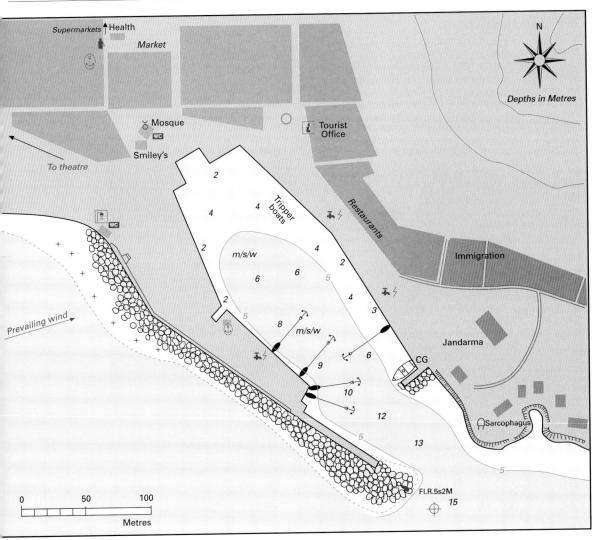

Supermarkets ↑ Health

Market

Mosque
WC

Smiley's

To theatre

Tourist
Office

Depths in Metres

N

Restaurants

Tripper
boats

2

4

2

4

4

6

2

6

5

4

2

3

Immigration

8

m/s/w

6

Jandarma

9

CG

10

Sarcophagus

12

5

13

5

Prevailing wind

Fl.R.5s2M

15

0   50   100
Metres

KAS
⊕ 36°12'·57N 29°38'·29E WGS84

well-charted and some are marked with cardinal marks, though be warned these come and go and may not always be in place. One error on many charts is that of Siren Rock, lying close southeast of Saribelen Adası. Most charts note the depth as 46m, when by my reckoning it is in fact 4.6m. For approaches from north or south, though, it is just a case of careful pilotage, keeping track of rocks and islets as you go.

The headland of Çukurbah Yarimadası is easily recognised with villas and hotels built around the steep slopes. On the end is an aquapark. Once under the headland it is a straightforward sail to Kan town sitting in the northeast corner. Care is

needed as you get to the harbour as a substantial swell is pushed into the bay.

Mooring Try for a berth on the northeast quay just inside the entrance or look for a spot on the breakwater quay. Smiley, who has a restaurant near the quay, acts as the unofficial 'harbourmaster' finding berths for yachts and helping them tie up. (Smiley's ☎ 0555 356 1863.) The harbour is normally very crowded with *gulets* and tripper boats and it can be difficult to find a berth in high summer. When dropping your anchor take your time to find a spot clear of other anchors. Large *gulets* drop an anchor just about on the opposite side of the harbour. Crossed

Ancient Antiphellus

Kaş has been identified as the site of Antiphellus, a Greek name in which *'phellos'* means 'stony ground', an epithet as true today as it was then. The *'Anti'* refers not to an opposite as might be supposed, but to an associated or sister-city geographically removed from the other. Antiphellus was the harbour-city for Phellus, a city on a site in the mountains near the village of Cukurbağ. However, during Roman times when sea-power and a safe harbour were important, Antiphellus prospered while Phellus declined. Apart from Büçak Limanı, it is likely there was a small artificial harbour on the eastern side of the isthmus where the small harbour of Kaş is sited today.

Little remains of ancient Antiphellus except for a number of sarcophagi and a delightful little theatre on the peninsula. It is well worth a wander around here to watch the sunset over the sea and islands. Once dusk has fallen a number of rock-tombs in the cliffs behind Kaş are illuminated with concealed lights, like ancient giant glow-worms bringing the Lycian dead into the 21st century. There are a number of sarcophagi around the town and one at the harbour, but the numbers are considerably less than when Spratt was here in the 19th century: he counted over a hundred lying around the site. Most have probably been broken up and used as handy building materials by the locals. You can see bits incorporated into houses and other buildings and a few bits like the cistern under Smileys that escaped being recycled.

One of the spin-offs of tourism in Turkey and indeed in the eastern Mediterranean generally, is that it has made ancient bits of stone of value as tourists come to see them, and thus they are something to be valued and cared for, since tourists spend money and keep the local economy going.

Kaş – all carpets and sarcophagi

anchors are a fact of life here, but almost everyone is good-natured about it. Good shelter once you find a spot.

Charge band 3.

Note There are plans to lay mooring lines in the harbour. Although they may not all be in place, the main mooring chain has already been laid down the centre of the harbour.

Facilities

Services Water and electricity on the quay. A card system operates – sort of. Showers and toilets (very sort-of).

Provisions Good shopping for provisions in town. Several larger supermarkets up at the crossroads leading out of town and to Kaş Marina. There is often a good market on the road to Kalkan just before you get to Kaş Marina, usually on Friday. In the middle of town there is also a more permanent market.

Eating out Smiley the unofficial 'harbourmaster' has his restaurant next to the mosque at the root of the breakwater. His food is good, the welcome warm, and underneath the restaurant you can look at an old Lycian cistern. It's worth a drink just to take a look at it. Around town

Kaş harbour

The Lycian cistern under Smiley's restaurant

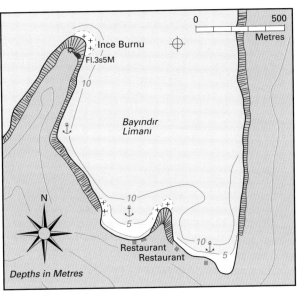

BAYINDIR LIMANI
⊕36°10'·9N 29°38'·8E

there are any number of good restaurants from local good-value *pide* places to more upmarket restaurants. The Bahçe serves good food and in town try Chez Evy which has good French-Turkish food.

General

South of Kaş lies a maze of islands and reefs with the largest island, Kastellórizon (in Turkish Meis), the lonely easternmost outpost of the Greek archipelago. On the shore opposite lies the village of Kaş, formerly Greek until the exchange of populations in 1923. It looks like a Greek village, with a cluster of whitewashed houses around the harbour. Even the mosque was formerly the village church, only now it sprouts a minaret instead of the Orthodox cross. Kaş is the only place of any size between Fethiye and Antalya with the exception of Finike. Because of its situation in the 'middle' of the Lycian coast it has become a centre for land and waterborne visitors, though in a thoroughly pleasing and modest fashion.

Kaş is a recent name for the town that was known as Andifli until last century. Formerly a small town to the north, Kaş Kasaba, was the administrative centre for the region, but when it declined the centre was moved to Andifli and the name Kaş came with it. The port, and particularly Büçak Limanı (formerly Port Vathi) on the western side of the isthmus, was used for shipping timber from the interior.

I have spent many happy days in Kaş and I always enjoy returning here. There is something very comfortable about the place that invites you to stay – not doing anything in particular except regaining that feeling of being human.

BAYINDIR

In the southeast corner of Kaş Limanı there is a sheltered bay affording reasonable protection from the *meltemi*. Anchor where indicated with a long line ashore. The holding is bad in places so make sure your anchor is properly in.

There are a number of rock-tombs and a few ruins on the summit of the hill above the anchorage. Be warned that the climb up to the summit is difficult and in places dangerous. George Bean identifies the site as Sebeda, a small settlement of no consequence and hardly mentioned by ancient writers. Until recently the bay was still called Port Sevedo on Admiralty charts, a name that reflects the ancient name of the place.

ASAR AND APERLAE

On the west side of Kekova a long peninsula juts out and its name, Sicak Yarimadasi, meaning the 'hot peninsula', adequately reflects the temperatures here in the summer. Ashore are the ruins of ancient Aperlae.

The anchorage in Asar can become uncomfortable and even untenable with the *meltemi*, so for peace of mind it is best to go to the western end of the bay enclosed by Kekova Island and anchor in Pölemos Bükü. See details in the Kekova section for anchoring here. It is a half-mile hike across the isthmus from this anchorage to the site – wear sturdy footwear and take some drinking water with you.

The oldest known shipwreck

Off Ulü Burun a short distance to the southeast of Kaş, Dr George Bass and the underwater archaeology team from INA, the Institute of Nautical Archaeology, have excavated what is now believed to be the oldest known shipwreck. From 1984 until recently a team of divers have been at work mapping and photographing the layout of the wreck and then systematically removing, item by item, in a carefully scheduled way, the artefacts below. It has not been easy to work on the wreck which lies more than 45m (150 ft) down. Divers could spend only a maximum 20 minutes working on the wreck because of the danger of a nitrogen build-up and the risk of narcosis, or worse, 'the bends'. To complicate matters the wreck, off Ulü Burun is in an exposed and windy spot and the dive-ship *Virazon* had to be securely anchored on four sides to keep it in place. The members of the expedition established a camp on the bare rocky slopes of Ulü Burun itself and lived at the camp throughout the summer while diving was taking place.

The wreck was located by a Turkish sponge diver who in 1982 noticed a pile of copper ingots on the sea-bed. Investigations by INA divers based in Bodrum soon established that this was a wreck of some importance and in 1984 excavation began in earnest. It wasn't long before some of the finds from the wreck established it as one of the most important excavated yet. Two bronze swords with inlaid hilts have been found: a gold chalice; cobalt blue glass; ingots; a gold pendant with a nude goddess grasping a gazelle in each hand; silver bracelets; ivory; a carved rock crystal cylinder seal with gold caps; a solid gold scarab. While these may be the sort of finds which make the headlines, for the archaeologists working on the wreck the most exciting finds are of a more mundane nature.

Parts of the keel and planking of the wreck itself have been discovered and from this the construction method, using mortice and tenon joints, pushes back the known period when this method of boatbuilding was used by some 200 years. From the pottery found on board the date of the wreck can be established to be around the 14th century BC. The copper ingots that originally

Replica of the 14th-century BC trading boat discovered off Ulü Burun

betrayed the presence of the wreck came to a staggering total of 200, each of them weighing in at around 27kgs (60 pounds). There is an interesting coincidence here. George Bass relates how, months later, he came across a passage on an Egyptian tablet of the time mentioning a promised gift of 200 talents of copper from the King of Cyprus to an Egyptian pharaoh. As it happens, a talent weighs in at around 27kgs, and George Bass wondered if it was just possible that this cargo ... but the coincidence is probably too great. However, the boat was evidently bound to or from Egypt, as evidenced not only by the gold scarab bearing the name of Nefertiti (incidentally the only gold scarab ever found naming the mysterious Nefertiti), but also a large quantity of yellow resin stored in amphorae. This yellow resin is probably from a tree related to the pistachio nut tree and was used in Egyptian burial rites. It was probably used as a base for perfumes and incense, thus its use during burial to disguise the smell of mortal flesh in a hot climate.

The vessel itself was around 15m (50ft) long and the valuable nature of its cargo indicates it was no ordinary trading ship. The diversity of the origins of the cargo is staggering. The copper ingots probably came from Cyprus, the glass and the amphorae from the Canaanites in what is now Israel and the Lebanon. Tin ingots found on board may have originated in Afghanistan, a vase is of Mycenean origin; unworked ivory may have come from Syria or North Africa. Most incredibly of all, amber beads found on board are of a type of amber originating in the Baltic. From wrecks like this it is necessary to revise the limits of the known trading world and accept that goods travelled greater distances, more frequently, than was previously thought. The Ulü Burun ship carried a cargo from the four corners of the ancient world and quite possibly a crew of mixed nationalities. The excavation and analysis of the finds has pushed back our ideas of the extent of trade in the ancient world to more than 3,300 years ago, as well as giving us a window onto the ships and the men and the cultures of the times.

Cut-away exhibit at Bodrum Underwater Archaeology Museum showing the Ulü Burun wreck

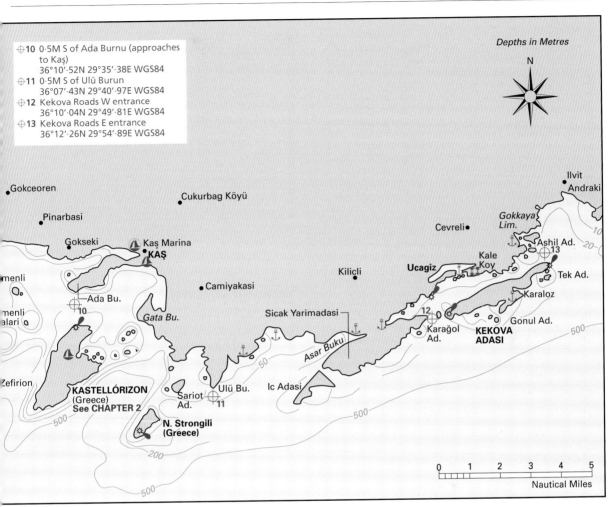

⊕**10** 0·5M S of Ada Burnu (approaches
to Kaş)
36°10′·52N 29°35′·38E WGS84
⊕**11** 0·5M S of Ulü Burun
36°07′·43N 29°40′·97E WGS84
⊕**12** Kekova Roads W entrance
36°10′·04N 29°49′·81E WGS84
⊕**13** Kekova Roads E entrance
36°12′·26N 29°54′·89E WGS84

Depths in Metres

TO KEKOVA

Kekova

Kekova Adası is the long thin island enclosing a stretch of water between it and the much indented mainland coast. It takes its name from Kakava, in Greek 'the island of the partridges', though I've not seen any in the area. The island has popularly given its name to the whole area which is referred to as simply Kekova. The Greek name for the area was Tristomo, 'the three mouths', so called from the three entrances: two at the west end of Kekova Island, and the entrance at the eastern end. The Turkish name Üçağiz itself means 'the three mouths' echoing the Greek Tristomo. The area enclosed by Kekova is also known as Ölü Deniz

'the dead sea' like its namesake further north because it is so calm inside.

Within the area enclosed by Kekova Island, there are many anchorages and coves and a number of appealing sites of ancient and more recent habitation. When Beaufort visited here during his survey of the coast in the early 19th century he recommended it as a fleet anchorage: … its great extent, its bold shores, and the facility of defence, may hereafter point it out as an eligible place for the rendezvous of a fleet. Unlike Marmaris it was never used as such, though local folklore tells of a Turkish submarine that evaded the Allies in the First World War by hiding in here.

Aperlae

At the head of the long inlet on the western side of the peninsula are the ruins of ancient Aperlae. It was never a great city in ancient times, but it was of some consequence as the leading city of this region. Part of the interest in the place is that the quay and harbour streets are now underwater. Either the sea level has risen or the land subsided to submerge this part of the city; the latter is the most likely. Ashore there are parts of the city wall and the ruins of buildings, and a number of sarcophagi. The ruins of Aperlae in this deserted landscape have a great deal of appeal.

You have to wonder why a city was built here and survived for a thousand years when it does not have good drinking water or a good harbour. Why not build it on the opposite side in Pölemos Bükü where there is a good sheltered harbour? Large cisterns here collected water and solved the drinking water problem, but still, why build the city here? One theory put forward is that the wealth of the city was built on the sea snail *murex* which is crushed and macerated to produce a purple dye. The Phoenicians controlled much of this dye production around Tyre and Sidon, so perhaps Aperlae was a client Phoenician colony. The purple dye was much valued and was used almost exclusively by nobility, especially during Roman times. By the 1st century BC the city would have been under Roman control and it appears to have survived until the 6–7th centuries AD. After that it is likely that piracy along the coast made it untenable and its history ends with a last-ditch conversion of the church to a mini-fort to protect the inhabitants, probably from Arab invaders from the east.

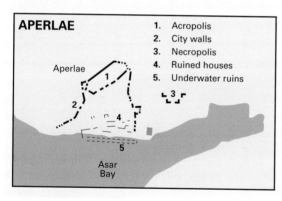

APERLAE

1. Acropolis
2. City walls
3. Necropolis
4. Ruined houses
5. Underwater ruins

The area around Kekova is home to a lot of tortoises and they do wander onto the roads

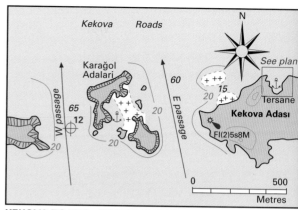

KEKOVA ROADS – WESTERN ENTRANCE

⊕12 Kekova Roads W entrance
36°10'·04N 29°49'·81E WGS84

Western Channel

The western channel leading in behind Kekova Adası has two islets connected by a reef sitting plumb in the middle. Yachts can pass either west or east of the islets. If you are using the east passage care is needed of an isolated reef on the eastern side – don't veer off to starboard too quickly but keep going straight into the roadstead. *Gulets* sometimes anchor for lunch or a swim between the two islets in the entrance behind the reef. Care is needed if you proceed into here and you should have someone up front conning the way in.

PÖLEMOS BÜKÜ

The long inlet running west from the western channel. Anchor where convenient along the coast or right at the western end of the inlet. The bottom is mostly mud and good holding. Good shelter from the *meltemi*. There is only maquis and olive trees ashore and blessed peace and quiet, but a half-mile over the isthmus are the ruins of Aperlae.

WOODHOUSE BAY

A small bay with the islet off it near the northern entrance to Pölemos Bükü. Keep east of the islet and reef at the entrance and the approach is free of dangers. Anchor in 12–15m on mud. Good shelter from the *meltemi*.

Ashore there is just a rough track leading up to the remains of a fort and a church which is claimed to date from the 2nd century AD. The track meets up with a path at the top which leads to Üçağız some distance away.

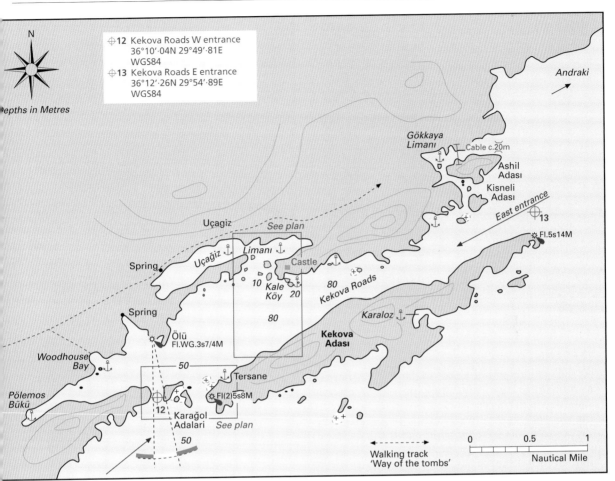

⊕**12** Kekova Roads W entrance
36°10'·04N 29°49'·81E
WGS84

⊕**13** Kekova Roads E entrance
36°12'·26N 29°54'·89E
WGS84

N

Depths in Metres

Andraki

Gökkaya Limanı

Cable c.20m

Ashil Adası

Kisneli Adası

East entrance

⊕**13**

Fl.5s14M

Uçagiz

See plan

Uçağiz Limanı

Castle

Spring

10 Kale Köy 20

80

80 Kekova Roads

Spring

Karaloz

Ölü
Fl.WG.3s7/4M

Woodhouse Bay

Kekova Adası

Pölemos Bükü

50

Tersane

Fl(2)5s8M

12

Karağol Adalari *See plan*

50

Walking track
'Way of the tombs'

0   0.5   1

Nautical Mile

KOVA ROADS

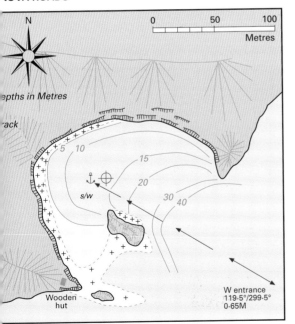

N

Depths in Metres

Track

0   50   100

Metres

5 10

15

20

30 40

s/w

Wooden hut

W entrance
119·5°/299·5°
0·65M

Karağol Adalari and the western channel into Kekova (left)

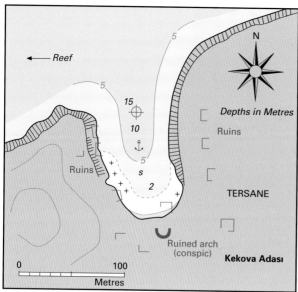

TERSANE
⊕36°10'·4N 29°50'·9E

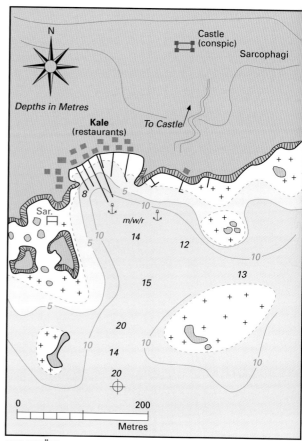

KALE KÖY
⊕36°11'·18N 29°51'·63E WGS84

TERSANE

At the western end of Kekova Island itself there is a miniature cove with the apse of a church standing on the beach. Anchor with a line ashore to the west side of the cove where there is reasonable shelter from the *meltemi*, although it can get a bit rolly in here. It is also popular with tripper boats though they disappear by late afternoon.

Around the shore and partially underwater are the ruins of other buildings of what was a small Byzantine settlement. Like its namesake in the Gulf of Fethiye, Tersane means 'boatyard', so presumably the inhabitants were engaged in building and repairing boats. The settlement was deserted by the early 19th century, if not earlier, as Beaufort mentions a deserted village with a small chapel on Kekova Island which Greek sailors used for their devotions. Today the lonely apse on the beach gives the place a haunted quality, a reminder of the long-forgotten souls and the busy little community that once existed here.

KALE KÖY

Once into the calm waters between Kekova Island and the mainland, the most conspicuous object is the medieval castle above the hamlet of Kale Köy (Castle Bay). Several cardinal buoys have been laid to aid navigation around the rocks and reefs in the approaches to Kale Köy, but they should not be relied on to be in the correct position, or to

Sunken sarcophagus in the sea near Kale Köy

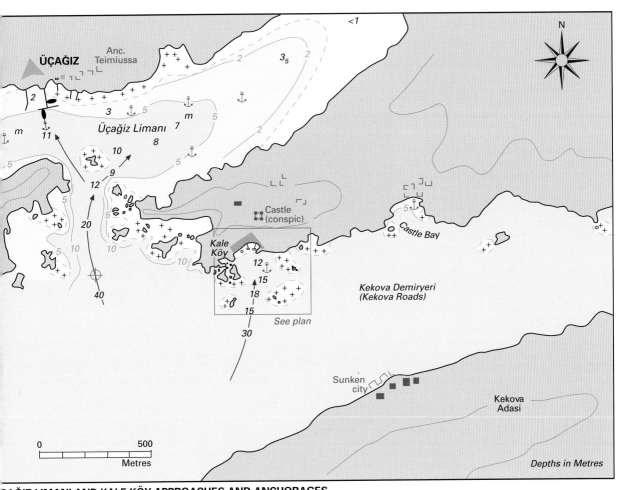

ÜÇAĞIZ

Anc.
Teimiussa

Üçağiz Limanı

Castle
(conspic)

Castle Bay

Kale
Köy

Kekova Demiryeri
(Kekova Roads)

Sunken
city

Kekova
Adasi

0   500
Metres

Depths in Metres

ÇAĞIZ LIMANI AND KALE KÖY APPROACHES AND ANCHORAGES
36°11'·36N 29°51'·11E WGS84

Looking across the
anchorage and yacht
jetties in Kale Köy. The
entrance to Üçağiz is top
left of photo
Kadir Kir

Kale Köy and Simena

The castellated ramparts of the tiny castle silhouetted against the blue sky on the ridge above the ramshackle houses of the hamlet can melt the heart of even the most unromantic and most people are captivated by the romance of the castle in this rocky wilderness. It gets better. As you pass into the bay between rocks and reefs on either side, what appeared to be a craggy rock reveals itself to have steps cut into it and the top levelled off flat. The general explanation for this is that the rock was quarried for construction purposes, and although other islets around the coast have been quarried for this purpose, why should this small lump of rock be worked when there is rock more easily accessible on the

Kale Köy with the mini-Genoese castle perched above

hillsides nearby? Given that the sea level has risen, or the land subsided in this region, as evidenced by the submerged harbour precinct here at Kale Köy and elsewhere such as at Aperlae, it is likely that this structure was a watch-tower or a defensive structure, or possibly a purely frivolous platform for diving and swimming off. There is no reason to suppose the ancients did not go swimming to cool off in the heat of summer just as we do.

Part of the attraction of Kale Köy is the mixture of ancient and medieval on the one site, with the houses of the hamlet tucked in between and on top of the site. The buildings of the hamlet are a sort of architectural palimpsest, with a bit of ancient stone here, a bit of medieval masonry there, and the family livestock safely tucked up in a rock-tomb. Along the waterfront are numerous (for such a small place) restaurants, with jetties out over the now-submerged quay and streets of ancient Simena. In the shallow water to the west a sarcophagus sits in the water like an elegant man-made dinosaur basking in the sun.

From the shore it is a steep, though short walk, up to the castle. It is thought to be largely of Genoese origin with later Turkish improvements, but it undoubtedly sits on the site of a more ancient structure. Inside the walls is a small theatre with just seven rows of seats entirely hewn from the rock of the hill. It probably held around 300 people at a squeeze, a reflection on the modest population of ancient Simena.

Over the hillside are scattered numerous sarcophagi, some tilted at crazy angles, some exactly where they were placed more than two thousand years ago. I remember watching one of the village women working a carpet loom near the castle, hemmed in by the walls and sarcophagi, with a view right out over the water to Kekova Island, a scene that could have popped out of everyday life two millennia ago.

As ancient sites go, Simena was not an important place. It was one of three demes under the control of Aperlae. Apart from the miniature theatre and the sarcophagi, little else remains. There are two rock-tombs, the ruins of private houses, part of the city wall, and the remains of a baths dedicated to the Emperor Titus. The Genoese castle is well preserved and the view from the top out over the landscape and enclosed waters of Kekova is alone worth the climb. Down below the restaurant owners do a roaring trade slaking the thirst and satisfying the appetites of visitors.

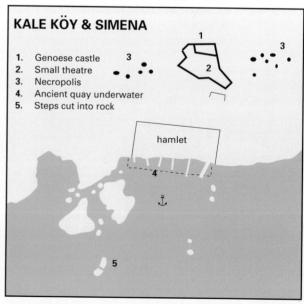

KALE KÖY & SIMENA

1. Genoese castle
2. Small theatre
3. Necropolis
4. Ancient quay underwater
5. Steps cut into rock

hamlet

be there at all. This is no place to rely on anything other than eyeball navigation. There are a number of catwalks off the restaurants on the shore, and although they tend to come and go, the three at the western end are open to yachts. Go alongside wherever there is room or at whichever one you like the look of. The restaurant owners will come out to wave you in and help you tie up. Depths come up quickly towards the shore, but there is room for two or three yachts alongside in good depths on each pontoon. The afternoon breeze sends a bit of a popple across the bay onto the pontoons, but it usually dies off for a calm night. Water and electricity is usually available here.

If there is no room on the pontoons you will have to anchor off in quite deep water, commonly 12–15m. The bottom is mud and weed and rock and the holding is bad. Make sure your anchor is well in.

By day there is a near constant procession of trip boats and *gulets* churning the waters from Üçağiz to Kale Köy to Gökkaya and back along the north shore of Kekova Adası before returning their cargo to Andraki or Üçağiz or Kaş. By the evening the throb of diesel engines has ceased, leaving only the promising clatter of dishes and pans as the restaurants prepare the evening meal.

ÜÇAĞIZ AND TEIMIUSSA

From the waters enclosed by Kekova a narrow channel, with an islet and reefs in the middle, leads into another large and totally enclosed bay. The place is called Üçağiz after the three entrances to Kekova and Üçağiz itself or because this bay

Üçağiz. Note the new municipal pontoon is not shown here
Kadir Kir

Ancient Teimiussa

Immediately east of Üçağiz a number of sarcophagi are scattered in gay abandon over the low slopes of the coast. This is the site of Teimiussa, a small settlement under the control of Aperlae. Little remains except the numerous sarcophagi and a couple of rock-tombs, the remains of a fort that is really no more than a fortified tower, and part of a quayed area. The latter is quite remarkable, being hewn from the rock with a narrow track at the back separated by a rock gateway from the quay.

Sarcophagi in the necropolis of ancient Teimiussa at Üçağiz

has three mouths: the channel divides into two around the islet in the middle. Although it looks treacherous, the passage into Üçağiz is really quite straightforward with a little care and someone up front conning the way in.

Once into Üçağiz you can anchor in several places around the enclosed bay. It tends to shallow up at the eastern end and right at the western end, although it is all soft mud so if you proceed slowly in the shallower water you shouldn't come to much grief. The soft mud can make anchoring difficult so take some care over getting your anchor to hold.

Off the hamlet there is now a T-pontoon where yachts berth. Yachts go either stern or bows-to or alongside. There is a marinero who will direct you to a berth. There are some laid moorings though in some cases you will have to use your own anchor. There is a catwalk to the west of the pontoon but this is exclusively for trip boats. Good shelter and some yachts spend the winter afloat here. Water and electricity on the pontoon. Charge band 2/3.

Nineteenth-century travellers

In the early 19th century a remarkable group of British travellers explored this part of Asia Minor and identified many of the sites scattered around the wild landscape. These early travellers had to cope, not only with inhospitable terrain over which they rode or walked when it got too rough for the horses, but also with bands of brigands, wily pashas, malaria, smallpox and cholera. Thomas Spratt and Edward Forbes were accompanied on their trip through Lycia by ET Daniell, a young clergyman who was to study the antiquities of the area. Daniell stayed behind after Spratt and Forbes left to rejoin the *Beacon*, and fell ill and died. Spratt himself fell ill of the same disease en route to his ship and nearly died; the disease left him debilitated for years. Captain Beaufort, while surveying the Cilician coast in 1812, was severely wounded when some Turkish soldiers opened fire on the ship's boats. A midshipman was killed and for a while it was thought that Beaufort would die too. Fortunately he recovered. That he and others did survive is remarkable given some of the cures of the time for the maladies. For diarrhoea *The Traveller's Medical and Surgical Guide* of 1888 advises the use of a lead and opium mixture, and for boils Baker suggests the use of a paste made of gunpowder and sulphur. On a lighter note, Lord and Baines in their *Shifts and Expedients of Camp Life* (1876) suggest the following treatment for blisters:

"... it not infrequently happens that the feet of those not thoroughly accustomed to hard tramping will become blistered. When the eggs of either poultry or wild birds are to be obtained, it is a good plan to break one or two, according to their size, into each shoe before starting in the morning."

The thought of these early travellers tramping over the countryside with eggy shoes is an amusing one.

Between 1810 and 1812 Captain Francis Beaufort was engaged in surveying harbours and anchorages along the Turkish coast for the Admiralty. Until recently Admiralty chart 241, *Anchorages on the South Coast of Turkey*, still used plans from Beaufort's original survey and apart from obvious manmade changes, the construction of roads, hotels, houses, chimneys, and a number of artificial harbours, his meticulous surveys are still accurate. Beaufort, in the mould of the times, was an amateur historian, archaeologist, and naturalist, and while on his tour of duty he explored the interior and wrote an entertaining book on the region: *Karamania ...* 'or a brief description of the south coast of Asia Minor and of the remains of antiquities collected during a survey of that coast in the years 1811 and 1812.' He had an eye for detail and for a good tale, and the book is packed with interesting description and anecdote. After his tour of duty Beaufort went on to become Hydrographer for the Admiralty and was largely responsible for reorganising it and making hydrographic surveys and charts an important part of the Admiralty's business. He is, of course, the same Beaufort who invented the Beaufort wind scale for wind and sea conditions that still bears his name and is used to this day.

Sir Charles Fellows, Thomas Spratt and Edward Forbes together 'rediscovered' Lycia in the 1840s. Charles Fellows was the British Consul in Asia Minor in the 1830s and 40s and during his time there he explored and examined a large number of ancient sites. He was largely responsible for revealing the splendours of Ephesus and Knidos to the interested western world, but his greatest accomplishment was the rediscovery of Lycia. On horse and foot he visited many of the sites of Lycian cities and proved beyond doubt that Lycia as a separate entity and culture existed. With the help of the British navy he carried off many fine pieces of sculpture and entire friezes to Britain, most of which are in the British Museum. He didn't mess around and even the huge lion (all eleven tons of it) at Cnidos was crated up and shipped off. In Lycia his prime objective was Xanthos and here, with the help of British sailors under the command of Spratt, he dismantled and removed some of the finest Lycian monuments known and shipped them on the navy's ships to Britain. The most well known is the Nereid Monument displayed in the Nereid Room of the British Museum. Freya Stark, musing on British sailors in this remote part of the world, wonders whether they played cricket here in the camp they set up under the ruins of the ancient city, and if so was this the first time cricket was played in Asia Minor. At any rate it didn't catch on in the way football has in modern Turkey. Fellows' travels in Turkey resulted in a number of volumes on his discoveries, much of which was collected together in an abridged edition: *Travels and Research in Asia Minor* (1852).

After the statues and friezes from Xanthos had been loaded on the *Beacon*, Spratt, Edward Forbes, a naturalist on board the ship, and Daniell remained behind for a journey into the interior. This was not as unusual as it might seem. The commander of the *Beacon*, Thomas Graves, actively encouraged his junior officers and surveyors to look beyond the coasts they surveyed and to take an interest in the interior, in the history and culture of a region, and especially in ancient history. The trio of Spratt, Forbes, and Daniell visited many sites inland and their travels are recorded in a book Spratt and Forbes wrote: *Travels in Lycia, Milyas, and the Cibyratis* (1852). As I have mentioned, Daniell died of fever in Antalya and Spratt very nearly died on his journey back to rejoin his ship. They were an eccentric bunch, these early travellers. Edward Forbes, the naturalist, is recorded in a later memoir as a colourful character roaming 'like a native around the countryside on his forays':

'... in these rambles it was his delight to encase himself in an old shooting-jacket, full of pockets; his long hair, surmounted by a 'Jim Crow' hat, hung down to his neck; his feet were shed with a pair of primitive country boots, into which he tucked the loose ends of his trousers; a botanical vasculum was slung across his shoulders, and a stout hammer supplied the place of a walking stick. Thus attired, he wandered over the hills and valleys ... dined and danced with the natives, pitched his tent on the hillsides, dredged among the bays and inlets, and plied his hammer along its shores'. *Memoir of Forbes* Wilson & Geikie.

These travellers are not as well known as the likes of Byron, Lord Elgin, Hobhouse or Edward Lear, but in their own fashion they were more adventurous and contributed much to our knowledge of Asia Minor and ancient civilisations, even if on hindsight we can criticise their scavenging of ancient sites. There were other later travellers and in the 20th century the redoubtable Freya Stark travelled around Lycia by jeep, on horseback and by foot, exploring Lycia and following in the footsteps of Alexander the Great to give us that travel classic *Alexander's Path* (1958). Likewise George Bean, who I have already talked about in Chapter 2, explored and recorded sites in Lycia to give us the definitive books on the Graeco-Roman sites along the Turkish coast.

Today the region is comparatively easy of access, at least to the major sites, though there are still small demes tucked away in the mountain fastness of the interior or perched away from the main roads on the rocky coast. Beaufort might have envied those on board yachts and *gulets* with reliable engines, and Fellows would certainly have envied the good roads and new *pensions*. In his journal he offered this advice to future travellers:

'A tent is the first requisite, the old cities and places of the greatest interest being frequently distant from the modern towns or khans; and a good tent makes the traveller quite independent of the state of health of the town. It is desirable that the tent should be of waterproof material.' *Journal 1839* Sir Charles Fellows

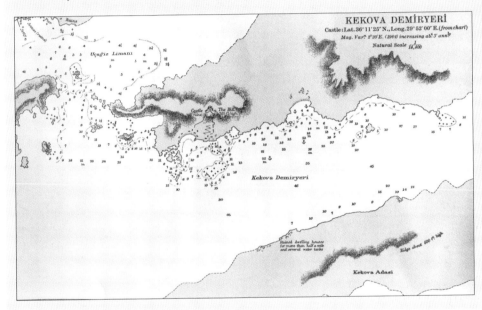

One of Beaufort's original survey plans of Kekova

On the shore stands the hamlet of Üçağiz, a small farming community that has adapted to the waterborne invasion with lots of restaurants and bars. I well remember on my first visit in the early 80s, being chased off by a villager for trying to take a photograph of his young daughter – times have changed and photography is now seen as part and parcel of the tourist trade. In former times the hamlet was only inhabited in the winter. In the summer the villagers retired to a *yayla* in the mountains to escape the summer heat and where there is grass and fodder for the livestock.

Nowadays the hamlet plays host to dozens of tour buses that disgorge every nationality in Üçağiz for a trip boat tour of Kekova. There are touts, tour guides and people everywhere. Fortunately the tour buses all depart by the evening and the place is more peaceful and recovers at least some of its charm.

CASTLE BAY

Around 600m east of Kale Köy there is a cove affording partial shelter from the *meltemi*. Anchor and take a long line ashore. There are numerous ruins at the head of the bay.

KARALOZ

This narrow and somewhat forbidding inlet lies on the southern side of Kekova. The entrance is difficult to see from seawards although closer in a cave on the northern entrance point will be seen.

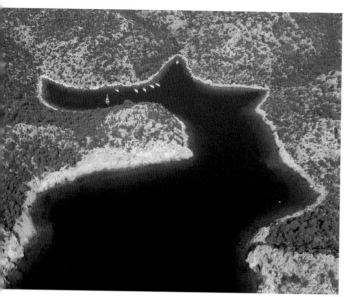

Karaloz on the southern side of Kekova Adası   *Kadir Kir*

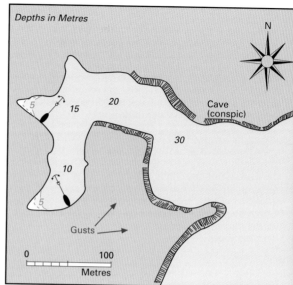

KARALOZ
⊕36°11′·4N 29°53′·4E

There are good depths in the entrance and right the way in and in fact you will normally have to drop anchor in 10–15m. It is a wonderfully peaceful place except when a local *gulet* is in. It is so quiet in here that when a generator is started, or the television or hi-fi turned on in visiting *gulets*, the noise seems to boom around the anchorage. Savour the place if you get it to yourself.

MARTINIS REEF

Note that Martinis Reef is not in the position shown on the old Admiralty chart 241. It lies off the small island in the southern approaches to Gökkaya as a reef extending E of the islet. A search within the area where the Martinis Bank is supposed to lie failed to locate it.

Coda A friend of mine, Harry Potts, has spent some time looking for the elusive Martinis Reef and believes he has found it more or less in the position shown on the chart. Depths over the reef were around 5m. Care should be taken in the vicinity of the Martinis-Potts Reef and any future reports are welcomed.

GÖKKAYA LIMANI

At the eastern end of Kekova lies a group of islands and above-water rocks with channels winding in and out of them.

Gökkaya is a fascinating place to explore from the water and in a yacht you can find your own

little place to anchor in. There are numerous coves and bights where you can tuck into with a long line ashore. By day it is busy with *gulets* and trip boats, but by late afternoon they will all have departed. Ashore the restaurants come and go, depending on whether the authorities clamp down on those who don't have permission. Most recently they had all been closed down, but the derelict buildings remain, and by the time you read this they may well be open again.

There are a few ruins ashore and on the mainland a short distance to the west there is another Genoese castle guarding the eastern

Anchorage tucked into Gökkaya Limanı

approaches to Kekova. The Genoese seem to have wrested this bit of coast from the Venetians. They controlled Kastellórizon up the coast, and in fact its name is a corruption of Castello Rosso, ('Red Castle'), after the Genoese castle on the island. The struggle between Genoa and Venice to control this important trading route bringing valuable commodities from the east to the west (the humble peppercorn being one of the most important items) was a long and hard struggle, with Venice now controlling one part of the coast, Genoa another; and not until the impending hegemony of the Ottomans did the Genoese and Venetians begin to co-operate – a little.

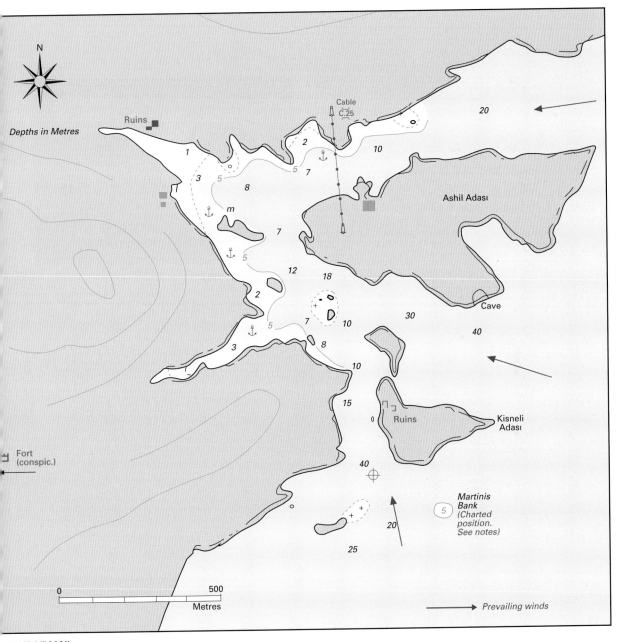

GÖKKAYA LIMANI
36°12'·08N 29°53'·92E WGS84

Myra and Andraki

Approximately two miles to the east of Gökkaya is the beach of Andraki, an open anchorage formerly the port for the city of Myra. In calm weather a yacht or *gulet* can anchor off and ashore you can get a taxi to the site of Myra, about 5km away. However, as the anchorage is uncertain it is better to do the trip from somewhere like Kaş or Finike.

A trip to Myra is well worth the effort. The theatre here is well preserved and there are a group of easily accessible rock-tombs behind it. The area around is a sea of plastic-covered greenhouses growing early tomatoes in the rich alluvial soil for export and the home market. The theatre is partially buried by alluvial soil and is an excellent example of just how a river not only silts up a harbour, but can bury a city. As you go into the theatre there is a stall space with an inscription above it reading 'Place of the vendor Gelasius', where friend Gelasius would have sold whatever the inhabitants of Myra munched on as they watched the show. Close to the theatre are a group of remarkable house-tombs, the best examples around, and easily seen close up. One of these has a series of interesting reliefs sculpted around the entrance showing (presumably) the man buried here, his wife and sons. Around the corner on the northeast side of the hill are another group of tombs and one of these has the remains of paint on the frieze. This frieze shows the life of the man and his family indoors and out and is quite one of the most remarkable rock-tombs in Lycia.

Down in the village of Demre, through which you pass to get to Myra, is the church of St Nicholas of Myra. Nicholas was born in Patara around AD300 and became famous in his own time and was duly made a saint. He is patron saint of an unlikely lot of characters: of sailors, merchants, pawnbrokers, scholars, those wrongly imprisoned, and by travellers everywhere. He is patron saint of Greece and Russia. His bones no longer lie in the church and indeed it is unlikely that the tomb the custodian shows you was in fact the final resting place of

Demre, where our Santa Claus started life

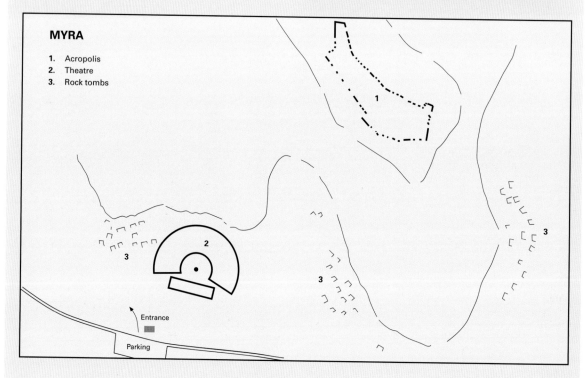

MYRA

1. Acropolis
2. Theatre
3. Rock tombs

Rock tombs at Myra

the saint. In 1087 his bones were stolen by sailors from Bari in Italy and removed to that city, where they now allegedly rest. However, the Venetians also claim to have the bones of the saint, as do the Russians, and the museum in Antalya. Wherever they are, the spirit of St Nicholas survives throughout the Orthodox world and has penetrated the young lives of most of us: from St Nicholas of the Orthodox world he has metamorphosed into the Santa Claus of the secular world.

Medusa at Myra

When at Myra he is said to have provided dowries for the daughters of an impoverished citizen by dropping three bags of gold down the chimney at night. The daughters were drying their stockings by the fire and in the morning discovered the gold in each of their stockings – an innocent enough tale of a saint who seems to have only good attributed to him and who provides legitimisation for the tradition of putting stockings out for Father Christmas to fill on Christmas Eve. Whatever the truth of the wondrous works and miracles attributed to him, he was well-loved in his own time.

At Andraki, in ancient times Andriace, the port of Myra, there are a number of ruined buildings and a granary of Hadrian, much similar to the one at Patara, but not as well preserved. It is here that the Apostle Paul, now a prisoner of the Romans, changed ship on his way to Rome and his trial. It was to be the last voyage this hardened traveller made, though there were many incidents and accidents along the way before the Romans finally had Paul safely locked up in Rome.

THE APOSTLE PAUL

Of all the apostles, Paul stands out as the one who was the traveller *par excellence*. His journeys through the length and breadth of the ancient world are nothing short of remarkable and, given the difficulties of travelling in these times, let alone the animosity and danger he faced trying to convert populations to the new faith, it is a credit to the endurance and tenacity of the man that he accomplished as much as he did. Paul, originally Saul, was born in Tarsus in what is now southern Turkey and after converting changed his name to Sergius Paulus. He is traditionally represented as a stocky little man, with a bald head and a grey, bushy beard. He made three great missionary journeys before being arrested in Jerusalem and taken to Rome, where he was beheaded in AD62.

On all of his journeys he travelled along the coast of Asia Minor and there are many places along the coast I have described where he stopped and taught, or changed boats, or sheltered from the weather. The Book of Acts covers most of his exploits and journeys as well as his last voyage as a prisoner to Rome.

One of the most well known incidents on Paul's travels is the riot of the silversmiths in Ephesus. On his third journey Paul stayed over two years in Ephesus, preaching every day in the synagogue. He was a canny man and knew that he had to convert the old pagan centres of worship, and Ephesus was one of the oldest, if this new Christianity was to survive. Towards the end of his time there Paul preached that '… gods made by human hands are not gods at all', a direct jibe at the silversmiths who made silver statuettes of Artemis and her temple for sale to pilgrims and tourists. Sales soon began to decline and one Demetrius, a leader of the silversmiths, led a group of artisans against Paul, who said '… the sanctuary of the great goddess Diana will cease to command respect; and then it will not be very long before she who is worshipped by all Asia and the civilised world is brought down from her divine

pre-eminence.' His speech caused an uproar and the band of silversmiths, and likely a number of merchants worried about the decline in business, rushed into the theatre shouting, 'Great is Diana of the Ephesians'. Paul was not forced to leave the city by the authorities after this riot, but he evidently decided it was prudent to do so and set off for Macedonia.

It was in Jerusalem after this third missionary journey that the authorities finally decided they could tolerate Paul's activities no longer and arrested him. He was put on a ship at Adramytium bound for the coast of Asia Minor:

'And putting to sea from thence, we sailed under the lee of Cyprus, because the winds were contrary. And when we had sailed across the sea which is off Cilicia and Pamphylia, we came to Myra, a city of Lycia. And there the centurion found a ship of Alexandria sailing for Italy; and he put us therein. And when we had sailed slowly many days, and were come with difficulty over against Cnidus, the wind not further suffering us, we sailed under the lee of Crete, over against Salamone; And with difficulty coasting along it we came unto a certain place called Fair Havens; nigh whereunto was the city of Lasea.' Acts 27: 4–8.

It was by now the beginning of winter and the voyage onwards was beset with strong and adverse winds. From Crete a gale blew them down to Malta where the ship was wrecked in what is now called St Paul's Bay. Eventually a ship brought them to Rome and there Paul was tried and beheaded in AD62. It is apocryphally told that when Paul was beheaded milk, not blood, flowed from his body. However dubious this may be, few could have predicted what the result of Paul's work was to be as Christianity went from strength to strength to become the dominant faith in the very country where he met his end.

Andraki, where the Apostle Paul was put on a ship bound for Rome

Appendix

I. USEFUL BOOKS
This is not a bibliography but a list of a few books readers may find useful.

Turkey
General
Discovering Turkey Andrew Mango (Batsford). Not a guide book but a good general introduction to things Turkish.

The Western Shores of Turkey John Freely (Tauris Parke Paperbacks). Entertaining guide to Turkey, originally published as Collins *Companion Guide to Turkey*.

Turkey: A Travel Survival Kit Tom Brosnahan (Lonely Planet). Good useable guide.

Turkey: A Short History R H Davision (Eothen Press). Good concise guide to the history from Seljuks to Republic.

Europa Minor Lord Kinross (Travel Book Club). Erudite and entertaining.

Atatürk: The Rebirth of a Nation Lord Kinross (Weidenfeld & Nicholson). Tells of the birth of the Turkish Republic; a good read.

Stamboul Sketches John Freely (Redhouse Press). As much about things Turkish as Istanbul.

Improvise and Dare: War in the Aegean 1943–1945 J S Guard (The Book Guild).

Birds Without Wings Louis de Bernières. (Vintage). Largely set in the now-abandoned Greek village of Kaya.

Snow and *My Name is Red* Orhun Pamuk (Faber & Faber).

Archaeology
Turkey Beyond the Meander and *Lycian Turkey* George Bean Bern (Murray). Much mentioned and lauded in this book, these are the guides par excellence to the Graeco-Roman sites. For the coast to the north there is *Aegean Turkey* and to the south *Turkey's Southern Shore*.

Ancient Civilizations and Ruins of Turkey Ekrem Akurgal (Haset). Good compact guide.

Alexander's Path Freya Stark (Murray). A travel classic around Lycia.

The Jason Voyage Tim Severin (Hutchinson). Follows the Jason voyage to Istanbul and along the Black Sea coast of Turkey.

Nautical
Turkish Waters & Cyprus Pilot Rod Heikell (Imray). Sailing directions and background for the Turkish coast.

Mediterranean Cruising Handbook Rod Heikell (Imray).

The Adlard Coles Book of Mediterranean Cruising Rod Heikell (Adlard Coles).

Sailing in Paradise: Yacht Charters Around the World Rod Heikell (Adlard Coles). Covers charter areas worldwide as well as general advice on chartering.

Mariner in the Mediterranean John Mariner (Adlard Coles). OP. Visits to Turkey.

Greece
General
Travellers' History of Greece Timothy Boatswain & Colin Nicolson (Windrush Press). With a name like that how could a sailor resist it?

The Greek Islands Lawrence Durrell (Faber). Good photos and eloquent prose.

The Greek Islands Ernle Bradford (Collins Companion Guide).

The Rough Guide to The Dodecanese Mark Dubin. (Rough Guides). Down-to-earth guide.

Rhodes and the Dodecanese. Robin Barber. (A&C Black).

Fortresses and Castles of Greek Islands and Fortresses and Castles of Greece Vol II Alexander Paradissis (Efstathiados Group). Detailed guides, available in Greece.

The Venetian Empire Jan Morris (Penguin). Readable account of the Venetian maritime empire.

A Literary Companion to Travel in Greece Ed. Richard Stoneman (Penguin).

The Ulysses Voyage Tim Severin (Hutchinson).

Eleni Nicholas Gage (Fontana/Collins).

The Colossus of Maroussi Henry Miller (Penguin). Arguably his best piece of writing, fiction included.

The Hill of Cronos Peter Levi (Zenith).

Flowers of Greece and the Aegean Antony Huxley and William Taylor.

Flowers of the Mediterranean Antony
   Huxley and Oleg Polunin. Both the above
   have excellent colour photos and line
   drawings for identification.
Trees and Bushes of Britain and Europe Oleg
   Polunin (Paladin).
*The Hamlyn Guide to the Flora and Fauna
   of the Mediterranean* AC Campbell
   (Hamlyn). Good guide to marine life.

Nautical

Mediterranean Pilot Vol IV (BHO) Covers the
   Aegean Sea.
List of Lights Vol E (BHO) Covers the
   Mediterranean, Black and Red Seas.
Greek Waters Pilot Rod Heikell (Imray). Covers
   all Greek waters in a single volume.
The Ionian Islands to Rhodes HM Denham (John
   Murray). Covers the Ionian islands through
   Crete to Rhodes. Classic guides, though no
   longer revised and kept up to date.
Mediterranean Cruising Handbook
   Rod Heikell (Imray).
*The Adlard Coles Book of Mediterranean
   Cruising* Rod Heikell (Adlard Coles).
*Sailing in Paradise: Yacht Charters Around the
   World* Rod Heikell (Adlard Coles).
Imray Mediterranean Almanac Ed. Rod Heikell
   (Imray). Biennial publication covering all
   major Mediterranean harbours and marinas,
   though not in detail.

II. COMMON GREEK AND TURKISH WORDS USED IN THE BOOK

Greek terms and abbreviations used in the text and plans

Greek	*English*
Ákra (Ák)	Cape
Andí (Anti)	Opposite
Áyios (Áy)	Saint
Dhíavlos	Strait or channel
Dhiórix	Channel or canal
Dhrómos	Roadstead
Fáros	Lighthouse
Ífalos (If or I)	Reef
Isthmós	Isthmus
Kávos	Cape
Khersónisos	Headland
Kólpos	Gulf
Limín (L)	Harbour
Mólos	Breakwater or mole
Moní	Monastery
Nisáki	Islet
Nísos/Nisí/	
Nisía (N)	Island(s)
Nótios	Southern
Órmos (O)	Bay
Ormiskos	Cove
Óros	Mountain
Pélagos	Sea
Pírgos	Tower
Porto	Small harbour
Potamós (Pot)	River
Pounda	Cape or point
Stenó	Strait
Thálassa	Sea
Vórios	Northern
Vrakhonisis	Rocky islet
Vrákhos	Rock

Turkish terms and abbreviations used in the text and plans

Turkish	*English*
ada (adası)	island
boğazi	strait, channel
burun, burnu	cape, headland
cami	mosque
dağ	mountain
deniz	sea
eski	old
göl	lake
hamam	Turkish bath
imam	cleric who presides over prayers at mosque
iskele	landing place
kale	castle
kapi	gate, pass
kara	black
Kayası	rock or reef
Kızıl	red

Turkish	English
Körfezi	gulf
Köy	cove, creek
Köyü	village
Küçük	small
liman	harbour, port
muezzin	cleric who gives call to prayer in mosque
pazar	market
saray	palace
šehir	town
sisar	castle or fort
su	water
vilayet	province
yarimadasi	peninsula
yeni	new

A few useful words in Greek

General

English	Greek
yes	né
no	ókhi
please	parakaló
thank you	efharistó
OK	endaksi
hot	zeste
cold	krió
here	ethó
there	ekí
hello	herete
goodbye	adío
good morning	kalaméra
good evening	kalíspera
good night	kalíníkhta
good	kaló
bad	kakó
today	símera
tomorrow	ávrio
later	metá
now	tóra
I want	egó thélo
where is	poú inai
big	megálo
small	mikró
one	éna
two	dhío
three	tría
four	téssera
five	pénde
six	éxi
seven	eptá
eight	octó
nine	eniá, enéa
10	dheca

Shopping

English	Greek
apples	míla
apricots	veríkoka
aubergines	melitzána
baker	foúrnos
beans	fassólia
biscuits	biscóttes
bread	psomí

English	Greek
butcher	hassápiko
butter	voútiro
carrots	caróta
cheese	tirí
chicken	kotópoulo
chocolate	socoláta
coffee	kafés
cucumber	angouri
eggs	avgá
fish shop	psaróplion
flour	alévri
garlic	scórdo
green pepper	piperiá
grocer	bakáliko
ham	zambón
honey	méli
jam	marmeláda
lamb	arnáki
lemon	lemóni
margarine	margaríni
meat	kréas
milk	gála
mutton	arní
oil	ládhi
onions	kremmídia
oranges	portokália
parsley	maïdanós
peach	rodhákino
pepper	pipéri
pork	khirinó
potatoes	patátes
rice	rízi
salt	aláti
sugar	zákhari
tea	tsái
tomatoes	domátes
veal	moskhári
water	neró
watermelon	karpoúzi
wine	krassí
yoghurt	yaoúrti

A few useful words in Turkish

General

English	Turkish
yes	evet
no	hayir
please	lütfen
thank you	teşekkür ederim
excuse me	affedersiniz
it's nothing/ that's all right	birşey değil
where?	nerede (dir)?
when?	ne zaman?
how?	nasil?
today	bugün
tomorrow	yarrin
left	sol
right	sag
big	büyük
small	küçük
open	açik
closed	kapali

English	Turkish
goodbye	Allahaismarladik
	(the one leaving)
	Güle güle
	(the one who remains)
good morning	günaydin
good afternoon	tünaydin
good evening	iyi akşamlar
good night	iyi geçeler
I don't understand	anlamiyorum
one	bir
two	iki
three	üç
four	dört
five	beş
six	alti
seven	yedi
eight	sekiz
nine	dokuz
10	on
20	yirmi
50	elli
100	yüz
1,000	bin
Sunday	Pazar
Monday	Pazartesi
Tuesday	Sali
Wednesday	Carsamba
Thursday	Persembe
Friday	Cuma
Saturday	Cumartesi

In the restaurant

English	Turkish
appetiser	ordövr
baked	firinda
beef	sigir
beer	bira
bread	ekmek
breakfast	kahvalti
butter	tereyagi
chicken	piliç
chips	patates (kizartmasi)
cheese	peynir
coffee	kahve
croquettes	köftesi
dessert	tatlilar
fish	balik
fried	tavada kizarmis
fruit	meyve
grilled	izgara
ice cream	dondurma
ketchup	keçap
lamb	kuzu
lemon	limon
lettuce	marul
liver	cigeri
meat	et
meatballs	köfte
mineral water	maden suyu
milk	süt
mussels	midye
mustard	hardal
oil	yag
olives	zeytin

English	Turkish
omelette	omlet
pepper	karabiber
rice	pirinç
roast beef	rozbif
roasted	kizarmis
salad	salata
salt	tuz
sandwich	sandviç
seafood	deniz mahsulleri
soup	çorba
spaghetti	spagetti
spicy omelette	menemen
steak	biftek
stuffed	dolma
tea	çay
vegetables	sebzeler
veal	dana
vinegar	sirke
(iced) water	(buzlu) su
wine	şarap
wild boar	yaban domuzu paçasi
yoghurt	yogurt

Shopping

English	Turkish
apples	elma
apricots	kayisi
aubergine	patliçan
bakery	firin
beans	fasulye
beef	sigir
biscuits	bisküvit
bread	ekmek
butcher	kasap
butter	tereyagi
carrots	havuç
cheese	pyenir
chicken	piliç
meat	et
melon	kavum
milk	süt
oil	yag
onions	sogan
oranges	portakal
peaches	seftali
chocolate	çikolata
coffee	kahve
cucumber	salatalik
eggs	yumurta
fish	balik
flour	un
garlic	sarmisak
grocer	bakkal dükkáni
honey	bal
jam	reçel marmel
lamb	kuzu
lemon	limon
potatoes	patates
rice	pirinç
salt	tuz
sugar	şeker
tea	çay
tomatoes	domates
water	su
wine	şarap

Greek alphabet and pronunciation

Α α	Alpha	a	a as in father
Β β	Beta	v	v as in vote
Γ γ	Gamma	g	g as in go, but before vowels such as iota and epsilon, y as in yet, and before gamma, kappa, xi, or chi, n as in sing
Δ δ	Delta	d	th as in then (but not thin); contrast theta below
Ε ε	Epsilon	e	e as in set
Ζ ζ	Zeta	z	z as in zoo
Η η	Eta	e	ee (/i/) as in meet
Θ θ	Theta	th	th as in thin (but not then); contrast delta above
Ι ι	Iota	i	ee (/i/) as in meet or y as in yet
Κ κ	Kappa	k	ck as in sack
Λ λ	Lambda	l	l as in light
Μ μ	Mu	m	m as in mouse
Ν ν	Nu	n	n as in nose
Ξ ξ	Xi	ks	ks as in kicks or x as in ax
Ο ο	Omicron	o	o as in tote or boat
Π π	Pi	p	p as in pan
Ρ ρ	Rho	r	r more like the Spanish trilled r than English r
Σ σ	Sigma	s	s as in sister
Τ τ	Tau	t	unaspirated t as in stop (but unlike top)
Υ υ	Upsilon	u or y	Like German ü
Φ φ	Phi	ph	f as in fan or phone
Χ χ	Chi	ch	Not found in English. Much like Spanish 'j'
Ψ ψ	Psi	ps	ps as in lips
Ω ω	Omega		o as in tote

Turkish alphabet and pronunciation

a	as in father
b	as in bat
c	as j in joke
ç	as ch in choke
d	as d in dote
e	as eh in met or Áy in stay
f	as f in fat
g	as g in get
ğ	a soft g, something like y or uh
h	as h in hat
ı	as u in circus but also as uh, i, or cc depending on the sounds preceding it
i	as i in sit or ee in meet
j	as zh in measure
k	as k in key
l	as l in lot
m	as m in me
n	as n in nip
o	as o in boat or aw in saw
ö	as er in sitter
p	as p in pay
r	as r in bray
s	as s in sea
ş	as sh in shall
t	as t in tea
u	as oo in soon
ü	as ew in pew
v	as v in very
y	as y in yes
z	as z in zest

BEAUFORT WIND SCALE

B'fort No.	Wind Descrip	Effect on sea	Effect on land	Wind speed knots	mph	Wave ht (metres)
0	Calm	Like a mirror	Smoke rises vertically	less than 1		
1	Light	Ripples, no foam	Direction shown by smoke	1–3	1–3	–
2	Light breeze	Small wavelets, crests do not break	Wind felt on face, leaves rustle	4–6	4–7	0·2–0·3
3	Gentle breeze	Large wavelets, some white horses	Wind extends light flag	7–10	8–12	0·6–1·0
4	Moderate breeze	Small waves, frequent white horses	Small branches move	1–16	13–18	1·0–1·5
5	Fresh breeze	Moderate waves, some spray	Small trees sway	17–21	19–24	1·8–2·5
6	Strong breeze	Large waves form, white crests, some spray	Large branches move	22–27	25–31	3·0–4·0
7	Near gale	Sea heaps up, white foam, waves begin to streak	Difficult to walk in wind	28–33	32–38	4·0–6·0
8	Gale	Moderately high waves	Twigs break off trees, walking impeded	34–40	39–46	5·5–7·5
9	Strong gale	High waves, dense foam, wave crests break, heavy spray	Slates blow off roofs	41–47	47–54	7·0–9·75
10	Storm	Very high waves, sea appears white, visibility affected	Trees uprooted, structural damage	48–56	55–63	9·0–12·5
11	Violent storm	Exceptionally high waves, wave crests blown off, badly impaired	Widespread damage	57–65	64–75	11·3–16
12	Hurricane	Winds of this force seldom encountered for any duration in the Mediterranean.				

USEFUL CONVERSIONS

1 inch = 2·54 centimetres (roughly 4in = 10cm)
1 centimetre = 0·394 inches

1 foot = 0·305 metres (roughly 10ft = 3 metres)
1 metre = 3·281 feet

1 pound = 0·454 kilograms (roughly 10lbs = 4·5kg)
1 kilogram = 2·205 pounds

1 mile = 1·609 kilometres (roughly 10 miles = 16 km)
1 kilometre = 0·621 miles

1 nautical mile = 1·1515 miles
1 mile = 0·8684 nautical miles

1 acre = 0·405 hectares (roughly 10 acres = 4 hectares)
1 hectare = 2·471 acres

1 gallon = 4·546 litres (roughly 1 gallon = 4·5 litres)
1 litre = 0·220 gallons

Temperature scale
t°F to t°C : 5/9(t°F–32) = t°C
t°C to t°F : (t°C×9/5) +32 = t°F

So 70°F = 21·1°C   20°C = 68°F
    80°F = 26·7°C   30°C = 86°F
    90°F = 32·2°C   40°C = 104°F

IMRAY-TETRA CHARTS: AEGEAN AND TURKEY

G3   **Aegean Sea (South) – Passage Chart**
1:750,800 WGS 84
Plan Approaches to Ródhos

G31   **Northern Cyclades**
1:200,000 WGS 84
Plans Órmos Ay Nikolaou, App to Finikas,
Órmos Naousis, Mikonos and approaches,
Órmos Gávriou

G32   **Eastern Sporades, Dodecanese and
the Coast of Turkey**
1:200,000 WGS 84
Plans Kusadasi, Yalikavak Limani, Limín A. Kirikos,
Steno Samou, Órmos Parthéni, Órmos Patmou

G33   **Southern Cyclades (West Sheet)**
1:190,000 WGS 84
Plans Stenó Kimólou-Políagou and Stenó Mílou-
Kimólou, Órmos Náxou (N Náxos), Órmos Livádhiou
(N. Sérifos), Stenó Andipárou

G34   **Southern Cyclades (East Sheet)**
1:200,000 WGS 84
Plans Ó. Analipsis (N. Astipálaia),
Órmos Iou (N. Ios), Vlikadha (Thira)

G35   **Dodecanese & the Coast of Turkey**
1:190,000 WGS 84
Plans Bodrum, App. to Ródhos
(N. Ródhos), App. to Kós (N. Kós),
App. to Turgutreis, Órmos Simi (N. Sími)

G36   **Marmaris to Geyikova Adasi**
1:200,000 WGS 84
Plans Marmaris Limani, Skopea Limani, Göçek, Fethíye,
Approaches to Meyisti and Kas

G37   **Nísos Kriti (West)**
1:190,000 WGS 84
Plans Kali Limenes, Órmos Ay Galinis, Palaiokhora,
Órmos Gramvousa, Ormos Soudhas, Rethimno

G38   **Nísos Kriti (East)**
1:190,000 WGS 84
Plans Iraklion, Sitía, A. Nikólaos, Spinalonga

G39   **Nísos Karpathos to Nísos Rodhos**
1:190,000 WGS 84
Plans Órmos Pigadhia (N. Karpathos), Órmos Tristoma,
Órmos Lindhou (N. Ródhos), Limín Fri andLimín
Emborio (N. Kasos), N. Khálki to N. Alimía

G40   **South Coast of Turkey – Kas to Antalya**
1:200,000 WGS 84
Plans Geyikova Demiryeri, Kemer Marina, Finike,
Kekova Roads, Setur Antalya Marina

Imray Digital Chart ID70 The Eastern Mediterranean

Eastern Mediterranean & Aegean Seas

Charts included:

M20, M21, M22, G13, G14, G141, G15, G2, G21, G22
G25, G26, G27, G28, G3, G31, G32, G33, G34, G35, G36,
G37, G38, G39, G40

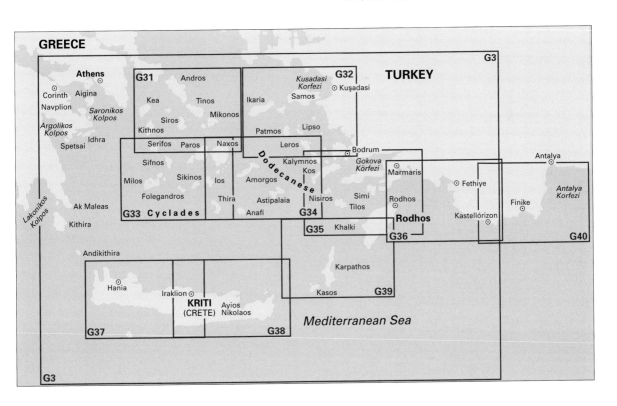

Index